# DELAWARE INTEGRITY

Rituals, Removals, Reforms

by

Lenape Indiens

Jay Miller, PhD

# HONORED TEACHERS

Nora Thompson Dean

Lucy Parks Blalock

Vincenzo Petrullo                    Fred Washington

# DELAWARE INTEGRITY
## Rituals, Removals, Reforms by Lenape Indiens

# contents

# contents

# PREFACE

The Delaware, justly famous in American literature and history, are also one of its best and longest documented native peoples, both by others and by ourselves. They are familiar to most from many sources, including the novels of James Fenimore Cooper and the records of the Moravian mission upon which his "good guys" image of the Delawares was based; through Sir Thomas West, third Lord de la Warre and 1610 Governor of Virginia, whose title became applied to a cape, a river, and a people who call themselves Lenape; through a century of academic research by scholars like Mark Harrington, Truman Michelson, Frank Speck, Gladys Tantaquidgeon (a Mohegan), and Regina Flannery; and through Delaware authors, albeit educated Christians, like Richard Adams. Moreover, for over three hundred years, Delawares holding onto their own traditions, languages, and religions kept a strong voice, written down by others, in preserving all facets of their culture.

This culture had and has an **integrity** and a logic all its own, clearly and recurrently seen during these centuries, and surmised – by analysis of meanings, symbols, and linkages – for over millennia. This logic is based on the pan-species genders of Man and of Woman, linked by the sharing of Mind or human intellect and best depicted by the Delaware themselves in their Origin Saga (genesis) in which the Creator ("the one who thought us into being") acted upon a Turtle, with the Earth island on its back, and a Cedar Tree, which sprouted at its very center.

Furthermore, the engendered creation came to the fore each year at the Gamwing (Big House Rite) which, over time, became the epitome of traditional culture. It became the beacon that guided and guides right-thinking Delawares through tempestuous change and cataclysm. As Delawares were driven away from the river routes of their homeland, forced ever westward to present locations in Ontario and arid Oklahoma, the meaning of and nostalgia for the Gamwing grew. In particular, for Delawares, every past event of any moment was believed to have occurred during a Gamwing. This rite and the Big House building (aboriginally, a chiefly home and community hall) were a public forum for national sentiments, so anything of lasting import became located within its confines. With the same inspiration, all of my own research throughout Native North America has also involved contrasts with Delaware practices.

Indeed, the rite was so well integrated into Delaware culture that claims by Anthony Wallace, Vernon Kinietz and others that it began about 1805 must be discounted (Miller 1996). While the rite was reformed during this time, its ancestry is deeply rooted in Delaware identity of heartfelt thanksgiving. European colonization fragmented Delawares along a spectrum of sentiments with, at one end, traditionalists adhering to some version of their aboriginal religion and, at the other, Christians (variously Lutherans, Moravians, Baptists, Methodists, and Catholics) espousing pro-European and American desires. What had once been the aboriginal population density and diversity of many Delawares, dwelling over a huge region, shifted to a great variety of political and ideological stances among the few survivors. An ancient range of aboriginal geography became an array of historical ideologies. At the core of each constituent, however, was a form of worship, native (like the Gamwing) or novel (like the Moravian love feast), whose beliefs and practices impinged on the others, since relatives were found throughout all the factions. Yet, sustaining what was special about Delawares was the core group, the successors of the aboriginal elite, who were devoted to the Gamwing. More succinctly, their range included the extreme stances of a "defender" of tribal traditions to a "merger" (absorbed into European society), with "blender" (using selective give and take) midway.

Once a year, after the harvest and before the hunt, communities gathered to renew the world as they knew it and to give thanks for continued bounty. For twelve days, because twelve levels separated the earth from the highest heaven of the Creator, prominent individuals – visionaries gifted by particular supernaturals – danced, prayed, and sang to evoke their first encounters with these immortals. In this way, various spiritual bonds were reaffirmed and the world was renewed for the benefit of all beings.

After Delawares were devastated by epidemics and driven from their homeland, the rite took on even greater significance as it reformed to become the epitome of all that the Delaware cherished in their culture. Pushed ever westward, the Gamwing became, more and more, the repository for the essence of Delaware identity and culture. Each new community built a special building – a model of their universe. A bare oval floor represented the back of the giant turtle "who" carried the earth and a single central pillar symbolized the world tree linking sky and earth. Seating places along the sides were assigned to each of the three clans – Turtle, Canine, and Fowl – inherited through the mother. The exact placement of these seats depended upon which matri-clan was hosting the service. At least once in the history of the rite, when Delawares were living in western Pennsylvania, the overall arrangement of such seating shifted from the far end to the middle of one side, matching the room-length pews of a Moravian church, German Pietistic Protestants who founded Bethlehem, Pennsylvania (Chapter 9).

Because rituals represent beliefs in action, the rite could and did survive each successive dislocation and resettlement. In every sense, literally and symbolically, the Gamwing defined Delaware personal and social identity. A person reaffirmed his or her Delawareness by participating in the rite as a visionary or as a worshipful spectator. The Delaware community thereby maintained, in public view, its membership and continuity. As one way of emphasizing such tribal identification, babies might be named during the rite.

From their beginnings as a distinct culture until a last gasp in 1924, the Gamwing sustained the Delaware community. Forced from their riverine and coastal homeland, Delawares moved ever westward, always expecting that each new home would be permanent. Instead, they moved across Pennsylvania and into Ohio, where they survived the American Revolution.

In the later 1790s, most of the Munsee (Monsi) or northern Delawares settled in Ontario among the Iroquois who had supported the British cause. The Unami or southern Delawares moved on to Indiana, where unsettled times led to a religious fervor that recast the Gamwing into its most familiar form (Miller 1994). From Indiana, the Unami were forced to Missouri and Kansas, before settling in Oklahoma in 1869, where most of the community remains.

In addition to these movements by the Munsee and Unami majorities, small pockets of Delawares remained in each prior location until merged into the local populations, albeit preserving some memory of their Lenape ancestry as a family tradition. Over time, pressures to conform eventually led Delawares to convert to (sometimes nominal) Christianity, although the use of the Lenape language for hymns and sermons kept these congregations singularly Delaware.

Eventually, the Thanksgiving aspect of the Gamwing became expressed, more and more, in Christian terms, while the stability once provided by the annual rite shifted to rely on accumulated memories about their new abodes. Thus, while the rite had sustained and supported Delawares for centuries, it was this deepened sense of place, by several generations belonging in Ontario or Oklahoma, that allowed the Gamwing to fade. Assurances that the communities would survive in each place confirmed Delawares in their sense of self, publicly expressed in modern churches and annual powwows without need of the Gamwing, which had done its reform work of sustaining them during displacement, distress, and despair.

In all, therefore, the Gamwing exemplified and sythesized major elements of the Delaware universe. It was, in brief, a conjoining of **process**, **persons**, **place**, and **portals** to allow intercommunication among all beings.

Process dealt with time, particularly the seasonal movements devoted to farming, hunting, fishing, and garnering — since the Gamwing was held at the juncture between harvest and hunt that marked the shift from women's importance in the economy to that of men. The daily actions of the rite moved the participants in a widening upward spiral through twelve sky levels, expressed as four segments of three days each, to the abode of the Creator himself.

The persons included all expressions of being extending from Our Creator through deities and humans to anything with the spark of lively intelligence. As organizing categories, these persons were divided into clans of Wolf, Turkey, or Turtle; tribes of Unami, Munsee, or others; the nation of Lenape speakers, and, overall, the genders of Man or Woman.

In terms of place, the big house building was a microcosm of the universe itself, relying on the turtle and cedar of the creation saga as represented in the central oval and post. Flowing down the center of the roof was the Milky Way, while the Delaware River itself, a major tributary, or a later waterway drew together the members of a congregation upon the earth.

Facilitating these acts of salvation were various portals that linked components together more closely. Among the most important of these were the east and west doorways, associated with entrance and exit (life and death), so that the Oklahoma west door was kept closed throughout the rite. During earlier versions, leaders probably sat as a block in front of it. The Munsee suspended masks over these doorways, while the Unami carved them into the side posts. The fires themselves also provided transmitting passage for offerings and actions, as a larger expression of the spark of life that united all of creation. In particular, the side and center posts, each with the carved face of a sky keeper leading upward to the Creator, provided the major axis for Delaware salvation during the rite.

The Delaware language, here called Lenape, like all Algonkian grammars, was pervaded by a distinction between the animate and the inanimate. As the terms imply, animacy was somehow concerned with life or the living, but in ways that have long baffled scholars. For example, Lenape anatomical terms include a word for the entire body which is animate, composed of many body parts which are inanimate (Miller 1977: 151; Appendix B). A few, however, were animate, namely those for the neck, knee, calf, genitals, blood vessels, kidney, and heart. While Charles Hockett argued that Algonkian animacy had to do with the ability to speak, Mary Black (1969) found that it had to do with volition and self-propulsion. The plurals of these and other Lenape terms similarly indicate that motion, particularly as pulsing (including rhythmic knee jerks and neck bobs), was the defining characteristic of animacy.

Yet flux, flow, and motion were consequences of a more basic motivation that can best be called "mind," which had its source and summary with the Delaware Creator, "the one who thought everything into being."

The remarkable story of how the Gamwing defined the Delaware, even served to reform and restore them, after each displacement is the subject of this book. It is the text that has most obsessed me, being intimately my very own concern from cradle to grave.

# ACKNOWLEDGMENTS

This study, based on the interplay of documents, interpretative devices, and Delaware memories, has incurred many debts over several decades (stretching across a new millenium). Foremost, gratitude is due to the late Nora Thompson Dean, an extraordinary woman well versed in Unami Delaware traditions. She made me feel a part of her family - Charlie, Louise, Jim - and named me, becoming my aunt in the Wolf clan. Her brother, Edward Leonard Thompson, also supplied memories of his childhood before he left Oklahoma to work in Denver. Through Nora, I met other people devoted to the Delaware, ranging over several generations, including that of new scholars.

Lucy Parks Blalock and her family (Jake ~ Rosemary, Sonny, Sissy, Jerald, Ruthe, and their own families) have been kind and considerate over the years, particularly when I visit Quapaw, Oklahoma.

Other Delawares who shared with me were Tom and Irene Wilson, and Annie Brown Parks.

Around Anadarko, gratefully appreciated help was provided by Linda Poolaw, Lillie Hoag Whitehorn, Esther Hoag Homovich, Willie and Bessie Snake, Lawrence and Dorothy Snake, Georgia Chisman Gallegos, and Edgar French.

Staff at the American Museum of Natural History, for the Tefft Collection; at the Harvard Peabody, for materials excavated by Ernest Volk; and at the American Philosophical Society, for Frank Speck correspondence, were most helpful. Pamela Hearn at the University of Pennsylvania Museum aided my search for Delaware materials and their Big House model. At the Bartlesville Public Library, over the years, Wilma Berry, Ruby Cranor, and Susan Box have encouraged my efforts.

Among colleagues, Drs Lorraine Williams, Janet Pollak, Sue Roark, Duane Hale, Linda Poolaw, and Bruce Pearson gained my well deserved thanks. Prodding and provocation has come from Bob Grumet, Mel Thurman, Ives Goddard, Fritz Jennings, C. A. Weslager, Fred Gleach, and Marshall Becker. Drs Ray Fogelson and William Fenton did much to improve my text and thinking, while occasionally driving me to drink.

Friends in Seattle and Saratoga, Wyoming, helped to make travel and trials less wearisome, particularly Marilyn Richen, Ann Schuh, Connie Jump, Tammy Jackson, Gilmans, Blairs, Chesnins, Bernsteins, and Monday Nite. At the Newberry Library, Ruth Hamilton, Michael Kaplan, Harvey Markowitz, Helen Tanner, John Aubrey, and other associates kept me working toward this goal.

Again, Amelia Susman Schultz has been proofreader extraordinaire.

# TERMINOLOGY

The Delaware genius and people have always been a crucial part of my life and I hope that this holistic study will reflect my own appreciation for a culture well lived. Nora Dean encouraged the use of Delaware instead of Lenape to refer to her own people because the European word, derived from the title of Thomas West, Lord le la Warre and governor of Virginia, was less likely to be mispronounced. She always said that the phrase Lenni Lenape had a childlike redundancy about it and she discouraged its serious use. Delaware will be used in the singular because the Gamwing or Big House Rite was quintessentially about being Delaware. The native term Lenape will mostly be used to refer to the language spoken by Delaware.

Similarly, most of these people identify as natives of the Americas, usually spelled Indian, erroneously derived from India, so to respect this selfdesignation and make it globally understandable, the name is spelled here **Indien**, for the Indies as in French.

In the further interests of understanding, the spelling used here of Manitu and Masing are not technically correct since the first vowel is a schwa, the short and weak sound at the end of "sofa" to produce Mənitu and Məsing. Writing it as "i" or "e" creates unfortunate linkages with similar English words that are avoided by the use of "a" as a good compromise.

Editorially, native words are _italic and underlined_, and, wherever possible, the English has been bent to express native meanings rather than the much more common reverse Anglophile arrogance. Direct translations are marked by equal sign '=' and single quotes

As John Heckewelder (1876: 413, 15 August 1816) wrote to Peter Duponceau about Delaware usage of _len-_, the root of Lenape,

> They also say _lenni m'bi_, "pure water;" _leneyachkhican_, a fowling piece, as distinguished from a rifle, because it was the first fire-arm they ever saw; a rifle they call _tetupalachgat_. They say, _lenachsinnall_, "common stones," because stones are found everywhere, _lenachpoan_, "common bread" (_achpoan_ means "bread"); _lenachgook_, a common snake, such as is seen every where (from _achgook_ a snake); _lenchum_, the original, common dog, not of a species brought into the country by the white people. I think I have sufficiently explained the name "_Lenni Lenape_."

Therefore, a better translation of the term Lenape would be "standard people," rather than 'original, common, or real', since the Delaware, especially when addressed as "grandfathers," were regarded as the exemplars of dignity and goodwill by other tribes. For a time, they were also addressed as "women" in contrast to Iroquois "men" in an engendered world.

Footnotes provide brief information, while longer disccusions appear as a few chapter endnotes. Bibliographic abbreviations appear at the start of the final list of references.

Linguists use the term "deictic" to refer to features of Native American languages where time and space fuse. A deictic center would therefore be a point where time and space conjoin, as in that ultimate being, the Delaware Creator. Such a point also served as a pivot in the cosmos, but it has never been properly distinguished in the literature and might best be called a "tysic," based on the initial letters of **T**ime, **S**pace, and **C**enter. Thus, the Delaware Creator can properly be called a tysic of their universe, whose mind animated it.  For Delawares, the mind was localized not in the head but in the heart, the tysic of the body.

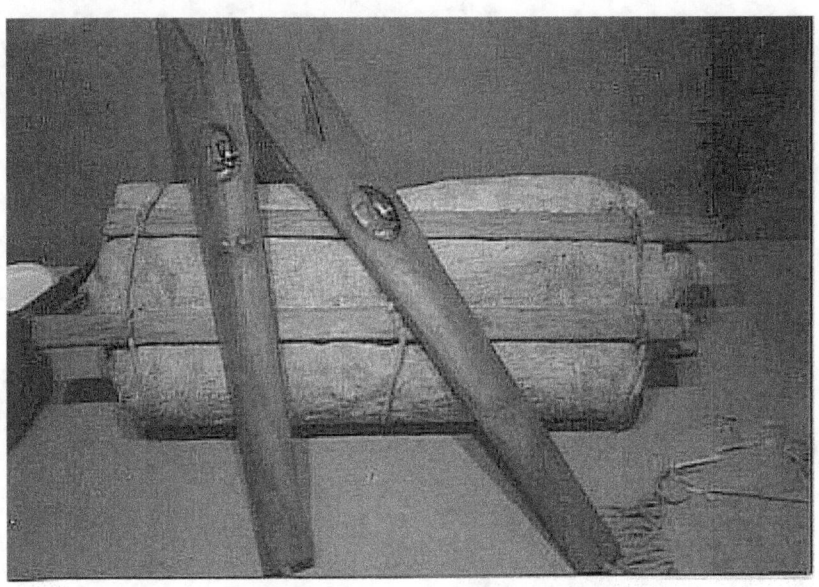

Image #1  folded deerskin drum
woman ~man special forked drumsticks for Gamwing finale

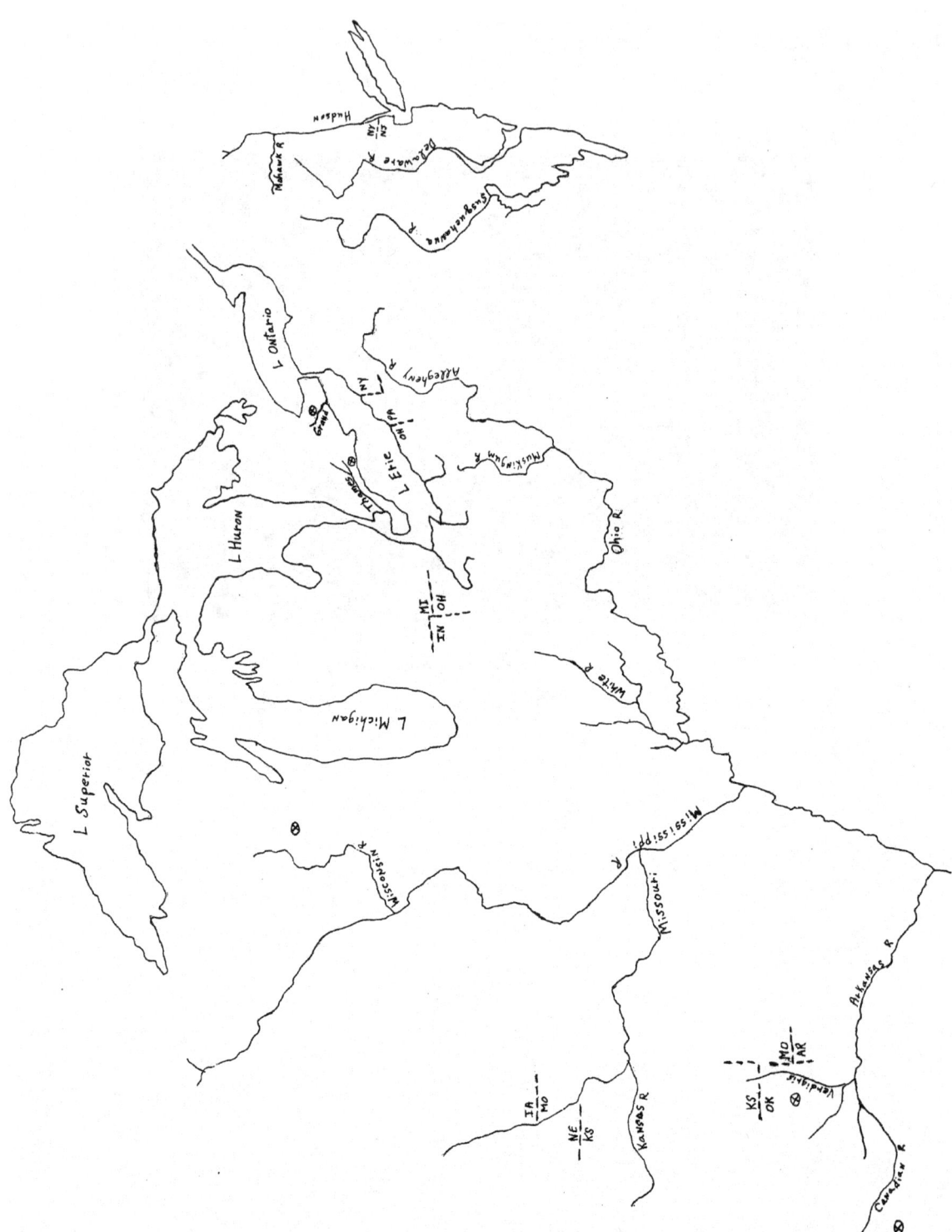

Image #2 ~ Drainages of Delaware migrations
today's communities marked by a circled X ⊗

## INTRODUCTION ~ 1

During their ordeal since Europeans arrived in their homeland and we began migrating westward, the *gamwing* (Big House Rite of Thanksgiving) became the epitome of Delaware culture, defined, sustained, and redeemed by their religion. Thirty years ago, when I asked elders in Oklahoma about traditional beliefs, activities, and institutions, their replies were based on memories of this ceremony, last held in 1924 near Copan, Oklahoma on lands now flooded.

For twelve days, Delaware (*Lenape*) families worshiped in a special building which symbolized their universe, renewing spiritual ties with all of creation. As a community, people defined themselves as Delawares by joining together under the sponsorship of one of the three clans (broadly Wolf, Turkey, Turtle) inherited through the mother, and by witnessing how a series of men and women evoked their visions (personal encounters with a spirit power) in song, gesture, and dance. Simultaneously, the entire congregation symbolically rose each night through one of the twelve layers between earth and heaven, finally reaching the abode of the Creator ("the one who thought us into being") on the last night.

By thus giving thanks to the Creator and all of creation, the Gamwing made manifest Delaware beliefs about their own world – in which the earth island rested on the back of a giant turtle with a cedar tree growing in the center of its back. Men and women were created by initial movements of the cedar and thereby the universe was engendered in such a way that everything became either male or female, or, pan-species Man or Woman, as Lenape – the Delaware language – specifically expressed these terms for gender. All of life has a basically human form – with head, hands, and legs – variously cloaked by an outer covering that makes things appear differently on the outside.

For Delaware, therefore, the fundamental categories which pervade the universe are the concepts of gender and of Mind because the Creator, the apex of everything, functions through Thought. Delaware culture derives from this basic equation of Woman and Man mediated by Mind.

Yet these terms are not strictly balanced because, like all languages, Lenape nests them within a graded threeway relationship involving a specific, a generic, and a generalized categoric. In terms of the Delaware expression of gender, therefore, Woman is specific, a special case of Man, the generic, while Mind is the categoric.

For example, when Delaware pray and give thanks to water, the form determines what kinship terms will be used. Thus, water in wells, cups, and containers is addressed as "mother," while free flowing water in rivers and lakes is called "grandfather." Subsuming all forms of water is the vast sea, surrounding the turtle holding the earth, and infused by the Creator with some of his thought at the beginning of time.

With the creation of space and time, the ordering of the universe was founded and the Gamwing also celebrated this work of the Creator. Held during early October when tree leaves changed color before falling off, the rite marked the transition from harvest to hunt, from the crops farmed by the women to the meat supplied by the men.

These themes of **creation**, **gender**, **clans**, and **seasons** stayed integral to Delaware society and culture. All four were expressed while the Delaware lived in their homeland along the Atlantic coast and the drainages of the river that still shares their name. With the arrival of Europeans exerting pressures to move west, the Delaware, through a series of prophets, used the Gamwing as a means of preserving what was important in their beliefs and lifeways. Various other rituals, based in families, clans, and towns, became subsumed into the Big House Rite over succeeding centuries.

After most Delaware were forced from homelands in New Jersey and eastern Pennsylvania, major revisions and restatements of the rite were worked out in Ohio and Indiana. The Munsee or northern Delaware took the rite with them into Ontario, where they now reside as Christians, while the Unami or southern Delaware continued the ceremony as they were driven from Indiana to Missouri, Kansas, and Oklahoma, where their descendants also now live as Christians. A splinter group of Unami left Indiana and settled in Texas among the Caddo and Wichita, abandoning the Gamwing in favor of southern Plains traditions, until they too were driven to find refuge in western Oklahoma.

## Scholarship

The Delaware are represented by a rich ethnographic tradition covering several hundred years, although the bulk of Delaware ethnography has been collected in Oklahoma, as indicated by checking the bibliography under the names of the scholars mentioned below.

Sponsored by eastern museums, Mark R. Harrington visited Delaware communities in Ontario, Kansas, and Oklahoma during 1907-10, collecting representative artifacts and important data dealing with technology, kinship, and religion, especially the Gamwing and the Big House building, which have been invaluable. His 1908 data from Oklahoma are consistent both with those of Charles Trowbridge from the 1830s and my own from the late 1900s. In addition to articles, a book on the religion, and an unfinished monograph, he is best known for a fine novel (Harrington 1963 [1948]) set among the early historic Delaware.

Truman Michelson, long interested in the comparison of the Algonquian languages (including Lenape), visited Oklahoma, Kansas, and Canada in 1912, collecting texts which included important descriptions of the Doll Dance, Otter Rite, and an important account of the Big House translated from the words of Chief Charlie Elkhair and treated in the chapter on Native Oklahoma Accounts.

The premier scholar of comparative Eastern ethnology, Frank Speck, began his Delaware research about 1928 and arranged for the fieldwork of students such as Vincenzo Petrullo and Claude Schaeffer. Unfortunately, Speck worked most closely with Charles (Charlie) Webber, a Delaware who sought him out but whose information was not always reliable. Webber's ancestry was mixed, including Munsee and Cherokee, but he did grow up among eastern Oklahoma Unami before he traveled extensively. He dictated, in Philadelphia, an account of the Big House Rite to Speck (1931) that has become the "classic" source, despite some obvious errors (Miller 1976b, 1980a). Particularly useful are his letters to Speck from Oklahoma, mentioning what was happening among the traditionalists. This correspondence, now in the American Philosophical Society Library, provided several details crucial for my analysis.

Eventually, Speck was interested enough, however, to become familiar with other members of the Delaware community. As a result, his Delaware descriptions gained in thoroughness and insight. His 1937 treatment of ceremonies, feasts, and dances corrected some of the fumblings in the Big House account, benefiting from personal fieldwork with several Delaware elders well versed in Unami traditions.

Speck was also the only researcher to send graduate students into the field, expanding the coverage of Delaware studies. Among these were Gladys Tantaguidgeon, herself a Mohegan, who worked with Webber on Delaware herbalism. Her study is surprisingly good because Hannah Stykes Webber, his mother, was an active herbalist. Anthony Wallace combed archives and did some Canadian fieldwork to produce a sketch of Delaware society (1947), a biography of Tedyuscung (1949) – known to elders in the 1970s as Tendayuskung [*tenday* = 'fire'], and several articles, including the classic one in 1956 tracing the acceptance of different religions among the Delaware in twenty year cycles, although he erred in dating the Gamwing only from 1806. Clinton Weslager devoted himself to several popular accounts concerned with things Delaware, based primarily on historical documents, although he gained the goodwill of many Delaware elders.

Summary treatments pulling together much information include the trait tables of Regina Flannery (1939) for Coastal Algonkians and composite syntheses by Mary Herman (1950) using published literature, by Vernon Kinietz (1946) basing his 1938 Oklahoma fieldwork on the 1823 Lewis Cass questionnaire used by C. C. Trowbridge, and by William Newcomb (1956) combining these other sources with extended 1951-52 fieldwork. While Speck (1948) gave Kinietz a scathing review, he was too harsh. Although scattered in long tabulations and sometimes in disjointed commentary, Kinietz provided some important information.

Newcomb has become the standard reference on the Delaware, but it is biased by its resort to socio-functional theory. While culture is a word used in the title, any symbolic content and meaning, particularly the cohesion provided by the gender echo, received no attention. My own work, therefore, provides a complement to his emphasis on society (social forms).

Decades ago, several Delawarists of my academic cohort became active. Ives Goddard and Bruce Pearson wrote dissertations on Lenape verbal morphology and the semantics of the grammar. James Howard wrote on music, dance, and costume as part of his interest in tribal and pan-Indian traditions. Susan Roark-Calnek (1977, 1978, 1980) studied the networks of intercultural and ethnic identities in Oklahoma from the standpoint of Delaware "moral transactions" to enhance personal prestige and worth. Robert Adams wrote a thesis on Unami music with information from several elders now deceased. Terry Prewitt (1981) examined population trends, rural farming techniques, impact of boarding schools, and ritual for an environmental impact statement on the Copan reservoir built by the Army Corps of Engineer. Robert Grumet's dissertation (1979) on the native strategy behind early land sales in the Delaware homeland allowed for greater social complexity than most other works. Marshall Becker (q.v.) engaged in considerable if dubious speculation, and is now well remembered in Oklahoma. Together with the older historic works interspersed throughout the following discussion, these scholars have provided the basis for understanding both the Gamwing and the Delaware in long term perspective.

The Katonah Gallery (Brawer 1983) display of Delaware artifacts and photographs was dedicated in May of 1983 by elders and leaders from all the modern communities.[1] In 1988, Delawares and scholars were invited to participate in a landmark conference during June 2-5 in

---

[1] A less successful attempt at a reunion of Delawares occurred in 1972 at Seton Hall University in New Jersey (Kraft 1974), where I first met Nora Dean and family.

New Philadelphia, Ohio, near the former Moravian villages of Delaware and Mahikan converts along the Tuscarawas River. Other gatherings were held during the 1990s.

The richness of the literature about Delaware extends to articles written by tribal members. Like the summary of Richard Adams, in Native Oklahoma Accounts, which was flawed by his Christian bias, Horace McCracken (1956), then Chairman of the Delaware Business Committee, wrote on the Big House, but his data were imperfect. Most of his dates were wrong, and he misunderstood information provided by the elders (such as claiming that clans were passed through the father), but he did record what became of the last vestiges of the building and its ritual artifacts.

Ruthe Blalock Jones (1973), daughter of Lucy Blalock and Professor of Art at Bacone College, interviewed, for a research paper at University of Tulsa, fifteen of the Delaware elders who had attended or heard about the Gamwing as children. While she relied on Wallace for her history of the rite, her summaries of information from the elders, as a member of the community, added significantly to our appreciation of the ceremony.

Nora Thompson Dean (Miller and Dean 1978) dictated her recollections of the Gamwing during one long night and these were edited to produce "the fullest ... and most accurate" description available for the last years of the rite. By comparing her version with older sources, modifications in the ceremony could be more easily traced. In her account, Nora described the rite in terms of process – the assembling of people and provisions. Throughout the present book, however, descriptions have followed the format of Richard Adams, the first Delaware to publish on the rite, by starting with the architecture of the building and moving to the personnel and events, and of Chief Charlie Elkhair, the last traditional leader to lead the rite, by expressing personal and tribal faith.

At the millennium, with the support of scattered Delaware communities in the US and Canada, a compendium of Big House accounts, most extracted from scholarly works, along with heartfelt personal commentaries, highlights most original native sources by name (Grumet 2001). Largely descriptive, it includes better understandings of contexts and linguistics. The century of political complexities and difficulties of the Delaware majority dominated by the Cherokee Nation have also been examined (Obermeyer 2009).

## Only Connect (to Good)

Delawares are key representatives of the eastern branch of the Algonkian language family. Kenneth Morrison (1992: 202-203) has been exploring an Algonkian theology, with wider application for Native American religions, which relies on existential postulates based on the triple concepts of Person, Power, and Gift to demonstrate that "ritual performance is at once a duty and a responsibility." His triadic structure, however, is that of Judeo-Christian beliefs, lacking the fourfold structure usual for the Americas.

Therefore, despite Euro-American insistence, there is no supernatural, as a distinct category, but, instead, the universe is populated by various persons (only some of whom are human) with a religious duty that is based, as expressed for the continent by Great Basin Numic, on "a self-accepted obligation of some kind, eventually in the form of ceremonies and rituals" (Liljeblad 1969: 52).

Because native languages are generative rather than representational, emphasizing process rather than product, notions of cause and effect derive from <u>personal intentionality</u>, both human and other-than-human, which can only exist by being tangibly expressed in some manifest manner perceivable by any of the senses. In other words, the sensory system of another person must receive this intention for it to be effective.

What distinguished beings within this expansive concept of <u>person</u> was access to power, including knowledge and its application. Power itself was neutral, so it must be used and directed by such intentional activity.

<u>Gift</u> was the result of moral processes through which a human would benefit from some compassionate being, often called a spirit. A "good" person will use power in helpful, co-operative ways to benefit a wide range of people, while a "bad" person will use it for selfish and self-interested purposes. "If all persons share the same ontological essence, and power to a relative degree, then gift dictates that reciprocity is the performed heart of cosmological and social order" (Morrison 1992: 204).

The inspiration for this view of the world as populated by persons, both human and other-than-human, was the work of A. Irving Hallowell among the Algonkian-speaking Ojibwe of the Great Lakes straddling both Canada and the United States. Others have confirmed these conclusions for other Algonkians, including the Cheyenne (Strauss 1976). Yet it is important to note that these Algonkians harvested from nature. Comparisons have not been drawn with Algonkians like the Delaware, who had a farming tradition and a much more complex conception of beings – only some of whom were persons.

In his most explicit, yet fittingly posthumous, statement about the Ojibwa category of person, both human and other than human, Hallowell (1992: 64-66) noted that each of these beings had an enduring vital part (a spirit or soul) and an outward form (appearance) with attributes of intelligence, will, and speech, enabling all of them to communicate. Each form was merely typical rather than absolute since any person could metamorphose between coverings. For example, the actual "person" of each species was its "owner" (or boss), possessing speech and transforming abilities that were lacking among the ordinary biological members. Similarly, transpersonal perceptions varied by species, although each had parallel traditions specifying proper homes, customs, and foods. For example, Thunder Birds hunted Great Snakes and Great Frogs, which they regard as their "beavers."

In prayers and pleas, all such other-persons were and are addressed by native humans as "our grandfathers" because they were predominantly both male and older members of the same moral universe. Similarly, the High God was and is the embodiment of pity and benevolence, both before and after Christian influence.

Children, usually boys, quested to meet such a person by fasting and praying in a "nest," a platform built for them high in a tree. At the encounter, the "supernal patron" gave explicit, life-long rules for the child to follow in order to be successful and maintain continuing access to power. These obligations were "so highly individualized, personal, and secret, their fulfillment reinforced self-reliance, particularly since they were under an implacable disease sanction. At the same time, this severe penalty [ill health, death] emphatically underlined in principle the importance of the fulfillment of obligations and reciprocal relations [particularly sharing food] in <u>all</u> interpersonal conduct. Herein lay the moral unity in the entire Ojibwa world," relying on inner controls rather than outward coercion (1992: 97).

## Persons

Nora Dean and other Delaware elders fluent in their language applied a set of 8 alternative classifications to the "living" of their world, variously based, beginning with the most frequent, on criteria of form, habitat, color, motion, sound, use, kinship, and appearance (Miller 1975: 436-41). All of these life forms had the ability to move, most often by breathing.

Overall, however, membership among the living was based on four criteria, although most beings had only the three of thinking, speaking, and reproducing themselves. Other beings, considered more complete, had power, either in their own right as a spirit(s) known as *manitu(wak)* or as humans who received it by transfer, phrased as a gift. Power and reproduction, along with other aspects of mortality, were inimical because spiritual beings were immortal and could be offended by anything with the reek of mortality. Most rigorously, humans had to be chaste, clean, and "pure" of food or filth when dealing with power.

Further, each species differed from others according to whether or not it had a spark-like soul and/or a ghost that looked like a transparent skeleton. The source and summary of all souls and of all power was Our Creator, who was an old man with white hair who sat eternally in the twelfth and highest level, which was heaven.

Form or shape distinguished seven subsets of 1) deity – centered on the Creator, 2) person – each with thought, language, reproduction, soul, ghost, and mobility on two legs, 3) maize corn – with thought, speech, and a soul, 4) animal – with thought, reproduction, four legs, and fur, 5) bird – with thought, reproduction, wings, feathers, and a language all their own, 6) tree – with thought, reproduction, leaves, language and power uniquely their own, and a special kinship with Delawares, and 7) plant – without attributes except for the ability to grow everywhere. Instead of all plants, salient attributes belonged only to the subset of medicine plants – with thought, their own language, and power to cure or alter events for good or evil. For Delawares, 'plants' were shorter and 'trees' were taller in size than adult humans.

The animal and bird forms, further separated into 'wild' or 'tame', involved more complexity since Nora believed that dogs, eagles, crows, and otters also had language, power, and souls. Although mute, all animals could take pity on a human and ask a deity, especially its species spirit "boss," to give the gift of power. Thus, among animals and birds, some species had special attributes that made them more significant.

For comparative Algonkian studies, it is vital to note that the Delaware word for "person" referred only to bipeds, while maize had an separate existence because "she" had to be treated with the utmost respect because she was easily provoked to anger, withdrawing her bounty (Bierhorst 1995: 44 # 67, 91-92). Such regard, of course, reflected the role of maize in Delaware life and, thereby, stood in marked contrast to the Ojibwa and Cheyenne concept of the person, where an economy of hunting and some 'wild' harvesting placed greater emphasis on animal spirits. Nonetheless, while the word "being" better reflects the Delaware sense of these life forms, readers are more likely to respond to "person" in this context. After all, even the Ojibwe category of "person" was not labeled overtly by a native term (Hallowell 1967, 1992; Fogelson 1976: 357-390).

The other classifications (Appendix A) were by habitat (above, land, water, woods, underground); color (red, black, green, yellow, blue, white, grey, purple of pokeberry); actions (crawlers, hoppers, fliers, walkers, climbers, trotters, runners, swimmers, baskers); sound (crowers, barkers, criers, howlers, singers); usage (medicine, food, drinks, smokes, materials, tabooed, useless); kinship (grandfathers, grandmothers, mothers, father, elder brother, male friend, female friend); and outer appearance (feathers, fur, shed skin, hide, naked [humans, worms], teethed, clawed, tailed, leafed).

Of these alternatives, that of kinship also had particular bearing on attitudes toward many other beings, as listed here using the proper Lenape terms of "man" and "woman" instead of the expected English words of "male" and "female." In concept and terminology, all beings had a infrahuman essence possessing hands, head, and feet.

> **Our Grandfathers**: tobacco, Thunderers, fire, Masing, man bears, man turtles, man doll spirits, whirlwind, water in large bodies or running free, and the directions of north, east, and west.
> **Our Grandmothers**: woman bears, turtles, and doll spirits, along with the direction of south.
> **Our Mothers**: Maize corn, the earth, and water in wells, springs, or containers.
> **Our Father**: Creator.
> **Our Elder Brother**: Sun
> **My Male Friend**: trees and medicines addressed by a man.
> **My Female Friend**: trees and medicines addressed by a woman.

All of these kin terms refer to relatives in the line of descent who have authority over an individual and, appropriately, were applied throughout the domain of interrelated life forms to indicate obligations and responsibilities by and to humans.

All of these persons had animacy (as indicated by the plural grammar of their names), a sense of being, and moved by a mindful act of will. Above all, they had minds with volition to permit intentionality. A person was good if their mind connected in useful ways, but bad if it did not. A good Delaware life was clean, holy, and chaste, while a bad one was selfish, slovenly, and promiscuous. In ritual, this distinction was expressed by the use of tobacco to well connect cosmically, while a smudge of red cedar needles disconnected from bad, wrong, or hurtful manifestations of various beings, situations, or thoughts.

"For Ojibwa, all the values implicit in a life free from hunger, illness, and misfortune are in part contingent upon help ... indirectly or directly from other than human persons. The Good Life is expressed by the term *pimədaziwin*, which is often articulated in ceremonies when a tobacco offering is made by turning a pipe in all directions [east, south, west, north] of the cosmos" (Hallowell 1992: 82). This Good Life involved "a feeling of security and confidence in facing the hazards of existence by being able to cope with all eventualities. Good dreams helped to promote this feeling as did good social relations. All this promoted ego strength, part of the price of which was self-control through self-discipline."

A person should want to lead a life that connected with others and most did. For those who did not, there were consequences that included divine retribution. Actions had consequences (Miller 1977: 156). After mistreating a cat, boils filled with hair were sure to inflict that person.

Improper conduct during a ritual, particularly letting the mind wander, inattention, or bad thoughts, led to insanity or deformed children. If a family inherited the bundle obligating them to host a ritual and did not do so, its members would begin to die off. Paralysis was the result of contact with a ghost, the severity depending on the mental attitude at the time. Tampering with a grave or eating in the dark if ghosts were about led to a twisted mouth.

Other illnesses with a spiritual or moral cause were danger for a man from contact with menstruation, eye contact from someone who has just looked at a corpse or had sex, unhealthy food because someone has tasted or craved it too much, or failure to observe various taboos and restrictions on diet, bathing, and appearance after an incident of mortality such as birth, puberty or death.

Strong will or desire could adversely effect situations and were avoided. Anyone coveting food was sure to receive it to ease their mind and prevent further disagreements. Most dangerous of all was any expression of violent public anger or disagreement (_k^wulakan_), which was forbidden because it led to spiritual retribution upon those unleashing such hostility.

Three examples of _k^wulakan_ reported in the 1970s included promised venison that was given with such reluctance and bad feelings that people refused to eat the deer because they suspected that the meat had become harmful, a family fight over an inheritance that was only settled by selling the land to take it out of harm's way, and the ownership of the home of a wealthy Osage that was bitterly contested among his children until it was destroyed by lightning. In each case, the harmony expected by the overseeing deities was breached and turned to super-charged hostility until the balance was reset by removing or destroying the object or property that was the basis of contention so that both those involved and bystanders would not be further harmed (Miller 1975: 46). Since European encroachment upon Delaware lands often led to the frustration and anger of _k^wulakan_, they kept moving westward to avoid its consequences.

For all these actions, intent was important because it indicated the degree to which the mind was involved in the process. Full mental control during the casting of a 'hex', dicta, or wish for long life had serious consequences beyond the intended outcome. For this reason, during all rituals and prayers, spectators in an audience had a vital role to play in lending their good thoughts, pulsing from their hearts, to that common purpose. Only Delawares were allowed to attend the Gamwing because other people might not respond with the proper mental regard and respect. The very effectiveness of the rite, of course, benefited from this consensus, collective action by a congregation of concerned and intentional believers.

## Thoughtful Light

If the basis of Delaware faith was the manifestation of connectedness, how was thought made "real" in the human dimension? Fortunately, by the lucky survival of an important text and by a comparison with other native beliefs, a ray of light can literally be shed on the mind.

Before I was drawn to serious Delaware research, I finished a dissertation on Pueblos in New Mexico. After moving to the Northwest, I began research among Tsimshian and Salish, both Coast and Interior branches. Later, while in Chicago, I taught the grammar of Ojibwa and Menomini to tribal members and learned about the Midwest tribes. In particular, my Delaware experiences made me pay attention to the manner in which tribes who were fortunate enough to remain in their homelands regarded these ancestral territories.  The Salishan Colville tribes living along the Columbia River suggested how the Delaware related to their namesake river.

Such breadth of information has been important for interpreting the voluminous materials about Delawares.  A major insight into the functioning of the Delaware cosmos, and the pivotal role of thought in it, arose from such a comparison.  During fieldwork in Oklahoma about 1910, Mark Harrington was told the story of an abandoned boy who was raised by bears.  One day, light shone into the tree den, but the mother bear "licked" it off and then remarked that some nearby hunters would not be able to find them.  Another time, however, the light came in and persisted until hunters arrived, killed the bears, and "rescued" the boy and a female cub, who was released with an offering of tobacco tied around her neck (Bierhorst 1995: 49 # 87).  The boy became a successful hunter and taught Delawares how to respect bears and other game animals.[2]

While the Bear Boy story is important, so too are its details.  What was the light that harkened doom to the bears?  To identify it, we must move across the continent to the coast of southwestern Alaska.

In two versions of "The Woman Who Married the Bear" epic from the Tlingit, Bears know that hunters are looking for them because beams of light reflected into their den.  Once, a Bear delayed the inevitable by snapping the beam to have it rebound outside, but eventually the hunters did have their way.  In their sensitive translation, Nora and Richard Dauenhauer (1987: 179, 225) explain that these beams are both the hunter's eyesight (a light reflected off the hunter's lens to be seen by the Bears) and, more especially, their "right" thoughts, which can not be deflected.  Indeed, Tlingits, along with Delawares and most other nations, stress "the importance of right thinking as well as right speech and right action in relationship to the natural and spirit worlds.  Human thoughts can be detected by bears, to whom they appear as "beams of light," which, according to the specific native term, came from an "artificial" source of pure light alone without the combustive heat of fire or sun (1987: 377).

---

[2] Among the Munsee of Ontario, this saga was the charter for the Bear sacrifice ceremony which they held in their own big house as the equivalent of the Unami Gamwing.

# PERSPECTIVES ~ 2

Any study of ritual should properly begin with religion, the wellspring of native or First Nations cultures. Delawares, in particular Unamis, were reported to be intensely religious people. Although the expression and meaning of such belief has yet to be explored in scholarly works, in largest part Delaware acts of faith were manifested in the Gamwing — the Big House Rite of Thanksgiving and Renewal.

Recently, as scholars in religious studies have looked to traditions without an official book, liturgy, and hierarchy — namely, the cultures most closely associated with anthropology, they have focused on the religious aspects of these traditions, faulting anthropologists and others in the human sciences for trying to "reduce" these beliefs and actions by treating them as expressions of more "fundamental" techno-economic or political institutions. Tribal and other religions have therefore been regarded as somehow more derivative than defining of transcendent worship and belief among human societies.

For anthropology, it has been sufficient that Delawares did this and other rituals and have been doing them for centuries. The interest, like God, is in the details. The Gamwing provided a window, a panorama, into Delaware culture. While I tried not to intrude on the beliefs and personal faith of Delawares, I listened when they professed them. Nora Thompson Dean, my mentor in all things Delaware, graduated from high school in 1924, the same year the last full Gamwing was held in Oklahoma. She talked with great feeling about women crying and wiping their eyes with their aprons during that last rite. She and they knew that it would be the last one and so they wept in sadness.

Religion was important to Nora. Her family upheld the Big House and other Delaware traditions for as long as possible. As an adult, Nora joined the Catholic Church, although she chafed at the patronizing instruction she received. Frank Speck (1931: 28) had noted a parallel between Delaware belief and Catholicism that I discussed several times with Nora, who insisted that these systems be kept distinct. Still, my questions provided a forum about faith and deeds. Most of the time, however, we discussed Delaware language, culture, and traditions in their own right.

Nora was an idealist who lived in accord with practices which have been consistently reported from Delawares for over 300 years. She consciously acted as the last of the well-trained elders, complemented by the knowledge and support of Lucy Parks Blalock. Together, these two women provided me with background and commentary on the published record, warning about its inaccuracies and misinterpretations, where willingness and availability to provide information did not guarantee that it reflected mainstream or "traditional" Delaware culture. Some of these errors about the Gamwing are treated later. Indeed, unlike many modern scholars, I firmly hold with Nora and Lucy that there are approved and disapproved sources on a culture. Traditions are meant to hold a group together and, for good reason, reside in the custody of recognized leading families. Everyone has and is entitled to personal opinions, but only some have the force of community support and these best reflect the culture.

# Anthropology

While originally inspired by sensitivity and genuine concern for other ways of life, the needs of imperialism and colonialism to control and trade with other people produced academic anthropology. Though motivated by the tainted concerns of missionaries and diplomats, those who espoused its ideals sought to understand human differences. In time, under academic auspices, it became professionalized as a scholarly discipline, and, for some, a new kind of universalist religion.

In the United States, after the Civil War, museums and public schools purveyed a sense of order as bastions of certainties while "focus shifted noticeably from the natural wonders of God to the artificial inventions of man, especially the material achievements of the Anglo-Saxon. Industrial museums and expositions displayed the superiority of civilization, and museum anthropology made the same point by exhibiting the inferiority of other peoples" (Hinsley 1981: 83). By looking at human inventiveness, scholars like Otis Mason could insist that "the true history of our race is written in things ... the material expressions of the human mind." Thereby, tribal histories became a means for indicating the ever-perfecting thoughts inexorably approaching the mind of the Creator (Hinsley 1981: 89).

After training in other disciplines like zoology or in careers like newspaper reporting, early American anthropologists without private incomes found government sponsorship through the Bureau of American Ethnology, founded in 1879. Academic programs, set in a context of the German university tradition, began before World War I and blossomed after World War II. Initially, American anthropologists were "moralists and citizens before they were scientists ... reflexive, [in] an exercise in self-study [of] a moral, reforming enterprise [when] biblical truths and religious orthodoxy [were] no longer personally persuasive or socially effective [for] White historical identity and national destiny ... lending an urgency to Indian studies [in] expressions of "salvage ethnology:" a unique blend of scientific interest, wistfulness, and guilt" (Hinsley 1981: 8, 23).

With the rise of anthropology went a corresponding sense of institutionalized homelessness. "Conformist abroad and critic at home, the anthropologist struggles constantly with ambivalence toward his own society and those he studies" (Hinsley 1981: 192). All discussions include comparative information that have led other scholars to diagnose a disease unique to anthropologists known as "amongitis" because such cross-cultural examples always begin with that preposition, as follows.

Among the Zuni Pueblos, for example, Frank Cushing, widely regarded as a genius, gloried in their cleverness as a means of enhancing his own. "He was an insider telling the rest of the world something it did not know. For later anthropologists the approach was more often that of scientists telling one another things about a group of people which the people did not know about themselves" (Hinsley 1981: 224).

Yet always and everywhere, with the full recognition of the doctrine of cultural relativity, each group had to be treated as valid in its own terms without any of the obvious ethnocentric "moral judgments" favored by historians (Washburn 1976: 479). Indeed, among anthropologists the highest compliment is reserved for a scholar such as Father Berard Haile, a Franciscan priest among the Navajo who worked closely on that language with Edward Sapir, but, to his credit, "tried to present Navajo ideology without using foreign concepts" (Darnell 1990: 259).

Above all, the danger to be avoided is any sort of evaluating judgment, such as the statement that, while engrossing, the study of "the many varieties of totem and taboo, magic rite and fetish ... may also be depressing. The variety comes down to endless variation on a few rudimentary ideas, a monotony that reveals an essential poverty of imagination, a death of spirit, a pitiful but degrading fear.... It may blur the all-important distinctions, the source of high values, by its implication that all cultures are equivalent" (Muller 1958: 71), which, of course, they are indeed.

The anthropological intention, therefore, is to be ecumenical rather than universalist, to be broadly comparative in the same way that Lionel Trilling described good literature as "the human activity that takes the fullest and most precise account of variousness, possibility, complexity, and difficulty" (Muller 1952: 24).

## Religious Studies

While anthropologists interpret tribal religions in their own terms, a notable exception has been the British scholar E. E. Evans-Pritchard, himself a convert to Catholicism, who took great care to phase the religion of the Nuer of the African Sudan in terms understandable to Christian theology.

Moreover, the emerging field of religious studies has undertaken such a task, not always with the approval of anthropologists or others concerned with the explicit integrity of these traditions. As always, the danger is that a universalist theory can only hold its own by distorting a comparative one. Nevertheless, it is clear that the Gamwing was an example of a larger class of tribal rituals, all sharing similar features of thanksgiving and world renewal.

Thus, the Shoshoni Sun Dance, and the older Father Dance, were "basically a thanksgiving ceremony in which the Supreme Being is thanked for the year that has passed and petitioned to guarantee a happy and healthy year to come, a year of plenty. We find such annual thanksgiving ceremonies among many North American tribes" (Hultkrantz 1987: 66). In their modern Sun Dance belief, "the center pole symbolizes Christ, the peripheral twelve poles his apostles, the buffalo head the Old Testament and the eagle the New Testament" (Hultkrantz 1987: 71). Moreover, the ancient Father Dance "was a round dance in which men and women formed a circle around a cedar tree, clasping hands and shuffling sideways" (Hultkrantz 1987: 66).

Those scholars seeking to define this academic study of native religions look at the Americas in avowedly religious terms rather than "the social science reduction of religion to social functions. Our concerns are with the religious functions of what we consider religious data. And these concerns complement and extend, rather than replace, current styles of academic study" (Gill 1987: 140-41). For anthropologists and others, religion has been "a window into other facets of culture such as the related systems of economic exchange or social and political systems" (Gill 1987: 6).

Rather, religion, in its own right, is best defined broadly to include, among other aspects, "those images and actions that to some person or persons both express and define the extent and character of the world, especially those images and actions that provide the framework in which humans find meaning and the terms of life's fulfillment" (Gill 1987: 152). Important for understanding both an event and its characteristics are signs, a manifestation signaling a relationship, "whose specific function it is to actualize — that is, to engage the world, to engage other persons, objects, and entities in the performance of the actions" (Gill 1987: 161).

In defining this field, Sam Gill (1987a) caused no end of furor by committing a kind of matricide in his study of Mother Earth, arguing that she only became a "goddess" in the recent political climate of native rights. Natives have been outraged by his treatment, presuming that he was denying their cherished beliefs, and those in Native Studies have been baffled at his stance since many tribes, including the Delawares (above), addressed the earth in their kinship systems as a "mother," sometimes a "grandmother." Of course, from a religious studies perspective, based in Judeo-Christian theology where assessment of god-like qualities are a major concern, Mother Earth was never a goddess in the European sense. Still, Gill could only make his point and highlight his emerging field by ignoring or denying linguistic (and thereby highly technical) and ethnographic details. At the expense of a universalist theory of religion, he has defaulted on the comparative one.

From a religious studies perspective, however, Native American religions are problematic because, for those interested in "Book" religions like Judaism, Christianity, and Islam, native tribes have "no written history, no dogma, no records, no written philosophy, no holy book. Our usual approaches to the study of religion were largely unusable and inadequate" (Gill 1987: 6). Gill might better have noted that there was no "established church led by a hierarchical priesthood" to impose an allegiance to a canon, locating religion in personal and institutional action.

Comparisons, nevertheless, are informative, and ritual, in and of itself, conveys a sense of order and purpose. For example, "Confucius emphasized the supreme importance of li, or ritual, ceremony, propriety. _Li_ corresponded to the order of the universe, as music did to its harmony; through constant ritual men came to realize their proper place in the natural and social order" (Muller 1952: 341). In addition to using ritual to live out belief, both Native Americans and Chinese experience such order and orderliness so that it may be perpetuated throughout the universe. "The plainest requirements for good human relations are sympathy, tact, forbearance, the art of compromise" (Muller 1952: 341).

Overall, the history of the loss of the Delaware Gamwing and the big house itself recalls that after the AD 70 destruction of the Jerusalem temple, Jews had only Torah, the written word of the Almighty and his Law, to sustain them (Muller 1952: 94). In an analogous situation, the Delaware returned to the occupied land itself as the wellspring of their continuity as a tribal community.

As the Delaware make clear, their epic of creation served the same function as a canon, particularly as actualized in the Gamwing when the tribal congregation annually re-created and thanked their universe.

Ironically, in lieu of regarding such creation sagas as the canon of and for a tribal tradition, Gill referred to them as merely a "paradigm" from which knowledge given in the creation stories permeates the life of the people (Gill 1987: 17). While central roles are played by core aspects such as the Blessingway, mountain earth bundles, and Changing Woman for the Navajos (Gill 1987: 23), these were not the equivalent of the Delaware Gamwing, which reflected the greater formal organization and denser population of a farming society.

Most recently, Gill has reminded his colleagues that since writing is an extension of thinking, they have "been interested in thought at the expense of action" as observed in performance, behavior, and, therefore, ritual (Gill 1987: 8, 9). "These acts themselves are creative in a primary sense, they define and shape reality; they literally make life possible" (Gill 1987, 44).

Bodies and spirits must join together. Both the material and the spiritual must be present for power to be made manifest. The material alone is drama or art, while the spiritual by itself is void. "The spiritual must reside in some manifest form to be held in common by the community" (Gill 1987: 35). For this reason, "Our words mask and impersonate [to?] suggest that these ritual processes are somehow artificial, illusions, enactments of something else which is being imitated or represented. I have been little comforted that these performances are described as reenactments of the events of the gods in the primal eras. I feel strongly that, rather than reenactments or dramatic performances, they are the actual creation of reality" (Gill 1987: 42).

However, any sensing of this conjunction had to involve <u>portals</u> to allow actual contact between the dimensions, a point overlooked by Gill in the following observation: "The performance of a sand-painting rite is in a way comparable to the shaking of hands to seal a social relationship.... in the context of a formal ritual of establishing relationships, handshaking performs an essential role by assuring each party of the acceptance of the privileges and obligations of the relationship. It marks the transformation from a relationship discussed to a relationship established and made operative" (Gill 1987: 32).

Most especially, therefore, in parallel with the theory of linkages outlined for the Delawares, both handshaking and dry painting create a conduit between previously separate entities and diverse flows. Indeed, a break in these connections was dangerous. For Navajos and other native peoples, illness is a moral and spiritual condition. "The illness suffered is attributed to the impairment of spiritual relationships. The physical symptoms of illness are only the manifestation of this situation" (Gill 1987: 122).

Again, among Navajos, as among other native communities, the best or most effective link was that through the mind, sharing thought with other beings. For example, Ted Brasser found that animal effigies on pipes from the Northeast faced the smoker "as aides in the concentration of thought" and meditation (Gill 1987: 41). Similarly, during a Navajo sing, the singer in charge of that rite usually oversaw the making of a dry painting (Gill 1987: 47), but did not apply colors himself because he had the more important role of maintaining the good thoughts and good will necessary for the whole ceremonial to be effective.

This same force of mind was highlighted throughout the Delaware creation epic, as summarized in the Creation and realized in the Gamwing. Equally important is the sense of consciousness, of mental alertness derived from the Creator for the Delaware but present in some form among all Native American communities.

## Delaware and Yup'ik Awareness

Along the west coast of Alaska, relying on 20 years of fieldwork, Ann Fienup-Riordan (1994, 50) has been exploring the intricate richness of Yup'ik (Inuit ~ Eskimo) culture, which is based less on essences and substances and more on the respectful maintenance of boundaries and passages between human, animal, and spirit worlds. As with other peoples, the Yup'ik name for themselves derives from *yuk* "person" and *-pik* "real or genuine."

Because they have remained in their homeland, outnumbering the foreigners among them, and managed the outside ideas imposed on them, the Yup'ik provide a remarkable example of how other tribal communities functioned within their religious system, articulated by a mindful awareness, genders, and series of rituals.

In contrast to the Western ("only connect") sense of society defined by Hobbes as "a diversity of individuals ultimately united through self-interest" (Fienup-Riordan 1994: 46), the Yup'ik lived in a primordial, undifferentiated universe with shifting and permeable boundaries that depended "on human action to keep them in place. The rules for living and ritual activity — both public and private — focused on the construction of boundaries and passages to circumscribe and control the flow of activity...." Such human attention to the rules, especially for sharing food and other gifts, was an "act of participation necessary both to create difference and maintain connections" (Fienup-Riordan 1994: 48). Again, intention, especially good intentions, was a vital aspect of a life well lived.

Through missionized by Russian Orthodoxy in the 1830s, Moravians since 1885 (in the guise of an ordained Delaware), and Catholics after 1888 and now shareholders in their own regional Calista Corporation (meaning "worker," from _cali-_ work) for the Yukon-Kuskokwim Delta, Yup'ik cosmology remains vital and integral to their lives as hunters and earth stewards.

Fienup-Riordan's earlier books were more historical, dealing in particular with the Yup'ik encounter with John and Edith Kilbuck, life-long Moravian missionaries who wrote volumes of letters and journals for each other. The irony is that John Kilbuck was a Delaware Indian (in the patriline of the Ohio Chief Netawatawas and Killbuck), who was raised and ordained by Moravians and, thereby, estranged from his own traditions while remaining sympathetic to a sense of community, native or otherwise.

In the end, Yup'ik became Christians by restating European notions of responsibility and accountability in terms of awareness, and of salvation in terms of rebirth not as separate individuals but within a community of believers. Only the doctrine of original sin had to be wedged into their basic beliefs (Fienup-Riordan 1991: 367).

Fienup-Riordan is careful to illustrate her analytical points with native texts, translated into English, from Yup'ik elders who regard "their words as the conduit for immortal facts about the way the world is" (Fienup-Riordan 1994: xii), firmly believing "people must not be stingy with their knowledge. They must give away what they know or it will rot their minds" (Fienup-Riordan 1994: xvii).

A good hunter focused on making a passage, a clear way, between himself and the animals he hunted, constantly thinking about and working hard to attract their attention. By his clearing of snow away from openings, these animals got a clear view of his face and decided to benefit him by offering their flesh. After the animals died and their outer remains properly treated, the spirit of that animal was reborn in another body. Indeed, for Yup'ik, existence was an endless cycle of birth and rebirth, with the same "persons" (both human and nonhuman) interacting over eons. At death, the constituents of the human body separated into mind, breath, feeling, life, warmth, shade, and name soul.

The most important aspect of all of these relationships had to do with the quality of one's mind, as revealed through the senses to enhance "awareness." Appeals to these senses opened passages between worlds. For example, the "ghosts" of humans and seals craved fresh water, which was provided by the living during rituals. The dead craved fresh water because their own was salty from all the tears shed by their mourning kin.

Until 1900, Yup'ik men and woman lived separately, the families in a sod house (*enet*) and the men in a lodge (*qasgiq*) that was "sweat house, hotel, workshop, medicine lodge, and dance hall" (Fienup-Riordan 1991: 53). Since the lodge represented the community of all persons and beings, man was the generic category, while "woman" was specific, as in English and Lenape. Women and children provided food, clothes, and support. The family or woman's house was variously associated with a womb, the moon, and the holy homes of *tuunraat*, spirit keepers of animals.

Everything in those worlds had a *yua*, an in-dwelling, human-like, fully-aware being. Those of animals, at death, contracted into their bladder to await rebirth. Each human had breath, mind, vitality, shade, and a name, inherited within its own immortal cycle of rebirths. These names were not gender-specific so each rebirth, often as not, was cross-sex.

Among the Inuit Eskimo of the Canadian central Arctic, children were dressed according to their namesakes until a definite gender was assumed. If a child had names from both men and women, it might be dressed as a boy one day and a girl the next or wear a boy parka over girl pants. Possible confusion was lessened because, unlike the understanding of modern physiology where all fetuses first develop as females, all beings for Inuit had a basic male form. For example, after the world pillars collapsed and destroyed the world, two men emerged from hummocks on Igloolik Island and married. The one that became pregnant was sung over to split into a woman and give birth to a son, who repopulated the earth (Saladin D'Anglure 1994: 95).

The foremost connection among all Inuit persons was a mindfulness or "awareness" (*ella*), whose ubiquity included that of the universe itself (*ella yua*) and of every other item. Today as in the past, Yup'ik out on the tundra still "feed the land" by burying food and offerings to show their regard from this larger awareness. Everything had to be done with slow, careful deliberation to avoid giving offense. Berries were picked with individual regard, and a good person always turned driftwood to "give it relief from the tedium and discomfort of lying in one position" (Fienup-Riordan 1994: 59).

The universe and everything else watched for proper behavior and this watchfulness was represented by the circle and dot motif ⊙ which decorated many human-made objects (Fienup-Riordan 1990: 55), the ringed center portraying the universe, often with the five levels above the earth ⊙[5] represented by that number of rings.

Each dot was, of course, as tysic, a nexus of time, space, and affect. In Yup'ik this temporal and spatial union was reflected in words such as *ciuliaq* = ancestor, leader derived from *ciu-* meaning 'the forepart of a body, front area, or time before'; in contrast to *kingu-* meaning 'rear end, back area, or time after' (Fienup-Riordan 1990: 202, 212).

Children, in particular, had to be taught to use all their senses and synthesize information each and every day. Upon waking, they were sent outside to take in a sense the wind, weather, and wayfarers. The aim of childhood was *ellange-*, to obtain awareness as a lasting memory of experiences.

Marriage negotiations focused not on beauty, wealth, or status, but on whether the potential partner handled food in a careful, honest, and respectful manner. The foremost rule of any marriage was not to "injure each other's mind" (Fienup-Riordan 1994: 175). A husband restricted his activities every time his wife was in menstrual or postpartum seclusion.

The primordial world was thin, allowing all beings, from humans and animals to extraordinary creatures, to interact more easily, but now it is hardening and thickening so humans have a greater duty to act responsibly in this moral universe because "Illness was, first and foremost, a moral state ... the body's physical response to the way a person chose to live life" (Fienup-Riordan 1994: 189). If standard treatments did not work, the patient was given a new name so as to start over.

Passages were blocked by thoughtlessness, including being clumsy with a knife, sleeping late, eating and drinking carelessly, bumbling through a door, being noisy, or wasting personal abilities. A proper person was ever concerned to restrict his or her breath, sight, thought, speech, and, with the help of restrictive belt and hood, body movement. Weapons, tools, and containers were carefully made and decorated both to please the artifact itself and to encourage game animals to give themselves up to such an attractive lure.

In everything, Yup'ik observed their duty to carefully perform "acts of differentiation — cutting, binding, covering, circling — to create the possibility of future relation" (Fienup-Riordan 1994: 355). "Men and women engaged in opening the boundaries between worlds protected themselves from merging with the spirit world by covering their bodies with gut parkas or by painting themselves with soot, clay, and urine. Or they might place grass mats or skins between themselves and the thin earth lest they slip through" (Fienup-Riordan 1994: 360).

This attitude toward a thin primordial world resonated in renewal rites throughout the Americas, distinctly for the Barasana of Colombia (Hugh-Jones 1979) and by implication for Delawares. Initiations, in particular, were intended to put youths in touch with this more vital universe where interactions among all beings were more easy and productive.

The five major rituals of the traditional Yup'ik celebrated such renewals. The Bladder Festival, when men evoked their spirit helpers in song and dance for five days, ended by returning to the sea the bladders of all animals slain the previous year so they could be reborn. Each year, with greater elaboration every ten years, a Feast for the Dead invited these shades into the qasgiq to receive fresh water, clothing, and sustenance. The Kelek masked dance invited animal spirits into the lodge and entertained them, with men and women reversing roles. At the center of most masks was a tiny humanoid identified as the "thinking part" of the being. The Messenger Feast hosted a visit from another village, and the Asking Festival celebrated cross-sex cousins (FZch, MBch)[3] within the community.

Each ritual focused on relations with a particular kind of "person," human or other-wise, giving attention to the major facets in the mosaic of their universe. As each part is given careful respect, so awareness increases of the greater interconnected totality.

Always, the probity of Yup'ik actions confirmed their constant awareness of human duties toward this moral universe, where they would "only connect" as community members (not as isolated or alienated individuals) fulfilling their obligations to other persons by supplying their desires. "According to Nelson Islanders, animals desire things they lack — seals that live in the ocean crave fresh water, belukha whales, which cannot crawl out on the ice to sun themselves, desire light and heat; and fish that swim in the river crave dry land" (1990: 186).

---

[3] Key kin terms are F = father M = mother B = brother Z = sister S = son D = daughter ch = child.

Emphatically, to Yup'iks, "people were social beings first and individuals only if they forgot themselves, in which case their downfall was assured" (1990: 76); survival, intellectually and physically, involved everyone in common cause, working and thinking together.

## Mindful Universe

All said, the best and purest form of connection among all beings was thought. Public gatherings were successful because all shared the same mind, the same heart, and the same intention. Contact with other dimensions through portals was vital to survival and goodness, but to involve humans these links had to be made somehow obvious to the senses.

While humans and other persons shared the same mind, what distinguished each was the manner in which their mind was put into motion. In all cases, the vital duality was that of men or of women. Men were active and far ranging in the outside, while women were modest and decent inside. All beings had gender and, therefore, two basic kinds of mobility.

In this regard, Delaware religion, as others rooted in an ancestral landscape, was not as concerned with transactions, relying on the meaning of trans- as "going across so as to change," but rather on sympathy as "coming together in experience." The intention was not so much to transact, "to climb across" in the sense of going above, but rather to trans-send, "to send across" to make contact and allow for power to pulse among persons, both transient humans and immortals transmitting increments of power.

For the Inupiaq Eskimo at Point Hope on the Alaskan North Slope, Edith Turner (1994, 77) found the same belief. "Then traditional healing, concerned with bodies, is a universal medium of connectedness, for we all have the body. In hands-on Inupiaq healing, the trouble is taken out by the connection of the hands of the healer with the sick tissues of the patient; bodies connect, they 'converse' in a way hard to describe, for the healing involves spirituality. The moment of healing is the mutual moment of awareness, a moment of concrete 'sym-pathy,' 'feeling with', although not without some community sanctions. Among Paiutes, "In diagnosing the disease, the doctor and the community pass a certain type of judgment on the patient and often they also judge other members of the society" (Whiting 1950: 53).

In sum, for Delawares, salvation meant that good life, good will, and being of good mind were all connected, most especially during the Gamwing held in the Big House, their most cosmic tysic (cf p9).

# DELAWARE CULTURE ~ 3
## Creation Matrix Echo World

## Creation

With this cultural background and advance summary, the predominant origin saga of the Delaware, first written down in 1624 and actualized in the Gamwing until 1924, will now be presented in detail.

"The One Who Created Us By Thought" (*Kishaylamukong*) sat, as he has always been sitting, and decided to create the world, which thereby began to take shape and substance. Initially, it was like a globe with the bottom half filled with water and the top half filled with sky divided into twelve levels. By directing a beam of his thought into the sea, He caused a gigantic turtle to rise to the surface. As the water rolled off its back, the clinging soil began to dry out.

The shell reflected the curve of the globe, its bulge matching the sky dome and its lines the levels of the sky. Possessed of its own intelligence because it sprang from the thought of the Creator, the turtle became the earth, a miniature of the universe. Like all turtles, it looks west, facing the direction of the sunset, death, and completion.

At the center of its shell, the intersection of a weblike pattern of plates, the Creator thought an enormous tree to spark into being. An evergreen with red veins, emblematic of life, it became the red cedar, serving as the upright (axis mundi) connecting sky, earth, and sea. Main roots at its base formed a cross pointing north, south, east, and west, making this trunk the universal nexus (a tysic).[4] Ever since, cedar wood, sprigs, and needles have been especially pleasing to the Creator and served as crucial offerings, particularly as rising smoke, for getting His attention.

Encouraged by the Creator, the turtle and cedar undertook the creation of the First Man and First Woman, the parents of all life. The cedar sprang upwards to sprout the Man; then it bent down and touched the earth, connecting and engendering the Woman. Associated with the upward expanse of sky and Creator, Man became unlimited – open, unbounded, and outside, providing an active form or container, while Woman was limited to the earth – associated with the closed, confined, and inside, as modest contents and contained. Both properties complement each other, and, via the Creator, they shared qualities of Mind differently put into motion.

The earth-turtle became the earthly abode of humans, animals, plants, and deities arranged in a great web of being with the Creator at the apex, the ultimate source of energy, thought, and life. Diversified into many different species and lifeways, each creation was instructed to uphold its own customs for the wellbeing of all. The Creator maintained his closest ties with the Delawares, known to many other tribes as Grandfathers, and provided the *Lenapehittuk* (Delaware River) as a homeland, where the Delawares long prospered.

After whites arrived, however, Delawares were abused and displaced, moving ever westward along the back of the turtle, seeking new homes. According to prophesy, if the Delaware

---

[4] Again, tysic (p9) stands for **T**ime **S**pace **C**enter with the **Y** pointing down and the **I** up.

nation ever reaches the Pacific sea, their stay on the earth will be over and everything, deprived of Delaware intercession, will end because "the entire continent will become _kʷulakan_ and will be destroyed" (Miller 1975).

## Echo

Delaware elders insist on the continuity of their culture, while recognizing that, as traditions passed from everyday usage, they became ritualized within the Gamwing. Hence, their link with the past and this ritual became mutually interdependent, as revealed by examining the threeway interchange among the Delawares themselves, the documents, and the interpretive device called the struckon.

This model, contracted from structural configuration (Miller 1979), presents a relational framework for portraying a culture as an integrated whole in terms of an **echo** reverberating throughout a series of component matrices, which are context sensitive for each set of inter-relationships. In some situations, for example, the body is named upward from feet to head to suggest upward growth, but in others it is named downward from head to feet, as in birthing. More encompassing categories tend to appear in multiple contexts, while highly specific ones occur in isolation.

Because so much of Delaware culture, and its traditions, have been previously treated in piecemeal fashion – cut up and divided by topics and interests – such a holistic approach is necessary to understand the process whereby Delaware have survived against impossible odds. Such disjointed considerations make Delaware survival all the more baffling to outsiders, but not to the Delaware themselves.

Culture is a coherent system, worked out by debate and compromise, conferring meaning and order on the world. It is articulated both by the linkages of an atemporal structure (or template) and by historically variable permutations (or configurations) transforming over time. Human Culture, therefore, becomes particular cultures as each concentrates on a particular tension having ramifications through ecological, personal, sociological, and cosmological expressions which are influenced by time, place, and external pressures. Over the long run, however, certain distinctive semantic categories, such as core notions of the person (the self, Miller 1991a) and of internal boundaries (separating local social institutions from those of neighboring tribes), continue unchanged.

An axiomatic tension pervades all categories of a culture and influences the character of its society (social forms), while also being dependent upon biological aspects of gender, age, and ability. Previously, Miller (1979) adopted the term paideuma from those interested in configurations, although, in its original sense, it referred only to a single all-pervading category. To make clear that this tension is dynamic, pervasive, and reflexive, this tension is now called an "**echo**" to indicate its reverberating quality throughout a culture.

As the cultural hallmark, the echo provides emphasis, variety, and overall cohesion to traditions. The echo and all of its emanations are expressed as relationships within a matrix, a threefold nested sequence composed of members which are specific exclusive, generic inclusive, or categoric inclosive.

The first two parts of a matrix are regularly paired as opposites, such that the exclusive represents disjunction, difference, restriction, the definite, and the specific; while the inclusive expresses conjunction, similarity, integration, the indefinite, and the generic.[5]

For Delaware, Woman is the most constrained, specific, limited, marked, and exclusive; Man is unconstrained, generic, unlimited, unmarked, and inclusive. Mind is categorically open, permeating, limitless, and inclosive. Of note, for Iroquois, these definitions are reversed, with man a special instance of woman.

Each opposition is integrated by mediators, which share some attributes of each of the pair, together with features distinctively enabling them to provide closure, linking themselves and all the opposites together into a whole system of relational categories. Claude Levi-Strauss (1969: 469) regarded such a triad as fundamental to human thought and culture: "conjunction, disjunction, and mediation each illustrated by empirical modalities … remain definable as relations [and] become the terms of a combinatory system operating on a higher level … as the beginning of a veritable logic of propositions."

Other scholars have also recognized these relations, though variously interpreted, as the crux of a culture. For Rodney Needham (1973, 1980), opposed categories were symmetrical equals, while Fadwa El Guindi (1973: 17) defined the binary opposites as closed and the interrelating mediators as open. E. E. Evans-Pritchard (1974: 245 #2) noted that such relations can occur across cultural boundaries as well as within them by arguing why the spiritual leaders of the Nuer and the Dinka, neighbors in the African Sudan, were named for different spears: "Whereas among the Nuer the fighting-spear is the symbol of the clan [as] exclusiveness and opposition, among the Dinka the fishing-spear is the symbol of spiritual leadership [as] inclusiveness and unity."

For Delaware culture, which was and is remarkably triplex, the members of a matrix were asymmetrical, nesting within ever more expansive categories. The exclusive is closed, the inclusive is open, and the inclosive is pervasive, forming an inter-nested matrix. These matrices could be and were manipulated to broaden, narrow, or neutralize their interrelationships, while their polarities could be and were reversed or repositioned within a ranked series to create variety as conditions called for new solutions.

In each case, inclusive and exclusive involved substitutions within a set (paradigmatic) of metaphors whose representatives replace one another within the same category. For example, universally human equations link

$$\text{Right} = \text{men} \;\; = \text{animals} = \text{night}$$
$$\text{Left} \;\; = \text{women} = \text{plants} = \; \text{day}$$

On occasion, however, these elements could and did switch alignments, as among Delawares, which suggests that the interrelated series formed something like a double helix spiralling out into time and space.

---

5. In linguistics, this distinction is called the marked or unmarked, as indicated respectively by plus or minus (+ / - or A / not-A).

Categorically inclosive mediators were sequential (syntagmatic), their commonalities were those which aligned a series of categories. Depending on the echo involved, mediators acted as links within a sequential hierarchy of higher and more pervasive relationships.

In terms of a helix, the exclusive was a tight inside strand alternating with a looser inclusive one. Covering them, so that it shared some of their attributes while maintaining others uniquely its own, was the inclosive. In specifically Delaware terms, as can be seen from art designs and the shapes of traditional graveposts, the exclusive was like a bar (-), the inclusive like a cross (+), and the inclosive like a crossed circle ⊕.

While the echo and matrix help to explain Delaware culture as represented by the Gamwing, this model is intended to be universal, an aspect of Culture as everywhere defined by its tensions and structurings. As suggested by Levi-Strauss, the global human tension is Culture / Nature, the latter conscientiously ordered and the former accidentally randomized. Culture is itself part of Nature because it is the species-specific adaptation of humanity. In terms of a matrix, Nature is inclusive and Culture exclusive.

Generally, their mediator might be Society, because it derives both from natural behaviors and from cultural constructs. For Levi-Strauss, however, the universal mediator is Mind, bridging the physiology of the brain and the rationality of thought. Interestingly, moreover, this view is not limited to French academe. Many American tribes believe in the same ultimate mediation (Miller 1980b), as do the Delaware. Mind provides mediators with a special quality, enabling them to permeate and unify the whole. Often this quality is also symbolized by fire, a natural force put to cultural use during the processes of cooking, smoking, and heating.

Among Delaware, the Mind, especially as Memory, was deified as the apex of their pantheon, *Kishaylamukong*, "the one who created us by thought" by engendering the universe. The Delaware echo, therefore, was inclusive Man and exclusive Woman, as complementary yet distinct categories. Man was defined in terms of form, container, and the outside; while Woman was content, contained, and inside. For example, in the native view of anatomy, the heart belonged to the category of Man (that is, it was manly), while blood was womanly. Water was all-pervasive and intelligent, because the Creator suffused it with his thought (Mind) at creation. As a mediator, water shared qualities of both Man and Woman, representing them in different contexts. During rituals and prayers, water in streams, lakes, rivers, and seas was addressed as Grandfather, while water in wells, springs, or vessels was called Mother. One was free flowing and unconstrained, but the other contained.

For the echo, Woman was nested within Man, and both were inclosed by Mind. Thus, gender and memory were vital aspects of the Delaware cosmos that survived the vicissitudes of many dislocations. This triad has defined and will define the Delaware for as long as they have been able to maintain their own traditions, socialize their own children, and speak Lenape. At the heart of these abilities, moreover, was the strategy of including everything essential or meaningful into the Gamwing, making it a superb cultural summary of the Delaware lifeway. Once a year, at the Big House, Delaware entered sacred time and space to relive in thought and deed the distilled epitome of their culture.

During the ceremony, Delaware were re-presented with significant metaphors and mediators expressive of sensory, interpersonal, and cosmic concerns. Each of the three components had a characteristic pair, which was also important across cultures. For the sensory, it was right/left; for the interpersonal, man/woman; and, for the cosmic, night/day and animal/plant.

## Culture

| Woman | Man | Mind |
|-------|-----|------|
| exclusive | inclusive | inclusive |

## Sensory

| right | left | heart |
|-------|------|-------|
| bloodroot | black | crimson |
| charcoal | wampum | sticks |
| cedar | tobacco | incense |
| laughter | silence | vigil |
| sweet | salty | spicy |
| 1 | 3 | 4 |
| inside | outside | fire |

Sensory emanations, because they relate to mind-body interactions, include colors, sights, sounds, silences, smells, styles of cooking, foods, tastes, hand (laterality) priority (and by extension, tactile expressions in shapes, textures, and manufactures), physiological states, and even pattern numbers because they are often used to bring order to sensory experiences (Miller 1979: 793).

## Interpersonal

| women | men | gifted |
|-------|-----|--------|
| farming | hunting | fishing |
| (Winetkok) | Munsee | Unami |
| Turkey | Wolf | Turtle |
| home | hall | stockade |
| Bear | Otter | Doll |
| Maize | Football | Məsing |
| town | forest | hearth |

Interpersonal emanations, because they represent the collective interaction of individuals, including various institutional contexts such as technology, economy, polity, descent, life cycle, religion, and language (Miller 1979: 793).

## Cosmic

| plants | animals | fish |
|---|---|---|
| Thunderers | Sun | Məsing |
| Pleiades | Comet | Moon |
| Cannibal | orphan | hero |
| Red Snake | Drawer-Under | Turtle |
| Tree | Sea | Creator |

Cosmic emanations, involving humans within their total environment, include symbolically charged biota, terrain, geography, meteorological phenomena, celestial bodies, myth characters, temporal progressions, philosophical tenets, and other-worldly dimensions (Miller 1979: 793).

## The Delaware World

In sum, the Delaware earth rests on the back of a giant turtle with a giant cedar tree growing at its center. Above it are the twelve levels of sky, each with a keeper,[6] and the Creator sitting in the highest one. Around and below the earth is the sea.

When building a sweat lodge, each of the twelve ribs is dedicated to a particular being, which gives a relative sequence for understanding the make up of the Delaware universe. In order, these are 1) Creator in heaven, 2) sun (day orb), 3) moon (night-orb), 4) earth, 5) fire, 6) water, 7) shelter, dwelling, house, 8) maize (Indian corn), 9) west, 10) south, 11) east, 12) north.

The cosmos itself consists of six types of mortal beings, according to Nora Thompson Dean (Miller 1975). Each type has attributes that might include thought, language, ability to reproduce, soul, ghost, and species-specific characteristics, such as bipedalism for persons, leaves for trees, and feathers for birds. Other diagnostic contrasts include male/female, day/night, wild/tame, and good/bad. Direct translations of Lenapi words are in single quotation marks (' '), while the native word itself appears italic inside parenthesis after an equal sign (= ). Inside parenthesis or as a second term is the plural, ending in a vowel for the inanimate <*skikw(o)*> or a vowel before a final K for the animate <*awɛn(čik)*>.

---

[6] Since only the faces of the Sky Keepers appear on the side posts of the Big House, and the lowest one nearest the earth is *Məsing*[w], wearing bearskin, it may be that each Keeper wore the skin of an appropriate species and acted as its "boss." Within the Big House, these keepers witness the ceremonies, facing inward. The faces on the four door sideposts are smaller than those on the six support posts, which may mean they were farther away. Since visionaries had the fire on the left side, the sequence of faces should be a spiral from east to north to west to south. North to south to east to west is also possible, since west is clearly the end.

From most widespread to more specific, these beings are plant(s) ("grasses, weeds" = *skikw(o)*), which are indistinct except when they serve as medicines; tree(s) (= *hıttuk*ʷ, *hıtkuk*) with thought, reproduction, close kinship with the Delaware, leaves, and a language and powers of their own; maize corn (= *xʌsk*ʷ*im*), called "Mother Corn," with thoughts, a language, and a soul; bird(s) with thought, reproduction, wings, feathers, and a language of their own; animal(s) (= *-xʌm*), with thought, reproduction, four legs, fur, and a willingness to take pity on people and ask deities to bestow power on them; and person(s) (= *awɛn(čik)*).

A person has three souls, one in the blood, one in the bone, and one suffusing the entire body. At death, the body soul goes back to the Creator, the bone soul becomes a ghost, and blood forms a ball that lurks in dark recesses and is dangerous if encountered. A twisted mouth or paralysis is the result of encountering a ghost without proper spiritual protection.

Animals are further categorized as land mammal(s), turtle(s), snake(s), lizard(s), frog(s), toad(s), literally "waist," fish(es), sea mammal(s), shellfish(es), and bug(s). Persons include figures from legend such as a giant cannibal (= *hmuwe*), "pimply face" (= *məkihape*), an orphan finally taken in by an old couple who watched him grow into a wise hunter and scout, and a humorous but wise man (= *wɛhixamukɛs*) noted for the fact that he always mistook metaphors as being absolutely literal.

Immortal beings (= *manituwak*) dispense power to other beings in the world. Their association is with particular dimensions or habitats, and will be so divided below.

At the apex of the system is "the one who created us by his thoughts" (= *kišelamukɔng*), the Creator, eternally sitting in the twelfth or highest heaven, who alone can create things and events by his very thoughts. Also in the sky are the Thunderer(s) (= *pɛthakhuwe(yok)*) – large birds with the heads of old or young men who live in the sky, controlling thunder and lightning; "war spirit" (= *ilawənıtu*) – any comet; Jupiter (= *kečipənɛs*), Mars (= *mʌxalʌng*ʷ), "bunched together ones" (= *asisktayɛsʌk*) – Pleiades, who were originally seven Delaware boys lifted into the sky by their purity or innocence.

In the waters are red snake (= *məxaxkuk*) – an enormous, horned red snake who lived in the ocean until he was killed and pieces of him divided among various tribes as tribal palladia; drawer(s) under (= *wewtunəwɛs(ʌk)*) – serpentine male spirits who live in all bodies of water after they were born of a girl who neglected to cover her genitals when she bathed.

At the edges of the world are the four directional spirits (= *ɛlantuwiɛkw*, vocative name), who are Grandfather North (= *luwanʌntu*) – closely associated with snow and icicles (When these are bothered, he sends more snow and cold weather); Grandfather East (= *wɛhɛnjiopvng*); Grandfather West (= *ehəliwsikakw*); and Grandmother South (= *šawnaxawəš*). Alternating warm and cold blasts of wind mean that South and North are trying out their powers.

On the forested land are "all over the woods one" (= *wemahtekənis*) – a leather-clad man, conferring powers of strength and stamina, about three feet high who is very agile and lives wherever he can find a wooded area; "the one who leads people astray" (= *tehtaongələmhaləwes*) – the will-o-the wisp; *mʌsing*< – sky keeper, fur-covered like a bear, nearest the earth and guardian of game animals and vegetation; dolls (= *ɔhtasʌk*) – portrayed as carved wooden dolls formerly inherited in certain families and believed to be alive; whirlwind (=*ɔwiyalahsu*); cyclone, tornado (= *kaoxən*); little people (= *manitutətʌk*) – about a foot high, able either to cause painful injuries or to grant great stamina or the ability to cure without the aid of medicines.

A likely import from Christianity, living below, is bad spirit (= *mahtantu*), the Evil One or Devil. While there were and are bad, nasty, and harmful spirits, especially in deep water and remote, dark regions, they did not have the European connotation of evil or demonic.

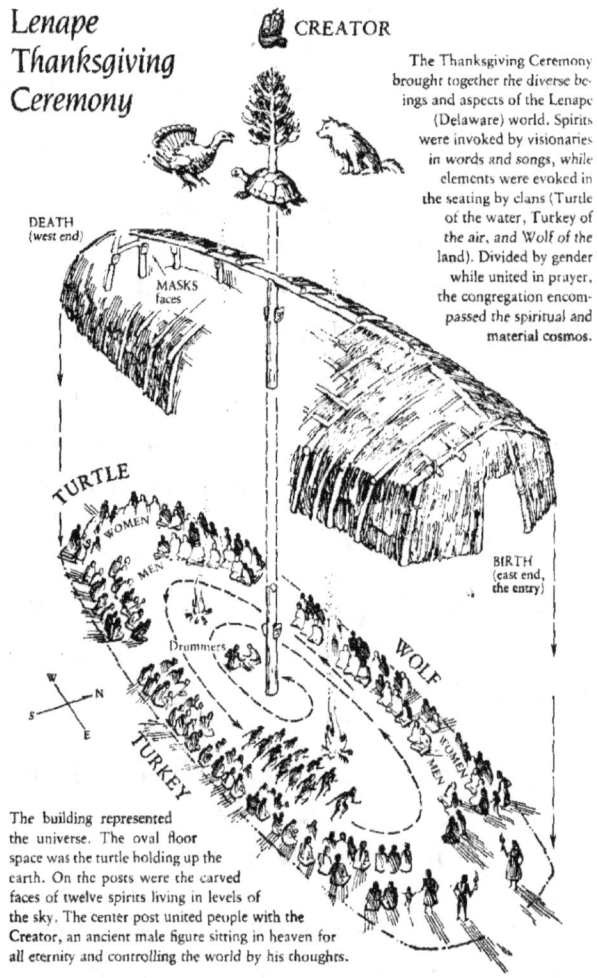

Image #3 ~ Gamwing Cosmology (by Hugh Claycombe)

# FEASTING ~ 4

## Visionaries

Since leadership involved all members of important families, public aspects of politics among the Delaware were traditionally in the hands of men, while women controlled private and domestic matters. Such families formed an elite made up of sanctioned visionaries, as distinct from the members of families who were "empty."

Every species, from ants to zebras, was believed to have their own prototypical boss, regardless of whether or not these creatures were actually known to Delaware. Also, there were unseen and unnamed forces that occasionally appeared to people in visions. All of them were sapient, having human emotions and sensibilities. Traditionally, in the telling of it, Delaware kept any such encounter as vague as possible. Visionary recitations were always deliberately sketchy since immortals were more powerful than humans. To name them called them forth, potentially causing harm. Each of them required special taboos and treatment, such as accepting only certain offerings and rejecting others. Collectively, all of the visionaries propitiated a vast range of immortal beings. Each alliance was an aspect in the array of all other bonds, everyone of which benefited every Delaware and intertwined the entire cosmos. In return, humans gained secular authority, prestige, and wealth derived from these spiritual links. The relations between those gifted and those empty were not exploitative; they were supportive, reciprocal, and fluid, or, at least, permeable.

Only visionaries were eligible for all of the positions of civil and religious leadership. Since they also had the ability to confer names, they admitted new members into the community. Nora Dean initially objected to any division between social levels, thinking that it made the "empty" people seem inferior. After further discussion about access to authority, however, she agreed to a difference between the "gifted" and the "empty" because those with a gift from an immortal were bound to succeed.

In general, attitudes toward visionaries were emotionally charged, ranging from admiration and respect to outright fear that the gift could be abused. After an immortal had provided access to potency, the person was free to use it to help or to harm. Some, hopefully few, visionaries became selfish or murderous with their power, using sorcery to take vengeance. Most, however, used it in support of the community.

Both boys and girls at puberty could acquire an immortal ally, but only boys were publicly forced to quest. In consequence, male visionaries outnumbered females, as "empty" people outnumbered "gifted" ones. Once a vision was received and contact established, the experience was not made public, and, even then, only in the vaguest terms, until the person was past middle age. In maturity, continued success convinced public consensus that the gift was genuine.

The elite formed an oligarchy, therefore, in which older members, families rather than individuals, represented many generations devoted to public service. Understandably, children of these families were also included in the elite, in expectation of and training for their own successful careers. Often, children were sent to the same places for the same gifts as their ancestors had ventured. The hallmarks of a gifted person generally were age, wisdom, maturity, prominence, oratory, and success. In addition, generosity was expected, with most honor coming to those who shared with those most destitute.

There were no rigid social classes or other hard distinctions between the two types of people, at least historically. The elite were never aloof to their obligations (noblesse oblige), while the most destitute might eventually gain help from a supernatural and receive belated social recognition. In public and private, everyone worked together, with the elite planning, guiding, directing, and encouraging others. Every Delaware performed tasks necessary for all of them to survive. Society as a whole consisted of a wide variety of role types: gifted and empty, leaders and workers, elite and average, rich and poor, domestic and religious.

Thus, Native curers or doctors also had political authority, particularly if they were members of chiefly families or worked in close conjunction with a leader.

## Leadership

As throughout Native America, Delaware leaders drew their strength from family and personal associations with specific places, often the holy homes of spirits. At least three official leadership positions were recognized among Delaware. In the distant past, these would have been positions within a town, grading into regional levels of leadership, if not also a national one. The three positions were those of councilor, captain, and chief, each held by families whose male and female members constituted the elite.

The councilor ("wise man" in Lenape) combined respect, authority, and proven relations with the supernatural. He earned respect because of his friendly personality, manifest kindness, acknowledged wisdom, and strong sense of responsibility. These men formed a council, deciding by consensus and influencing both the community and its leader. Since the chief also sat with the council, he, in turn, could personally influence their decisions. For important meetings, councilors shaved their foreheads as a reminder to act with cautious wisdom.

Published sources mention only "wise men," but modern Delaware also has a term for "wise women," although these female equivalents never met in public council, as they did among the Iroquois. They were female members of leading families, raised to take a prominent role in community activities, particularly in tasks involving women. While all women could attend councils to listen, any comments they contributed were made for them by a man, generally a father, brother, or husband. Women believed this was necessary to maintain a reputation for modesty. Similarly, when women recited in the Big House, they were accompanied by a male visionary. In symbolic terms, of course, women were exclusive so when a woman acted in public, a male speaker gave form to her thoughts and statements.

The avowed exception to the modest demeanor expected of women was the "old ladies," who acted with the freedom of men – and then some. They had great license and high seniority, adding weight to their opinions, wishes, and decisions. Also, a long, healthy life proved access to immortals. Old people could use these contacts to help or to harm others, especially when angered or displeased. Even so, the words, thoughts, and collective opinions of these old women were presented in formal council by men. Informally, they seem to have done much as they pleased, licensed by general awe and an enjoyment of their bold, sometimes bawdy, humor.

While councilors formed the supporting majority of the tribal elite, outright leadership was shared between the complementary positions of war captain and of chief, the martial and the civil authorities.

The protector of clan and town was the captain (*ila* "warrior," garbled as *kitartilax* "head warrior" in Speck APS #921), who earned his position on the basis of personality, prowess, and supernatural sanction. The late Anna Brown Parks insisted that the captain was really only a "scout" (*netupalis*) who led the war parties after someone else organized or recruited them. The majority of sources, however, say that there was a head warrior who took charge of such expeditions, after rising through the ranks himself. Any career, including military ones, had to be initiated by a vision appropriate to that task. If a boy received such a gift to be a warrior, he strove to organize war parties, gain victories, and have none of his recruits slain. If a death occurred, he atoned to the grieving families by giving them booty, wergild (blood money), or captives to be adopted in place of the deceased. Inauspicious results refuted his claims to a vision. By and large, these captains were younger, stronger, and more impetuous than the chiefs, who were noted for great forbearance.

While consensus recognized several coterminous captains, there were formalized roles for three of them, one for each of the matriclans. The clan warrior replaced the clan leader during periods of extended conflict. These captains and chiefs alternated the leadership of the clan or community, a common feature throughout Native America.

Because the Colonial period was spent in almost constant warfare, war captains had a strong role in historical documents. Such alternation of authority between chief and captain supported the statement by Herman (1950: 59) that a single clan or clan segment occupied or "owned" a single town, an extension of the bond between women and land. Adams (1906: 298) suggested that each clan town was located near enough to the other clans for their leaders to meet. "The three clan chiefs acted the same as three judges for the whole tribe. In council the opinion of two was taken as final. The clans were always traced from the mother's side, and lived in separate villages in olden times, but now they live together. Each chief had his war chief or head warrior under him." Lawrence Hicks (IPH 5: 44) also said that each clan had its own town or settlement and that if a man of one clan wanted to marry a girl of another, after the legal age of 15-16, he had to secure permission from the councils and chiefs of the two clan towns.

The clan captain led revenge raids to retaliate for the killing or maiming of clansmembers. The other captains supervised the protection, tactics, and defense of the whole community. While chiefship was hereditary, the roles of captain and shaman were filled by those with appropriate abilities and family ties. During colonial times, several such men rose to prominence. The best known of these was Teedyuscung, who maneuvered himself into a position of tribal leadership among the holdouts along the Susquehanna River (Wallace 1949, Miller 1999b). While such tribal and national leaders appear to develop gradually in the historic record, they probably had prehistoric antecedents.

Presumably, such tribal and national captains would have supervised intertribal expeditions, or protected the community during seasonal moves to the coast or large riverine fisheries. Historically, men joined war parties, or indicated their willingness to do so, by "striking" a red-painted post set up at a war dance, during which recruits heightened their enthusiasm, resolve, and adrenalin.

Although war was a male prerogative, Oklahoma Delaware recalled at least one woman who "stopped the drum" at war dances to recite her deed of valor. As "striking the post" promised participation in an expedition, "stopping the drum" enabled warriors to boast of their exploits with public approval. For a woman to do this meant that she was publicly recognized as a warrior. This woman had killed a man who was trying to steal her horses, and she was rumored to have killed others with less provocation. Interestingly, her more extensive participation in the war dances and military events became curtailed by other women, who resented her notoriety.[7]

Although the information is sometimes confusing, there are considerable data on the role and status of the chief (*sakima*), or, better, of chiefly families. Heckewelder (1876: 52, 107) wrote that each town located along a river or a stream had its own chief, and that these were subordinate to a national council of high chiefs. These great councils assembled once or twice a year for deliberations, which presumably also included formalized mourning for deceased leaders and the installation of new ones, as was done by the League of the Iroquois at Condolence Councils. At these meetings, the sacred fire of the Delaware was kindled, tribal history recited, and archives inspected, including tally sticks, wampum belts, tokens, and other mnemonics.

Nora Dean said a chief was followed because people respected him, not because he could apply sanctions or punish offenders. Based on his family background, clanship, and abilities, a Delaware chief had authority but no coercive power; his actions supposedly followed from decisions made by the council. Although the office was inherited matrilineally, it was only effective if supported by council and community consensus. Kinietz (1946: 56) reported that a chief was selected from the possible heirs within a lineage by a general council of chiefs and councilors. During the twentieth century, the Oklahoma Delaware elected their leader, replacing consensus by majority rule. In all, during the past, a proper chief had to have physical stamina, seniority, oratorical fluency in Lenape, and the goodwill of his constituents.

Only Trowbridge (TC) implied that a chief governed by a kind of divine right or favor, probably an overstatement of the supernatural sanctions needed for this career. He wrote that the Creator once lived on the earth and directly led the Delaware until he left for heaven, selecting "a person possessed of all His own virtues" to become the first chief.

Wallace (1947: 6) reported that each Canadian Munsee clan had a matron who selected a candidate from her own chiefly lineage to fill a vacant position, recommending him for approval by the clan council. Since this is also the Iroquois system, additional outside influence reinforced the Munsee practice of elite women selecting leaders from their own families.

In the homeland, since this office was passed through a matriline, the selection of a chief was probably made by a clan council of senior men and women. Their decision was announced to the community or the tribe, then later approved by a council of other clan chiefs. Robert Grumet[8] suggested an aboriginal gradient for this practice among the early historic Delaware such that Munsee were more matrilineal and southern New Jersey groups more patrilineal, but this may be a bias in the documents. Certainly, for the entire East Coast the gradient was patrilateral in the north

---

[7] Such resentment by other women may have also been a factor in the resignation of Beata in Indiana.

[8] Robert Grumet, personal communication.

and matrilineal in the south. Moreover, Munsee seem to have functioned with moieities of Canine and Fowl, while Unami had the full triad that also included mediating Turtle.

Grumet (1979: 23-25) also suggested there were three levels of chiefly authority in colonial times, consisting of village, district, and tribal leaders, together with their families. He also suspected a level intermediate between village and district, probably associated with drainage. Sites mentioned in documents seem to have favored fishing, hunting, and defense rather than agriculture, but this may reflect a native willingness to sell off such resource areas in favor of continuing their free mobility, as well as holding off European's greed for available native farmland to save them the labor of clearing their own fields for wheat and other imported crops.

Harrington (ms.) said clan chiefs inherited their offices through women, but the tribal chiefs were elected, so it was possible for a son to succeed his own father if he had the necessary qualifications. By the end of the last century in Oklahoma, each clan advanced a candidate for the tribal chiefship, and one of these was elected by Delaware adults to fill the office. Most of these chiefs belonged to the Wolf clan as did most Oklahoma Delaware. While these were the chiefs recognized by federal bureaucracies, the traditionalists also elected their own chiefs: Simon, Jackson, and then Elkhair. These men led activities ranging from trading parties with the Osage, to namings, weddings, and funerals, in addition to the Gamwing. According to Nora Dean, a chief could not be younger than his late forties, nor older than his late sixties because he needed to be actively involved in everything.

These traditional leaders were fondly recalled by the Big House people, who called the others "paper chiefs" because they had warrants from the American government. Famous among these national leaders with "papers" were William Anderson, James and John Conner, James and Charles Ketchum, John Sarcoxie, and Charles Johnnycake (Journeycake) (Weslager 1972: 422). Anna Parks always insisted that a man could not be chief of the Delaware without a paper from Washington, D.C. As appointed representatives, paper chiefs proliferated throughout the world wherever colonialists have insisted that a single individual be responsible for carrying out their demands among his own people. Traditionally, however, leadership rested on social consensus and communal needs, not on limited personal authority conferred by an European overlord.

Such Euro-American manipulation of Delaware leadership (Jennings 1965), included, about 1747, a refusal by Colonial officials to recognize Pisquetomen, the legitimate Delaware heir, which transferred the office to his brother Shingas by 1752. The chiefship, as always, was the responsibility of an elite family, not just an individual. Records refer to Pisquetomen, Shingas, and another brother Tamaqua (Beaver) as members of "the Delaware royal family" (Jennings 1965: 197), but this status was not limited to men. Regrettably, even Hugh Gibson (1837: 142), an adopted captive of this family from 1756-59, mentions only seven brothers, remaining silent about sisters, if any, who nevertheless conferred just this chiefly status on their own and succeeding generations.

Often, the wife of a chief was herself the daughter of one. Such women were responsible for coordinating the tasks of townswomen, acting in cooperation with their husbands. Zeisberger (1910: 113) specified that an officiating chief gave a wampum belt to a new chief's senior wife, who accepted it with a promise to "obey" her husband "in the name of all the women." Heckewelder (1876: 269) reported the respect and honor shown at the funerals of the wives of a chief or captain, particularly those who "were descended themselves of a high family."

Trowbridge (in Weslager 1972: 478) added that some women could assume a kind of superiority over female activities based on their own innate capacities, regardless of whether or not they came from chiefly families. Given the elite status of visionaries, leading matrilines actively tried to have all of their members receive such a gift. Women with innate abilities gained prominence in specialized tasks, but their skills were attributed to supernatural assistance. Moreover, mothers with visions were better able to benefit their progeny.

Oklahoma Delaware kept a special hat, now at the Museum of the American Indian, which was bestowed annually on a woman selected for her high moral character and contributions to community wellbeing. This "tall hat" was in a felt stovepipe style, decorated with ostrich feathers, just like that worn by Osage brides (Wilson 1988: 101). Harrington (1921, Plate 1) illustrates it being worn by Susie Elkhair, wife of Chief Charlie Elkhair, which was probably not a coincidence. Sarah Wilson Thompson, Nora's mother, was awarded the hat at least twice. These women were very much involved in the social and ritual life of the Delaware around Dewey and Copan, which was no easy task because there were many ritual obligations but surprisingly few traditionalist women. In fact, a tenth (Adams (1906: 299) says a fourth) of the Delaware population, for a time, was maintaining a full range of rituals that had formerly been sponsored by the entire nation of thousands.

In hindsight, however, this perseverance was not unexpected. From comparable cases, we know that aboriginal elites have often devoted much effort to perpetuating complex traditional rituals. By clinging to these observances, they continued an identity, despite invasion, colonialization, and missionaries insisting that they assimilate into the lowest grade of the dominant society. The Mandan of North Dakota are a particularly poignant example since, after 1837, thirty people committed themselves to conducting rituals once performed by several thousand. Among Delaware, these traditionalists were probably descended from the elite of the aboriginal and proto-historic society, and, therefore, unwilling to give up their inherited rank for one of lesser worth in American society.

As Homer Barnett (1953: 404-5) remarked: "When cultures meet, the majority of those who switch allegiance are individuals with the least opportunity for full participation in the most valued activities of their own society ... those who had nothing to lose by their defection – the social props and pawns of the elite."

By implication, some members of the elite never converted; others did, especially when kept from the highest native positions or actively seeking new challenges. The aboriginal Delaware probably included many positions known from other tribes, such as speakers, heralds, messengers, acolytes, and a variety of others at the family, household, lineage, clan, town, tribal, and national levels. Basically, these officials were elaborations of the three positions of councilor, captain, and chief just discussed.

While serving as staff to the leaders, some were heirs in training, others were filling the office permanently, and a few were recruited on the basis of outstanding ability. Such staff positions, while prestigious, would have been frustrating to those with greater ambition, who eventually satisfied it by becoming Christians.

Delaware society was also led by religious specialists (Miller 1977) who were finely graded on the basis of their gifts of differential access to supernatural potency. Along with this sanction, each specialist blended psychological, political, and medical abilities, together with membership in the elite families of clans. Among Delaware, medico-religious knowledge ranged from various home remedies to specialized cerebral techniques. Their home medicines generally functioned as laxatives, which needed no religious sanction, and could be used freely by "empty" people, those without visions.

While all adepts were gifted (had visions), they were variously known as "herbalist," "sweat doctor," and "shaman." The herbalist, "someone who understands plants (and their uses)," had an extensive knowledge of plants, permitting her to gather them at the moment when they were most effective. Nora Dean was an herbalist and provided some of her knowledge to the general public (Weslager 1973). The "sweat doctor" used liquid medicines and the sweat lodge to effect cures. The shaman or shamaness, "dicta (hex, spell) man or woman," had the ability to cure without using any medicines. Each relied entirely on supernatural gifts, although in less serious cases they sometimes used the same treatments as the other two practitioners. Some exceptional visionaries had the ability to cure without any aids at all. Among these was Sally Thompson, Nora's mother. In all, then, such specialists formed a matrix of exclusive herbalist (shaman) sweat doctor.

In addition, there were special gifts that came from the ownership of mystic bundles, ranging from those for medicine and love to those for witchcraft or sorcery. Medicine bundles were used for general and specific cures, as stated when the bundle was first bestowed by an immortal. Love bundles were used to join, rejoin, or divide spouses and lovers, but they could never be used for the personal benefit of the owner, only to help others in need. Personal use was selfish, encouraging sorcery. Witch bundles contained a "bad thing" used to harm, hurt, or kill people. The owner used it, sometimes in return for pay, but more usually out of her or his own sense of anger, jealousy, envy, hatred, nastiness, or disregard for others.

Along with personal bundles, there were also public ones passed down through the women of a matriline. Primary among these were the bundles for the Family Rites, which were led by brothers or sons of the key women. Among Dewey Delawares, these Family Rites consisted of the Bear (Doll) Otter Rites, as described in Chapter 7. Other bundles and prerogatives were associated with the Tribal Rites of Green Corn or Maize (Masing) Football games, involving the inheritance of a ball or a mask and costume.

## Gamwing

Moreover, the role of gender as the echo of Delaware culture suggests that a summary ritual would have been celebrated annually to dramatize the complementary reciprocity of men and women, whose participation was based on personal contact with a supernatural (*mənitu*), who provide a text, song, and array of evocative gestures to that visionary. Aboriginal recitations, therefore, were much more animated than the staid recent ones, probably influenced by dour Protestant practices.

Such a rite would have been celebrated in the fall because this was the season when harvest and hunt overlapped, allowing both men and women to exchange their economic staples. Timing was decided by the end of harvesting, by the leaf color change of deciduous trees, and by celestial factors. In her account of the Indiana revival of the Big House, Nora Dean ended with a legend of the creation of the Pleiades, and Speck (1931: 171) included another version of this tale in his account of the Big House.

Earliest sources refer to the annual worship as *Cantico* and *Gamwing*. According to Brinton (1888: 41), Cantico, a jollification, assimilated to Latin <u>cantare</u>, came from the Lenape term "<u>*gentkehn*</u>, to sing and dance at the same time." As a religious ceremony, it was distinct from a feast. Zeisberger (1887: 72) listed "*n'gamuin*, to feast," and the Brinton-Anthony dictionary (1888: 95 #9) had "*Ngamuin*, to keep a feast in Indian style."

As the feast exchanging hunt and harvest, the Gamwing epitomized the importance of gender for Delaware culture by sharing such foods after their consecration by visionaries who gave thanks to the Creator and creation while moving everyone higher through the cosmos.

As applied to the annual festival in the Big House, therefore, the term Gamwing probably signified "The feast among all others," and was held in the village council house, with two or three fires, whose "only permanent occupants were the head chief with his wives and children" (Brinton 1888: 40). Thus, chiefly homes also served as temples decorated with faces of deities inside and emblems of the clan over the doorways.

## Big Houses[1]

As a focus of communal sentiments, a big house, probably also the home of a clan leader, was long a feature of Delaware towns. Indeed, community houses, town halls, and rotundas generally served cohesive functions throughout Native America.

Along the Delaware River, ancient towns were seasonally occupied, relying on hunting and harvesting, since the Archaic, which Ritchie (1969: 32) dates to 6500 years ago for the Northeast. The Late Archaic site of Wapanucket #6, dated to 4300 years ago, in present eastern Massachusetts, indicated a central base for a foraging (non-farming) community which included circular house floors, 30-45 feet across, and one that was 66 feet across, "a probable ceremonial structure" (1969: 35). Its size suggests a prototype for the later rotundas which were the focus of corporate towns throughout the Americas, whether Southwest kivas, Plains earthlodges, or California roundhouses.

Between the Archaic and Historic periods, there was a shift from rotunda to hall in the Northeast. For Delaware, while a rounded hall would be more evocative of the World Turtle, a longhouse was better adapted to a large population characterized by intensive farming, matri-households, and leaders directing complex rituals. As necessary, adding compartments to a longhouse was easier than enlarging a round building.

In tribal societies where consensus was the rule, the forum for unanimity was a community building, often also serving as the home of the leading family and the focus of a larger region rather than a single community. While Delaware regional groupings are not well known, Arthur Parker (1922: II, 706, note 17) implied that the Esopus, northern Munsee speakers occupying several towns, had a tribal grand council house "at the junction of Vernooy Creek and the Roundout just southeast of Warwasing village and opposite Port Benjamin." Among Delaware, Iroquois, Shawnee, and others, as the day-to-day use of the Big House faded, its essence survived as a rectangular spot of ground sanctified by its ties to on-going community sentiments.

The Big House, a separate building that increasingly became the focus for scattered and dispersed settlements, represents a response to change that had parallels among neighboring Northeastern tribes. Even New England towns themselves grew up around town squares, a kind of psychic center.

Among the Iroquois, the innovations from Handsome Lake included separate buildings, modern frame longhouses, where the Good Word is preached and rituals celebrated (Trigger 1978: 455). There, the metaphor of the common longhouse of all the Iroquois maintained its currency into the present. Daly (1985) argued that this "housing metaphor" contributed much to Iroquois survival during recent history.

Among the Powhatan to the south, dispersed homesteads have been typical of the historic period. Just prior to the 1600s, however, stockaded town clusters were characteristic. As the Powhatan chiefdom gained superiority (confidence), it seems, homesteads dispersed and a temple remained the only community focus. Each temple was either located among the scattered homes or isolated away in the forest. A temple in the forest was the likely site for the Huskenow, a male puberty initiation with nine months of specialized training for leader or priestly roles, marking a rebirth into adulthood.

At each one, a sacred fire was maintained by priests. Unlike the Big House, however, entrance was restricted to Powhatan temples, which were hallowed places for the elite dead and for the protection of treasured goods and tribute. These temples were ranked, as were the towns. Foremost among them was the temple of Uttamussak at the mouth of the Pamunkey River (Roundtree 1989: 133, 177), which signified the whole nation.

After Robert Beverley (1947: 196) and his friends invaded a temple, which he called a Quioccasan, he wrote "Round about the House, at some distance from it, were set up Posts, with Faces carved on them, and Painted." In a dark interior room were three mat bundles on shelves. The first was filled with human bones, the second with carved and painted tomahawks, and the third with the wooden segments for assembling an articulated human figure that served as an idol.

Powhatan Temple posts had "carved and painted beasts" apparently depicting humans and animals. Other images decorated posts set up around the outside (Roundtree 1989: 134). This arrangement suggests that the Delaware Big House may have also had exterior decorated posts in prehistoric times and that these images provided inspiration for the faces on the outside supports of some Big Houses.

While the Powhatan ritual series is not well known, Purchas (1617: 951) described events that seem to parallel Delaware ones, particularly the vision recitation. "Their devotion is most in songs, which the chiefe Priest beginneth, the rest following: sometimes he maketh invocations with broken sentences, by starts and strange passions, and at every pause the other give a short grone."

The Iroquois League was expressed in terms of a symbolic longhouse, east to west across central New York. After 1800, through the prophecies of Handsome Lake, their sustaining religious beliefs became centered within modern versions of a longhouse. Thus, these self-designated "People of the Longhouse," even as they gave up bark-covered buildings housing matrilineages, increasingly concentrated their cultural concerns into community halls and symbolic structures expressive of the all-pervading importance of the longhouse (Campisi 1974: 19).

For Delaware, in their own view of history, important events are remembered as occurring during a Gamwing celebration, probably as a way of indicating significant public impact. Thus, at significant junctures of time or place, Gamwing provided a public declaration of what it meant to be Delaware in the fullest sense of that designation.

Hints from different areas of Native America indicate these sentiments also included an equation of the cosmos, the settlement, its community house, and its leader. For instance, among the Californian Yuki, each new chief was confirmed in office by the construction of a new rotunda whose central support post was a tree carefully cut down while the new chief stood securely within its branches (G. Foster 1944: 178).

Evidence that the Delaware also made this equation rests on the fact that once the Delaware had moved to Oklahoma in 1867, the traditionalists built two Big Houses in succession, each during the tenure of a different ceremonial leader, first Colonel Jackson and then Charlie Elkhair. Earlier, new halls were specially built for ceremonies instituted by rising prophets, such as the masked one met by David Brainerd in Pennsylvania and Beata in Indiana, or were promised for the service of new religions such as Mormons in Missouri.

## Global Renewals

Lastly, other evidence that the Gamwing was indeed an aboriginal rite comes from its parallels with other major rituals in the Americas, particularly among fellow Algonkians. There, the center pole of the Big House, the annual recreation of the universe, and the ritual definition of tribal identity have far-flung reflexes.

In a fascinating article, Schlesier (1990: 13, 14) argued for an 1660s formation of the Oxheheom ("Creator Lodge") ceremony of the Suhtai, an Algonkian speaking tribe which later merged with the Cheyenne. This "New Life, or World Renewal Ceremony" inspired various Plains ceremonies collectively (if erroneously) called the Sun Dance, whose uniform feature was "erecting a pole within a circular encircling structure before which votaries dance" (Leslie Spier quoted in Schlesier 1990: 12)). Of particular note (1990: 12): "The Suhtai Oxheheom does not represent a break with religious tradition or a completely new invention [but] is based on an ancient Algonquian world perception … expressed in such distant New Year or World Renewal ceremonies as, for instance, the Big House of the Delawares or the Yurok Wohpekumeu ceremony".

Within the overall context of the Americas, moreover, the role of ritual in defining social identity and perpetuating culture, as illustrated by the Gamwing, was explained by the Barasana of Colombia as a triumph of continuity over change (Hugh-Jones 1979: 139):

As the Barasana view it, as [generations] pile on top of one another like the leaves on the forest floor, human beings are in danger of losing touch with the beginning and source of life, the world of myth [so] the object of the HE house is literally to squash the pile so that the initiates … people of another pile (*gahe tutiana*), are brought into contact with, and adopted by, the first HE people.

As evocative as this explanation was for a tribe in South America, it was equally apt for the Delaware, a people tracing ancestry to the tip, leaves, and branches of a great Cedar Tree.

---

Endnote

[1] Today, the best place to get a sense of what the Gamwing was once like, as I well know, is in the far Northwest on the US/BC border among communities of Coast Salish. There, every winter, starting the day after US Thanksgiving, an individual's guardian spirit returns to occupy their body and make them "sick to sing" (Miller 1999a). This phrase means that the song given that human at the initial encounter with the immortal rises from the chest cavity and lodges in the throat, where it must be sung for the wellbeing of that person and the community at large. Family members will know that song and rally around the person when he or she begins to make sobbing, moaning noises that seek to move the song up and out through the mouth. The larger Salish community will also know this song and rally to sing it a public gatherings all winter long.

The spirits move through the Coast Salish region along a counterclockwise route that takes them around the "Salish Sea" along Vancouver Island and Puget Sound, across BC and into Washington state.

While spirits come to their human at their present homes, winter weekends are spent traveling to a series of large public buildings on reserves and reservations throughout the NW. Called Smokehouses as a consequence of the large open fires that heat and light them, they are a continuation of the large communal cedar plank homes that go back to the earliest human occupation of this region. Fed by abundant runs of salmon and served by the multiplex utility of tall straight-grained cedar trees (providing everything from boxes, canoes, tools, and clothing to the planks that covered these houses), this was and is a land of plenty. And for that bounty, people gave thanks to the powers that be.

Smokehouses are huge, easily holding several hundred visitors. Because they are built of huge timbers and wooden planks, they are rectangular. This is also the shape of historic Delaware big houses, though prehistorically when they were built of poles and bark, they seem to have been long ovals.

Salish smokehouses have dirt floors for the sake of the, often barefoot, dancers, and open fires, generally two in the middle of the floor space. Most do not have center poles, though they do usually have huge, carved and painted side support posts. Most often, these are full figures of ancestors and spirits important in the pedigrees of leading families associated with that smokehouse. They are never carved faces like those in the big house. The Saq$^w$bix$^w$ [Sauk Suiatle], however, far upriver and in the high mountains, do indeed have a single central post, but their smokehouse is much smaller than those downriver. For Saq<bix<, the center post is a symbol of their unity and courage in the face of some horrific events in their past.

Dancers wear paint and clothing appropriate to their spirit patron, though the correspondence is rarely direct so as to protect both the human partner and the source of power from hostile acts by malevolent shamans. Today, when someone says simply "I wear paint" that means that he or she is an initiate of the smokehouse. The belief itself is known as Siyowin, but that term is not often heard outside of the native religious community. These paints can be either red or black, though a white paint seems to have once been worn by powerful native doctors. Black paint is associated with 'fierce' protective, warrior powers, often from the saltwater region; while red is linked with 'calm' healing, curative powers, often from the high mountains, devoted to community good.

# PLACING ~ 5

## Shared Waterway

Beliefs about gender, divinity, and ritual emerged in (and, in a greater sense, out of) the Delaware homeland, providing a basis for an aboriginal Gamwing that reshifted with each removal. Originally, along the middle Atlantic slope, Delawares were a river people, named in English and in their own language for Lenapehittuk, the Lenape (Delaware) River.

For earlier, proto-historic times, the largest clusters of Delaware villages and bands were near the mouths of the Lehigh and Schuylkill, especially the latter, with the Falls at modern Trenton between them serving to restrict interchanges until the founding of Moravian towns and missions. Those people at the confluence of the Schuylkill and Delaware Rivers became the nucleus for the historic amalgam resulting in the Oklahoma Delaware.[9]

As the major Delaware tributary, the Schuylkill and its survivors would have played a similar role in the formation of the historic Delaware, specifically the Unami now resident in Oklahoma. As a necessary corollary, the marine rivers along the Jersey shore, occupied by smaller, unconnected, and more diverse bands – on the Passaic, Raritan, Rancocus, Maurice, Mullica, and others – would have contributed fewer survivors. The Unalachtigo group, however temporary, was probably formed of survivors from these coastal bands.

Aboriginal Delaware complexity became fragmented, if not actually shattered, by the diseases and disruptions of the European onslaught. Some stability was provided, however, by their common links to the drainages of the same river. Even in folktales, people spoke of rivers before terrain. "Shortly after this the Chief called his people together and announced his intention of going to another river, two days journey to the westward, where there were fertile valleys and game, and there to start a new village" (Adams 1906: 42).

In a brief history of his tribe, this same Richard Adams (1890: 297) focused on the various riverine abodes of the Unami Delaware.

From ... Pennsylvania, Delaware, and New Jersey, they moved up the Susquehannah river and over the Alleghanies, down the Monongahela to Wheeling. Then by treaty in 1789 lands were reserved to them between the Miami and Cuyahoga rivers, and on the Muskingum, Kihoga, and Upper Sandusky rivers in Ohio ... Delawares went from Ohio to

---

[9] While many other tribes, especially in the East, went through much the same process, a particularly well documented example of re-amalgamation after depopulation was provided by the Twana Coast Salish along Hood Canal, residents of the Skokomish Reservation on the Olympic Peninsula of Washington State. Each of eight Twana winter villages was situated at the confluence of a tributary with Hood Canal. A ninth consisted of a cluster of five or more villages on the Skokomish River. The largest of these was at its fork. After the Twana were ravaged by disease and raids, more people survived from these Skokomish towns than from any of the others. The reservation established for all the survivors, therefore, was dominated by the Skokomish and bears their name.

Indiana, and in 1812, joined the Shawnees in the battle of Tippecanoe. In 1818 the Delawares ceded all their lands to the government and removed to Missouri, near the headwaters of the Merrimac and White rivers, near the present Springfield. While there, they joined the Tehe band of Cherokee Indians and overcame the Osages, who were on the western boundaries of Arkansas and Indian territory. In 1829 they sold their lands and made a treaty for land in what is now Kansas, but some of the tribe did not want to go there, saying that the two rivers (Kansas and Missouri) came together near their new lands, looking too much like a white man's trousers, and there was a division in the tribe, and part of them went to Indian territory and settled with Kiowas and Wichitas, where they now are.

While flawed on details and fanciful about the trousers, his repeated emphasis on rivers was distinctly cultural. After they arrived in Oklahoma, Delaware tried to settle near running water, no easy feat in this dusty terrain. During the past decade, several Delaware have explicitly stated this preference in interviews (Chouteau, Redman), with forceful statements by Anna Davis (T-298, B-6) "The Delaware are always close to water" and Fred Falleaf (T-512-1: 17) "Delaware liked to settle near streams."

While data are slim, Delaware in their homeland probably had much the same orientation and usages of their drainages as did other Native Americans (Schrabish 1930, Volk 1911, Wacher 1968, Williams 1980). To investigate this, a patchwork of the Delaware River was assembled from road maps, government reports, local records, and fieldnotes to suggest comparisons between the Delaware and tribes still living along their own rivers, particularly the Columbia and Skeena of the Northwest where I have worked and published on local ethnography.

At present, four states border the Delaware River, each having some jurisdiction over sections of it. Not until 1946, recognizing the need to consider the entire river, was the Delaware River Basin Commission established at Trenton, dividing the drainage into twelve sub-basins, as though haunted by the Delaware use of the number 12. When this coincidence was mentioned to Delaware elders, they accepted it as inevitable because of their strong spiritual links with the waterway, although the possibility that these sub-basins were also the basis for the importance of twelves among the Delaware cannot be ruled out. These sub-basins and an excellent map of New Jersey (1972) drainages suggest that prehistoric Delaware were consistent with the rest of the continent, despite previous intensely regional treatments.

Delaware have long been primarily associated with New Jersey (see Newcomb 1956, Map 1) and sub-tribal names have been slashed across its surface – ignoring the contours of its hills, dales, streams, and valleys. According to the Delaware Basin Commission, half of its concern lies in Pennsylvania, a quarter in New Jersey, and another quarter is divided between New York and Delaware State, with eight square miles in Maryland. The size of the domain in Pennsylvania relates to the magnitude of the Schuylkill, draining 1,893 square miles, and of the Lehigh, draining 1,364 square miles. Within New Jersey, the largest tributaries dwarf in comparison: the Rancocus (340 square miles) and the Maurice (386 square miles) on Delaware Bay. Major villages were most likely to have been located at confluences of the Delaware and its many tributaries.

United by their sharing of the same fresh water, aboriginal Delaware also took full advantage of Atlantic resources, either visiting the Jersey shore or trading with people who lived along coastal rivers for salt and seafoods.[10]

In addition, some areas did not drain into the Delaware River at all and so were comparatively independent, particularly several rivers in New Jersey. Among these, the largest were the Raritan (1106 square miles), Passaic (949mi), Hackensack (201mi), or the coastal Mullica (570mi) and Great Egg Harbor (338mi) rivers. Such ecological separateness must have coincided with political and social domains.

## Watersheds

The most cogent discussion of the native American riverine mode of orientation was a general model developed by Marian Smith (1940: 7), based on her fieldwork with tribes along the rivers draining into southern Puget Sound, near Seattle (Miller 1999a). Her model considered increasing levels of integration, explicitly recognizing that the greatest allegiance and loyalty coincided with the entire drainage system. She later abandoned the riverine model for one that emphasized topography, so as to include prairies important for edible roots and horse pasture (Smith 1941: 198), but unfortunately her revision does more to reflect needs developed after European contact. Nevertheless, as elsewhere, rivers provided the primary orientation, and fish remained the staple food. To the credit of her riverine model, moreover, other scholars have continued to adopt it, generalizing it for the continent. In a footnote (1940: 7, #1), Smith cited corroboration from Alfred Kroeber, relying on his knowledge of Native California and the Northwest: "The Native point of view seems to be throughout that a group owns the stream with whatever flows into it from both sides." Additionally, Kroeber mused that the width of the Lower Columbia might have been an exception, but Chinook and Sahaptian villages were definitely located along both banks.

For Native America, the only exception was also the most likely: "While rivers do not as a rule constitute cultural barriers ... the Mississippi seems to have been such" (Wheeler-Voegelin 1944: 371). Other possible exceptions are found in the Southwest, where the lack of watercraft set tribal boundaries along the few rivers with a steady flow of water.

Thus, the riverine model of embedded loyalties might be projected throughout the continent, if not also much of the pre-industrial world.[11] Within a watershed, group affiliations became

---

[10] Based on the archaeological survey of the outer coast of Vancouver Island, the historic practice of natives leaving their winter villages to harvest seasonal resources far and wide would have been unlikely during prehistoric times when the large, dense population meant that these lands were fully occupied and trade rather than transhumance (seasonal shifts) was the means and manner of moving around local resources.

[11] While not discussed here, the social organization of a drainage was a consequence of beliefs about topography. Thus, among the Cubeo of Colombia (Goldman 1963: 44, 4), the Vaupes River was a waterway supplying food, linking clan lands, and providing a source of power from antiquity. Clans were distributed such that neighbors formed phratries of linked clans, with the highest ranked clan nearest the mouth of a tributary, the most strategic position. Natural features such as rapids, bends, and confluences served to define boundaries, and locate the holy home of spirits. Overall, Cubeo unity was expressed by a genesis in which groups

increasing more expansive in terms of (a) hearth mates or commensal families, (b) households under one roof, (c) birthright locals - those born there in contrast to affines, visitors, and foreigners, (d) settlement locations or seasonal camp sites, (e) community networks, (f) tributary drainages, and (g) the entire watershed.

From the beginning, Delaware derived their cohesiveness from a common land, language, and lifeway, as articulated by the lifeline of the Delaware River (Dunlap and Weslager 1958). With their loss and dispossession of their overall drainage, cultural means were used to maintain cohesion. In particular, these included the belief in the Creator who acted via thought; the use of the Big House as community hall, chiefly residence, ceremonial lodge, and guest house for each town; and the ability of their leaders, as civil or religiously sanctioned visionaries, to motivate their communities. These cohesive forces had the advantage of being portable, carried in the head and heart, until successively realized in new towns. Once settled again, a new Big House was built and the community leaders resumed their roles. Eventually, however, even the Big House existed only in memory, albeit vivid and compelling enough to provide cultural cohesion for the last generation of elders to worship as children and to speak Lenape.

## Seasonality

For Delaware, the ancient economy was composed of hunting by men, farming by women, and fishing by both. For aboriginal Delaware, women were associated with soft materials, farming, plant and meat processing, and the household; men with stone and other hard materials, hunting, animal by-products, and the forest. Of their tool kits, men were most closely identified with their bow and arrows, women with their mortar and pestle. Men did the routine hunting and fishing, engaging in continuous activities with male partners and groups (Witthoft 1967). Women, by season with the help of children, gathered wild seeds, nuts, and berries, in addition to farming plots of maize, beans, squash, sunflowers, and other crops (Wheeler-Voegelin 1941). At one time, women and old men made mats, ropes, tumplines, and baskets (Newcomb 1965: 28). Old women grew tobacco, a crop otherwise associated with men in ritual contexts.

---

were distributed along the river by a sacred Anaconda acting as a canoe to carry ancestors to these specific locations.

Along the Columbia River of the American Northwest, Coyote's journey upriver bringing the salmon provided a unity for Salishan and Sahaptian tribes. For Haida Gwaii (Queen Charlotte Islands of Northern British Columbia), each stream had a Creek Woman living at its source. Along the Missouri, the river itself was a boy hero who transformed into a snake.

Among the Ainu of northern Japan, rivers and tributaries were regarded as parents and children, with each waterway the abode of a spirit (kamui) of the same name, which also applied to the humans living along it (Watanabi 1973: 70ff). The most important Ainu deities were located at mountain peaks, catch points for rain falling between earth and sky. Humans, spirits, and drainages were closely linked. Someone from another area who wanted to use local resources asked permission to do so from the resident headman, who then supervised the manufacture of appropriate ritual offerings for the patron spirits of fire and waterway. After a successful venture, some of the resources taken by the outsiders were given to the headman as a token of appreciation.

On several occasions during the year, men and women worked together during communal hunting drives and seasonal fish runs, using nets and traps. Harrington (1913: 222) indicated that Munsee used a fish poison of pulverized green walnuts, but Newcomb (1956: 16) did not think that this usage was aboriginal. Yet fish poisons and stupefiers were an areal feature of the Southeast, near enough to the Delawares to permit borrowing or overlapping use. The Unami, who lived between the two regions, apparently lacked a fish poison, though they did have a huge fishery at the Fall that amply supplied their needs.[12]

Among techniques for fishing, Adams (1906: 3) wrote "They caught fish with fishhooks made of bone and dried claws of birds, and also used brush nets." Munsee mentioned "making fish traps in rivers by running a close fence of posts driven firmly into the bottom from bank to bank, but leaving a narrow aperture in the center with a net behind so arranged that the fish could enter but not escape when driven downstream by beaters above" (Harrington 1913: 222).

Fishing techniques continued in use during the Delaware juggernaut westward to Oklahoma. There, Nora Dean, as a child, saw a similar "fence net" across Hogshooter Creek, east of Dewey. It was called by a generic term (*aswiikʌn* = dip up + instrument) applied to both a weir and a dip net. Elsie Brock (IPH 16: 396) said her brother jigged every night, attracting fish with a fire. Along the larger Neosho River, fishing remained important. There, Cyrus Washington (IPH 11: 245) recalled his father George (aka Wahooney) using a seine lent to him by Mr. Pratt, an Indian agent, a spiked arrow to shoot fish at 4PM (helped by shadows?), and a fish trap. Sturgeon up to 150 pounds could be taken from the Grand River near Miami, Oklahoma.

These vestiges of fishing's importance harkened back to the fact that their Atlantic homeland had "some of the best food fishes of North America ... in quality, and in quantity ... the province is surpassed by no other in the continent" (Rostlund 1952: 74).

In addition to river mouths, aboriginal Delaware also located their villages at waterfalls because these were good locations for fish weirs (Thurman 1973b, 40). In his important survey of freshwater fishing techniques, Rostlund (1952: 87, 170, 183) found evidence for Delaware use of weirs, tidal traps, spears, torchlights, claw hooks, arrows, and, particularly, small dip nets and grapevine drags, but no clear data for true seine or gill nets. For Delaware, available aquatic foods included fish, eels, mollusks, and, significantly, sturgeon because: "The center of abundance on the Atlantic coast appears to have been the region of the Delaware and Susquehanna Rivers, with a tapering off in numbers both northward and southward" (Rostlund 1952: 10).

Concerning fish resources, "The time of the shad and herring fishery was spring or early summer [to] spawn on a rising temperature and do not enter the rivers until the water temperature has risen to about 60F ... Seine nets were much used during colonial times for catching shad in the Delaware and Susquehanna Rivers ... When the Connecticut settlers of the Susquehanna Company first took up residence in the Wyoming Valley in the 1760's their chief subsistence for

---

[12] There is real possibility that the Unami rejected the use of fish poison for some cultural reason, perhaps having to do with a religious regard for life and pan-species mental alertness, much as the Cheyenne refused to drive bison over cliffs as being disrespectful of life and used impounds instead (Schlesier 1987).

a long time was shad [and on a] "widow's haul" ... on the first Sunday after shad fishing began ... between Wilkes-Barre and Plymouth 10,000 shad were caught (Rostlund 1952: 14).

The Delaware River had three annual runs of shad:  March for three weeks, April-May for fish averaging twelve pounds, and again in early June.  Similar runs occurred in the Susquehanna, where, at Wyalusing, on 18 May 1768, Moravian converts caught 2,000 shad (Thurman 1973b: 41).

## Naming Land and Water

As always, the greater context for these shifting social relations was the on-going community composed of hamlets, towns, districts, and overall regions.  While we lack complete information to delimit prehistoric Delaware bands and villages, a Delaware capitol or religious center, the place where their sacred fire burned, was known.  For Unami, it was located at the extensive archaeological zone known as Abbott Farm, near the Falls of the Delaware, more accurately an extended rapids, at modern Trenton.  It may not be entirely accidental that this is now the state capitol since Albany, New York was similarly located across the Hudson from the site where the Mahikan tribal fire burned.  New arrivals in an area adapt themselves to existing patterns, so these capitols seem to be carry-overs from the proto-historic situation.

The Falls at Trenton, which lie 130 miles upstream from Delaware Bay, were the limit of the tidewater, and a major obstacle for shad and other anadromous fish runs important to the ancient Delaware.  Any river travel required portaging there, so it was a well-known stopping place.  Like Columbia River waterfalls at the Dalles, Chelan, Nespelem, and Kettle Falls, it would have been an important intertribal fishery, an extensive arena for economic, social, political, and ritual activities.

The very size and complexity of the site has perplexed American archaeology from its beginnings (Fitting 1973).  The Abbott Phase (AD 150-550) was defined at the Falls of the Delaware, with related sites scattered throughout central and southern New Jersey (Pollak 1971: 115-118, 1976).  External influences included early Illinois Hopewellian traits such as zone-decorated ceramics, mica caches, birdstones, platform pipes, and several stone tool types.  More exotic goods like earspools and shells might have also been present.  Another insignia of rank was the remains of deer antlers found in some graves (Cross 1956), suggesting the antler headdress associated with Iroquois League Chiefs (*royaner* in Mohawk).  Together, these occurrences indicate that Abbott Farm was a major Middle Woodland site of proto-Delaware, if not Unami, ancestry.

Apparently, the site included a large settlement in the bottomlands with a concentration of religious activities on the bluff, evidenced by cache pits of argillite "Fox Creek" blades, mica, copper, and other scarce goods, sometimes laid out in patterns.  The bluff may have also featured earth mounds, long since plowed down, and other distinctions, such as a log tomb.

As the Delaware religious center, close parallels between this site and Illinois Hopewellian manifestations suggest that there was a vast network linking together a Middle Woodland (BC 300 - AD 500) trade and ceremonial tradition.[13]  While not as accessible as Sandy Hook, as specified by John Heckewelder (below), the Trenton area abounds in archaeological import for Delaware political and religious organization.

---

[13]  Heckewelder's report of Mandan remnants among the Unami and Unalachtigo might just hint at this network or Siouian participation in it.

Above the Falls, the other major topographical feature along the river is the constriction called the Delaware Water Gap, which also influenced Delaware settlement, by analogy with the Canyon of the Skeena River on the north coast of British Columbia.[14]

Like this canyon, the Water Gap served as a valve in the transmission of cultural patterns, both as a buffer and a filter permitting only determined access across its constriction. The degree of influence apparently depended on the difficulty or speed of the current, availability of portage, desire for contact, and ease of overall transport. In general, it appears that the easier it was to make the passage, the more the constriction served as a filter, rather than a buffer. Since riverine tribes generally have a more complex social system near the mouth and a more diffuse one upriver, the area near this constriction would have been a transitional zone (Miller 1997: 1999).

An analogous group along the Columbia River was the Met-how, historically adopting downriver patterns of the Columbian (Moses) Confederacy, while serving as a buffer between the Okanogan or Wenatchi chains of the Interior Salishan languages. Along the Delaware, the people at the Lehigh Forks, just below the gap, probably held a similar position.

In their summary of the later archaeological record from the Upper Delaware, Fischler and French (1991: 155-6) found only seasonal use (AD 100-900) by groups who fissioned into the hinterland after fusioning around Abbott Farm for the spring fish runs. This was particularly evident in Fox Creek lithic materials (AD 325-450) and the use of shell-tempered ceramics. With the shift to more intensive farming (AD 1050-1200), settlements became more permanent in what would become the Munsee region, especially with the adoption of a maize economy after AD 1200.

The riverine environment of the Delaware was also addressed in a recent summary of Delaware materials by Ives Goddard (1978: 213-23). According to his reading of the linguistic materials, the major break between Lenape dialect chains (taking this phrase from Interior Salish) came at the Water Gap, with Munsee spoken in the north and Unami in the south. Important grammatical and vocabulary differences between these two speech communities (Voegelin 1939) include an inanimate plural suffix of -al for Munsee and of -a for Unami. Both used -ak for animate plural. Within Unami, Goddard saw internal divisions at the Falls between Unalimi, Forks, or Northern Unami – spoken at the confluence of the Lehigh and Delaware Rivers until forced out by the 1737 Walking Purchase, and Southern Unami, along the lower Delaware River – whose speakers "had particularly close relations with one another" (Goddard 1978: 221), especially after they were displaced and had regrouped on Tulpehocken Creek off the upper Schuylkill River.

Given the two obstructions along the Delaware at the Falls and the Gap, and given the greater cohesion of the downriver Unami, it seems likely that Unami was being adopted by upstream villages, with the Lehigh Forks as the transitional zone between Unami and Munsee. Unfortunately, such a blend is best attested in the translations of the Moravians, which the great Algonkianist Truman Michelson (ms-b) said were defective exactly because they jumbled together different dialects. Although an intermediate blending into Unalimi seems plausible, its existence

---

[14] The Skeena was the river of the Tsimshian, with Coast Tsimshians flourishing below the canyon, in recognizable form for several thousand years (Inglis and MacDonald 1979), and Gitksan Tsimshians above the canyon, heavily mixed with Athapaskans who became Tsimshianized through trade and intermarriage. Over time, Gitksans adopted coastal forms of moieties, kinship, chiefship, cremation, and language (Miller 1997).

remains problematic because missionaries, especially before this century, were often imprecise linguists.[15]

The Moravians assembled a similar hybrid language, derived from a mixed population of converts. Both Nora Dean and Lucy Blalock, Lenape speakers, said they found Moravian liturgical translations confusing because they contain inappropriate native words, some made up and others used out of context. For instance, the ordinary word for "mirror" was adopted by the Moravians to mean the Christian soul, to distinguish it from the three other traditional Delaware souls.[16]

In fairness, this missionary language was much richer and varied than the trade jargon of uninflected Unami forms, analogous to the Chinook trade language of the Northwest, that spread among white and outlying native populations under the stimulus of the fur trade. In the East, the fur trade and Dutch expansion gave the Delaware jargon considerable currency. The Delaware themselves retained bits of this jargon until a century ago since Colonel Jackson's native name was _ponaetet_, the word for "little boy" (# 230) in the Salem Record, a 1680s list of jargon words (Prince 1912, Tomason 1980).

Tulpehocken Creek, the early Delaware refuge mentioned above, indicates another significant aspect of the relationship between language and territory: the contributions of place names for understanding land use patterns. Tulpehocken was derived from the Unami _tulpe + haking_ (turtle + land) because these reptiles were abundant there. Although many place names became undecipherable, their true forms were probably intended to provide ready identifications – as locales, labels, and memory aids – for the transmission of tribal knowledge about terrain, supplies, history, and folklore.

In other words, places were and are named for some distinguishing feature, and meshed with tradition by making reference to mythological events, religious rituals, and/or the seasonal cycle.[17] Yet all that remains of the prehistoric Delaware pattern are a few suggestions made by Nora Dean. Navesink may derive from _namēsing_ "fish place," and Mullica from _maalokok_ "snow geese."

After retirement, John Heckewelder (1833) tried to reconstruct Lenape place names, but his Moravian vocabulary undoubtedly influenced his etymologies (Donehoo 1928, Reichel 1872,

---

[15] A recent example was "old Father Griva," as the elders of the Colville Reservation refer to a polyglot Jesuit priest who could not always keep his many languages, native and European, distinct and so used vocabulary from all of them during a sermon. Even when he wrote grammars and religious texts in native languages, he sometimes jumbled distinct words and languages together. Out of respect for his sacred calling and dedication to their welfare, however, the Colville dutifully learned to use his texts, relying on their own linguistic fluency to sort them out.

[16] Each Delaware has three souls, respectively in the body, in the blood, and in the bone (Miller 1992).

[17] For example, Nespelem places translated as "corrugated rocks" or "paint" south of Grand Coulee Dam were named for obvious characteristics, but their specific locations were also kept in mind because they figured in the series of Coyote stories that map the landscape in terms of his journey. "Corrugated rocks" was further noteworthy because of the fine-flavored camas roots that Coyote left there for people to dig up every spring. As camas was a Salishan staple, its many locations could not each be called "camas," so other hallmarks were used to distinguish the various plots.

Nelson 1904). A full review of his text with the remaining native speakers needs to be done to salvage other examples of place name significance. Mahr (1959) began this undertaking with a semantic analysis of stream names from Ohio and Pennsylvania, showing that each made practical reference, as hint or warning, to local conditions involving travel, terrain, and resources for hunting, fishing, or farming. He made the important point that the mouth of a river or stream was often specifically named, "revealing to travelers on river or trail what was to be expected ahead" (1959: 367). This name was usually extended to the entire water course.

Because tribal identity and riverine settlement coincided, both banks were shared by the same group, unless other factors change the "natural" situation. For example, Goddard (1978: 215) claimed that the western side of the Delaware River was abandoned because of Susquehanna raids, even though "Somewhat puzzling is a 1654 account that names only six village bands for both banks, all of them within or very near the present city limits of Philadelphia" (1978: 215) on the western side. As these were at the mouth of the Schuylkill, the largest of the Delaware tributaries, such clustering could be expected. According to Nora Dean, the Schuylkill was known in Lenape as "elegant river," a reference both to its beauty and the sophistication of its Delaware aboriginal inhabitants. As an adult, she was able to visit the river, ocean, and homeland of her people. In the case of some modern place names, she was able to see the locale and grasp how the original Lenape names had been anglicized.

Goddard (1978: 73) identified the controversial Unalachtigo "tribe" as the Unalimi residing on the Jersey side of the Delaware: "Unalachtigo probably differed little from the form of speech preserved in an early word list from the Sankhikan of the Trenton, New Jersey area." He (1978: 236) also said that Unalachtigo was "The Munsee name for the Unami speakers of west-central New Jersey," but its "translation is unknown." The pan-Algonkian term Wapanaki (*ooppanahki* 'Easterners') "was once said to be the Unami name for the Unalachtigo ... but phonologically it cannot originally have been a Unami word," although Goddard thought it might be derived from Munsee.

The only Sankhikan vocabulary was collected by De Laet (1967) about 1633 near the Falls, which was a gathering place for people from all over, a fishery and crossroads for the region. Thus, De Laet could have collected words from many Lenape dialects. According to Grumet (1979: 29), "the term Sanhican applied to both the Falls of the Delaware River at Trenton, the area around Newark Bay, and an Upper Delawarean maximal organization located somewhere between these two points." As a name, however, Sankhikan suggests fascinating semantic ramifications.

Rather than being one of a series of equivalent but distinct subgroupings within Unami, the Sankhikan may have had a priority over the others. By analogy with the Salishans, the Unami, if not also the Delaware, expressed their solidarity by joining in rituals under the direction of a hereditary line of priestly leaders with appropriate supernatural allies. For the Salishans, this collectivity was most clearly expressed by the scope of attendance at the First Salmon and other Return Food Rites. Among the Delaware, however, solidarity was probably expressed in a series of rituals related to farming and harvest, culminating in a prehistoric version of the Gamwing, not in its modern form but as a generalized world renewal rite focused around the tribal sacred fire, archives, elder priest, and other "national" symbols set in a context of gender and seasonal exchange.

My interpretation relies on a possible translation of the word Sankhikan, which others have tried to associate with the term for flint or stone, used for an arrowhead in the old days and a gun flint after firearms were introduced. Yet this reference only includes the first part of the word. Instead, it seems significant that a similar term was used for the pump fire-drill rotated by a chaste man to kindle the sacred fires in the Big House. According to Nora Dean, this word was a special term referring only to this instrument and, as such, distinct from the usual word for a fire starter, _tǝndaywiikan_ derived from _tǝnday_, "fire." Nora gave the etymology of _sɛnghikʌn_ as "whirring noise implement," and her brother Leonard Thompson said that the sound of the drill in action inside the Big House was like a dull roar, heard throughout the camp, warning women and children to keep away from the building. Furthermore, this sound might have equally evoked the noise of cascading water, linking together people, fires, and waterfalls.

This drill consisted of a large disk pierced by a central post, spun by the action of a doubled leather strap running between the top of the stick and opposite sides of the disk. In profile, it looked like the earth surface with the cedar tree axis at the center. The drill, therefore, was also a model of the Delaware universe, an appropriate symbol for use in a world renewal rite. The rushing sound would have also represented the waves of the primal sea, with which the falls was also washed.

The drill served to summarize all of the attributes of a cosmic mediator, part of a continuum that began with the heart of the person and rippled outward through the household hearth, sacred fire of the capitol, sun in the sky, and to the Creator in heaven. Its use in the modern Big House fully expressed this symbolism.

While the earth was a constant presence, the Delaware had to especially create a reminder of the cedar tree, their mystical and mythic parent. This was the center post with carved faces that stood in the Big House. Such posts with carved faces were found widely throughout the Northeast (Krusche 1986), as in the ring of seven such posts in a 1585 watercolor by John White depicting the community of Secotan (coastal South Carolina).

Such a single standing timber with carved human faces was distinctly Delaware, especially with the faces painted half red and half black. After a lifelong study of masking iconology in the East, Speck (1950: 55, part VIII) concluded that stationary face-images were so well integrated in Delaware culture that they were the most likely source for the greater regional masking complex. "The religious representations of spiritual forces by stationery face-images is so deeply rooted in diverse groups of the Delaware cultural complex that the latter may be posited as a center of development for masking phenomena of the stationery image type ... Iroquois share in its antiquity, [as a] bifurcation into the employment of prosopic [facial] masks." A Delaware inspiration for this imagery also helps to explain why so many other tribes were willing to address the Delaware as Grandfather, a source of ancient wisdom and imagery.

Certainly, this use of the face was very daring in native religious terms since many tribes believed that all of life had a basic human form, with the face, as the most distinctively human feature, deserving very careful respect. For example, children were not allowed to put faces on their dolls or toys to avoid possible mockery of powerful supernaturals. Rocks and plants with face-like impressions were considered sacred and treated with reverence. Usually in Native America, the power given to someone was proportional to the strength and difficulty needed to acquire it. By daring to use the face on a sacred post, without suffering consequences, the Delaware impressed other tribes with their great power. Some of the faces on the Big House supports had wrinkled brows to indicate their great age and wisdom, so, in a sense, these carved grandfather faces expressed a kinship with the supernatural that became further applied to all of the Delaware when they were collectively called Grandfathers.

Like the fire-drill, these faced posts served as summarizing symbols for integrating Delaware culture, uniting the vertical axis with the symbolism of earthbound Man and Woman, represented by faces and the respective black and red colors. Therefore, to mark a Delaware ritual center, a post might have stood near the Falls of the Delaware, probably on the bluff surrounded by special caches. If placed on a mound, it would have looked like the world cedar on the back of the great turtle.

If a world renewal ceremony and sacred fire was found among the Sankhikan, serving a regional population engaged in farming, hunting, and, especially fishing, its spiritual leaders or priestly elders, like those among Powhatans who supervised similar activities, were implied by the names of two early "chiefs." If a priest for all the Delaware existed, it is unlikely that references to him would appear in written records. As a religious leader trafficking with the supernatural for the benefit of everyone "drinking the same water," he needed to live a very secluded and contemplative life, one largely devoted to fasting and prayer. While visitors would see and meet lesser public leaders, the most sacred figures might have been carefully sheltered and protected by their communities.[18]

While I have occasionally written of the Delaware Nation, implying a collectivity of the different tribes and languages, and have been unjustly criticized for creating a political entity where none existed, a prehistoric national "congregation" or "mystical unity" nevertheless seems likely. In addition to spiritual centers and shrines, seasonal communal rituals, and ancient family lines of leadership, Delaware shared a common language and culture, pivoting around the "gender echo" (see Chapter Four). For the protohistoric Delaware, however, any sense of spiritual bond and shared identity was shattered by epidemics, dislocation, and despair before direct European arrival. Yet a sense of prior unity remained with the Delaware until they were able to reconstitute it in Ohio and Indiana.

Chiefs noted among the Unami at Tulpehocken included two called Sassoonan (died 1747), also known as Alumapes (Olumapies), and Manɛngy (from *mɛnjis* "left-hand). Heckewelder (1833: 385) clouded our understanding by translating Sassoonan as Shassuna ("our uncle") and listing him as a chief at the Forks, while listing an Olumapies (from Olumapisid "well tied, bundled up") among the Susquehanna chiefs and councilors. Other sources indicated the same man had both Delaware names. While it is possible to derive Sassoonan from terms for a mother's brother (*ziis*) and for "our," it is not clear which of the two plurals, exclusive or inclusive, was intended, although the inclusive would be more appropriate for a chief.

The term Olumapies is more intriguing because it can also be derived from *olamon* "red ochre" and *-ape* "biped" – as in the self-designation of the Lenape, a combination of *len-*, "common,

---

[18]  An analogy here is the Southwestern Pueblos, each having a cacique, the supreme religious leader of a community, intimately concerned with farming cycles and cosmic harmony, who went underground for much of the 400 years of Spanish, Mexican, and American occupation. While Pueblos were more institutionalized than Delaware, both had farming cycles to regulate their lives. William Fenton (2000, 714) observed that Thadoda:ho', the shamanic 'wizard' first among equals of the Iroquois League, is rarely if ever mentioned in colonial documents.

standard" and -*ape* "biped." The reference to tying-bundling used by Heckewelder might be a reference to a keeper of the tribal archives and wampum, possibly associated with a Walam Olum "scored red," a proper Delaware term even if the known version of the record was a fraud or historic fabrication during the Indiana furor.

Is this title a hint of a Delaware spiritual leader, known as Olamon-ape, who kept a tribal record marked in red ochre? Among Delaware, red was emblematic of the inside, the community associated with blood and kinship. Historic wampum belts in white and purple beads which made up much of the tribal archives were mnemonic emblems of pledged agreements. Combining white and dark colors, they symbolized diversity and boundaries, a combining of insiders and outsiders. When sent to recruit war allies, such belts were smeared with red paint to represent both closeness and battle wounds.

The nucleus of Unami Delaware may have moved from Abbott Farm of the Middle Woodland Period to the important cluster of villages on the lower Schuylkill during the Late Woodland-Early Contact Period, fostering the eventual growth of Philadelphia as a social and political center. Yet, the Falls probably remained a religious site until the early epidemics. According to Nora Dean, Chief Left-Hand [Manɛngy] was often praised in the Oklahoma Big House, harkening back to "Managy, whose name appears a number of times in Pennsylvania provincial records, was formerly a chief of one of the Delaware bands settled near the falls of the Delaware in the Trenton vicinity" (Weslager 1972: 176).

Clearly, a leader fondly recalled after 250 years must have played an important role in the tribal past. Initially, I assumed that his memory became more important after Neolin introduced the priority of the left into Delaware ritual, but that now seems hasty. Left-Hand was resident at the Falls and a leader, probably a religious one. If aliens called him a chief, they might have been deliberately led to misunderstand his religious role, which is suggested by the recognized link between the left hand and the heart. His seniority entitled him to great authority. If not himself a priest, he may have been a front for this office.

Neolin, therefore, may have only been reemphasizing a left priority, then in decline, by preaching that the left hand was sacred because it was closer to the heart, the center of the person and Delaware locus of thought, emotion, and blood. Such integration suggests antiquity, binding together self and society within a Delaware integrity. Much as the Gamwing changed from a validation of the internal elite rankings as visionaries toward a confirmation of Delaware national identity by a democratization process increasingly emphasizing the greater community over the privileged ranks, so Neolin may have popularized a usage of the left by native priests into a general Delaware custom that continues to set them apart from other tribes.

If Manɛngy passed the priestship to Sassoonan, this would provide a link between a sacred fire at Trenton and the holder of an Olamenapes title. While speculative, this argument derives from comparable situations elsewhere in Native America during early contact periods.

# PEOPLING ~ 6

By analogy with other tribal beliefs, every being in the Delaware universe had a home of some sort. These varied from the solitary abodes of spirit persons to the camps, houses, and towns inhabited by humans according to season. Such housing was the means for linking persons to places, with those in the most important positions leading and governing the wider community. These leaders acted for constituencies of dwellings, clans, and genders.

## Housing

Regardless of settlement, Delaware women "owned" the houses and controlled the domestic economy. In the ethnography, houses are described as conical, domed, and rectangular, but we know very little about housing, except for post hole patterns at archaeological sites in the most marginal areas of the homeland. Various house types may have been occupied at different seasons, or by communities with different functions. Our best hope for such data is the responsible excavation of enough Late Woodland sites to reveal a full range of Delaware housing and seasonal activities. Regrettably, urban sprawl has probably destroyed most of such evidence.

Symbolism relating to houses can be surmised. Generally, the long rectangular houses, located in the large summer towns had manly associations, while the smaller domed ones were womanly, especially since the smallest versions of these served as birthing and menstrual huts. Zeisberger (1910: 170) said Delaware longhouses had peaked or gabled roofs, unlike the quonset or rounded roof of the Iroquois longhouse. When I asked Nora to sketch a house, she spontaneously drew a rectangular one. When I asked her why, she said that she had always thought of this form as the proper Delaware house. Certainly, the Big House represented such a glorified longhouse, an impressive council hall for the leaders and assemblies in larger communities. The smaller domed menstrual and birthing huts were located behind the longhouses or at the edge of the settlement, away from foot traffic for the protection of men and their gear. Women had power of their own at such times, dangerous to men.

Seasonal camps, aside from rockshelters, probably used the round, domed, or "beehive" house (*wikwam*), the abode of wife and children while the man was hunting. In general, attitudes of ancient Delaware were probably much like those of modern Ojibwa, fellow members of the Algonkian or Algic language stock.

The hunting lodge (usually a birchbark wigwam or canvas and bark tent) [stood] at about the center of the game range. It "belonged," in Ojibwa parlance, to the wife, who occupied it with the young children. The woods and the hunt "belonged" to the man, who … might remain away days or weeks at a time, and return home only to rest (Landes 1968a: 7).

In addition to camps, Delaware had substantial summer towns unlike Ojibwa informal clusterings. Lenape has words for town and hamlet, while Ojibwa simply call any settlement by a term meaning "lots of people." According to Delaware, each of these towns "belonged" to one of three matriclans $\frac{\text{Fowl}}{\text{Turtle}}\frac{\text{Canine}}{}$ or (Fowl (Turtle) Canine), and the houses "belonged" to resident women members.

Overall, then, tributaries of the Delaware River were probably used by localized bands and tribes of the collectivity. Each drainage was occupied by settlements that were "owned" by a matriline, matrilineage, or matriclan whose hereditary leaders (leading families of sisters and brothers) were most familiar with the resident spirit (manitu) of that place. These residential kinship units were probably the basis for the clan segments recorded by Morgan (1959: 1963) and Harrington (1913) among Delaware descendants living in Kansas, Oklahoma, and Ontario.

Such localized or village-based lineages also provided the context for the so-called Family or Household rites (like the Bear, Otter, and Doll Ceremonies) performed and described by Oklahoma traditionalists. Clusters of villages along major tributaries would have been tied together by intermarriages, trade networks, and joint participation in Tribal or Town rituals like those of Maize, Football, and Masing.

The conduct of these rituals was the responsibility of the leading families, whose residence varied. Adams (1905: 25, 44) reported "The Delaware Indians always lived in villages. The rich people would live in the centre of the village and the poorer people would live on the outskirts. Somewhere on the outskirts of the village, always near a creek or river, would be the lodge where the boys were trained." In a story, a departing chief announced to a man, "I give you my inheritance, the chieftaincy, my lodge and daughters and I will retire to the edge of the village and from now on you are my Chief." Speck (APS 912) wrote that the home of the chief was in the center of a town; Nora Dean said it should be on the edge.

Though they differ, these statements clearly indicated that the location was not random, and both may be valid. As host to visitors, the chief functioned on the "edge" of the community, mediating between insiders and outsiders. The official residence, throughout Native America, was centrally located to be the focus of a larger community. Perhaps some chiefs had a private home for a second wife on the periphery, while sharing the central council house with a senior wife. Such a second home in town would have been useful when the chiefly family had to move out of the hall during ceremonies with a large attendance.

## Kinship

Throughout Native America, as well as among Delawares (Miller 1991a), a person was only a facet of the larger community, a link within a set of relationships based in kinship, clans, tribes, and spirits. Each of these aspects, in turn, will now be considered for what they can indicate about the antiquity of Delaware beliefs.

Delaware ideology placed strong emphasis on notions of a consubstantiality of shared "blood" (hmuk$^{w}$). Delaware elders expressed genuine horror of incest, by which they meant a marriage between blood relatives of any known degree. This aversion was so strong that the last of the remaining full-blood Delaware preferred to marry outside the tribe, rather than risk the possibility of marrying a distant relative, which confirms that "blood" was exclusive, passed through women as mothers and shared by all offspring. Thus, the incest taboo extended to all relatives, those of both the father and the mother; even though the ideology of descent was matrilineal, a child clearly had two parents.

Indeed, derived from this matri-emphasis in the link between blood and women, the descent system was Matri-Hawaiian, a flexible bilaterality leaning toward the female. While clans were exogamous, Newcomb (1956: 109) found Oklahoma Delaware who claimed descent in the clans of both mother and father. Also, Harrington (ms.) noted that if both parents were Turtles, then their children were "full Turtles" and sat with the Turtles in the Big House. If the parents came from different clans, the children could sit with either clan, although a child specifically "belonged" only to the matriclan of the mother. Thus, the system was bilateral in function, but matrilineal in interpretation, except under extenuating circumstances such as a marriage between members of Turtle clans presumably from different tribes. At least, this was what I think Harrington meant by marriage between Turtles; otherwise the couple was committing incest in the Delaware view. Careful inquiry about seating in the Oklahoma Big House revealed that while a child could visit at the father's section, he or she belonged where the mother's clan sat. Young children were indulged by letting them sit with either parent, but with maturity came seating with the mother's clan.[19] They could visit with their father and his kin, sometimes for long periods, but they belonged with their mother if a girl or mother's brother if a boy.

Inheritance had the same personal and bilateral aspects. A Delaware owned only what he or she made or bought through personal efforts. Recently, if a woman had the money and bought the family car, then the family used it with her permission. While everyday utensils were inherited bilaterally, allowing that some items were more appropriate to males or females, specialties followed definite rules, often matrilineal ones. Thus, religious offices, paraphernalia, and rites usually passed through women, presumably because of the bonds existing between women, land, and clanship. These links ranged through the entire scope of life, including the farming cycle and other rituals of renewal. Sacred obligations were passed through women, but performed by men.

More personal possessions like jewelry and craft tools went to someone of the appropriate gender. Thus, Nora was given silver bracelets when an old relative died. Since the young were vulnerable to the dead, her mother Sally [Sarah Wilson Thompson] kept them until Nora was old enough to wear them safely. Clothing was too close to the dead (absorbing body essences) to be inherited by close relatives, so it was given to non-kin who helped at the funeral. No discord should occur for this would threaten the consequences of _k$^w$ulakan_ upon the heirs and everyone else in proximity (Miller 1975c).

All societies use kinship terms as a means of classifying special bonds within an ordered pattern. Among the Delaware and many other societies, the only true "person" was a "relative." Nora told me on several occasions that "over time even a friend comes to be considered a relative" (Miller 1975b: 441), as substantiated by my own naming, Canine clan membership, and role within the Dean household.

---

[19] This confusion about seating, of course, has to do with the phrasing of the question. When asked where they sat, elders thought fondly of sitting with either parent or any other of their favorite relatives because children were always indulged. When asked where they belonged, however, they always said with the people of their mother's clan.

Delaware kinship terminology has been carefully reviewed by Newcomb (1956, 43ff), and its linguistic aspects considered by Goddard (1973), who noted some derivations from Proto-Algonkian (Aubin 1975, Walker 1975). As the basis for social relations, kinship systems were sensitive indicators both of structure and of change. They meshed particularly closely with the techno-economy, since they enabled the cooperation necessary for effective task groups. Particular changes in the Delaware system were suggested by Newcomb (1956: 43), who attributed them to historical factors such as altered residence patterns, decreased polygyny, and increased surplus from the economic efforts of men.

The kinship system as first reported by Lewis Henry Morgan in 1859 conformed to the types called MacKenzie Basin by Leslie Spier and Hawaiian or Generational, particularly Matri-Hawaiian, by George Peter Murdock. Arguing from Delaware matrilineality, matrilocality, and the importance of female farming, Newcomb (1956: 47) reconstructed an earlier Iroquoian type of terminology, where cross-cousins (children of opposite sex siblings) were designated by a separate term but siblings and parallel-cousins (children of same sex siblings) were called by the same term.

Goddard (1973: 41) reviewed the full terminology and provided Proto-Algonkian reconstructions (hypothesized terms from the parent language of this stock) for sibling terms that were based on relative age. This suggests that Morgan's distinguishing of step-siblings and cousins from full siblings probably reflected the attitudes of Christian Delaware, who now observed strict monogamy. Traditionally, Delaware sibling terms distinguished only relative age and gender – "younger sibling," "older brother," "older sister" – indicating a fairly stable Matri-Hawaiian system based on twin distinctions of gender and age with a bias toward women.

With matrilineality and matrilocality important only seasonally, the flexibility inherent in the Hawaiian type allowed for the shifting importance both of summer farming by women and of winter hunting by men. The full system was skewed toward women probably because of the metaphysical bond provided by "shared blood" inherited through females, the long absences of men from the towns to hunt, war, trade, and travel, and the stabilizing influence of surplus crops provided by the women.

Delaware also included terms for male and female 'friend' in their kinship system (Goddard 1973: 52, Miller 1977), indicating that personhood was indeed based on kinship. Unami, and probably Munsee, recognized formal friendships between people of the same sex. In Unami Lenape, male friends called each other "*nitis*" and female friends used "*nichus*." Friends of opposite sex addressed each other by appropriate sibling terms.

Nora Thompson Dean added another aspect of this usage that was otherwise overlooked. Like all young women, Nora's family selected an older man to serve as her confidant, whom she always addressed as "*nichus*." Because there were no suitable older men among the traditional Delawares, her parents selected an Osage man. By way of illustrating the closeness between a girl and her confidant, Nora told me a classic tale about this relationship.

A young girl was washing clothes and happened to look down to see worms poking out of the ground. She thought they were looking up at her and became upset. Crying, she went to her nichus and told him the worms were trying to look up her dress. The man went back to the spot with her, pushed aside his loincloth and sat down at different places on the ground, announcing "Here, look here, if you want to see genitals."

When Nora told this story to other researchers, they remarked to her about its "Freudian" overtones, but she rejected such an interpretation as "way too whiteman," since the intent of the tale was exactly the opposite. Rather, it expressed the openness, helpfulness, and frankness, especially in matters of sex, that were proper to this special relationship. As Delaware women were raised to be extremely modest, such a male confidant must have provided an outlet for the uncertainty and confusion of teenagers and new brides. It contributed to the stability of Delaware society by easing the anxieties involved in courtship, marriage, and domestic relations, particularly since modest young females were kept very ignorant of human physiology. Puberty seclusion included lectures about personal conduct and work habits, but not about gynecology. There were no occasions for proper girls to learn about coitus or pregnancy; the bulk of their instruction was devoted to moral and ethical concerns. When Nora was reminded that children saw pets and livestock engage in biological functions, she insisted that animals were not the same as people. Better families did not and would not learn from such animal behavior. Animals had their own rules and laws to follow, established by the Creator and distinct from those of humans.

The male *nichus* nicely illustrates the inclusive characteristic of the category Man, applying the same term to both girls and men. There was no equivalent for boys, possibly because they were expected to have aged widows for their first wives, providing them with experienced advice about family life. Among the closely related Shawnee, some newlyweds were so unfamiliar with sex that the mother of the bride would instruct them the first time they had intercourse (Voegelin, Yegerlehner, and Robinett 1954). The trust assigned to older men and women support the importance of seniority in Delaware society; possibly the nichus man also played a role in the traditional oligarchy by giving older men some control over marriageable women.

Thus, in broad terms, Delaware kinship was flexibly bilateral, but specifically narrowed to uterine lines when land, farming, and social continuity were involved. Yet bilaterality was the predominant pattern both among Algonkians and the majority of Native American peoples (Driver 1961, Frisch 1977, Wherry 1979). Where it was otherwise, the complex requirements of agriculture, large towns, cooperative labor, and community defense were suspected causes for such unilineality.

"Delaware-Mahican matrilineality can be referred to the importance of horticulture in the area and perhaps [?] Iroquoian influence" (Aberle 1974: 74). Murdock (1965: 31) has designated "this distinctive type of bilateral organization ... recognizing its variability in regard to rules of residence ... the Salish type ... more widely distributed in North America than any other type of social organization, and there is reason to suspect that it is the original type from which most other North American systems have arisen by one or two steps of normal evolutionary development ... The Delaware could have developed their matrilineal system through the parallel process of matrilocalization and sib formation," presumably during the seasonal occupation of farming towns.

Wallace (1947: 9) argued that the Delaware were matrilineal and accorded high status to their women as a consequence of the intensive labor which females devoted to the maize crop. As a result, it was the women who produced a reliable surplus, although political reasons may have also been involved in the process. Trigger (1978: 62) proposed that neighboring Iroquois developed matrilineality and matrilocality when men began to spend much of their time away from the villages, engaged in warfare and diplomatic missions, leaving the women in charge at home. Since both female farming and male absence were factors of proto-historic Delaware society, these gender attributes might help explain why this nation assumed the title of Women for a time in the 1700s, at least when Iroquois overlords were nearby.

## Clans

In the Delaware homeland, a tribe included a number of towns, each "owned" by one of the matriclans, whose totemic designs have been discussed by Miller (1973, 1975a), Dean (1975), and Goddard (1974b, 1975). While there is general agreement on three named groupings, debate continues about possible internal subdivisions or subclan segments. In consequence, the same three groupings have been variously called phratries or clans, although the term matriclan clearly indicates membership through women. Nora Dean and other elders insisted that the clan names were generics, rather than named for individual species, and were symbolic expressions of the major elements in the cosmos. In this light, the clans form a set with the same associations and complexities as the tribes, though not the direct equations made by Heckewelder. While the antiquity of these clans is unknown, they do belong to a regional pattern. Neighboring Mahikan, Mohawk, and Oneida also had three clans: Turtle, Wolf, and Bear. William Fenton (2000: 353) even suggested that all Iroquois began with these same three clans, while those to the west added more matriclans with the adoption of captives from other nations.

The Unami clans were Turtle, Canine (also Wolf) and Fowl (also Turkey). Although Harrington (ms.) noted that the Munsee had only the Wolf and Turkey members, during the Munsee Big House ceremony the moieties were Turtles and Wolves (Speck and Moses 1945).

The Canine clan is called literally "round foot" in Lenape. Nora translated the name of the Turtle clan as "hole (hollow) in the heel," but agreed with others that there was no ready translation of the Fowl clan name, although "scratchers" and "doesn't chew" have been suggested. In terms of their physical characteristics, both canines and turtles were tailed quadrupeds, while both fowl and turtles lay eggs, indicating, once again, that Turtle was a mediator between the other two clans.

Oklahoma Delaware also used synonyms for the clans. Thus, Canines were called "red paint people" and were supposed to favor this color. The Fowl were "yellow leaf tree people" and considered loud and boisterous. Turtles were "lively people," considered agile, wiry, and full of energy. Nora was told by elders that there were more of these labels in the past, but she never learned them. Like that for the Turtles, some of these may have been humorous or ironic terms used in cross-sex joking. Morgan (1963, also in Newcomb 1956: 49) listed subdivisions for each of the three clans named by the Kansas Delaware, leading some to consider them phratries, larger units having constituent clans. These named subdivisions were probably vestiges of localized matrilineages or clan segments that occupied separate villages in the homeland. Nonetheless, the functional units during much of the historic period have consistently been the same three matriclans, whose membership has sadly dwindled over time.

Trowbridge (ms.) said each clan had four of these subdivisions, or twelve of them in all. Morgan reported that each clan had 12 sections, although he could learn names for only 10 among the Turtle. When Nora mentioned the possibility of other synonyms, I went over the list in Morgan with her. Only two could be identified. Her Canine "red paint people" were clearly the same as Morgan's Wolf (number six) "vermillion," and her Fowl "yellow leaves" was his Wolf (two) "yellow tree." Harrington (1913: 210) reported other names recalled by the Canadian Munsee, and suggested on this basis that each label made reference to an attribute of the clan eponym.

While the two names in Morgan belonged to the Canines, the "yellow trees" are now linked with Fowl, a shift explained, by luck, in Harrington's manuscript. After the Delaware settled in Oklahoma, the "yellow leaf tree people" were in danger of becoming extinct. Susie Elkhair – third wife of Charlie, mother of five children, three of them daughters, and a member of the Fowl clan – was offered membership in the "yellow leaf trees" in exchange for five strings of maize, presumably one for each child. When I inquired, I learned that her female descendants are in fact the living members of the "yellow leaf trees" of the Fowl clan. A strong motivation for perpetuating this grouping was its responsibility for organizing the Big House at Copan (Speck 1931: 17), because as the wife and daughters of the chief these women had important domestic and hospitality responsibilities during the rite.

According to Heckewelder (1876: 253), each clan had a standard representation of its eponym. A Turtle drew an outline of a turtle as seen from above, a Fowl marked an avian foot with three toes, and a Canine sketched a round foot attached to the outline of a wolf. He further noted attributes that recognized the Turtle as amphibious, the Fowl as stationary, and the Canine as mobile. Morgan (1959: 51) said the Canine represented animal life with hair, the Fowl those with feathers, and the Turtle those without hair, including fish. Adams (1905: 66ff) regarded Turtles as amphibious, Canines as great hunters, and Turkeys (Fowl) as omnivorous. Miller (1973b) argued that in general Canines = land, Fowls = air, and Turtles = water.

While these associations, folk etymologies, and random observations seem bewildering, they do represent a consistent matrix. The Canine and Fowl were diametrically opposed, mediated by the Turtle. Canine was characteristically quadruped, haired, widely roaming, terrestrial, carnivorous, viviparous, and tailed. In contrast, Fowl was bipedal, localized, feathered, herbivorous, and egg laying. The Turtle occupied an intermediate position as a shelled, amphibious, quadruped, laying eggs that hatched into self-sufficient toddlers unlike helpless baby birds.

Possible translations for the clan names were also intriguing as another possible matrix. Thus, "round foot" contrasted with "scratchers" as the whole foot contrasted with the toes, while "doesn't chew" contrasted the head with the feet. "Hole in the heel" emphasized the back of the foot together with a round space, in contrast to the round solid of the Canine foot.

The current associations of these clans with red paint, yellow trees, and agility provide a variant matrix. Thus, yellow was a color associated with men as warriors, and red was the only color used by women. Further, agility was not generally considered inherent to turtles, especially when they flail around when turned upside down. Instead, irony was probably intended since joking was expected between members of the different clans. "Among the Delaware, for instance, a Turtle man was teased about being slow and a Wolf would be told he could not pick up anything with his hands [forepaws]" (Kinietz 1947: 76). These deliberate reversals made such joking all the more vivid.

The standard matrix, therefore, is that Fowl was exclusive, Canine inclusive, and Turtle inclosive. Also, the complexity of these relations included some humorous reversals.

Zeisberger (1910: 93) attributed a political superiority to the Turtle clan over the others, and some have claimed that the Turtle chief had priority to the other two. As the inclosive, the Turtle clan had a special mediating status that had greater ramifications. Through time, however, any prominence of the Turtles was leveled out by the periodic leadership of one clan over the others during various meetings and rituals. The position of the Turtles, therefore, probably rested on their integrative role, rather than any special political dominance.

## Tribes

Often misunderstood by writers, particularly historians, Delaware tribes were usually known as Munsee, Unami, and Unalachtigo. Yet only the first two were well attested in both the historic and ethnographic literature, each characterized by distinctive territories, speech styles, rituals, and burial rites. Euro-Americans were remarkably oblivious to such features of indigenous social organization, which they were slow to grasp and report.

For example, the Unalachtigo remain dubious, particularly since this name first appears in documents of 1769 (Hunter 1974, Miller 1974c, Weslager 1975), although negative evidence before then is unconvincing. Nora Dean interpreted this name as "those detached from where there are waves" and remembered her mother mentioning them once when she was scrubbing the floor with her dress cinched up. Nora thought her mother was implying that their women wore short skirts (Miller 1976a: 248) to be able to enter the water. Limited mainly to Moravian sources, the Unalachtigo were probably a consequence of missionary activity – an ephemeral group of refugees, most likely, from the Jersey shore.

Instead of the Unalachtigo, Nora said that the Delaware recognized a third tribe called the Winetkok, an amalgam of many tribes, also known as the Nanticoke because these contributed heavily to the mixed population. Originally, the early Nanticoke were an independent tribe of the Delmarva peninsula. The Winetkok, then, were probably a tribal group, now extinct or joined with historic tribes like the Nanticokes, who had their origins along the Atlantic coast and closely interacted with ancestral Delaware or Iroquois.

The Munsee, Unami, and Winetkok were treated as comparable tribes, forming a nested set, while the Unalachtigo remain either anomalously outside of this system or a substitute for the Winetkok.

The Munsee supposedly derived their name from the contraction of the phrase "people of the stony country," but the term remains obscure, lacking even an accepted folk etymology.[20] Munsee funerals included a feast in honor of a deceased member, serving favorite foods, twelve days after his or her death. The Munsee were also called Wolves, not because they were all members of the Canine Clan as Heckewelder proposed, but because they were renowned warriors, fierce as wolves. They were courageous and brave backwoodsmen, said to look, act, and dress like disheveled bumpkins and to speak a harsher version of Lenape. Their tribal fire was kindled in the Upper Delaware River, historically on Minisink Island (Heye and Pepper 1915, Ritchie 1949).

The Unami were more spiritual, less aggressive – noted for their pleasant sounding Lenape, extensive religious activities, and thoughtful leadership. Their dead only took four days to reach heaven, so funeral feasts were held four days after a death. Their fire burned near modern Trenton, and may have represented all Delawares for some purposes.

---

[20] Distinctive Munsee artifacts were collected by Harrington (1908) for the Tefft Collection at the American Museum of Natural History in New York City.

The Winetkok, according to Nora, introduced the Unami to a form of witchcraft using a lethal "poison" that was capable of wiping out entire towns and depopulating regions. Their funerals followed the common Southeastern practice of exhuming the dead after a few years and reburying them in a communal grave after a night-long Skeleton Dance. Every decade or so, family members dug up all of their relatives buried longer than a year, cleaned the bones, and placed the pieces of each skeleton into a loosely packed bundle. Close kin carried their bundles to the open communal grave (ossuary). All that night, everyone danced while the bundles were shaken like a rattle in time to the songs. The next day all of the bundles were buried together (Howard 1975).

According to Unami perceptions, these tribes formed a matrix. The Winetkok were exclusive, avoided and feared for their poisons and sorcery, which also explained why they disappeared without regrets. Also, they were only dimly recalled in terms of their women, rather than the entire tribal community. The Munsee were inclusive, with very manly characteristics, and the Unami were inclosive, noted for being more integrative, reflective, and religious.

Further, this triad included some subtle internal variations. The Munsee were regarded as effective warriors but socially awkward, the Unami peaceful ritualists, and the Winetkok relentless, asocial sorcerers. The Munsee and Unami maintained themselves into the present, but the Winetkok became extinct, much to the relief of their former neighbors, although a fascinating transposition has filled their place in the matrix. Many Delaware, especially those living in Anadarko (Newcomb 1956: 70), attribute dangerous sorcery and the Skeleton Dance to members of the Canine Clan living around Dewey (Howard 1975). Conversely, some of the Dewey people look upon the Anadarko Unami speakers with suspicion.

In a few instances, Anadarkos have abetted this. In the words of Leona Parton (IPH 93: 55), "My mother has been a witch woman and she has her medicines which she keeps in a bag about 12 inches deep but never uses any more. In this bag is a can and in the can is a little image of a man. There is some Indian tobacco also in the can and if anyone bothers with it he will go crazy." She also mentioned that another woman had some witch medicine.

While not based in history, these claims derive from the internal logic of Delaware culture. Overall, the exclusive member of the matrix was replaced, appropriately enough, from the inclosive Unami, perhaps suggesting a hope that they would blend their sorcery with wisdom.

# OKLAHOMA ALLIED RITES ~ 7

At the 1877 payment, Oklahoma Delaware were recognized in terms of three riverine settlements: Cana [Caney] with John Sarcoxie, Verdigris with Charles Journeycake, and Grand River with James Ketchum.

As the Big House people led by Sarcoxie identified with the Caney River, so the Christians congregated on Lightning Creek, both tributaries of the Verdigris River in the drainage of the Arkansas. Although there were Methodist Delaware along the Grand River, the majority of the Lightning Creek "bunch" were Baptists, linked to Alluwe, the site of their church and the tribal payment ground, where treaty annuities, accumulated interest, and, in 1891, $900,000 from the sale of the Kansas lands were distributed.

According to Isaac Secondine (IPH 9: 193), early payments were made at Vinita and Chelsea "until the Delaware decided that they could use the Church House at Alluwe, Oklahoma as a payment ground." Every six months between 1885-87, it took a full week to distribute $30-40 per head. The money was hauled from Coffeyville, Kansas by an Indian policeman, with Bill Foreman as guard and Robert Owens was paymaster.

Ruth Parks (IPH 8: 73-74) repeated much the same information, and added "The money came to Coffeyville, Kansas by railroad express and it was transported to the payoff stations by horse and buggy. Seldom did more than two armed men accompany the money en route. It took at least a week or more to finish these payments." At the last payment in 1895, people got $600 each, much of it spent at the Alluwe store run by J.E. Campbell.

Discontent increased, and attempts were made to find a new home in the West or in Mexico. In December of 1898, ten Delaware men visited the Don Cailos Conan concession on the Yaqui River, seeking another haven. Some of the Anadarko Delaware did settle in Mexico for a time, and Jasper Exendine left the Caney area and settled in Anadarko and in Mexico for long periods.

Eventually, Christian settlements formed a series of towns along the 1889 north-south tracks of the St. Louis to Iron Mountain Railroad. These towns were named Delaware, Lenapah, Alluwe, and Nowata – the last three forming a Lenape phrase meaning "The Delaware know more about it." While they gave up most of their traditions, the Christian Delaware continued to use the Lenape language, well into this century, for hymns, sermons, prayers, and services. The best known of the Baptists was Charles Journeycake (Mitchell 1895, Roarch 1970), who was ordained and became official chief in 1877, serving until his death 3 January 1894. Since his death, Delaware affairs have been handled by a Business Committee composed of elected members. Delawares fought for and gained autonomy from the Cherokee Nation after, only to have a federal court return them to Cherokee overlords. On March 2005, Delawares had their federal funding cut off by order of the Cherokee government. Matters were not mutually resolved, not entirely to Delaware satisfaction, until a 2007 agreement (Obermeyer 2009).

Although the Delaware had already been allotted in severalty in Kansas, almost thirty years before, when the 1887 Dawes Act became federal policy, the Five Civilized Tribes (Choctaw, Chickasaw, Creek, Seminole, and Cherokee, including Delaware arrivals) were initially exempted. Constant pressure for land, however, led to 1892 legislation incorporating these tribes into the general allotment. Most Delaware agreed to this policy because it was in accord with their newly-espoused Protestant ethic. The conservatives, about ten percent of the population faithful to the Big House, strongly opposed this. Their protest, however, went unheeded.

By 1904, all Oklahoma Indian land was open for homesteading by whites, yet the Delaware allotment was not completed until 1907. Around 1900, Thomas Alford (1976 [1936]: 187) heard of a plan to move all Oklahoma natives to Mexico, where they would lack treaty rights. Fortunately, this ploy was disclosed to the public and halted. Otherwise, Delaware might have been forced to relocate again.

During the 1980s, the population of Unami elders well versed in their culture and language dropped from twelve to two. Nora Dean, Annie Parks, Fred Washington, Tom Wilson, Bill Shawnee, Ollie Anderson, and several of the Longbones have gone to their ancestors. Gratefully, Nora Thompson Dean and Lucy Parks Blalock, with whom I worked most closely, were best informed and longest lived.

At Anadarko and Ontario, Lenape speakers have been influenced, respectively, by exchanges with the Caddo and the Iroquois. Ironically, The Delaware Tribe of Western Oklahoma, descendants of the Plains Delaware forced to Anadarko, is now the only Delaware community federally recognized by the United States. Their elders are multilingual, but preserve in their spoken Lenape and legends many indications of Delaware culture unaffected by changes in the Big House Rite and the Indiana revival.

Incongruously, over the last decades, the number of enrolled Delaware among the Cherokee has increased dramatically as a result of the publicity surrounding the successful completion of the litigation of Delaware land claims. By July 1977, the tribal roll included 9,600 names, each of whom received a check for $1,339.59 drawn from a $14 million fund, with interest, in compensation for the inequities of the Kansas land sale. Shortly after, another check for $91.20 went to compensate for the 1818 Treaty of St. Marys, Indiana.

Of the minor rituals, only occasional funerals and the Naming (Name Giving) is still held with any frequency, albeit with greater creativity than when Nora Thompson Dean was alive and sanctioned traditionally by her own vision experiences. According to her, the name must be kept secret until a pure fire is kindled, an exorcising smoke raised from burning cedar needles, pure water drunk four times by the person named, and tobacco smoked to open a channel to the Creator. Then the name was announced several times to remind the Creator of the uniqueness of that individual. In the past, respected men named boys and elderly ladies named girls.

This ritual, although minute in comparison to the Big House, symbolized all of the relationships vital to Delaware culture: the cedar smoke segregated and excluded, qualities of Woman, while the tobacco integrated and included, qualities attributed to Man. The fire and water mediated and inclosed, binding together the universe as a whole. While all human cultures share such details, the particular relationships, along with the occasion and locale, distinguish the whole as Delaware.

Today, like other Oklahoma tribes, Delawares express their ethnic identity by hosting an annual powwow in June, a homecoming for those who live away and a chance to gather friends and relatives together at the same place and time.

## Annual Rituals

For over half a century, however, after settling in Oklahoma, traditional Delaware families continued to celebrate not only the Gamwing, but a full series of traditional rituals, which have been recorded by scholars. These annual rituals included family sponsored Grease Drinking Rites in honor of (1) Otter or (2) Bear and the (3) Doll Dance, all three probably held in the spring; and tribal sponsorship of (4) "Indian Football" games held from the first budding of vegetation (April) until mid-June, (5) the Məsing Dance held every fall and whenever else the need for it arose, (6) the Maize Preharvest (Green Corn) held when the crops first ripened, and, finally, (7) the Big House Rite celebrated when the leaves began to change color in mid-October.

Aside from the Big House Rite or Gamwing, the other six rituals once celebrated in Oklahoma can be viewed as forming two triads of Family or of Tribal rites. Each will be discussed in turn.

It is interesting that the Family Rites were held in the Spring when, aboriginally, people were returning from winter camps to the summer farming town, and reintegrating themselves into a community in which those families able to sponsor rites would be quietly able to assert positions of leadership. The Tribal Rites were mostly held in the Fall, when food was plentiful before groups left to winter in hunting territories.

## Family Rites

The Grease Drinking Rites (called in Lenape, "repeatedly rising up") for Otter and Bear belonged to certain matrilines, as did the responsibilities associated with the inheritance of certain carved dolls.

## Otter

Nora Thompson Dean would have inherited one of the Otter Rites if her mother had not sold the necessary bundle to Harrington, acting for the Museum of the American Indian, Heye Foundation, which preserves a receipt for the sale of the bundle but lacks any notes on the ceremony itself. These collections now belong to the Museum of the American Indian in DC. Chief Elkhair told Michelson (ms.) that Nora's brother Jesse died at 16 because his mother had sold the bundle, but Nora always said that Jesse died of appendicitis and the bundle was sold because no one could remember all of the songs, thus placing the family in danger because the Otter Spirit would be offended by such neglect. By selling the bundle, this onus fell on the buyer. Even so, family members still avoid contact with otters or otter pelts. This family's version of the Otter Rite was last held when Sarah Wilson Thompson's oldest son was two years old.

According to Nora, the rite was held every two years, usually on a spring afternoon in the open air. The speaker on the last occasion was Billy Wilson, Sarah's father, who began the rite by facing east, praying, and explaining the purpose and procedure of the ceremony. The bundle was an otter skin with a long slit in the neck area (cf. Pawnee warrior garb, below). The service involved visionary recitations by men, each of whom, in turn, wore the sacred pelt with the head resting on the chest and the tail hanging down the back, as illustrated by Harrington (1921: 178).

Each recitation duplicated those done in the Big House, using the turtle shell rattle with strap handle. Among these men, one was memorable because his dog walked around the fire with him and every time he shouted "Hoooo, Hoooo, Hoooo," the dog barked an echo. Meanwhile, a kettle of meat cooked over the fire, probably bear or deer in the old days, but pork in Oklahoma. Two men served as cooks, appointed by the host family to butcher the hog and make the watery soup. Toward the end of the recitations, one of the visionaries carried the hog head on a plate around the fire. After several circlings, he threw the head into the fire as an offering to Otter. Women and "empty" (visionless) men sat at the edges of the cleared area, offering their own personal prayers.

When the food was ready, a gifted man moved one way around the fire and one of the male cooks circled the opposite way, carrying the kettle full of greasy meat. When they met, the visionary would sometimes take a ladle of this soup and give it to a clansman, who had to drink all of it immediately. Towards dark, after the recitations finished, everyone was served a feast of hog meat. Finally, the two cooks were each given a yard of wampum for their efforts.

Speck (1937: 46) reported another version of the Otter Rite, but it seems doubtful since it included an unroofed brush arbor, probably a confusion with the den of the Bear Rite. Also, no otter pelt was used. Speck said this version of the rite passed from Colonel Jackson to his daughter Lizzie Half Moon, but elders are sure that the rite, whose details were forgotten, had been properly transmitted from mother to daughter.

## Bear

The Bear Rite was similar to that for Otter, and both were regarded as Grease Drinking Rites (Harrington 1921: 171, Speck 1937: 30). Jake Parks, husband of Annie Brown Parks and a Big House singer, said that Jackson and Old Mrs. Frenchman shared one type of Bear Rite, but it did not use a brush arbor. This is confusing because in other versions the enclosure represented the bear's den. Modern Delaware have not witnessed this rite, so I have relied on Harrington, who was generally a reliable source. The Delaware Bear Rite has added significance because it was a southern example of the circumpolar distribution known for such ceremonialism (Hallowell 1926).

The Bear Rite was held every two years within the confines of a brush arbor shaped like a small version of the Big House, 14 by 30 feet. A meat pole was put up to hold fresh bear meat before it was cooked. After bears became scarce, a black hog was used, then a decision was made to use any hog available so the rite could continue. Held at night, gifted men recited, wearing a string of wampum about the neck and using a turtle shell rattle. The hog head had two ribs stuck in its mouth and was placed on a platter near the center. At the end of the recitations, the head was thrown into the fire.[21]

After the service, everyone feasted on cooked pork. Any remaining fat or broth was added to the fire, while six women were asked to move apart and recite the prayer word "Hoooo" six times

---

[21] There is no explanation for these ribs in the mouth, but, given the legendary accounts of cannibal monsters, it may be that the rite also symbolized the triumph of Delaware ancestors over fierce beings like the naked bear.

[at the meat pole?], a significant act for determining its inclusive character when compared to the use of that sound by men in other rituals. Its use by women also indicated that bear and hog were more womanly meats than venison. The rectangular arbor probably represented an assimilation to the form of the Big House. Earlier, it may have been circular, more like a den and the earth. Among Algonkians generally, bear is a symbol of the earth.

Bear and Otter Rites had similar tales of origin. A child had a pet bear or a young girl had a pet otter that was released into the wild with wampum tied around its neck. Later, the child became deathly ill and a shaman diagnosed the cause as the animal being unable to care for itself and making the child sick in order to receive periodic offerings of food from its former keepers.

Image #4 ~ three dolls (1 man, 2 women) in 1938 (by Vincenzo Petrullo)

## Doll

The third rite in this triad was the Doll Dance, related to the Bear/Otter pair in complex ways (Miller 1976b). The dance ground had a fire in the middle of a cleared space and, on the edge, a tent where the doll(s) were dressed. Participation was open to all, gifted and empty. Speck (1937: 66, note 6) placed the Unami ceremony in the fall, when the Munsee ritual was held, but both Harrington and Nora Dean said it was held in the spring. It may be that various families held their versions of the rite at different times.

According to Nora Dean (Miller 1976b), the Doll Dance was held in the dusky dark. Each doll, tied to a stick, was passed along the line of dancers. Dolls were alive and sometimes dangerous, so the sticks must have provided mediating protection. Dancers were accompanied by singers using special songs and beating on a folded deerskin drum. Families who inherited one or more dolls kept them stored in trunks, which were opened once a year to provide each one with a new set of clothing. During the previous year, their clothing had become worn and frayed because they were believed to wander out at night. Dolls were inherited as a single female addressed as "Grandmother" or as male + female pairs addressed as "Grandfather" and "Grandmother," exclusively female or inclusively paired.

During the dance, normal gender patterns were reversed. Men danced as the inside ring near the fire, passing a Grandfather Doll from one to another, starting at the front of the line, at each verse change. Women in the outside line did the same with the Grandmother(s). During lulls, sticks holding the dolls were stuck into the ground in front of the tent.[22]

---

[22] Apparently, Vincenzo Petrullo was the only anthropologist to ever witness a Doll Dance, held in 1929. The last one of 1933 was reported to Frank Speck in a letter from Charlie Webber.

After twelve rounds of dancing, people feasted on corn gruel that had been cooked over the fire. Afterward, all night long, Delaware did social dances. Early the next day, a "scramble" was held. Everyone gathered around an area covered with leaves and tried to catch oversized cornmeal biscuits and a special large loaf called "Bear," which were thrown to the spectators by the doll owners. It was a feat to catch these biscuits in the air as they were so hard they hurt on impact. Most people waited for them to hit the ground and gathered them from the leaves.

Image #5 ~ Doll Dance camp, 1938, three dolls at far left tent (by Vincenzo Petrullo)

Together, the Bear, Otter, and Doll Rites formed a set with closure, representing the elements of land, water, and air. In this triad, Bear was of the land, Otter of the water, and the Doll was the mediator, carved from wood and sharing the associations of trees with sky. As the Doll Dance was inclosive, so the Otter was inclusive and the Bear exclusive.

Speck (1937: 61) said the Doll Dance was intended to appease Mother Maize, mentioning cornhusk dolls. Harrington, Nora Dean, and my own inspection of a doll indicate that they were made of wood, much like those of Great Lakes tribes (Skinner 1925). Rather than being emblematic of maize, these dolls represented trees, the World Tree, and the link between earth and sky. This was vividly displayed at the end of the rite when the corn biscuits and Bear loaf were thrown into the air to land among the leaves, as though they were falling from a tree. The bread evoked both plants and animals, maize and bear, while tying the dolls onto sticks placed them along the vertical dimension between earth and sky. Since only corn gruel was served at a Doll Dance, plant associations were singularly strong.

The extensive power of this rite is confirmed by the decision to hold the last Doll Dance in 1933. During a severe drought in northeastern Oklahoma, elders met at Chief Elkhair's home to decide how to bring rain. Elkhair had a rainmaking charm of dried frogs that came alive when a ritual was performed, but, instead, they held the 1933 Doll Dance with a Grandfather and two Grandmothers.[23] As Webber noted in a letter to Speck,[24] the dance was held on a Monday and the next Sunday there was a full day of rain. As a mediating and inclosive rite, the Doll Dance proved itself to be the better selection, calling down a rain storm to save the crop.

---

[23] These three dolls were buried together with a brother of the last owner.
[24] American Philosophical Society, ms. # 932.

Lastly, there was a suggestion in the account of the Doll Dance by Silas Longbone to Michelson (ms.a) that there were clan-based versions of this rite. Longbone remarked that the special loaf thrown up at the end could be in the form of a turkey, bear, turtle, or human, each linked with a "band," by which he meant a matriclan. This gives further support to the mediating role of the Doll as a nexus for several opposed categories.

## Tribal Rites

While the Family Rites were transmitted by women of elite families, the tribal rites involved the whole community, focusing on the economic cycle that started with the football games and culminated at the Məsing and Maize Rites.

## Football

Oklahoma Delaware football was played men against women, using an eight inch oval made of deerskin stuffed with deer hair. The playing field, about 180 feet long, had pairs of goal posts set six feet apart at opposite ends. Before the game, a bet string was taken around and wagers were added to it of money (singles or change knotted in a cloth), ribbons, cigarettes, and handkerchiefs.

The game began when a respected elder took the ball out to the center of the field, prayed, and threw it into the air. Whichever player caught the ball started the game. If a man, he started kicking the ball from the men's goal posts, but if a woman, she began play from the posts at the women's end. At the now-abandoned field on the Falleaf farm, men were on the south side and women on the north. At the White Oak Shawnee ground, currently in use, men are on the east and women on the west. To score, the ball had to pass between the posts of the opposite sex; the first goal won the game. Then, a new game would start. Total scores for all games, for both men and women teams, were kept by a man using counting sticks. The Delaware limited play to 12 games, on rare occasions to 24, and the side that won the most games was declared the winner for that day.

Lacking referees, players settled their own disputes, minimizing the need for judges by using certain strategies to handicap the men and keep the play friendly. Men could only kick the ball, while women could hold, run with, and throw the ball. Women would never kick the ball because that was considered immodest. As Nora Dean said, it was as though men were playing soccer and women football. The most a man could do was slap the ball out of the hands of a woman. If he became rough, grabbing or holding a woman, the other women would mob him to teach the men a lesson in manners. Therefore, a man avoided touching a woman during the game, putting males at a disadvantage. Sometimes, women would deliberately mob a man if the game were going against them, but the men dared not retaliate. At decisive moments, the ball was sometimes given to an ancient and vulnerable dame who was slowly and carefully guided by the women down the field and through the goal posts. The men could only stand by, never obstructing such a frail and defenseless opponent.

After the last game of the season, an elder prayed on the field before splitting open the ball and scattering the deer hair stuffing. The hide covering was kept in trust by a respected person or couple until the next year. The night after the last game, a stomp dance was often held. Games went on during the first few months of the spring to encourage the growth of vegetation, particularly crops. During the 1970s, traditional elders were confounded, however, because younger Delaware played football (at the Copan powwow grounds) all summer long, an excess harmful to healthy growth.

During a game, the exclusiveness of Woman allowed the female team to monopolize the field because men had to abide by restrictions applying to women. Speck (1937: 73) recorded that the games were held to advance vegetation, a womanly purpose, but otherwise his description was much less informative than that provided by Nora Dean.

## Məsing[w]

The Məsing outfit and bundle, sold to Harrington and never replaced, had been kept in a tiny house in the yard of a respected old man. After the annual rites lapsed, he would occasionally hear the sound of Məsing's snapping turtle rattle, like those used by the Iroquois in their rituals, but no one went near the tiny house because they had neglected Məsing. After a time, the custodian went "berserk" (lost his senses). An Indian doctor diagnosed the cause as Məsing insisting that his dance be revived. This was done and the man was cured, but no one wanted responsibility for the bundle so it was passed from one elder to another, each one concerned about the consequences that might befall his family for avoiding the rite. Its last keeper was George Bullitt and the circumstances of the sale to Harrington are discussed by Speck (1931: 43).

The bundle contained the entire outfit, a jacket and pants of bearskin, together with a wooden mask painted half red and half black, a snapping turtle rattle holding corn kernels, a walking stick, and a pouch, said to hold "snakes." Children proved their bravery by going up to Məsing and giving him tobacco to put into this pouch. Shy or weak children were especially encouraged to do so. When fully dressed, the impersonator held the mask in front of his face, gripping it through the mouth opening with the left hand. In his right hand were the cane and rattle. The fitted cap securing the mask over the face, as described by David Brainerd in 1745, apparently did not continue in use.

The Delaware loved Məsing because he was uniquely their own. In Oklahoma, many Delaware were angered by the sale of the Məsing bundle, but, in hindsight, most have decided it was safer for everyone because any danger was transferred to the new custodians, much as Sarah (Sally) Thompson decided to sell her Otter bundle to Harrington for $20.

Other tribes have also sold sacred goods to collectors or museums, preserving a source of mystical power while shifting any adverse consequences to the new keepers. Ever a concern was the danger in passing powerful items on to a younger generation, if they were unprepared to accept them or unwise in their use.

In some cases, the Delaware buried bundles or dolls with the last owner, but this could be dangerous because the residual potency of the bundle might be used by the dead to harm the living. Delaware believed in several souls (Miller 1992), one of which lurked on the earth. Any harm it intended would be worse if a bundle shared its coffin. In short, there were several ways of disposing of sacred items. Destroying them, usually in a fire, ended their utility, so this was often too extreme a solution; placing them in graves gave the dead a potentially dangerous advantage; while selling them to outsiders preserved them for the future while deflecting any harm.

The Məsing Rite was held in the fall (Speck 1937: 50) or in May (Harrington 1921: 152). More likely, it was probably held during the hunting season and whenever else the custodian felt it was needed. A dramatic figure, Məsing left a lasting impression on those who saw him. The mother of Charlie Dean saw the rite once and for the rest of her life talked about the "Devil Dance." This was not unusual because Məsing could be frightening, as vividly recalled by older Delaware and early Oklahoma settlers. At least once, while the messengers and Məsing were going around to announce the camping day for the Big House, the sight of him caused the horses of an on-coming buggy to bolt in terror.

Image #6 ~ Məsing outfit, as once displayed in New York City

The Məsing Dance was held at midnight in a forest clearing, accompanied by special hunting songs and a folded deerhide drum stuffed with dried grass. A water drum, with a hide cover drawn over a hollowed log partially filled with water, may have also been used since Nora had such a drumstick with a Məsing face carved at the end. A fire burned at the center of a clearing, with the men dancers forming an outside ring and women an inside one. Məsing danced "outside the circle of people, not with them. When they have finished, he dances twelve changes alone, which occupies the time until morning" (Harrington 1921: 154). At the end, everyone feasted on hominy.

For an earlier period, Richard Adams (1906: 299) reported

Across the fire and inside of the ring is a long hickory pole supported at each end by wooden forks set in the ground. On the east of this pole the singers stand; on the west end is a venison or deer, which is roasted. About daylight, when the dance is nearly over, all the dancers eat of the venison. They have a dried deer hide stretched over some hickory poles, and standing around it beat on the hide and sing. The dancers proceed around the fire to the right, the women on the inside next to the fire. After the dance is under way the Messingq comes from the darkness, jumps over the dancers, and dances between the other dancers and the fire. He makes some funny and queer gestures, kicks the fire, and then departs... He is a terror to little children, and when he comes to a house or tent the man of the house usually gives him a piece of tobacco, which the Messingq smells and puts in his big pouch, after which he turns around and kicks back toward the giver which means "thank you," and departs.

Məsing also appeared in the Oklahoma Big House Rite during the days of the hunt, while the Munsee parallel, called Mazink, appeared during the last half of the Bear Sacrifice. Instead of a single masked figure, the Munsee had a Mazink guild, limited to 12 members, which functioned like an Iroquois Falseface order (Harrington 1921: 158ff).

Speck and Moses (1945: 27, 29) also mentioned other feasts and rituals in the Munsee series, such as the Maple Sugar and Strawberry, which agree with or follow Iroquois practice. Delaware and Iroquois cultures were indeed very close, but their similarities were buffered by deliberate reversals. Thus, they could adopt features from each other without cultural dissonance, as the Munsee adopted the masking sodality. The same also applied to Delaware and Shawnee parallels, aided by their common Algonkian background.

## Maize

Contrary to A. F. C. Wallace's claim (1956: 3; Miller 1996), the Maize (Preharvest Green Corn) Rite did not lapse until shortly after the Delaware settled in Oklahoma. As a young man, Jim Thompson encountered two Excrement Daubers, wearing cornhusk masks, as they were going around announcing that the rite would begin in four days. They had to be given a gift immediately, otherwise they were at liberty to smear the ungrateful with a fecal mixture from their container. Jim quickly gave them his neck bandanna.

At the actual dance, the men dancers were led by the Daubers wearing cornhusk masks, while the women were led by two women without special attire. At the feast, only hominy and cornbread were served, exclusively made from maize. Drums and rattles accompanied the songs. All other sources describe Dauber masks as made of cornhusks, so the set of wooden ones made for Speck (1937: 80) by Joe Washington reflect a creative imagination (and assured sale). While Harrington (1921; 43) said "little remembrance of the details of her worship can now be found among the Oklahoma Lenape, his novel (1963: 179) detailed that the Daubers wore "ugly little masks of wood with cornhusk hair and their clothes were made of cornhusks: sleeveless jackets, leggings, and shoes coarsely woven."

Since their own Green Corn lapsed, faithful Delaware have danced with the Shawnee at White Oak, Oklahoma, but the Shawnee had no Daubers. Throughout the East, the ceremony was held preharvest, while the corn is still alive in the fields, allowing "her" to receive thanks directly.

According to Speck (1937: 79), the daubing with human excrement was a "punishment," but this was an overly fastidious explanation. Generally, human cultures used feces to represent disjunction, separation, chaos, and disorder. Often, it symbolized a switch in time. Therefore, the Daubers were not just announcing the rite, they were marking the end of an old year and the beginning of a new one, a time of uncertainty well represented by the symbolism of feces.

While the Green Corn marked the end of the agricultural year, the Gamwing was the summary of the entire annual round. Their functions were distinct, refuting Wallace's (1956) attempt to derive the Big House Rite from the earlier Green Corn.  Further, the two ceremonies continued, side by side, until Delaware reached Oklahoma.  There, the Big House steadily incorporated other rites, not all of them Delaware, including the Maize Rite.

## Other Rites

Comparative study of such external and intertribal influences can shed light on the rest of the ritual series.  For example, Speck (1937: 67) and Harrington (1921: 182) disputed that the Buffalo Dance was integral to the Delaware ceremonial cycle.  This dance is still performed at White Oak by Shawnee and participating Delaware, much as described by Speck.

At the 1975 White Oak Bread Dance, men danced the inside ring and women the outside one, moving around cornbread loaves and garden vegetables piled in the center.  Afterward, everyone feasted on meat, bread, and corn on the cob.  A week later the Buffalo Dance should have been held, but drought had killed the maize crop, so the dance was cancelled.  Ordinarily, the dance involved men (impersonating bison bulls) guarding two kettles of mush and "butting" the women (acting as bison cows) out of the way.  Everyone tried to grab some of the mush.  The Bread and Buffalo Dances were reciprocal, the first held for harvested plants and the second for products of the hunt and farm.  Delaware say that both these dances were like their own had been.

The Delaware Buffalo Dance seems to have been part of another matrix of rituals concerned with killing: Buffalo, War, and Opossum.  The Buffalo Dance was "intended for fighting men and hunters" (Speck 1937: 67), "usually given before starting on the chase" (Adams 1906: 299), with both men and women dancing.  The War Dance was held by men and a few unique women before departing for raids and battle, or later to commemorate their deeds of valor.  The Opossum Dance, named for an animal that "plays dead," emphasized women, since it featured a vision recitation by a woman, singers using a pottery water drum, and a row of female dancers.  "Other women, we are told, formed a line of followers behind her, and there is no mention of men in the column" (Speck 1937: 58).  The indications, then, are that the Opossum Dance was exclusive, the War Dance inclusive, and the Buffalo Dance inclusive.

Of the best known tribal rites, The Maize Preharvest Rite was womanly and exclusive, linked with Mother Maize, who was believed to be jealous and very sensitive (Speck 1937: 61).  She was set apart, treated carefully, and somewhat feared because her wrath would ruin the harvest if she thought any disrespect was being shown to her fields, crops, or bounty.

The ballgame was inclusive, played men against women for the part of a year transitional between hunting and farming.  The game encouraged the spring growth of plants, in sympathy with the rapid movement of people along the field.   The game used a ball made of deer products which was itself a mediator, passing between men and women, sky and earth, and the standing wooden goal posts.   Tribes of the Southeast and the Lakota equated a ball game with the quest for knowledge and wisdom.  Although this was not a ready Delaware explanation, it accords well with their attitude.

The Məsing Rite was inclosive, associated with sky and earth, animals and plants, hunting and farming.  In all, the tribal triad of Ballgame (Məsing) Maize parallels that for the Family Rites of Otter (Doll) Bear.

Speck equated Məsing with a widespread belief in a Game Boss (Owner), although he was more like a Keeper or Warden in that he did not "own" the resources or species, he only managed them. Məsing was believed to live in a mountain range floating above the earth. Anciently, he was probably the lowest one of the 12 skykeepers represented on the Big House posts. He received particular attention because he lived closest to the earth, and initiated the upward movement of prayers to the Creator. Unifying this chain of beings was the Mind they shared in common.

An unexpected reversal occurs between the Məsing and Maize Rites. Both rites used masks, a wooden one for Məsing and two husk ones for the Daubers. We should expect a single mask for the womanly rite and two for the manly one, but this was not the case, probably to emphasize the value of reciprocity, exchange, and complementarity among all the rituals. As Nora Dean said, "Just because it was called the Green Corn didn't mean that people did not also take time to give thanks for everything else." Thus, while directed to the approaching maize harvest, prayers were also addressed to all interrelated beings. In Canada, of course, there were 12 Mazink, each representing a skykeeper, so there was no reversal.

## Big Moon Peyote

Oklahoma also had its own prophets. Foremost among them was John Wilson (Moonhead, Nishkantu in Caddo), an Anadarko Caddo with a Delaware father who was related to Nora Dean's mother (Speck 1933, Thurman 1973a, Parsons 1941). Moonhead was profoundly interested in religion, serving both as an advocate for Catholicism and as a leader in the Ghost Dance. About 1895, he began to preach the virtues of the sacrament of peyote, a thornless cactus long important in the rituals of tribes in northern Mexico. His teachings formed the Big Moon Rite, now limited to the Quapaw and Osage. While Wilson is still acknowledged as the revealer of peyote ritual, the modern form originated with the Lipan Apache, Comanche, and Kiowa. Sometimes called Little Moon, it counted among its converts such prominent Dewey Delaware as Chief Charlie Elkhair. Incorporated as the Native American Church and granted legal status in various states, this modern form of Little Moon recognizes Quanah Parker as its founder. Anadarko and other Delawares, nevertheless, continue to revere the teachings of Nishkantu.

# EARLY REPORTS ~ 8

Almost 200 years ago, Delawares, answering a questionnaire for C. C. Trowbridge and Lewis Cass, were able to recall, on behalf of all survivors, that before they ever saw Europeans, a lethal darkness and stench came while they were gathering together, engaged in an ancestral version of the Gamwing (Weslager 1978a: 89).

#6.    What is the earliest incident they recollect in their history?

Previous to the discovery of America by whites they were in a large meeting house in their worship. The day of a sudden turned dark and a very bad smell was smelt apparently coming from the sea, shortly after they were all taken sick and a great number of them died, since that time all manner of diseases have been prevalent among them. Before that they had no sickness as they ever heard of.

Set against a festive occasion, this grim account conveys the impact of epidemics ravaging the East coast. Introduced into the Caribbean by the Spanish and others (and into the Northeast by Basques), diseases spread very quickly along the shore before moving inland, depopulating much of the Atlantic by 1500, and enabling colonies from western Europe to settle with only sparse native resistance. "Repeated epidemics wrought social and demographic disruption ... scythed Indian populations ... tore holes in the social fabric, induced migration and resettlement, and produced spiritual and psychological upheaval [as] Indian civilizations crumbled under the onslaught of recurrent pandemics" (Calloway 1987: 28).

Strained by such repeated tragedies, Delaware integrity nevertheless remained rooted in rituals which gave form to belief and substance to identity, once itself rooted in their homelands. Like so many other tribes, the Delaware constituted themselves as a community by means of ceremonial participation. Their religion and its rituals, therefore, were what provided overall comprehension of what it meant to be Delaware.

## Lindestrom

A glimpse of Delawares living in their homeland appears in Geographia America (1925) by Peter Martensson Lindestrom, who, in 1654-55, was an officer and fortifications engineer in New Sweden. A practical man, his descriptions were best for geography, such as the condition of fields and soils, and for objects rather than beliefs espoused by native culture. His description of houses and elite families match well with later evidence.

Since native houses had interior bunks that served as both seats and beds, Native visitors often regarded European tables as similar furnishings. "In such cases one must always have the table uncovered at the lower end, for when the savage [?] comes to his good friends, where he knows he has his free condition, he climbs up and seats himself with feet and everything on the table and crosses his legs and requests then of the food on the table which he fancies" (1925: 233-34). Similar bunks were described for the Ohio council house of Newcomer, and for Indiana.

Lindestrom implied the importance of chiefly families rather than individuals when he named tracts associated with specific leaders along the Schuylkill River, noting that Passaungh was where the principal rulers lived (1925: 126,128), and that every chief must have a wife "because his government exists as under a family," hence the wife of the sachem "is housekeeper for the whole crowd" (1925: 193, 255). For language use, he noted that, during times of war, new words were introduced by the leader in council to provide a code used among the partisans.

Amandus Johnson (1911: 1914), Lindestrom's translator, also summarized Swedish and Dutch records from 1614-1664, and was able to note other practical concerns, such as the planting cycle, clothing details, different types of canoes, including a seagoing outrigger with mat sails, and the manufacture of wooden tools, twine, bags, nets, and beads. Although its importance has recently been overdrawn, settlers did have to trade for native harvested crops in order to survive.

According to Johnson (1915: 280) "Sewan (wampum), or money, dark-blue and white among the Lenapes and red and white among the Minguas, was made in the winter time by specially appointed Indians. One man could make from 63 to 48 beads a day, valued at about one-fourth of a florin, perhaps 50 cents in our money." In Oklahoma, however, Nora Dean was told by her elders that wampum was manufactured by old women, each of whom could make up to 100 beads a day. Changes in time, location, or procedures may well account for this difference.

## Herrman Map

Augustine Herrman's Bohemia Manor, a barony of 20,000 acres in Maryland at the head of Chesapeake Bay, was granted in compensation for his careful survey and map of Virginia and Maryland. This map shows, in adjoining sections to the north, labeled as New Jarsy Pars, native dwellings on many of the drainages of south Jersey, a few much larger than the others.

Herrman spent 10 years and £200 assembling the geographical information, but one of the comments attributed to him about the final draft was that it was "slobbered over by the engraver Faithhorne defiling the prints with many errors." Modern geographers also agree that William Faithhorne did this work "in the wane of his glory" (Phillips 1911: 11, 13; Ristow 1972).

Since Herrman himself was critical of the final product, misplacement of native communities may have been a factor. Significantly, however, the loaf-shapes of houses varied in size, with the largest one near the center of upriver Remkokas or Mantaas. Several clusters also include a larger building, suggestive of a council house, if the arrangements were not totally arbitrary or purely decorative. Indeed, what we know of native settlement patterns would locate such halls in communities at the mouths or forks of these drainages, not among the uplands as on this map. If Faithhorne was at fault, he nonetheless achieved a certain aesthetic by scattering dwellings amidst the mostly blank interior.

## Danckers

In 1679-80, Jasper Danckers and Peter Sluyter, under the respective aliases of Schilders and Vorsman, came to New York seeking land for their much-moved Labadist community, led by the charismatic Jean de Labadie (1610-74), who had been in succession a Jesuit, lay priest, convert to Dutch Calvinism, minister, and founder of the sect that eventually settled one of the earliest Euro-

American communes in the New World. During their first trip, Danckers and Sluyter decided to buy land from Augustine Herrman, adding more land in 1684 to total 3,750 acres.

Danckers returned to the Northeast a second time to arrange the necessary documents and payment, then returned to live out his life in Europe (Danckaerts 1969). Sluyter was appointed bishop of the new community, a daughter church (<u>dochter gemeente</u>) under the archbishop of the mother church at Walta House in Wiewerd, but he became increasingly dictatorial. Membership dwindled until the manor became the private property of his family (Dankers 1966).

Given the inner, spiritual (Quaker-like) background of the Labadists, it was not surprising that the first well-articulated accounts of Delaware beliefs, enacted by 300 years of Gamwing rites, appeared in the journal kept by Danckers, who was careful to name locations and people encountered by month and day.

For example, on Saturday 30 September 1679, Danckers (1966: 124-5) and others visited a Najack household near Fort Hamilton (Brooklyn) that contained 20-22 people divided into 7-8 families dwelling in one house (60 X 15 feet). Its ridge roof had a six inch gap along the peak to allow for the escape of smoke coming from a row of fires along the middle of the floor. Residence in a peaked-roof longhouse during the Fall both indicates one type of season-specific housing, assumed for Delaware and other Eastern tribes with a farming economy, and enables the overall plan of the Oklahoma and Ontario Big House buildings to be projected back through several centuries.

Equally noteworthy was the remark by Adrian van der Donck,

> Their dwellings consist of hickory saplings, placed upright in the ground and bent arch-wise; the tops are covered with barks of trees, which they cut for this purpose in great quantities. Some even have within them rough carvings of faces and images, but these are generally in the houses of the chiefs (in Jameson 1967: 302).

The symbolism of the Big House itself, however, related directly to conversations Danckers had with two elderly natives, called Jasper and Hans in the diary, who lived around Hackensack.

On Monday, 16 October 1679, a man about 80 years old came from his home at Ahakinsack and visited with the Labadists. Local whites gave him the name of Jasper[25] (his native name was rendered as Tantaque) to single him out after he once relieved their famine with a gift of fresh fish. He was probably compelled to do this out of his own sense of their common humanity and early training in proper etiquette, but he admitted to the colonists only that he was told to do this by his personal spirit.

By contrast, Danckers, and presumably other contemporaries, did Jasper the disservice of equating this personal spirit (ally, guide, guardian, protector, partner = *manitu*) with Christian notions of the Devil (Dankers 1966: 149) and demons. Yet, shared piety, felt despite such religious prejudices, encouraged Jasper to reveal tribal beliefs about creation and the godhead.

---

[25] Grumet (1979: 133) suggested that Jasper was a village or district leader in the upper Hackensack River valley.

In words and sketches, Jasper explained that the various *manituwak* (deities) did the bidding of a Chief Above, who was otherwise removed from human affairs. Expressing the origin of the world, he drew a diagram in charcoal.

He was silent for a little while, either as if unable to climb up at once so high with his thoughts, or to express them without help, and then took a piece of coal out of the fire where he sat, and began to write upon the floor. He first drew a circle, a little oval, to which he made four paws or feet, a head and a tail.

"This," he said, "is a tortoise, lying in the water around it," and he moved his hand round the figure, continuing, "this was or is all water, and so at first was the world or the earth, when the tortoise gradually raised its round back up high, and the water ran off of it, and thus the earth became dry." He then took a little straw and placed it on end in the middle of the figure, and proceeded, "the earth was now dry, and there grew a tree in the middle of the earth, and the root of this tree sent forth a sprout beside it and there grew upon it a man, who was the first male. This man was then alone, and would have remained alone; but the tree bent over until its top touched the earth, and there shot therein another root, from which came forth a sprout, and there grew upon it the woman, and from these two all men were produced." We gave him four fish-hooks with which he was much pleased, and immediately calculated how much in money he had obtained (Dankers 1966: 150-151).

Later that afternoon, Jasper and a young man, probably a relative, returned intoxicated, caused some disturbance, and left for Long Island.

Danckers presented the lesson on creation and the drunken visit as different events on the same day, but they were probably closely connected because, typically, when native people have revealed sensitive information, they often go on a binge to assuage their uncertainties, if not remorse, about revealing beliefs to people who might misuse them. This doubt, I think, overcame Jasper and underscored the earnestness of the dialogue between these men from different cultures, indicating Jasper's own desire to share the "truth" with someone he hoped was willing to regard it seriously.

Similarly, when the Labadists met with Hans, who lived at Achter Kol (behind the Kol or Kil Van Kol in the general Hackensack area), their prior information from Jasper was enriched because Hans was placed in the position of helping them to better understand what they had already heard. As fieldworkers know only too well, the best way to learn fuller esoteric knowledge from a native philosopher is to present previously acquired information on the subject in an almost, but not entirely, correct manner. Since the knowledge has already been revealed, enough to permit a grasp, ordinary reserve has already been breached so the matter needs to be set right to prevent harm to or abuse by the believers. While the Labadists probably did not realize all this when they broached the subject of creation with Hans, their inadvertent questioning did much to clarify early Delaware belief.

On Monday, 4 March 1680, they mentioned to Hans that they had been told that the world proceeded from a turtle. In response, Hans countered that the first cause was not the turtle, but rather the Creator living above, whom he called Kickeron, a word from the trade jargon familiar to his foreign listeners. Hans explained further that he himself was a chief, captain, and shaman who was particularly qualified to speak about the Creator since he knew from his own attempts at curing that "medicines do not cure" if it does not "please Him to cause them to work" (Dankers 1966: 268).

This Creator, albeit under the alias of Kickeron, like the world on the back of the turtle, remained central to Delawares for over 300 years. In addition, this narrative implied the very core of the Gamwing, confirmed by the internal arrangement of the building and the movement of the rite through the twelve levels of the world tree and sky. In all, Danker's journal supports a great antiquity for the Big House among Delawares.

## Denton

For the area to the north, Daniel Denton (1937 [1607]: 7) noted that natives had small portable tents which were moved two or three times a year to hunting, fishing, and farming camps, although people had "their principal quarters where they plant the Corn." Such fields would have been along the lower courses of the watershed. While Denton mentioned no large buildings, he did note that a king or sachem sat in council guarded by armed men (1937: 11), while each spoke in turn on the topic under discussion, implying a large shelter, at least during harsh seasons of the year.

Denton, however, was not a sympathetic observer, as when he noted the impact that foreign diseases were having.

it is to be admired, how strangely they have decreased by the Hand of God ... for since my time, where there were six towns, they are reduced to two small villages ... that where the English come to settle, a Divine Hand makes way for them, by removing or cutting off the Indians, either by Wars one with the other, or by some raging mortal disease (1937: 6-7).

While Denton was not always describing ancestral Delaware practices, those he did mention had reflexes in Delaware rituals, particularly in the Gamwing where 12 sticks were used to beat time, a wooden bowl held wampum bead offerings, and highly dramatic posturings by the visionaries characterized worship during the colonial era.

They worship once or twice a year, also upon extraordinary occasions such as declaring war. Their usual time is about Michaelmas, when their corn is first ripe, the day being appointed by the chief priest or pawwaw, most of them go a hunting for venison. When all congregate, the priest sometimes asks for "money" offerings which he collects in dishes then set atop their low flat-roofed houses, invoking God to come and receive it, which with a many loud hallows and outcries, knocking the ground with sticks, and beating themselves, is performed by the priest, and seconded by the people (1937: 8).

Then a "devil" appeared, sometimes as a fowl, beast, or man, "and makes sure of the money." He described a Cantico and other dances which involved Antick Tricks, such as "wringing of their bodies and faces after a strong manner.  Some jump into the fire, others bite the glowing end off a firebrand" (1937: 11).

> Their custom is when they dance, every one but the Dancers to have a short stick in their hand, and to knock the ground and sing altogether, whilst they that dance sometimes act warlike postures, and then they come in painted for War with their faces black and red, or some all black, some all red, with some streaks of white under their eyes, and so jump and leap up and down without any order, uttering great expressions of their valour (1937: 11).

Over time, it seems that many individual sticks used as beaters were replaced by twelve carefully made prayersticks, which continued to convey the notion of branches of the world tree evoked during important rituals.

## Penn

Another religious intrusion among the Delaware was the 1682 charter for Pennsylvania given to the Quaker William Penn, in compensation for money his father had loaned to Charles II, whose feuding with Parliament kept his royal finances precarious.  His brother, James II, added to the Penn domain by leasing to him the three lower counties (modern Delaware State) for 10,000 years – an indication of his own sense of divine right.

Penn visited these lands in 1682 to set up a model government, based on Quaker principles allowing religious toleration.  He scrupulously transacted treaties with Delaware, probably both to strengthen his own claim and to counter opposition from Lord Baltimore's Catholic Maryland.  He collected ethnographic information about Delaware, using a questionnaire prepared for him by Sir William Petty (Fowler 1975), and discussed the data in a 16 August 1683 (Julian, Old Style) letter to the London Free Society of Traders, which treated the persons, language, manners, religion, and government of the natives (Weslager 1985).  During his discussions of housing and ritual, Penn compared the house to a barn, implying that both had gables.  "Their houses are Mats, or Bark of Trees (mostly chestnut) set on Poles, in the fashion of an English barn, but out of the power of the Winds, for they are hardly higher than a Man; they lie on Reeds or Grass" (Penn 1970, 27).

Worship rituals consisted of sacrifices, mostly of first foods, and of <u>Cantico</u>.  "The other part is their <u>Cantico</u>:  performed by round-Dances, sometimes words, sometimes Songs, then Shouts, two being in the middle that begin, and by Singing and Drumming on a Board direct the Chorus:  Their Postures in the Dance are very Antick and differing, but all keep measure.  This is done with equal Earnestness and Labor, but great appearance of Joy" (1970: 34).  This last description could also be applied to the Oklahoma Big House Rite, particularly its finale, although only the Canadian Munsee kept the drummers in the center.

Penn also noted that women used sticks, apt mediators, to eat with during seclusion, "when with Child, they know their husbands no more, till delivered; and during their Moneth, they touch no Meat, they eat, but with a Stick, lest they should defile it" (1970: 29).

His most sensitive statement deals with the importance of sharing and Quakerly regard for each other, "they never have much or want much: Wealth circulateth like the Blood, all parts partake; and though none shall want what another hath, yet exact Observers of Property" (1970: 30).

Yet, for all his goodwill, much of the warm regard that Delaware had for William Penn later vanished due to the avarice of his sons. Their need for money and land to sell led them to concoct, using an alleged 1686 deed, the infamous 1737 Walking Purchase (Jennings 1984: 333).

The suspect deed surrendered as much land as a man could walk in a day. To take full advantage, young men were hired to speed along a trail freshly hewn through the forest, encompassing half a million acres, most of the land along the Forks of the Lehigh still occupied by Delaware. This travesty angered the Delaware and gave the Penn family a bad name among them. Among the leaders active at this time were Tishkohan and Lapawinsawa, whose careful portraits were done in 1735 by Gustavus Hesselius (1682-1755), a Swede who settled in Philadelphia in 1711 as one of the first professional portrait painters. A lucrative skill in the days before photography, his son John (1728-1778) also took it up.

Another Swede who recorded details about the abandoned Delaware homeland was Peter Kalm (1972), whose 1747 visit under the auspices of the Swedish Academy of Science was devoted to the collection and classification of indigenous plants. He applied the system developed by Carl von Linne and returned to Europe with a representative botanical collection. Regrettably, he arrived in America after most Delaware had moved west, so his comments were based on residual traces or the hearsay of local whites.

## Paulus / Simeon Drainage as North – South Longhouse

The on-going challenge for Delaware research is our lack of certainty about aboriginal Delaware concepts and perceptions. One example of such a native viewpoint, however, is provided in a fascinating manuscript by John Heckewelder[26] reporting earlier testimony that questions our present map-based knowledge of drainage patterns as synonymous with aboriginal perceptions. After all, Delaware portaged among their rivers and streams in such a way to suggest that they regarded all waterways as interrelated (Wissler 1909, Hauptman and Campisi 1978). Indeed, the implications from Heckewelder are that the Delaware regarded tidal portions of the lower Hudson and Susquehanna as integral with the Delaware River.

This manuscript begins with a legend, sometimes reminiscent of the Walam Olum, of Delaware movement from the West to the Mississippi, and then along the Ohio River after defeating the "Talligewi" with the help of the Mengwe (Iroquois). The Lenape eventually settled on the Atlantic shores, "multiplying and living to a great age, (as they say they did in those days, and before the White People came among them)" (ms: 4). As their numbers increased, groups dispersed to create other tribes, all of these recognizing the Lenape as their Grandfathers, "having the exclusive right of kindling a large Council fire - of keeping the same always a burning" (ms: 5, original emphasis). Only the Delaware had the right to call a general council or declare war in the name of all their allied nations.

---

[26] American Philosophical Society, ms. # 890.

In the distant past, the figurative council house of the Lenape "extended from the head of Tide Water on the Mahicanittuk [Mahikani-hittuk, modern Hudson River], to the extent of Tide Water on the Patomac" (ms: 7). At the north and south were figurative doors opening to the Mahikan and to the Powhatan.

Within this house were three Lenape branches the Minsi - remote from the sea beyond the Lehigh Hills with their principle settlements and council fire at Minnisink, the Unalachtigo - adjoining on the south side, and the Unami - between these and the seashore. A few of a fourth tribe which failed to cross the Mississippi, most of whom became Mandan or Mantas, lived on the Delaware River before merging into the Unami and Unalachtigo.

From the converts Paulus, born at Amboy in Jersey, and Simeon, born in Philadelphia, Heckewelder received confirmation that Lenape territory stretched from Albany to Chesapeake Bay, with doors or gateways at the north and south for allies to enter and "smoke the Pipe of Peace" (ms: 12). Within, there was "one House - one Fire - and one Canoe" (ms: 13, original emphasis). The largest town was to the Southward of Amboy, at a place from which a Land-bar ran out to a great distance into the Sea ... At this Town, the great chief resided, and who was afterwards present at the first meeting of theirs with the White People at Manahattani ... on the Lenapewihittuk (Delaware River) we had many towns – The Minsi had their principle towns and settlements high up this River – from the Mountainous part upwards; while the Unalachtigo were settled from Lechauweek ["confluence," Easton, Forks of the Delaware] downwards – at Chickohacki on said River, the great chief of the Turkey tribe resided. This town was of long standing – older than any of our other towns. [Its meaning is] the spot of ground longest under cultivation ... this place was high up the Delaware, and on the East side of same, probably where Trenton is now (ms: 13-14).

As commentary, the manuscript adds that before the Walking Purchase fraud, the Lenape term for Whites was Wapsit Lenape [white humans], but afterwards the Minsi coined the term Schwanak [salt people]. As whites increasingly pressed the Delaware for their land, this became the preferred term for greedy and obnoxious Americans. Before the Delaware themselves were displaced, they provided refuge for some Shawnees.

Since Heckewelder drew upon individuals quite aged, their statements provide background to later vague claims for a Delaware leadership among the Atlantic slope Algonkians by describing a symbolic Lenape longhouse running north-south, sharing one fire, one canoe, and, by later accounts, one water – the Delaware River running down its middle (Hanna 1911: 99). Access to the north or south was through the Hudson or Susquehanna, suggesting a greater importance for a maritime, rather than riverine, orientation among the prehistoric Lenape.

While his attribution of a fourth remnant tribe to the Mandan, Siouians of the Upper Missouri, was impossible, Heckewelder's erroneous equation of Delaware tribes and clans is somewhat saved by the implications of his text.

Generally, clans have a localized population from which some members scatter via intermarriage and residential shifts. It is, therefore, likely that a particular clan may have predominated within a region of the tribal territory. If a clan was most numerous in a town, then its leader would also serve as chief. Heckewelder elsewhere linked the Unalachtigo tribe and Turkey clan but in this manuscript he located the Turkey chief at Chikohaking, which, from other evidence, was also the site of the Unami council fire and the Abbott Farm complexes near the Falls of the Delaware (modern Trenton). As an ancient site with many religious features, such a symbolic link with agriculture agrees with Unami attributes reported by modern Delaware. The expected clan association, however, is Turtle rather than Turkey.

The Munsee chief was at Minisink, where that tribal fire burned, suggesting an association with hilly uplands, hunting, and, by extension, carnivores like wolves. The linking of the Unalachtigo with the Forks is probably derivative. Moravian sources localized them in this region, but they seem to have come there as refugees from the coastal shore.

Unique to Heckewelder's manuscript was the placement of the Delaware national fire at Sandy Hook, which has a certain logical appeal. As central to the figurative longhouse, its shifting sands occupied a mediating position between land and sea, earth and sky, like the turtle in Delaware belief. This sandspit would have been an appropriate abode for the Turtle clan chief. In Lenape, turtles, fires, and the ocean are addressed in prayers as "grandfathers," a term used by other tribes for the Delaware themselves. A fire at Sandy Hook would manifest all of these associations. There was also the suggestion that the hook itself may have been conceptualized as representing the tail of the world turtle, believed to be facing west and carrying the earth on its back.

While these equations have a logical consistency, it may be that Paulus was giving expression to local pride, though I doubt this. The details are too integrated with other symbolic relations for it to be merely an idiosyncracy. Certainly, Delaware culture included a symbolic triad for their economy of hunting (fishing) farming, with modalities such as the locations of chiefs and fires at Minisink (Sandy Hook) Trenton and of capitols located among land (sea) river and island (spit) bluff.

## Recollections

Vivid recollections of their life in the Northeast survived among Delaware living in Oklahoma. Since they included features not otherwise known from the archaeological or ethnohistorical record, it seems worthwhile to summarize them here, to aid future comparative research and to suggest a general context where they would have been appropriate prehistorically.

Most of these memories were supplied by the late Nora Thompson Dean, along with a few others provided by Lillian Hoag Whitehorn of Anadarko, Oklahoma, who was the daughter of a Caddo chief and a Plains Delaware mother. An enrolled member of the Caddo tribe, Lillie grew up in a household where Lenape was the first language. While the Plains Delaware exchanged many Woodland patterns for Caddoan ones, they maintained their language and oral traditions. In her account of the origins of the Women Dance, Lillie included several details of aboriginal life, especially a chest tattoo, called _laksu_, on boys to identify their own matri-clans. Lilly described a husband, wife, and child living in a domed wikwam near their corn patch. The husband hunted turkeys, and the wife tilled the field with a hoe made of a deer scapula affixed to a handle. After the wife was killed by lightning, the husband and child sadly returned to the Turtle clan village to report their tragedy. In the village, young boys were described as having their clan emblem tattooed on their chests, so, if they got lost, they could be returned to the proper village. Each of the three clans – Turtle, Turkey, Wolf – had its own community. The Turtle clan village also included in-laws and members of other clans, who were there as guests.

Nora Dean mentioned another feature of ancient Delaware towns, often unspecified in documents. The "old heads" always told her that settlements were stockaded. Although there is little archaeological evidence of this, such is probably a reflection of the poor state of Lenape archaeology. Symbolically, these stockades served as the boundary between domestic and natural spaces. Since they were made of standing posts, wood again served to mediate between the realms of women and men, of home and forest, of culture and nature, or of community and wilds (Cf. Rohn 1975).

From the rivers of their homeland to their abodes of today, Delaware took with them relational sets based on the echo of genders and the mediation of mind, repeatedly expressed, recreated, and represented during settlements or dislocations. Sustaining a belief in their Creator; instituting a community hall evoking Sea, Tree, Turtle, and Sky; and acting upon divinely inspired instructions to their leaders; Delaware have cherished their culture and ritualized their past for three centuries, at least, and for hundreds more in all probability. While these concepts have been used creatively, Delaware have blended rather than "invented" them.

# MORAVIANS ~ 9

Of all Christian sects, the Moravians (*Unitas Fratrum*, Unity of Brethren) had the longest and closest association with Delawares.  In Europe, inspired by the 1457 Protestant Episcopal reforms attempted by John Hus,[2] Count Nicholas Ludwig von Zinzendorf at Herrnhut (in former East Germany) supported their revival from a "hidden seed" of believers (Allen 1981).  Missions were sponsored around the world, including one to Georgia in 1735-39 that was forced out because Moravians would not bear arms during a war between Spain and England (Schattschneider 1982).  Seeking a haven, the Georgia mission accepted a 1740 offer from George Whitefield, a Calvinist, to come to Nazareth, Pennsylvania.  Soon, however, theological differences, particularly over the doctrine of predestination, led to a falling out with Whitefield.  Moravians then settled Bethlehem in 1741, in time for a visit by Count Zinzendorf to Pennsylvania.  Throughout their history, with the advantage of hindsight, Moravians have carefully avoided further theological disputes (Nelson 1963).

The consensual ways of the Moravians, as a religion of the "heart" not the "head," appealed to Delaware.  Both could agree on basic tenets:  "In essentials unity, in non-essentials liberty, in all things charity" (Gray 1956: 23, Allen 1981: 6).  Further, Delawares could appreciate Moravian organization into Choirs on the basis of gender and age, with female Choirs the most distinctly marked by colored ribbons.[27]  Lenape vocabulary made similar distinctions indicating social statuses, roles, and duties, which could be particularly instrumental in entire family conversions.  The leaders of the matrilineages, clans, and towns looked after the complete spiritual and temporal welfare of their kin.  When one of them converted, his or her relations followed in the interests of their own moral safety and social solidarity.

Moravian rituals were either worship services or love feasts – where a roll and beverage (baked goods and moisture) were consumed and hymns sung.  The handshake of Brotherly Agreement also expressed sentiments understood and appreciated by the Delaware in terms of sharing.  Further, the selfless, if biased, dedication of Moravian missionaries was appreciated by many Delaware.

During the summer of 1747, Moravians built a small chapel at Shamokin (PA).  Later fortified as Fort Augusta, modern Sudbury, at the branching of the Susquehanna River, Shamokin was the most important native settlement in Pennsylvania from 1727 to 1756 (Weslager 1972: 282, 192).  Three hundred natives, half Delaware and the others Seneca and Tutelo, occupied an island and both sides of the river.

Under the date of 7 June 1747, the Moravian diary kept by Johannes Hagen mentioned a war party, off to fight the Catawba, composed of Delaware (wilde Dellaware) who arrived after all were asleep.  Roused, everyone gathered in council (*raht = rath*) in the big house (*grosse Haus*) where these warriors created a great din – dancing, singing, and sometimes striking a post carved with a human head and reciting their grievances against the enemy.  This idol (*gotce*) was the center of activity for half the night until, apparently, the Moravians were able to defuse the expedition by

---

[27] The ribbon colors for the Moravian female choirs were children = red, younger girls = pinkish red, single sisters = pink, married women = blue, and widows = white (Gray 1956: 141).

feeding everyone a substantial feast. Since warriors usually joined an expedition by striking a plain post painted red, the post carved with a human head suggests a center pillar like that later found in the Big Houses of Oklahoma and Ontario.

During the Revolution, Moravian missions were maltreated by British agents who suspected them of being quietly pro-American, although this was never official policy and church leaders valued their concessions from the British Crown, which officially sanctioned Moravians as a fellow Protestant sect. Finally, British allies, including the Munsee, confined Moravian converts near Detroit. During winter scarcity, ninety converts left Captives Town for Ohio and reoccupied the former Moravian Mahikan settlement of Gnadenhutten (Grace Huts) on the Muskingum. There, on 8 March 1782, they were methodically massacred using wooden mallets in the hands of irregular militia from Washington County, Pennsylvania, commanded by Colonel David Williamson.[28] "The carnage was horrible and has been regarded as the most brutal act of the American Revolution, performed not by Indians but by whites" (Grinde 1977: 117).

The massacre confirmed the worst suspicions of other Delaware that Christianity was only a ploy to soften them up for slaughter. When Moravians Abraham Luckenbach and John Peter Kluge tried to continue such a mission (1801-06) in Indiana, they met with sullen rejection and periodic threats. This was, of course, the time of the great revival when Delawares were agitated and seeking to recapture the spirit of ancient traditions (Miller 1994b).

All of the Delaware keenly felt the loss of the 90 converts, perhaps a fifth of their number. Two months later, they took partial revenge when they captured, tortured, and burned Colonel William Crawford, an officer in the regular army and a Virginia neighbor of George Washington.

After a failed attempt to reclaim their Ohio farms, the Moravian mission moved to Michigan, then went across the lake to Ontario where they built Fairfield (Moraviantown) under the supervision of Zeisberger in 1792. Later, some Delaware went back to Ohio to found the community of Goshen, where Zeisberger died and was buried. During the 1813 Battle of the Thames, when Tecumseh (Tekumtha) was killed, Fairfield was destroyed by Americans for alleged British sympathies. New Fairfield was established in 1815 across the river and survives to this day.

In 1837, two hundred natives from New Fairfield rejoined Delaware in Kansas, led by Reverends Jesse Vogler and John Kilbuck, an ordained Delaware (Romig 1910). In 1854, these Moravian Delaware settled the town of Westfield until White pressure forced them to sell out in 1859, and the group split up, some moving back to New Fairfield and others joining the Chippewa at Ottawa, Kansas. Rev. Kilbuck became a founder of the Yup'ik Moravian missions in Alaska (Fienup-Riordan 1991), which have since developed autonomous status with their own native bishop.

The most famous of the colonial Moravian missionaries, David Zeisberger and John Heckewelder, left important works about Delaware history and ethnography. Based on long residence, their writings nevertheless have a clear bias against the traditional theology and religion. Zeisberger wrote his most famous account, including a detailed summary of rituals, in Ohio during the winter of 1779-1780, sending it to Bishops John Ettwein of Bethlehem and George Henry

---

[28]   This was the second Gnadenhutten to be massacred. The first was on the Lehigh, where 11 Moravian missionaries were killed in 1755.

Loskiel in Europe, who included it in his history of the Moravian Indian Missions, which appeared in German in 1790 and English in 1794.[29]

David Zeisberger[30]

In general, Zeisberger's works were full of honest descriptions, but devoid of insightful analysis. Sometimes, his accounts were marred by confusing narrative, as when he treated the installation of a new chief and the various sacrificial feasts and rites. Since he was multi-lingual, some of this confusion may have been due to transferring his native German grammar into English syntax.

Moravian sources invariably defer to this account of feasts drafted by Zeisberger (1910: 136-140) to describe Delaware, actually Munsee, rituals, though with little sympathy. "That the Indians spoken of have some sort of religion and mode of worship, cannot be denied; but it is replete with gross absurdity [?], and entirely unconnected" (Loskiel 1794: 33).

John Heckewelder[31] (1876: 207) said the subject "has been almost exhausted by other writers (Loskiel), although I will not pretend to say that they are correct on every point."

---

[29] An English translation of Zeisberger's German manuscript was published in 1910.

[30] Born in eastern Moravia, Zeisberger followed his parents to the failed Georgia mission, and then settled in Pennsylvania in 1743. During his first mission among the Iroquois, he was adopted by the Onondaga, the firekeepers of that League. He served as their envoy in 1745, was resident there again in 1752-55, and, for several years, protected the League archives and wampum belts in his sturdy abode. Since the councils of the League meet at Onondaga, he had ample opportunity to watch the complexities of "forest politics." During formal meetings, the Onondaga led, joining with the Mohawk and Seneca as elders across the fire from the Oneida and Cayuga juniors. By 1760, Zeisberger had finished a grammar of Onondaga, together with a dictionary with translations into German.

From 1762 until his death in 1808, Zeisberger (1885, 1887, 1910) devoted himself to the Delaware missions, personally suffering their vicissitudes. He learned Lenape, after a fashion, and published a spelling book (1776), collection of hymns (1803), and sermons for children (1803). He also prepared a grammar, dictionary, and other manuscripts (de Schweinitz 1871: 686-92). These vocabularies were later studied by August Mahr (q.v.), who was a Moravian native speaker, to tease out some of the semantic dimensions of Lenape.

[31] John Heckewelder began writing about the Delaware after he retired from the missions. Briefly, he was born 12 March 1743 in England, came to Bethlehem in 1754, worked as a missionary during 1765-86, and retired to Bethlehem. He died 31 January 1823 and was buried in God's Acre behind Central Moravian Church and his own home (Rondthaler 1847, Wallace 1952, 1958). His works include a history of the missions (1820), an account of the Delaware (1819), a treatment of place names (1833), and an extensive correspondence about Lenape grammar with Peter Stephen Duponceau (1760-1844) of the American Philosophical Society.

His florid prose, describing events long past, invites skepticism. Overall, however, this distancing seems to have allowed him to draw some important analytical insights, developed in correspondence with intellectuals of his time.

His grasp of the significance of the animate/inanimate distinction in Lenape grammar (Black 1969, Miller 1977), based on the semantics of self-mobility (willfulness, autonomy versus inertia, immobility), has ramifications throughout the culture.

A century later, the same contrast between Zeisberger's careful descriptions and

Unfortunately, Heckewelder never clarified what was incorrect. In his own case, an inadequate understanding of social cohesion, has misled many into accepting his equation of the three tribes of Munsee, Unami, and Unalachtigo with the three matriclans of Canine-Wolf, Turtle, and Fowl-Turkey.

## Zeisberger

What Zeisberger mentioned as "four or five feasts" became "five" for both Loskiel and de Schweinitz (1871: 151-153), while Gray (1956: 446) mistakenly treated them as "five series of feasts, each lasting for days and each progressively worse." Except for the first, suggesting a prototype of vision recitation, the others, while once independent rituals of the Munsee or Unami, became absorbed, condensed, or evoked within recent Gamwing practices.

Zeisberger (1910: 136) had no doubts that Delaware rituals had great antiquity, though modified by recent influences.

> Worship and sacrifices have obtained among them from the earliest times, being usages handed down from their ancestors. Though in the detail of the ceremony there has been change, as the Indians are more divided now than at that time, worship and sacrifice have continued as practiced in the early days, for the Indians believe that they would draw all manner of disease and misfortune upon themselves if they omitted to observe the ancestral rites.

During this period, prohibitions particularly condemned alcoholic disruptions; a century later, such injunctions concentrated on sexual misconduct.

> At these feasts there are never less than four servants, to each of whom a fathom of wampum is given that they may care for all necessary things. During the three or four days they have enough to do by day and by night. They have leave, also, to secure the best provisions, such as sugar, bilberries, molasses, eggs, butter and to sell these things at a profit to guests and spectators. Festivals are usually closed with a general drinking bout. There are rum-sellers present on such occasions who make large profits. As a result of the drinking there are generally several fatalities, for, among the Indians that gather from various places, such as wish to work off an old score are ready to make use of the opportunity afforded by those occasions (1910: 139).

Since the major feast was held every two years with four aides appointed, only two clans seem to have been involved. As events like a Summoning and a Gathering were mentioned, these clans were probably Canine and Fowl. In recent times, the Munsee had only Wolf and Turkey clans, which functioned like moieties or tribal halves.

---

Heckewelder's occasional insight was repeated in the anthropological work, respectively, of M.R. Harrington (1908, 1910) and Frank Speck (Hallowell 1951).

According to Zeisberger, major or minor feasts were distinguished according to the extent that food was shared.

Besides these solemn feasts of sacrifice there are many of less importance, for individuals arrange them on their own account. They invite guests and prepare a feast of deer or bear's flesh. The guests consume the whole meal, the host and his family being mere spectators. At the great feasts all who are present partake of the food (1910: 139).

Using Zeisberger's manuscript and other Moravian sources, Loskiel (1794: 33) reaffirmed that "religious notions of the Indians differ in many respects from those of their forefathers." but insisted

These sacrifices are of very ancient date, and considered in so sacred a light, that unless they are performed in proper time and in a manner acceptable to the Deity, they suppose illness, misfortunes, and death itself, would certainly befall them and their families. But they have neither priests regularly appointed, nor temples. At general and solemn sacrifices, the oldest men perform the offices of priests, but in the private parties, each man bringing a sacrifice is a priest himself. Instead of a temple, a large dwelling-house is fitted up for the purpose (1794: 39).

The first feast described by Zeisberger suggests the celebration of a Gamwing in a community with two clans (or moieties), like the Munsee. The religious duties of senior matrikin was clearly understood.

In the manner of sacrifice, relationship, even though distant, is of significance, legitimate or illegitimate relationship being regarded without distinction. A sacrifice is offered by a family, with its entire relationship, once in two years. Others, even the inhabitants of other towns, are invited. Such sacrifices are commonly held in autumn, rarely in winter. As their connections are large, each Indian will have opportunity to attend more than one family sacrifice a year. The head of the family knows the time and he must provide for everything. When the head of such a family is converted, he gets into difficulty because his friends will not give him peace until he has designated some one to take his place in the arrangement for sacrificial feasts.

Preparations for such a sacrificial feast extend through several days. The requisite number of deer and bears is calculated and the young people are sent into the woods to procure them together with the leader whose care it is to see that everything needful is provided. These hunters do not return until they have secured the amount of booty counted upon. On their return they fire a volley when near the town, march in in solemn procession and deposit the flesh in the house of sacrifice. Meantime the house has been cleared and prepared. The women have prepared fire-wood and brought in long dry reed grass, which has been strewn the entire length of the house, on both sides, for the guests to sit upon. Such a feast may continue for three or four nights, the separate sessions beginning in the afternoon and lasting until the next morning. Great kettles full of meat are boiled and bread is baked. These are served to the guests by four servants especially appointed for this service. The rule is that whatever is brought as a sacrifice must be eaten altogether and nothing left. A small quantity of melted fat only is poured into the fire [by the oldest men according to Loskiel (1794, 41)]. The bones are burnt, so that dogs may not get any of them. After the meal the men and women dance, every rule of decency being observed. It is not a dance for pleasure or exercise, as is the ordinary dance engaged in by the Indians. One singer only performs during the dance, walking up and down, rattling a small tortoise shell filled with pebbles. He sings of the dreams the Indians have had, naming all the animals, elements and plants they hold to be spirits. None of the spirits of things that are useful to the Indians may be omitted. By worshipping all the spirits named they consider themselves worshipping God, who has revealed his will to them in dreams. When the first singer has finished he is followed by another. Between dances the guests may stop to eat again. There are four or five kinds of feasts, the ceremonies of which differ much from one another (1910: 137).

Another sacrifice, though treated separately under the title of _'ngammuin_, suggests recent Big House features like a Summoning, a Gathering, and the concluding episode where elders were given the hides of deer killed by the official hunters. Certainly this was one of the few occasions when ten or more hides would have been available at the same time for use by the community instead of sale in the fur trade.

At a third kind of feast ten or more tanned deer-skins are given to as many old men or women, who wrap themselves in them and stand before the house with their faces turned toward the east, praying to God with a loud voice to reward their benefactors. They turn toward the east because they believe that God dwells beyond the rising sun. At the same time much wampum is given away. This is thrown on the ground and the young people scramble for it. Afterward it is ascertained who secured the most. This feast is called _'ngammuin_, the meaning of which they themselves are unable to give (1910: 138).

Loskiel also described another feast which also had parallels to the Gamwing since it involved the sharing of meat and corn, along with a Summoning and the use of six marked prayersticks to select those who tossed the ears of corn, as was done with biscuits at a Doll Dance. These six aides suggest that this was a Unami rite with three clans participating. While the anointing of the host with bear oil was distinctive, the likelihood was that he was praying for the wellbeing of all rather than serving as an oracle.

Two of the missionaries were once present at such a feast, and seated in a corner of the house appointed for them, but not understanding the language of the Indians, they could not observe the order of the feast. In the middle of the house lay a heap of Indian corn in the ear, around which were placed pieces of boiled deer's flesh upon bear-skins in rows according to their families.  Then four men went out before the door of the house, and made a short howl in a mournful strain:  As soon as they returned, the whole company, consisting of about one hundred persons, joined in a short song.  An old man then rose and sat down at the fire, in the middle of the house, where he was anointed by a woman with melted bear grease.  She first poured it out of a bottle upon his head, and then proceeded to anoint his breast, shoulders, and arms, [with] a general silence prevailing.

Soon after the old man began to pronounce short sentences as oracles, which were heard with genuine attention.  Having returned to his former seat, the whole crowd then joined in a song.  After this, six servants were chosen, each guest drawing a blade from a bundle of grass, six of which were marked.  These placed themselves immediately behind the heap of Indian corn, and upon a sign given by the old man, made a proper distribution of the deer's flesh lying upon it.  This being eaten, all joined again in a third song, which was followed by another sign given by the old man; upon which the servants began quickly to throw about the ears of Indian corn among the guests, who scrambled with great haste and alacrity, every one endeavouring to snatch up as many ears as he could.  The feast was then concluded by burning the [deer] bones (1794: 43-44).

Another rite has no clear parallels in the ethnography, although the 1760 spring rite, with dancers painted and bedecked with flowers according to the report of John Hays and Christian Frederick Post (Chase 1982), suggests a resemblance.

In another kind of feast the men dance clad only in their Breech-clout, their bodies being daubed all over with white clay.

The eat-all feast of bear meat was wide-spread among Woodlands tribes and attested for the Delaware when there were ample bears to hunt.

A fourth kind of feast is held in honor of a certain voracious spirit, who, according to their opinions, is never satisfied.  The guests are, therefore, obliged to eat all the bear's flesh and drink the melted fat.  Though indigestion and vomiting may result they must continue and not leave anything.

The fifth rite was a ceremonial sweating, performed by Delaware at least until they lived in Kansas (Harrington 1921: 122-126), possibly by Munsee descendants among the Unamis.[32]  Its use had been encouraged by the prophet Neolin during his preaching in Ohio.  The last one was hosted by John Sarcoxie (Harrington 1921: 122).  Because fasting was integral to the sweat, the twelve men would not have eaten when the rest of the congregation feasted.  The repeated use of twelve, of course, was characteristic of the Gamwing.

---

[32]  De Schweinitz (1871: 352) garbled the name as Machtugu.

A fifth kind of festival is held in honor of fire which the Indians regard as being their grandfather and call <u>Machtuzin</u>, meaning "to perspire." A sweat-oven is built in the midst of the house of sacrifice, consisting of twelve poles each of a different species of wood. These twelve posts represent twelve <u>Manittos</u>, some of these being creatures, others plants. These they run into the ground, tie together at the top, bending them toward each other; these are covered entirely with blankets, joined closely together, each person being very ready to lend his blanket, so that the whole appears like a baker's oven, high enough nearly to admit a man standing upright. After the meal or sacrifice, fire is made at the entrance of the oven and twelve large stones, about the size of human heads, are heated and placed in the oven. Then twelve Indians creep into it and remain there as long as they can bear the heat. While they are inside twelve pipes full of tobacco are thrown, one after another, upon the hot stones which occasions a smoke almost powerful enough to suffocate those confined inside. Some one may also walk around the stones singing and offering tobacco, for tobacco is offered to fire. Usually, when the twelve men emerge from the oven, they fall down in a swoon. During this feast a whole buck-skin with the head and antlers is raised upon a pole, head and antlers resting on the pole, before which Indians sing and pray. They deny that they pay any adoration to the buck, declaring that God alone is worshipped through this medium and is so worshipped at his will.

Loskiel (1794: 42-43) provided greater detail on the symbolism of a sweat lodge in his account of how a boy offered the first game he killed. In this instance, the boy probably had received a vision from a Thunderer. Such first kill sacrifices were made at the start of a hunter's career and also by a reverent hunter when he had made his first kill of the year. They might also be sanctioned or demanded by a hunter's supernatural patron, as in this instance. Use of a large house with three fires suggests the building known from Indiana.

The missionaries had once an opportunity of seeing a burnt offering as performed by the savages [?] in the neighborhood of Friedenshuetten [Pa].
When a boy dreams, that he sees a large bird of prey, of the size of a man, flying towards him from the north, and saying to him, "Roast some meat for me," the boy is then bound to sacrifice the first deer or bear he shoots to this bird. The sacrifice is appointed by an old man, who fixes the day and place in which it is to be performed. Three days previous to it, messengers are sent to invite the guests, some of whom perhaps live at a distance. These assemble in some lonely place, in a house large enough to contain three fires. At the middle fire the old man performs the sacrifice and hangs up the skin; the other two serve to dress the meat [i.e. the meat is burned in the other two fires]. Having sent for twelve strait and supple sticks, he fastens them into the ground, so as to enclose a circular spot, covering them with blankets. He then rolls twelve red-hot stones into the enclosure, each of which is dedicated to one god in particular. The largest belongs, as they say, to the great God in heaven; the second, to the sun, or the god of the day; the third, to the night-sun, or the moon; the fourth, to the earth; the fifth, to the fire; the sixth, to the water; the seventh, to the dwelling or house-

god; the eighth, to Indian corn; the ninth, to the west; the tenth, to the south; the eleventh, to the east; and the twelfth, to the north.  The old man then takes a rattle or calabash, containing some grains of Indian corn, and leading the boy, for whom the sacrifice is made, into the enclosure, throws a handful of tobacco upon the red-hot stones, and as the smoke ascends, rattles his calabash, calling each god by name, and saying: "This boy N.N. offers unto thee a fine fat deer and delicious dish of sapan [cooked corn]!  Have mercy on him, and grant good luck to him and his family."  He then retires to the guests seated around the other fires to dinner:  Two men being appointed to stand at the skin, sing and repeat all their dreams and visions, and the words of the bird of prey, till all have eaten their fill.  Then another man rises, and taking the calabash, sings his dreams, skipping [!] across the whole length of the house.  Finally, the old man, seizing the skin, and extending it upon his arms with the head and horns towards the north, utters a peculiar inarticulate sound, and thus closes the ceremony.

These lesser sacrifices continued until the mid-1900s, along with the more guarded topics of witchcraft and rain making, which were also mentioned by Zeisberger and Loskiel.  Over two hundred years later, these same beliefs are still held.  In Oklahoma, witches are called 'night walkers' because they are believed to enter homes at night, put the inhabitants into a deep sleep, and steal whatever they desire.  For rain, someone with this gift went to a secluded spot, marked a cross on the ground with a circle around it, placed an offering of tobacco or special talisman (such as dried frogs that came to life for Charlie Elkhair) in the center, and prayed in an appropriate way.  Versions of this rite span the time from Loskiel (1794: 46) to Speck (1937: 70), and attest to its great age, suggesting that it and other rites extend into remote Delaware antiquity.

Rev Heckewelder meets Məsing[w] (by Hal Sherman)

# Endnote

[2] Moravians descend from the reforms attempted by John Hus (1369-1415), rector at the University of Prague, who preached from Bethlehem Chapel before he was tried for heresy and burned at the stake by the Roman Catholic Church. These Czech regions of Moravia and Bohemia, though originally converted to Orthodoxy, eventually became Catholic, aggravating such religious conflicts. In 1457, 60 years before Luther, the Moravian Church (Unitas Fratrum) emerged. A century later, during great persecutions, many Poles converted until a massive defeat at the 1660 Battle of White Mountain. During these crises, Bishop John Amos Comenius (1592-1670), from exile in England and Holland, led the Moravian church while also improving the techniques and textbooks used in general education.

A "hidden seed" survived these religious wars to find refuge with Count Nicholas Ludwig von Zinzendorf in 1722, settling Herrnhut at his Wachau estate. The count encouraged them to undertake a global ministry, "filling in" until other Protestant missions were available. They began in 1732 with the West Indies, added Greenland Eskimos in 1733, but failed with a mission to Georgia (1735-40). Bethlehem, Pennsylvania, was founded in 1741, as headquarters of the church's Northern province. Later, colonies, on the Wachovia tract in North Carolina, set up the headquarters of the Southern province at Winston-Salem. After a 1752 failure in Labrador, they established successful mission stations, from Nain in 1771 to Zoar in 1865. Their trading posts were especially helpful, until these were sold to the Hudson's Bay Company in 1925.

The Moravian Church of North America was established at the Unity Synod of 1848. Over time, the Northern Province came to include Eastern, Western, and Canadian Districts. After a thwarted mission to the eastern Arctic, founders of the 1885 Alaska mission included Rev John Kilbuck, of a distinguished Delaware chiefly family.

# REFORMATIONS ~ East ~ 10

Before settling in Oklahoma and Ontario, Delawares suffered repeated uprootings as they were forced westward from their ancestral waterways (Hoffman 1967). Each new community expected its location to be permanent, but each lasted only a decade or two before pressures from American expansion propelled Delawares onward to found other communities and to try again for stability. As hostilities increased each time, Delaware concern with _k^wulakan_ eventually led to decisions to relocate, beginning all over again. What redeemed and sustained Delawares throughout these ordeals, above all, was the Gamwing, though it was modified and customized as needed to provide integrity to these communities. More and more, the Gamwing took on the trappings of a staid Christian church.

From Pennsylvania, Delaware moved to Ohio, where the American Revolution forced the majority of Munsee into Ontario in the 1790s. Some Munsee stayed with the Unami and moved with them to Indiana (1800-1820), then Missouri (1821-29) and Kansas (1830-67), before finally settling in Oklahoma. A splinter group of Unami left Indiana and crossed the Mississippi River, forsaking the Big House tradition, and ranged through Missouri, Arkansas, and Texas before they were driven, with Caddos, to central Oklahoma in 1859. All along the way, a few Delaware families remained in each locality when everyone else moved on, as still recalled by local family traditions.

With each relocation, Delawares built upon their established beliefs. The Creator sustained them, as did their epic story of creation, and each new town built a Big House in which to recreate this Delaware universe, particularly during the annual thanksgiving rite. The Turtle's back was the oval dance area in the Big House, and the Cedar was the center post.

All of these beliefs – allowing for factors of time, place, and impinging forces – were logically developed in the Gamwing, which became, over time, the epitome of Delaware culture. Yet its virtues in sustaining Delaware identity over at least half a millennium have been misjudged by many prior researchers, and its redeeming qualities have been ignored.

## Pennsylvania

While Delaware vision songs, the basis for recitation in the Gamwing and other rites, were implied in early accounts, they were first reported for dislocated Delawares in two diaries from Pennsylvania. In his notes, Christian Frederick Post described what he heard, but apparently did not see, of a ritual held during the night of 30 August 1758, at Kuskusky (near New Castle, Pa., on the Beaver River), after leaders had gathered in a house.[33] Men outside shouted a long, drawn out "ho ho ho" six times, then a man inside sang until 5am "and they spoke often between the singing." Post, who spoke Lenape, wrote this song in two versions (Hunter 1974, Sept 14).[3]

---

[33] Post's published journal recorded only that on August 30th and 31st, "The Indians feasted greatly" (in Thomson 1759, 153).

In 1760, the province of Pennsylvania sent an embassy to the western tribes consisting of Christian Frederick Post, John Hays, Moses Tatamy, Teedyuskung, and others. They visited along the Susquehanna before being turned back by the Seneca Iroquois.

In his journal for 24 May, at the Munsee town of Assinisink (or Atsennetsing, now Painted Post, NY), John Hayes described details of a vision recitation which was part of a spring ritual (Hunter 1954: 68, 74) and included a feast of meat from three deer and two bears and dancing by at least eleven people painted and adorned with flowers. They first danced inside before filing out to greet the sunrise. The next day, Hayes saw a man shaking a shell rattle as he sang and danced for "A Great While" before portions of a wampum belt and hides were given to some men, who took them outside to pray toward the rising sun. On 5 June, a hog was sacrificed for what was obviously a Family grease drinking rite (see end of this chapter) and, on 9 June, a man held a feast consisting of the first deer he had killed that season.

The Post and Hayes glimpses of rites in progress serve to confirm the central importance of personal visions for Delaware religion, re-emphasized during the preaching by Neolin, the Delaware Prophet, a few years later in Ohio. Hayes also described the use of a turtle shell rattle and a Summoning by men given wampum.

In modern Pennsylvania, the Forks Delaware, living near the confluence of the Delaware and Lehigh Rivers, were the last to be forced off their river, following others who were then living on the Susquehanna River (Witthoft 1965; Kent, Smith, and McCann 1971).

## Jersey Holdouts

The few Delaware still left in New Jersey were Christians and had the dubious distinction of occupying one of the first state reservations (Larrabee 1976). Located at Bethel or Brotherton, it was occupied from 1758 to about 1801, when the Brothertons decided to join the Stockbridge and other Praying Indians recently settled by Rev Samson Occum among the Oneida Iroquois.

Occum was an ordained Mohegan ministering to his own peoples. On a tour of England, he collected funds for the education of natives that, despite his protests, were used to found Dartmouth College (Blodgett 1935). To safeguard his congregation, Occum gathered together various native converts and moved them away from the bad influences of white neighbors. After a time at Oneida, New York, he moved them again in 1824 to Green Bay, Wisconsin (Jones 1854, Davidson 1893, 1900), where their descendants remain (Mochon 1968). In 1832, the Brothertons sent Bartholomew S. Calvin, one of their own educated at Princeton, to negotiate with the New Jersey Legislature for a sum, eventually set at $2000, to extinguish any remaining treaty rights to hunt in New Jersey.

The best known of the missionaries serving the original Brotherton reservation was David Brainerd, who preached at Cranberry, Crosswicks, and the Forks from June 1744 until he died in October 1747. He counted as a notable success the August 1745 conversion of Moses Tatamy.

Months before, in May of 1745, there was a famous encounter, near the Conoy and Nanticoke town at Juniata (Grumet 2001: 30) between Brainerd and a Delaware, wearing a mask and bearskin, identified as a new prophet.[34] As noted by Wallace (1956), this prophet preached in a

---

[34] While Gregory Dowd (1992) and Grumet (2001: 30) assume that this masked man was probably Conoy, the role of a new prophet is to preach and his ensemble is too similar to the

newly built house. While the mask was described as awry, like that of a Munsee Mazink, the costume duplicated that of the Masing, who was impersonated by Delaware men in rituals until the early 1900s.

As the focus for a special ritual to gain his goodwill, Masing assured Delaware prosperity. He also figured prominently during the Gamwing when the official hunters went after fresh meat. The costume thus had a special significance for the Delaware; one that the new prophet was directing toward his own ends while preaching in the newly-made hall. Although this was the first published reference to such prophets, they had a long and significant role among Delaware survivors. As conditions worsened, others arose to preach and reformulate a meaningful tradition able to keep Delaware together, and culminating with the version of the Big House Rite revised while they were in Indiana.

Image #7 ~ Long Big House as a rectangle in Kittanning at Alleghany Bend

On the move westward, most Delaware established and abandoned a series of settlements, though leaving behind a few families in each one. Following the 1742 Treaty of Lancaster, those remaining along the lower Delaware River had to leave, joining the tribal majority already on the Susquehanna until whites moved into that area and hostilities again increased. Most continued on, except for those who gathered around Teedyuskung (baptized by Moravians as Gideon), a leader troubling to settlers until his suspicious 1763 death in a burning cabin at Wyoming (modern Wilkes-Barre) (Wallace 1949, Miller 1999b). Repeatedly, the Delaware backed out of disagreeable situations, motivated by a commandment of $\underline{k^w ulakan}$ to avoid any interpersonal conflicts on pain of divine punishment.

---

later Delaware Məsing to suggest he was other than Delaware.

## Goschgoschink

The majority moved next to the upper Allegheny River in western Pennsylvania, where a visit by Rev David Zeisberger to Goschgoschink, near his own mission at Lawunakhannek (Deardorff 1946), seems to have precipitated a rearrangement of the interior of the Big House.

On 16 October 1767, Zeisberger arrived at the council house, where the prophet Wangomen usually preached, at the middle of three settlements comprising the town of Goschgoschink, founded by Munsee in 1765. In anticipation of his preaching, the natives of the upper and middle towns arranged themselves to follow the layout expected within Moravian churches.

> Retaining the indispensable fire, which burned in the center of the building, they seated themselves in rows, men on the one side and the women on the other (de Schweinitz 1871: 330, 332; Cf. DeC Smith 1948: 163).

Since Moravian churches at this time divided men from women and "In the German Moravian scheme of church interiors the long communion table and the chair of the liturgist behind it were placed always by the longest wall and raised on a low platform two steps off the floor (Gray 1956: 133)," these Munsees may well have instituted the layout of the Big House later observed for both Munsee and Unami.[35] Prior to this, following native practice, leaders would have been located at the far end of the building opposite the east door, with men and women arranged in separate rows by clan along either of the long sides. Lingering hints of this ancient pattern included the blocked-off west door of the Oklahoma Unami Big House.

Thus, in the first documented reform of the Big House, under Moravian influence, these Delawares adopted an arrangement that aligned men and women with, respectively, west and east ends, as for the Ontario Big House. Important activities and people were located in the center or along the long sides of the building in proximity to the center post and fires. This arrangement thereafter remained unchanged even while other features of the rite were modified, displaced, or abandoned.

## Ohio

Dislocated from the Allegheny, Delawares resettled westward along other tributaries of the Ohio River, such as the Muskingum and its Tuscarawas branch. Other Delawares settled on rivers, like the Cuyahoga and Sandusky, leading into Lake Erie before most of the Munsee and Moravian converts moved around Lake Erie, after the American Revolution had taken its toll, to settle in the 1790s along the Thames River in Ontario.

---

[35] During Easter week of 1988, I attended the Passion liturgy at Central Moravian Church in Bethlehem and, knowing the earlier arrangement, became aware that Moravian churches, as ancient Delaware, now locate officiants at the end of the long space. Afterward, I realized the significance of this quoted passage from de Schweinitz. My hosts included Rev. Linda Strohmeier, Rev. Ted Wilde, Rev. Tom Miner, and other staff at Moravian and Lehigh Colleges.

The Old Northwest (D. Miller 1979), particularly Ohio, provided the cradle to nurture and revive the Delaware as an organized polity, preliminary to their religious rebirth in Indiana. Delawares were temporarily isolated from whites during this time, the result of a British attempt to confine the colonies to the east coast to better exploit American manufacturing and trade. The 1757 Treaty of Easton briefly prohibited settlers from entering the Ohio region. Once the area was broached, however, a 1775 treaty tried to keep whites from moving west of Ohio. After winning the French and Indian War, England tightened its control on Canada and America. Lingering sentiment for the French coalesced into the 1763 alliance forged by Pontiac, but that too was defeated. Would-be native allies of the British, therefore, were enticed with the 1763 Royal Proclamation confirming their land rights under English Law, as still upheld in Canada.

Restrictions imposed by the British on Americans included the 1774 Five Intolerable Acts, the last of which moved the boundary of Quebec into Ohio and allowed tolerance of the Roman Catholic Church. Until their recent deaths, a few of the surviving Big House worshipers had a special affinity for Catholicism, whose ritual was particularly appealing, encouraged by continuous exposure to its doctrines and practices in the East, Ohio, and again in Oklahoma.[36]

About the time that Newcomer died, espousing but never joining the Moravians, Delaware moved their capitol to Coshocton at the junction of the Tuscarawas and Walhonding. In 1774 Newcomer had passed the chiefship to White Eyes, whose own son, Killbuck, founded an important line of leaders using this patronymic, although they became estranged from native traditions and closely allied with the Moravian church, eventuating in Rev. John Kilbuck, the missionary to the Alaskan Yup'ik. It would be fascinating to know if a new community hall was built after White Eyes became chief, thus upstreaming the link between chief, clan, hall, and community further back into the historical record. Certainly, there was a clear need for one in the new location.

During and after the American Revolution, conflicting loyalties and strategies divided the Delaware into several factions, each with its own leaders. Those pro-American were living with Killbuck and White Eyes near Pittsburgh, those pro-British were with Captain Pipe on the Sandusky in northwestern Ohio, and neutrals drifted west into Indiana and Missouri, hoping to stay out of harm's way.

Once the American Revolution began, Delawares lost ground. Trying to legislate safe conduct for an American force under General Lachlan McIntosh intent on attacking Detroit, the American government signed its first Indian treaty, with the Delaware, on 17 September 1778. Article Six proposed a fourteenth state, made up entirely of natives with the Delaware at its head. This was a heart-felt desire of White Eyes, while also reflecting the Delaware view of themselves as mediating peacekeepers among all nations. The American expedition was never sent, the treaty never ratified, and White Eyes himself was probably murdered by an American by 10 November 1778. Earlier, during the 1774 Lord Dunsmore War with the Shawnee, White Eyes had distinguished himself by working to keep the Delaware neutral, despite their close ties to the Shawnee, which continue even now.

---

[36] Speck (1931, 28) also noted "the worship of the Supreme Being and the lesser deities in Delaware offers a noteworthy correspondence to old adoration in the Roman Church – to latry and dulia", but he overlooked evidence of a Catholic presence among Delaware (Miller 1989a).

In 1782, American borderers, perhaps those returning from the Gnadenhuetten massacre, attacked the Delaware living on Smokey or Killbuck Island near Pittsburg. In the confusion, the Delaware tribal archives of wampum belts, mnemonics, and other tallies were lost in the river. As they were never replaced, the Delaware lost this important source for national cohesion.

By the end of the Revolution, Delaware were concentrated in Ohio and intended to remain there with other tribes, forming native republics (White 1991), despite continuous white encroachment. After renewed hostilities began, the native alliance was initially victorious, soundly defeating the expeditions sent in 1789 under General Josiah Harmar and in 1791 under General Arthur St. Claire. This alliance consisted of Miami with Little Turtle, Shawnee with Blue Jacket, Delaware with Big Cat and Buckongehilas, and other tribes. Briefly a member of Big Cat's family was John Bricknell (1842), captured in 1791.

Helen Tanner (1978a) vividly reconstructed the intercultural dynamics of this Ohio, especially at the confluence of the Maumee and Auglaize Rivers in 1792, the hub for the native confederacy after both victories (Harmar and St. Clair). There, a population of 2000 was scattered in towns of Shawnee (3 in number), Delaware (2), Miami (1), and British-French trading communities, along with some Nanticokes, Chicamauga Cherokees, and Mingo [Ohio] Iroquois. Other Cherokees were frequent visitors (Tanner 1978b).

The remarkable Mohawk widow, Coo-coo-chee, of the Wolf clan, lived in a solitary cabin and served as a religious force in the area (Tanner 1979). Shawnee was the language of her household, as described by Oliver Spencer (1968 [1834]), a captive there for seven months. In addition to providing oracles, she hosted important rituals, such as the Green Corn and a Feast For The Dead, when her husband's bones were reburied. Such a blending of traditions in a single, albeit important, household suggests some of the influences, present in these communities, bearing on the variety of religious change and prophetic traditions.

These intermeshed settlements disbanded after their 20 August 1794 defeat at Fallen Timbers (near Perrysburg, Ohio) by General "Mad Anthony" Wayne and his disciplined forces. That land was formally conceded by the 1795 Treaty of Greenville, forcing them to abandon Ohio and move west to Indiana.

Despite all of these increasing external strains, Delawares while clustered along Ohio's Muskingum River (Heckewelder 1884) made every effort to reforge a political unity under Netawatawes, or Newcomer, who died in 1777. This unity seems to have revived (and reinvented) an aboriginal one lost during the decimation wrought by diseases, conflicting loyalties, and dislocations from the Atlantic.

Newcomer's Town, also called Gekelmukpechin ('Still Water') and Negh-ka-un-que ('Red Bank') on the Tuscarawas, had 100 houses, both log cabins or elm-bark wikwams, while the chief lived in a two-story house with shingled roof, stone chimney, wood floors, and staircase (Weslager 1972: 291). Rev. Charles Beatty (1962: 60), a Presbyterian missionary, described the big house of Netawatawes, whom he called Nettautwaleman, in his entry for Friday 19 September 1766, noting "a turtle pictured ovr the door at each end & on every Door post is ingraved on ye inside the face of a grave old man." In his published account of this mission, his description indicated the persistence of older housing forms with bunks along the inside walls and honored seats at the extreme end, where the chief presided (Weslager 1972: 293).

During his mission to Ohio in 1772-73, David Jones (1865: 104, 106) also visited Newcomer's Town and reported that the council house was 60 by 24 feet and "had one post in the middle, and two fires," confirming a center post overlooked in Beatty's account. Jones also noted a ceremony suggestive of clan thanksgiving rites in which the three clans alternated in hosting a rite, each one sponsoring the rite every third year.

## Neolin

Prophets appear in human societies after times of despair and trouble to preach a new way for integrating life and expectations, buffering a hard dose of reality. Anthony Wallace similarly found that Delaware prophets became active after a traumatic time, rather than concurrent with the immediate time of upset. These visionaries revived morale when it was slow to recoup, preserving the framework of old ways while accommodating to the new pressures caused by European colonists and missionaries. Delawares increasingly became demoralized, a condition aggravated by diseases, especially the severe smallpox epidemics of 1756-59, and by alcohol. At the Forks of the Delaware River, Papoonan tried to preach a new solution, but decided that the simplest strategy was to convert by accepting the teachings of the first missionary he encountered – who was David Zeisberger in 1765. Conversion, however, was not the ready solution Papoonan hoped it would be.

The best known of the Delaware prophets was Neolin ('Four') from the Cuyahoga River settlement south of modern Cleveland on Lake Erie (C. Hunter 1971). In 1762, he preached a return to the old ways, especially advocating four practices: (1) purges to keep the body pure, (2) priority of the left hand because it was closer to the heart, (3) kindling a fire only with a pump drill since this was the ancient and sacred way to avoid the use of imported steel and flint, and (4) the sale of maps showing the way to heaven painted on deerskins so the souls of the faithful could readily find their way there.

These maps are described by John McCullough (1888: 274), who was a Delaware captive in 1756-64 when he learned "their prophet taught them, or made them believe, that he had his instructions immediately from _Keesh-she-la-mil-lang-up_, or a being that thought us into being, and that by following his instructions, they would, in a few years, be able to drive the white people out of their country (1888: 273, original emphasis).

> I saw a copy of his hieroglyphics, as numbers of them had got them copied and undertook to preach, or instruct others. The first, (or principal doctrine), they taught them, was to purify themselves from sin, which they taught they could do by use of emetics, and abstainence from carnal knowledge of the different sexes; to quit the use of fire arms, and to live entirely in the original state that they were in before the white people found out their country, nay, they taught that fire was not pure that was made by steel and flint, but that they should make it by rubbing two sticks together, which I have frequently assisted to do ... (1888: 272-273).
>
> [T]hey also taught, in shaking hands, to give the left hand in token of friendship, as it denoted that they gave the heart along with the hand ... (1888: 275).

McCullough also noted that some Delaware, in a belief that continues today, linked a soul with the Creator: "as soon as their _Lin-nap-pe-oc-can_, or soul, leaves the body, it takes its flight to _Keesh-she-la-mil-lang-up_, or a being that thought us into being..". (1888: 287, original emphasis).

When the corn was green, a buck deer was killed to make a feast for "twelve of the oldest persons in the town, to wit: six men and six women" (1888: 288). Twelve portions of meat and of corn gruel were served to them. When the meal was over, these elders prayed with a long, drawn out "hoooo" twelve times. The skin of the buck was given to the most deserving male elder, and its worth in wampum was given to a deserving woman elder. These set [walk] out of doors and sit down, facing east, to pray "hooo" twice." The head of the first buck killed in a season was sacrificed in a fire while people sang accompanied by a turtle shell rattle. Lastly, mention was made of a council house with the note that "they have one in every town" (1888; 290).

The 1761-1763 journal by James Kenney (1913), a Quaker trader, included more details on the prophet, his new doctrines, and a rite with reflexes in the modern Big House. He also saw a map to heaven and described it as "Portrayed on a Dress'd Leather Skin & some on paper" (1913: 171). His detailed description of it mentioned a line from Earth to Heaven and a series of "Squairs," like the rectangular shape of the Big House. Delawares were dancing, feasting, kneeling, and praying daily to a "little God who carries ye petitions & presents them to ye Great Being ... too High & mighty to be Spoke to by them; this little God lives in some place near them."

On the first day of the third month (by Quaker count), James Mokesin, a Delaware from Kuskusky, told Kenny that the tribe had decided to follow the teachings of the prophet for seven years. In consequence, boys would hunt with only bows and arrows. Everyone would live on dried meat and a "Bitter Drink," a "Physick" to purge out all white ways and natures. If any but Delawares took this emetic, they would die. Women and ancient men would raise and eat corn. After seven years, Delaware would "quit all Commerce with ye White People & Clothe Themselves with Skins" (1913: 188).

John Doubty, an old Indien born in the Jerseys, told Kenny (1913: 165) about a legend that said the first grain of corn was found between the skin and ribs of a special deer. Its discoverer planted it and "had great increase." Since then Delaware have held a feast of boiled venison and corn to return thanks to the Creator, apparently a reference to the Gamwing since only plant foods would have been served at a Green Corn.

On the 5th month, 10th day, James Kenny reported that some traders from Salt Licks Town on Beaver Creek in Ohio (Kenny 1913: 196, also Tanner 1987: 50) had said

ye Delawars had held a General Feast, there ye Provision for it was 24 Bears 24 Deer 24 Turkeys & 24 Squirrels, by report they Hold this feast Yearly but last year had mist [missed it] so this year they provided Double ye Quantity of Provission, ye Yearly alowance being but 12 of a Sort, & ye manner of performing it is - They Choose 6 Men head Councilors & 6 Young Men 12 in Numr which bring 12 Stones & make then red Hot in a fire, on which Stones they Burn ye fat of ye Creatures, in this manner, they bring 12 poles or long rods with Which they make a Booth cover'd with Blankets, in this Boothe they have ye Hot Stones & burn ye fat in it where they Swet, & at ye same time Spake out to ye People, in ye following manner: Hear all of you & take Good Notice that in this manner Your Grandfather's perform'd their Worship, ye others give ye Approbation, so ye Old Men in ye Booth make a huming Noise as by way of adoration or Prayer, & the Whole is finished with Singing and Dancing (1913: 196-97).

Kenny suggested that an elaborate sweatbath began the feast celebration, purifying the participants. Afterwards, the mention of humming, singing, and dancing implied vision recitations and clan rites. His remarks underscore the importance of repetitions by 12, although he did not specify that duration for the actual Gamwing. Further, Neolin's use of the sweat lodge also explains later references to sweatings in a Big House context.

After his message was thwarted, Neolin faded from the record except for Charles Beatty's (1962, 64) mention of him at a Sabbath service of 21 September 1766.

among these was Neolin a young man that says he had some thing like a vision about 6 years agoe while he was alone by himself musing & greatly concerned about the evil ways he saw prevailing among the Indians. Since which time he has at times Spoke to them & endeavoured to perswade & instruct them as well as he can [. T]he vision was the apperanc [appearance] of a man who came to him by night while he sat by the fire alone and perfectly awake & told him these things he was thinking of were right & that all who follow evill ways should goe to a Miserable Place aftr they died but that those who hated all Evill & lived agreable to the mind of God should aftr Death be taken up to God & made happy for Ever [.]

All of Neolin's teachings have expressions in modern Gamwing, particularly emphasis on purity in the use of the left hand. Two sacred fires were indeed kindled with a fire drill with only men present, and the rectangular form of the building duplicated the form of heaven on his maps.

Around 1805, such features were reinforced during the revival that took place on the White River in modern Indiana. Priority attributed to the left is fairly unusual in human societies, where the right is almost universally recognized as the more important. Even now, traditional Delaware still move around a fire in a counter-clockwise circuit so that the left side is toward the center, so integrated a practice suggesting that left priority was ancient among the Delaware, variously used either to distinguish themselves from the Iroquois, from Christians sitting at the right hand of God, or from both.

## Endnote

3   Of these verses, Nora Dean was able to suggest tentative translations only for lines 5 "They gave away three" and 8 "new leaves."

| | | |
|---|---|---|
| 1 | Jack un daja bugen | Jack un daua bugunu |
| 2 | | - - - - - - - - no |
| 3 | Jack un daja knock | Jack in daja kianock |
| 4 | - - -- - nahanock | - - - - nahanock |
| 5 | Jacha meka nahamack | Nachamechanahamack |
| 6 | Jack und aga buguno o ne | Ajaquela hahama |
| 7 | Kak wapele lahame | Kak Wapelelahame |
| 8 | Wes ke pache | Weskepache - - - |
| 9 | | Wach und a jakajana |
| 10 | | Neck undaja ajana |
| 11 | | Wack unesabugune |
| 12 | | Kakaboginahana |
| 13 | | - - - ne |

# REFORMATIONS ~ Indiana ~ 11

The Unami Delaware majority left Ohio and joined a vanguard already in Indiana, settling along the White River, between present Muncie and Indianapolis, from 1800 to 1820. While there, a religious fervor – inspired by prophets from both within and without the tribe, such as the Moravian apostate woman known as Beata, Tenskwatawa (the Shawnee Prophet), and an unnamed Nanticoke sorceress – strengthened their cultural reintegration as detailed in Miller (1994b).

## Luckenbach

In his autobiography, Abraham Luckenbach, ill-fated Indiana Moravian who later served at Goshen and New Fairfield, provided our best description of the Big House building there (Gipson 1938: 611-12), complete with split log walls, side bunks, gabled roof, and three fires at the middle and ends.

Luckenbach also described dances held in honor of protecting deities (guardian spirits), who appeared as in a dream and told the person of his or her career and fate. If the information was grim, "they did not sing their dreams but sadly related them." Those with hopeful dreams recited them at the dances, shaking a turtle shell filled with corn kernels and speaking, "amid many grimaces ... by fits and starts, the contents of his dream, or the manner in which his god appeared and what he told him."

Others joined him in his dance, "arranged in a row," and wearing deer-hooves and noisy silver trinkets on legs and arms, making a jarring sound at every step. At the side, two men sat and beat time on a dried deer skin. Everyone moved forward with short, regular steps "at certain abrupt intervals," repeating his words.

> The leader cuts many capers and jumps up and down, followed by men first and the women following. When they reach the starting point, all gather around the post or pillar standing in the middle and upon which the roof rests. Upon both sides of this pillar are cut men's faces, provided with hair and painted, making a hideous appearance. In conclusion, all stretch out their hands toward the totem, and with a terribly shrill yell the dance comes to an end, whereupon all take their places again.

After a pause, another began to recite. Such dances occurred only at night and often continued for weeks. At the end, a sacrificial feast was held of deer and bear, "provided by all joining in a common hunt, the women furnishing a store of corn bread ... bread is arbitrarily thrown among the guests, and each one catches as much as he can." Finally, two old men were each given a beautifully tanned deerskin. They hold these "toward the sunrise, in front of the house of sacrifice, and spread them out, while murmuring something." They thanked the Creator for long life and health.

Before he could grasp Lenape, Luckenbach watched part of this ceremony only once, while in the company of John Conner, at the town of Woapikamikunk. His account is faithful because

Conner, who was a participant himself, probably was careful to explain events, including family camps with tents like those later used in Oklahoma.

The chiefs gave speeches against alcohol, fornication, adultery, stealing, lying, cheating, murder, and, in their stead, urged hospitality, love, and unity. Among the great tragedies of this period were the deaths of chiefs such as Buckongehilas on 24 May 1805 and, more grievously, the Turkey chief, who died entirely alone just after a 1 April 1803 rite held for fellowship and long life (Gipson 1938: 221; Miller 1994: 253).

The mission diary provided other details of a ceremony held 28 April 1805. Delaware were called together "by the loud cry of two servants appointed for the purpose, and entered the large house newly built for the sacrifice. Inside were two fires, and straw [hay] scattered around the sides. Visionaries recited, one after the other, each in a loud voice accompanied by a turtle shell rattle. The audience repeated both the song and the chant, with "the leader making all sorts of gestures and jumping up and down, which those following him then imitated as best they could. In the middle of the house, they had erected a post on which were cut, on both sides, a human face painted in Indian fashion." At the end of each recitation, "they gathered about this post, stretched out their hands toward it, and sang a song which they closed with a howl" to thank God for the fulfillment of the vision.

A letter of the same date (Gipson 1938: 531) mentioned disapprovingly the urging of the woman prophet [Beata?] "that the Indians must live after their ancient manner, keep the sacrifices and by no means believe anything else ... in which connection they spend eight days and nights in sacrificing and dancing and drinking. They live in constant fear, because the old woman told them that they would all perish, if they would not live up to the letter in everything that she said."

Even so, things did not improve. Early in June, an epidemic ravaged the Indiana communities (Gipson 1938: 359), with famine and bilious fever expected. Nothing was certain except further hardships. The Moravian mission was harassed by visitors who begged for or stole food. Jacob, the senior convert, was chastised by the missionaries for participating in a Delaware feast where he held up a buckskin to the Sun and called aloud 12 times to 12 spirits (1938: 375), as old men did at the end of the annual rite.

## Johnston

During the War of 1812, the Delaware were relocated from Indiana by order of William Henry Harrison to Piqua, Ohio, under the care of John Johnston, Shawnee agent from 1812-30 (Hill 1957: 72). About 900 Delaware stayed in Ohio between 1 February and 1 December 1813.

Johnson contributed to the first ethnographic and linguistic studies, good by modern standards, conducted among Delaware and other tribes by Charles C. Trowbridge, using a questionnaire prepared by Lewis Cass, governor of Michigan Territory (McLaughlin 1891). The reliability of these data is impressive, closely agreeing with those of Nora Dean and Lucy Blalock 150 years later.

Johnston provided an account of the Gamwing (Kinietz 1946: 93-97, #41) as one of three responses about the Delaware to an 1821 ethnographic questionnaire (Kinietz 1946: 16-17) when, in 1822, he sent answers concerned with Shawnee and Delaware. Trowbridge, a special agent employed to collect ethnographic and linguistic materials, spent December 1823 through March of

1824 in Indiana, after the Delaware had left there, collecting data from William Conner (Thompson 1937: 138), along with Captain Pipe, a Delaware on a ten-day visit from Sandusky, Ohio. In 1824, Cass and Trowbridge alternately recorded information from Captain Chipps, a Canadian Delaware or Munsee visiting Detroit. Kinietz (1946: 38) felt that Chipps was probably a Moravian, favoring Christianity over traditional rituals. Hence, there was no account of the national worship rite from him.

According to Johnston (Kinietz 1946: 93), the Delaware national worship, filling 12 days and nights, "keeps the world from coming to an end," and was "attended with very great expense at procuring wampum and provisions."[37]

It was held in a large building, 25 feet wide and 50-60 feet long, with a door at each end. The men and women sat separately in rows along the inner walls. At each door sat a man and a woman, the former as doorkeeper and the latter "to sweep between every exercise." Pure fires were made by rubbing sticks together, kindled anew each day to prevent contamination.

Before the assembly, young men were appointed hunters to acquire sufficient deer to feed those attending. Their kills were skinned, cooked, and served by special butchers. When all was ready, the one who prepared for the meeting got up and shook a turtle shell containing pebbles. This was a signal for the whole assembly to arise. He began to tell his vision and "the whole congregation repeats it after him in one voice word by word till he says he heard a voice singing to him and begins to sing," immediately upon which two men "commence beating with flat sticks on skins folded together." When he stops singing, he and the assembly make 10-12 jumps as a dance. After a sudden halt, he recites and the others repeat in one voice after him. He sings again, the beaters keep time, and then "the whole jump or dance." These alternations fill half an hour or more. When all are seated at the end, the women at the doors sweep the room. The reciter shoves the turtle shell under his legs to the next one, who, giving it a shake, begins reciting. He starts off sitting, but soon rises together with the assembly, and alternates text and song during a mimetic dance.

At intervals, twelve men were called by name and given a bit of wampum. They went outside to "make a doleful noise which is similar to howling but they term it making twelve prayers. Then they return to the meeting and the foreman, who was called first, divides the wampum into 12 parts." Such recitation and praying continued for 12 days and nights, "abstaining themselves from women and every thing whereby they think they could be defiled."

Every evening a man was appointed to dress in bearskins and appear very frightful. He pointed out those guilty of improper conduct and the accused was escorted from the meeting by the doorkeeper, forbidden to attend any further. Fatalism was much in evidence.

> At a very large annual dance which the agent [Johnston] attended on White river, an aged chief remarked poor Delawares, pelotchahee mutta Wabenughka, that is, by and by, no more Delawares, alluding to the increase of mixed blood which the large assembly then present disclosed. Wabenughka [Wapenaki] is the Indian name of the Delawares, i.e. the people from the east or sun rising.

---

[37] Hence, Beata probably preached against the overuse of wampum to keep Delawares from depleting their resources or incurring debt from other tribes.

Since this 24 Sept 1840 letter to Benjamin Drake places Johnson at a Gamwing in Indiana, his description probably does not refer to any Gamwing he might have witnessed in 1813 Ohio.[38]

## Pipe

According to Captain Pipe, the Delaware "grand national worship" was called <u>Engomween</u>. Three or four families had the duty by inheritance to prepare for and invite others to their assembly. Each family hosted a service once in three years, sometimes more frequently.  Once the family decided on the time and place, the leading man sent a messenger to every village chief, who told the other residents this news.

A vast lodge was prepared and people assembled there, the women sitting behind the men. An old man gave them a speech about the importance of the ceremony and the need to abstain from all unlawful pleasures during this period:  "any connection with women is counted a polluting sin" (Kinietz 1946: 95).  The customs of their ancestors were described at length, this ritual foremost among them.

The head man of the clan then shook a turtle shell rattle as a signal for all worshipers to rise. In short sentences, he recited his dream and everyone repeated each phrase.  Then he sang, followed by the company, "relieved between the sentences by a chorus of singers beating on a deer skin stretched across four sticks." With his minute recitation of every circumstance of the vision and its fulfillment, "every person in the lodge takes him by the hand in a mystical manner and they all seat themselves." The men smoked in grave silence while the turtle shell was pushed to the right under the reciter's legs until someone gave it a slight shake and prepared to recite.  After meditating for a moment, he arose and shook the shell, joined by all the worshipers standing up, as previously.

Recitations occupied all night, from evening to daybreak.  On the last night, after adjourning for an hour or two, they recited the vision of a famous ancestor revered in tradition.  They ended at noon on the next day.

Menial tasks during the meeting were performed by 2 men and 2 women specially appointed, presumably from the other two clans.[39]   After every recitation, they swept through the council house.  Before the close of the ceremonies, they received wampum, which was contributed to the leading man by everyone who had the means to do so.

An old man with curing (juggling) powers was appointed to keep order and point out those who had connection with the opposite sex.  A man thus identified was removed by the men servants, a woman by the two females, and both were forbidden from further worship.  This old man was dressed in a bear skin and had a frightful mask.  Sometimes a visionary had difficulty speaking and the inquisition would scrutinize the assembly for the person whose improper conduct had caused this lapse.

At least once every night, the leader named 6 to 12 men and gave to the male servants a number of wampum strings equal to the number of males summoned.  These men went out of the

---

[38]  Lyman Draper Collection, Microfilm, Series YY, Volume II, 22-5.

[39]  Constant reference to two pairs of ushers suggests that they might have been determined by the two ends (doors) of the building, rather than two of the three clans.

building, facing east, "seat themselves upon their hams and commence a kind of howl, which they repeat in the same tone 12 times."

These men, only at the end of a night of worship, might also be asked by the leader to scatter wampum beads inside the lodge. Then the servants "are obliged to stand upon one leg and take it up with the thumb and finger, a slow method, affording amusement to the spectators." This posturing provided comic relief at the end of a long night of ritual and would be "improper at any other time."

Since Pipe came to Indiana from Sandusky, Ohio, he may have provided a description of the ceremony as performed there. In all essentials, he agrees with other accounts from Indiana and Kansas, while particularly specifying that sponsorship was by clan leaders. Thus, the families mentioned would have been leaders among the Turtle, Canine, and Fowl.

His treatment of the events (Summoning and Gathering) make it clear that the later versions became more dignified from a White standpoint. The earlier ones, as with the entire Gamwing, were more athletic and mimetic. The Summoning had men act the part of Wolves sitting on their haunches and howling. For the Gathering, aides behaved like fowl, particularly cranes and herons perched on one foot. If everyone involved in the Summoning was not a member of the Wolf clan, then the man named first almost certainly was. Similarly, the Gathering may have involved members of the Turkey clan or had their sanction.

Two other events in the Oklahoma ceremony were not mentioned, but were clearly comparable. One night had the Measuring, when owners of turtle shell rattles brought them into the Big House, where each was given a measure of strung wampum equal to the length of their shell. Here again wampum was given in compensation for the display of an attribute associated with a clan, suggesting a desire for bounty or plenty. The other event, mentioned for Kansas and Ontario, was the Incensing, the burning of quantities of cedar needles to fill the Big House interior with fumigating smoke. No wampum was exchanged because this was not associated with a clan. Rather, it recognized the common ancestry of everyone from the Sea and Cedar Tree.

During this time and later, some Delaware men ranged quite widely, bringing home knowledge of other rituals that seem to have influenced the Gamwing. Among the possibilities were similarities with the Midewiwin (Grand or Shamans Lodge) of the Great Lakes, reformulated by the Chippewa about 1700 from ancient and innovated practices (Hickerson 1970: 1988) and the Calumet or Eagle Dance, developed by the Caddoans and diffused among Eastern tribes.

Indiana was also supposed to be the 1820 source for the pieces of decorated bark acquired by a Dr. Ward, who may have been the botanist John Russell Ward, although the physician Malthus Ward (Barlow and Powell 1986) seems more likely. Ward passed them on to Constantine S. Rafinesque, a scholar of unsure reputation, who made them famous as the Walam Olum (Lilly 1954), which is purported to be an account of the Delaware migration across North America. While the Delaware, like other tribes, had a mnemonic system for keeping records, the Walam Olum remains dubious at best (Oestreicher 1994). It may be a white forgery, but it also could be an attempt by a Delaware, during religious fervor, to produce a native record analogous to the Bible – lending antiquity to the Indiana revival, instilling pride in tradition, and fending off missionaries by presenting basic beliefs as more like those of Euro-American churches.[4]

After 1806, the furor burned itself out, only to be revived by massive earthquakes in the central Mississippi Valley. Shocks began at 2am on 16 Dec 1811, with a severe series 23 January through 4 February 1812. The last severe tremors came at 4am on 7 Feb 1812 (Douglass 1912: 212-14, 224). Jared Brooks at Louisville counted 1,874 shocks between 16 December 1811 and 15 March 1812 (Penick 1981: 140). These earthquakes had a profound meaning for natives, some of whom attributed it to Tekumtha [Tecumsah] sending a sign to his confederates. Moreover, while more native people died than were recorded, in the official counts of deaths, Indians outnumber others 2 to 1 (two women, one black man, six Indians). Within the area of disturbance, there were many more natives than whites, encouraged to settle there by Spanish officials (Penick 1981: 109, 121), so casualties must have been more severe than reported.

While back in Ohio during 1813, although Delaware were encouraged to stay neutral towards whites, they did maintain active hostilities with other tribes. Between 1805 and 1830, their primary enemies were the Osage, encountered during bison hunts on the plains, trading forays across the Mississippi, or along the Missouri River.

---

## Endnote

[4] Another Indiana record also seems to have bearing on the modern form of the Big House. Reports by early white pioneers suggested there was a standing post with a carved face in Indiana, at least for the Munsee. Samuel Cecil and others (1905), Indiana farmers, reported their memories of a "torture post" that stood at the site of old Monseytown. According to Cecil, who owned the land for 50 years, its diameter was 8-10 inches and it fell over in 1836-38. Eddy, who saw it on the ground in 1842, said it was 8 feet long, with a hollow depression 5-6 feet up the post to fit the back of the prisoner's head.

Near the center of old town hill, Munsee "huts had been built in a circle with the Council House in the center where the post stood" (1905: 178). Since the post had been charred and at least one victim was said to have been burned there, these authors describe it as a "torture post."

Another local, Rev. W. C. Smith, however, described it as a 10 foot oak stake, "with the rough outline of a human face cut on either side." Ashes ringed the post about 5-6 feet away, and beyond this ridge was a circle hard packed from dancing. This makes the post seem much more like that at the center of a Big House. Moreover, the one reference to a hollow depression on the post might indicate that a carved face had been removed.

When prisoners were killed or burned at the stake, the restraining post was improvised, functional (ad hoc) rather than permanent. Certainly, embossed faces would have been inappropriate to such usage.

At the most famous Delaware execution, the burning of Colonel Crawford in revenge for the Gnadenhutten massacre, "The post was a stick of timber placed firmly in the ground, having an arm framed in at the top, and extending some six or eight feet from it, like the arm of a sign post" (Jemison 1961, 121). Mary Jemison's account also mentioned that the war post kept by each famous warrior was a peeled timber 10-12 feet tall, marked with a design for each campaign, scalp, and prisoner. Among Delaware and other tribes, a war post was set up whenever a war party was organized so that those volunteering could strike it, recite their deeds, and enlist. Barton (APS), who saw one at Kashkashkunkg (Goschgosching, Pa) on 23 October 1785 (Sunday) during the western boundary survey, described it as commonly a peeled or shaped sapling, 10 to 15 feet tall and painted red.

Thus, the Indiana timber with embossed faces seems more likely to have been an emblem of the world tree like that at the center of a Big House. Before it was destroyed by zealous converts, the center post of the Canadian Munsee was an unmodified tree trunk, a suggestive parallel for the "oak timber" of this old Munsee town.

## REFORMATIONS ~ West ~ 12

### Missouri

At the request of the Spanish governor, a Delaware and Shawnee vanguard settled in Missouri at Cape Girardeau by 1788 to provide a bulwark against raiding Osages. During twenty years, they were, in turn, subjected to Spanish, French, and American jurisdictions. This same group later joined the Caddo on the Red River of Arkansas and Texas, eventually exchanging many of their Woodland practices with those of Caddos, the only Mississippians west of that major river. While in Texas, these Delaware served as emissaries between Texan vigilantes and oppressed tribes until survivors were driven into Oklahoma, where Caddo and Plains Delaware have lived around Anadarko since 1859 (Hale 1984a, 1984b, 1987).

After Indiana became a state in 1816, white settlement increased. Remaining Delaware signed the 3 October 1818 Treaty of St. Marys and moved on to Missouri, where Chief Anderson had high hopes for their new lands. These remained unfulfilled, however, because he had not negotiated for food and funds to support Delaware as they tried to develop these lands. Their initial hardships could not be overcome before they were forced onward.

Most Delaware arrived in Missouri just after 1821 statehood and remained there until 1829, living along the wide floodplain of the James Fork of the White River (Schoolcraft 1854). The main Delaware community, south of modern Springfield, suffered because there were few game animals to hunt and their fields often flooded (Tong 1959). If there was a Big House, which seems likely, it would have been located here, but no description of it has yet been found.

On 21 January 1824, William Clark wrote from St. Louis to Richard Graham[40] that "The Delawares on White River as it appears from reports and letters from Anderson are nearly in a state of starvation." On 15 February, Pierre Menard, five days after visiting the James Fork, wrote to Clark "All the Dalaware except Anderson and five or six Famely [families] have goone to the wood to suporte them Self having No Corn nor games near their village."

Aside from describing such hardships, reports were largely silent on Delaware religious beliefs and rituals. During a tour of southern Missouri in 1824, Vincentian clerics thought they saw vestiges of Catholic ritual among Delaware and Shawnee, who "never buried their dead without planting a cross at the grave's head; and when they solemnly offered spring and autumn prayers for a successful hunt and a copious corn harvest, a veteran petitioner habitually held a cross uplifted" (Baynard 1957: 21). While this report suggests that crossed markers indicated the graves of Delaware women and thanksgiving rites were being observed, there are no explicit Big House references.

Eventually, Chief Anderson agitated for and signed the 14 September 1829 Treaty of Council Camp. There, he carefully negotiated for the long term welfare of the Delaware after their move to Kansas. For this trek, the poor were given 40 horses, six wagons were loaned for transport, and farm tools, saw and grist mills, and provisions for a year were carefully stipulated. Finally, all

---

[40]  The following two quotes occur in the Richard Graham Papers, Missouri Historical Society, St. Louis, Box 3-12.

terms were made subject to the prior inspection and approval of the new land, which was done by Baptist missionary Rev. Isaac McCoy and John Quick, a Delaware (below).

## Kansas

In eastern Kansas, Delaware lived on prime forest land from 1830-67, near Cantonment Leavenworth, which began in 1827 (Barry 1972, Cole 1912). Chief Anderson, who came to power in Indiana, died in late September of 1831 (G Foreman 1946, 58 note 32), assured that his people were prospering. With contentment came changes, however. After years of being faithful to their own religion and hostile to Christianity, some of the Kansas Delaware began to convert. Shortly after they arrived, Mormons attempted to establish a mission. By 1832, Baptist and Methodist missionaries preached among Delaware, who were then living on homesteads much like rural whites (Lutz 1906, Farley 1955, Unrau 1979).

## Nahkoman

On 21 November 1834, Nahkoman ("Answer") described some Delaware traditions to Rev. McCoy, a famous Baptist missionary, who wrote them down the next day (Miller 1989b). Foremost among these accounts was a description of the Gamwing at a crucial time in its history.

Nahkoman became head chief of the Kansas Delaware in 1839, after a far-flung career as a renowned warrior. By 1849, however, he was incapacitated by a wound from a "Pawnee" arrow received during the 1828 Battle of Blue River near Fort Towson, Oklahoma (G. Foreman 1930: 274). For his valor, he was voted a pension by Congress in 1833. George Catlin painted his 1842 portrait now hanging at the Gilcrease Art Center in Tulsa. In 1849, he passed leadership to Captain Ketchum, who later died in 1857 at the age of 77 (Ferguson 1972: 170).

In addition to confirming the national importance of the Gamwing and left priority for Delawares, his account also emphasized that women visionaries, because they were of the earth, began and ended the rite, a start that did not continue in Oklahoma but surely must go back to the Indiana reforms of Beata. Further, Nahkomen noted that the smoke from camp fires carried prayers upward to the Creator, confirming the mediating aspects of fire.

According to Speck (1931: 17), the scene for the events described by Nahkoman was west of the Delaware majority settled on the Missouri River since "The Delaware Big House stood about six miles east of Lawrence, Kansas, during the reservation days in that state (1830-67)" (also repeated by Muriel Wright in McCracken 1956: 184, # 1a).

In 1859, at that location, William Tomlinson (1859: 34) spent a night with the Delaware attending a "war dance" in a village about six miles from Lawrence, in a clearing perhaps near the Big House building. Since the dancers were both men and women, something other than a war dance was being celebrated.

## Morgan

The famous Americanist, Lewis Henry Morgan, father of kinship studies, toured Delaware and other tribes in 1859. While there, he saw an annuity payment and recorded details of clan (or phratry) subdivisions. It appears, however, that some of the old people misled him, probably because as recent Christian converts they had learned to disparage their own ancestral traditions in the presence of whites. Also, he may have stumbled into factional differences among the Methodist Ketchums, Baptist Journeycakes (or Johnnycakes), and Big House people.

His oldest source was Sally Journeycake, mother of Reverend Charles Journeycake. She was born in 1797, daughter of Mary Castleman, who was captured as a girl, and Abraham Isaac Williams.[41] Sally married Solomon Journeycake, a leader of the Ohio Sandusky Delaware, who joined the Kansas Delaware in 1833. In 1827 Sally hovered near death until God promised that she would recover. She did, using Christian hymns to testify to her revelation. Later, when missionaries became active among the Delaware, she and her family converted. Eventually, her son Charles Journeycake became a Baptist preacher, ordained in 1872, and, from 1877-93, the last Delaware principal chief before the institution of a business council (Weslager 1978a: 237).

Sally described for Morgan a marriage system among the clans that would have been incestuous, so she may have been underscoring the virtue of Christian marriage. As a member of the Sandusky Delaware who moved to Kansas, however, she may have been ill-informed about traditional practices among the majority. William Adams, a young man from the community, answered some follow-up questions that Morgan asked by letter, but his responses were those of an enthusiastic Christian who briefly gave up his Delaware membership before joining the others in Oklahoma. His son, Richard, published the first account of the Unami rite, cited above. While William began with the intent of the ritual and role of visionaries, Richard described the setting and then the sequence of the rite.

Calling it the Gum-mween (Morgan 1959: 56-57), William described the building with two fires and an east door where a Dreamer (*a-la-pa-cte*) hosted for six days, before another took over, and so on, for as long as a month. Participants sat by clan as Turtles, Wolves, or Turk[eys]. The singers each had a rolled up deerskin drum, while each reciter used a turtle shell rattle. William erred, however, in regarding their verses as extemporized instead of the ritualized texts they were. Lastly, he mentioned the deer hunt, cedar smoke incensing, and final prayer line to ask for longevity and health.

## McCoy

That many Delaware became Baptists in Kansas was due to the zeal of Isaac McCoy (Schultz 1972), despite initial hostility in Indiana, where he met with Delaware in November of 1818 to propose a Baptist Mission. On 18 December, he visited Chief Anderson, reporting half the Delaware lived in log cabins and the other half in bark huts (McCoy 1840: 53).

---

[41] This sketch of Sally Journeycake's life is based on unattributed notes in the Bartlesville Library and Archives.

He returned to Indiana for a council meeting on 31 May 1819, when Anderson's interpreter was a black man, probably his slave, while McCoy's was an aged woman. Encouraged, McCoy received instruction in Lenape from Ben Gray. Mrs. Christina McCoy, in turn, taught Mrs. Gray to knit and "become more neat." Among his lessons, McCoy learned that the Delaware "returned thanks to *Ke-esh-she-la-moh-ko*, (Our Creator,) for their food and drink, their clothes, and other good things." After death, Delaware went to Him and lived "in large houses, clean and comfortable, made of cedar, or some such wood, which emits a pleasant odor." This afterworld had plenty of fat deer, bear, and turkeys. Most of the time was spent singing. The bad, however, went to Muh-tunh-to [the Devil], where they were tormented and punished in ways to fit their crimes. Thus, a drunkard had to consume boiling hot whiskey.

Plans for an Indiana mission were abandoned, however, when local Whites opposed McCoy. When he saw better prospects among the Potawatomi, he started the famous Carey Mission in Michigan. Nevertheless, he continued sporadic contact with Delaware. When Mrs. Shane, a Delaware married to an Ottawa-French husband, was baptized, someone rebuked her for wearing trinkets in her ears. According to McCoy (1840: 88), she replied, "My religion is not in my ears, it is in my heart.... Nevertheless, I will converse with the missionaries, and if they say it is wrong to wear them, I will put them away." McCoy responded that

We never deemed it necessary to make innovations on the customs of the Indians merely for the sake of <u>form</u> or <u>fashion</u>. Their ornaments are esteemed a part of their dress. She was, therefore, told that the Great Spirit had not directed what should be the fashion of our dress. Different nations and different ages had their own various modes of dressing, both in regard to comfort and comeliness. Religion consisted of right disposition of the heart, rightly influencing our actions.

For this reason, McCoy distributed face paint and native-style clothing among his converts, earning general goodwill.

McCoy reactivated his association with the Delaware when, in anticipation of their move to Kansas from Missouri, he surveyed the new reserve. Accompanied by John Quick, a Delaware leader representing Anderson, they began on 16 September 1830 after approving the proposed land (G. Foreman 1946: 55). Once settled in Kansas, Delaware were served from the Shawnee Baptist Mission before a Delaware Mission was started by Ira Blanchard. William Lykins gained respect for this mission by inoculating Delawares and Shawnees during a smallpox epidemic.

In August 1833, Delaware baptisms began, during a time of hostilities with the Pawnee. On 6-7 August 1836, McCoy went among the Delaware to quiet their alarm about a growing split between "heathens" and Christians (1840: 505), stating that such unnecessary distinctions created an evil prejudice. For him, this contrast was minimal since he discounted any possibility of an aboriginal religion. Certainly, the Delaware contradicted his general characterization of native religion ("lacking worship of idols, regular mythology, and lax observances"), although their conversion to Christianity in growing numbers suggests that many had indeed become indifferent about ancient rituals.

According to McCoy, these "trifling, unmeaning" ceremonies so little influenced morals that it was unnecessary for missionaries to inveigh against them. Hence, McCoy probably recorded an account of the Gamwing from Nahkoman for intellectual reasons, rather then to suppress it.

Methodists from the Missouri Conference visited the Kansas Delaware Mission under the care of Brother Edward T. Perry (1846), but failed to grasp Delaware native beliefs, reporting instead a male winter god of the north and a female summer goddess of the south who was patroness of the Green Corn Ceremony (Patton 1954: 176, entry for Wednesday 9 May 1843).

Obviously, while Delaware culture was and is gender-based, no God and Goddess ruled their world, only the Creator. Instead, these Methodists misunderstood the deities of two of the four directions, particularly Grandfather of the North and Grandmother of the South. The Grandfathers of East and West received no mention, although belief in them continues in Oklahoma.

During their stay in Kansas, Delaware tried to complete their national unification. Envoys were sent to all the remnant groups left along the way to encourage them to rejoin the majority, and most did. About 30 came from Sandusky, Ohio, in 1833, including future leaders, and 200 Moravians came from Canada in 1837, to their regret.

Kansas Delaware abandoned communal villages in favor of family homesteads, and planted more wheat than corn (maize) for the first time in their history. Of their 924,160 acres in Leavenworth County, 1500 were cultivated. The full population numbered 1,085: 247 men, 315 women, and the rest children. The 108 additional females explains why modern Delaware recalled polygyny among their grandparents.

## Scouts

Kansas and Texas Delaware men spent considerable periods away from home, roaming along the frontier (Dodge 1882, Newcomb 1978). Delaware men played a significant role in American expansion in the West. The Chisholm Trail followed the route used by Delawares moving between their communities in Texas and in Kansas. In 1837, eighty-seven served as scouts in the Seminole Wars in Florida. Others were scalp hunters in Mexico until 1850, tracking Comanche and Apache raiders in the employ of James Kirker, who "in 1840 with a party of Americans (including Shawnees and Delawares) contracted with the governor of Chihuahua to exterminate the Apache of that state. After several forays Kirker collected more scalps (some allegedly were not Apache) than the governor could pay for" (Gregg 1974: 228, note 4).

Delaware were also active as scouts on the plains during 1855-75. On the 1857 summer campaign against the Cheyenne, Fall Leaf, a Munsee with many descendants still living in northeastern Oklahoma, returned with gold nuggets that helped precipitate the 1858 Colorado gold rush (Stone 1956: 227). Black Beaver (C. Foreman 1946), a famous Plains Delaware guide, led James Audubon and others to California.

John C. Fremont had Delaware scouts for his expeditions of 1842, 1843, and 1844. During the ill-fated one of 1845, these Delaware left Fremont because he started too late in the season. Julia Hall (IPH 63: 279), the daughter of Wahooney, a scout named George Washington by Fremont, recalled that the other Kansas Delaware scouts were Andy Miller, James Harrison, John Moses, Jacob Eneas, Good Traveller, Solomon Everett, John Smith, and John Wolf. Jim

Secondine, a Delaware chief, agreed to supply Fremont with 10 good hunters, each receiving $2/day, ammunition, a saddle, and compensation for a horse if it died.

A few Delaware were involved in historical events in the West. As members of a tribe long in contact with Euro-Americans, Delaware warned Western Indians about white avarice. Tom Hill, a famous Delaware warrior, was present at the 1847 Whitman Massacre in Washington State. An unnamed Delaware man lived briefly on the lower Columbia River and taught some Lenape to a Wishram Chinook trader. Big "Nicholas"[42] helped instigate the 1848 Taos Rebellion, then retired to Kansas, served on the tribal council, moved to Oklahoma, and was buried in a cemetery at Nowata.

Delaware scouts and mountain men were famous throughout the plains for the distinctive aroma of their tobacco smoke. Smelling it, friends and foes knew that Delaware were nearby. Francis Parkman (1964) remarked, upon seeing Kansas Delaware in 1846, that they were regarded as the most adventurous and dreaded warriors on the prairies, successfully taking on Sioux, Comanche, and other tribes. During the expedition of Captain Wilkes (1845: IV, 471), Horatio Hale reported "From some of the officers of the Hudson Bay company, I learned there were many Delawares and Shawnees among the Blackfeet, and the former, known by the name of the 'Shaved Heads' were much dreaded by the other tribes." The reference here was to the high foreheads, produced by shaving the front hair to the crown of the head, favored by older Delaware men as a mark of wisdom and maturity. This hair style was traditionally worn by councilors at formal assemblies.

## Pawnees

Scholars have been so concerned with tracing influences from Christianity and Euro-American institutions that inter-native borrowings have been ignored. Yet Delawares interacted more easily and more intensely with other tribes and nations. Certainly, some of the early Delaware practices seem to have been deliberate reversals of those of the Iroquois, distinctly setting apart these often hostile communities. Later ritual details also suggest reactions to Pawnee observances.

Kansas Delaware enjoyed a hunting outlet to the west, 150 miles long and ten miles wide into the Plains bison range (Abel 1904). Specified by treaty with the United States, the outlet cut into Pawnee territory. As a consequence, Pawnees then became the primary enemy of the Delaware. In 1832, a party led by Captain Shawannock, a son of Anderson, sacked a Pawnee village in retaliation for the killing of three Delaware. On 1 December 1835, a hunting party returned with 11 Pawnee scalps. Yet, despite hostilities, during an 1833 treaty conference among all the neighboring tribes, Delaware acted as mediators, continuing their long diplomatic tradition.

While Anderson had sent wampum to the Pawnee through their agent John Dougherty, he died before Dougherty could report in October of 1831 that the gesture was "well received by the Pawnee and that they would be glad to become acquainted with the new arrivals" (G. Foreman 1946, 56). Instead, the tribes became enemies, although bloodshed was not the only outcome of their contacts. Some parallels in the religious practices of the two tribes indicate that Pawnee rituals

---

[42] Strictly for the sake of historical accuracy, this was not his actual name, his alias of that time was "Big Nig."

relating to warfare, such as the New Fire Ceremony, were absorbed into Delaware practices. Commonly, hostile tribes will adopt each others rituals so as to diffuse some of the power available to an enemy. Captured bundles and ritual objects were also put into service by the new possessors.

Other features, however, may be related to universal patterns of human ritual. Thus, when the new fire was kindled by a Pawnee, the leading priest whispered to the sponsor that the firemaking shaft and board represented a procreating male and female (Murie 1981, 150), as in the Big House and many other Native American rituals.

More intriguing is a parallel use of folded hides as a drum. Among the Pawnee, a young man rushed into the circle of warriors, "folded his buffalo robe into drum shape and placed it upon the six willow sticks he held .... The warriors gathered round the robe and sang the wolf songs, beating time with the sticks" (Murie 1981: 139).

Also, the otterskin worn during one of the family versions of the Delaware Otter Rite recalled the slit otterskin worn by important Pawnee warriors.

A warrior's regalia consisted of a whole otter collar, a sacred pipe, an eagle feather, soft down feathers, a buffalo-hair rope, paint, and native tobacco. The otterskin was split through the middle so the warrior could put his head through. The head of the otter usually hung on the back. On the right shoulder the warrior wore a swift hawk and on the left hung Mother Corn. On his breast were two flint arrowheads, each encircled in a ring of sweetgrass (Murie 1981: 137).

Since a Pawnee hung the otter's head down the back and a Delaware wore it on the chest, such a reversal was probably deliberate (Miller 1974b).

## Osages

In Oklahoma, the Caney Big House people were on Osage lands and hostilities continued until formal intertribal gift exchanges called "smokes" established peace. In other words, further hostilities were averted by smoking and gift giving. As Nora Dean explained, the nineteen year old son of "old lady Wahooney" was murdered and scalped by the Osage. Katie Day (IPH 2: 473) said he was buried at the forks of the Caney. Eventually, annual "smokes" were sponsored by each tribe in alternation when everyone camped together to confer, visit, and trade. The Delaware hosted their smokes beside Post Oak Creek next to Highway 75, just north of Dewey, Oklahoma.

Additional information on the smokes appears in unpublished interviews. According to Charlie Webber (IPH 49: 103), those of the Osage were along Soldier creek "a stream running east and west along near the old round house [peyote chapel] reserve at Pawhuska." Rachel Green Hudson (IPH 30: 78) gave more detail: "The Delaware-Osage stomp dances and smokes were held near Post Oak, and would sometimes last a week. They always served barbecued beef and were highly insulted if we refused to eat with them. Lewis Tinker was the favorite dancer. These dances are still celebrated by the Delaware Indians, on the Halfmoon place near Post Oak." William Floyd Davis (IPH 105, 12) recalled that the small tent village was inhabited for 2-3 weeks, with everyone eating, gambling, and relaxing. Later, Ice Wilson hosted old time square dances at his homestead north of Post Oak. "Smokes" continued until at least 1900,[43] when "This time the Delawares were presented with 5 ponies and 500 yards of Calico by the Osage."

## Oklahoma Removal

The Kansas Delaware were directly in the path of whites moving west and their land was again taken away in sections. By the 1854 Kansas-Nebraska Act, the Delaware lost their hunting outlet and their reservation was reduced to twenty by forty acres, held in common. In 1860, this Diminished Reserve was allotted, with each Delaware receiving 80 acres. The remaining land was sold off to the Leavenworth, Pawnee, and Western Railroad for $1.25/acre.

Understandably, the Delaware decided to relocate, considering remote lands in Idaho, Utah, or Mexico, until, in September 1863, they opted to buy a new home from the Cherokee then living in Oklahoma. The tragic 1839 Trail of Tears forced most Cherokees from the Carolinas to Oklahoma, where they were rich in land but poor in money. The Civil War intervened, however, postponing further decision.

Delaware and Cherokee shared a long history of interaction, which had been hostile in their respective homelands. James Adair (1930 [1775]: 168) reported that Delaware once captured the Cherokee tribal ark, leaving them spiritually defenseless against misfortune.[44] In later years, after dislocations, they "respected" each other, according to the native idiom. When Newcomer died, Cherokees sent a delegation to Ohio to condole the Delaware. During a fight with the Osage at Claremore, Oklahoma, now the site of a Public Health hospital, Delawares reinforced the embattled Cherokee, who won the battle, which Grant Foreman (1930: 59) described as a glorified slave raid. Plains Delaware and Cherokee settled together in Texas with Chief Bowles, before they had to flee to central Oklahoma.

Eventually, the Cherokee-Delaware Agreement was signed on 8 April 1867, with Cherokees receiving handsome compensation. The tribal role of 18 February 1867 listed 985 Delaware, each of whom received rights in the Cherokee tribe and 160 acres, for a total of 157,600 acres. In return, the Cherokee treasury was paid $123 per Delaware, amounting to $121,824.28.

Prior to the move, the Kansas land was sold to the Missouri Railroad for $2.50 an acre. Disease erupted, however, preventing an orderly departure. As Delaware prepared to migrate, many people came down with a fever and ague that may have been malarial, such as that suffered by the Pawnee just before they moved from Nebraska to Oklahoma. Adding to their grief, local whites lingered around Delaware homesteads, ready to pounce on whatever had to be left behind. Some

---

[43] El Reno News, 7 July 1899, 3, column 6.

[44] This Cherokee ark was made of hickory splints shaped into a square, roughly two feet by one foot by one foot, that bulged on three sides. On the fourth side, it was flat to better fit the back of its carrier. The war leader or a special waiter who fed all of the members of the war party alternated in carrying it. Mooney (1900, 503) added that it had a dressed deerskin cover. Inside were several vessels made by beloved elderly women. One of these may have been a clay pot holding embers of a sacred fire. When not being transported, the ark was set on blocks to keep it above the ground and guarded by an armed warrior.

Delaware, already outraged by white greed and prejudice, mercilessly smashed up anything that had to be abandoned.

A few Delaware stayed in Kansas, choosing American citizenship by renouncing tribal membership. William Adams briefly took that option before deciding to move to Oklahoma as a missionary. Some Munsee and Moravian Delaware (Romig 1910, Weslager 1974) also remained, unwilling to join the majority because they felt misused by the tribal council after joining with the Kansas Delaware. When these Munsee and Moravians decided to join the Kansas Chippewa near Ottawa, their land on the Delaware Reserve was immediately purchased by Andrew Isaacs, a former Attorney General of Kansas, manipulating Senate approval to buy it without a period in the public domain, as federal law had previously required in all cases (Unrau 1978: 186).

## NATIVE ACCOUNTS ~ Oklahoma ~ 13

During the past century, Gamwing celebrations have been described by both scholars and Delawares. The most notable were two accounts by enrolled Delawares, one the son of a Baptist missionary, and the other the chief of the traditionalists who was official leader (host) of the rite. While that of Richard Adams is perfunctory and prosaic, Charlie Elkhair conveys a sense of what it was to be among the faithful.

After Munsee settled in Canada, their two communities, apart from Christian Moraviantown, celebrating the Big House were Munseytown and Smoothtown. Descriptions of these rites follow those from Oklahoma.

### Oklahoma

The earliest surviving description of the Gamwing by a Delaware was printed in the 1890 US Census Report, the first federal survey to include Indians. This summary was provided by Richard C. Adams (1890: 299), a man who devoted his life to advancing Delaware legal claims but whose identity and reliability leaned toward Euro-American rather than native Delaware values. Though a prolific writer, he was a Christian with a flawed understanding of Delaware aboriginal traditions.[45] In this case, however, credit is due him because he reached back to an earlier generation for his description, provided by his own father, William, who earlier supplied Lewis Henry Morgan (1959), the lawyer turned founding Americanist, with an account of the rite while the Unami Delaware were living in Kansas.

While William Adams briefly gave up tribal membership when the Delaware were moving to Oklahoma, he soon rejoined them as a life-long Baptist missionary. Father and son, therefore, were well aware of the importance of the Gamwing and, while they might condemn its observance as pagan, they at least shared a language and ancestry with these worshipers. The 1890 description seems to refer to Oklahoma practice, as compared to the father's account for Kansas events, given later in the chapter on Reforms and Revivals. Question marks [?] have been inserted to indicate statements at variance with other accounts of the rite.

### Adams

He begins with the building, then briefly considers the annual ceremony, when the Big House served as a redeeming beacon for the traditional Delaware. Every year, for about two weeks,

---

[45] "Richard Adams published voluminously and sympathetically (if not always accurately) on the religious observances of the traditionalist faction .... He was a Baptist, the son of Morgan's convert informant", according to Sue Roark-Calnek (1977: 332, note 6). Frank Speck (1937: 144, note 14) said Adams "assumed the honor of being the only descendant of Chief Captain White Eyes, and so had himself portrayed." Delawares said "his mother was a white woman and his father was scarcely more than one fourth Indian and that of Stockbridge (o'ppannu [easterner]) Mahikan descent adopted by the Delawares.

the building and environs became a busy encampment of adults and children renewing the world. In this instance, as usual, the hosting clan was Wolf (Canine).

During the twelve-day enactment, men constantly moved in and out of the building, women cared for their families, and everyone saw inside, or overheard from outside, the nightly ritual affirming Delaware continuity. Admittedly, those attending were only a portion of the total Delaware population. The others, the majority, were firmly Christian and had rejected many of their own traditions, save for their use of the Lenape language in hymns, prayers, and sermons.

A conservative tenth, devoted to the Gamwing, kept Delaware traditions alive, not in unchanged aboriginal form but in spirit and intent, by condensing the main cultural principles of their past into this all-encompassing rite.

{Why the Delawares went to Canada. – These are notes by William Adams, an aged Delaware, father of R. C. Adams, of Alluwe, Indian Territory}

THE WORSHIP DANCE OF THE DELAWARES ... We have several kinds of dances; the most important one is the "worship dance" which is carried on in a large building called a temple, which is rectangular and ranges from 60 to 80 feet long, from 30 to 40 feet wide, and is about 10 feet high. It is built of wood with 2 doors. The main entrance is at the eastern door, and it has only a dirt floor.

On each post is carved a human face. On the center post or one in the center of the building four [?] faces are carved; each face is painted one-half red and one-half black. All the people enter at the east and go out the same way. When they come in they pass to the right of the fire, and each of the three clans of the Delaware take seats next to the wall, the Turtle clan on the south, the Turkey on the west, and the Wolf on the north. In no case can any one pass between the center post and the east door, but must go around the center post, even to go to the north side of the temple.

This dance is held once each year, in the fall, and generally in October, in the full moon, and lasts not less than 12 days for each part. The tribe is divided into three clans, and each clan has to go through the same part, so the dance is sometimes 36 days long, but sometimes the second and third clans do not dance more than 6 days each.

The Turtle clan usually lead or begin the dance. A tortoise shell, dried and beautifully polished and containing several small pebbles, is placed in the southeast corner near the door in front of the first person. If he has anything to say he takes the shell and rattles it, and an answer comes from the south side of the temple from the singers, who strike on a dried deer's hide; then the party who has the tortoise shell makes an address or talk to the people, and thanks the Great Spirit for blessings, and then proceeds to dance, going to the right and around the fire, followed by all who wish to take part, and finally coming to the center post he stops there; then all the dancers shake hands and return to their seats. Then the shell is passed to the next person, who dances or passes it on, as he chooses.

On the third day of the dance all men, both married and single, are required to keep out of the company of women for 3 days at least. They have a doorkeeper, a leader, and 2 or 3 parties who sweep the ground floor with turkey wings, and who also serve as deacons.[46] The ashes from the fire are always taken out at the west door, and the dirt is always swept in the fire. In front of the east door outside is a high pole on which venison hangs. It is a feast dance and the deacons distribute food among the people. The officers and waiters are paid in wampum for their services.

In no case is a dog allowed to enter the temple, and no one is allowed to laugh inside it, or in any way be rude. Each person is allowed to speak and tell his dream or dreams or to give advice. It is believed by the Delawares that every one has a guardian spirit which comes in the form of some bird, animal, or other thing, at times in dreams, and tells them what to do and what will happen. The guardian spirit is sent from the Great Spirit.

Traditions say that 10 years before white men came to this country (America) a young man told his dream in the temple. This was on the Atlantic coast. He saw coming across the great waters a large canoe with pinions (wings) and containing strange people, and that in 10 years they would in fact come. He told this dream and predicted the arrival of the white men each year until they came and were seen by his people. Many of our people still keep up this dance, but the temple is not so large as it used to be, and the attendance now is not more than 100 people. Any Indian of any tribe can also take part in the dance, but no white man can.

When the dance is over all the people go out and stand in a single line from east to west with their faces to the south [?]. Then they kneel down and pray, and then go home. We do not know the origin of the worship dance, but the old Indians claim that the Great Spirit came many years ago and instructed it and also gave them the wampum. We, the Delawares, also have the bread dance, war dance, dole [doll] dance, buffalo dance, and human skeleton dance.

## Elkhair

At age 62, Charlie Elkhair (1912), the last chief of the Big House Delawares, described the Gamwing for Truman Michaelson, a famous linguist from Washington DC. While details of his account will be used below to analyze the rite, specific expressions of faith, particularly intention, should be mentioned now. Elkhair gave his account in the native language (Lenape) so the English cited is the translation by Silas Longbone. Under attack by Baptist Delawares, the Gamwing adherents adopted Christian terminology to defend their traditional beliefs, hence "God" was used as a synonym for the "Creator, the one who thought into being." More traditional is the word play, such as the doubling of "shook" and "will" for emphasis.

In his first sentence, Elkhair made clear that the "Delaware church" was given at the time when all nations were given churches "in case they wanted to live a good life and be with God." The sense then is that the Gamwing was the means of Delaware salvation, particularly by living a

---

[46] Delaware traditionalists borrowed terms from Christian churches to better explain their worship to outsiders. "Deacon" was such a term, still widely used by other tribes like the Creeks to refer to officials ("night deacons") at their square grounds, which are modern expression of ancient town rotundas and public plazas.

good life.  By using the word "good," Elkhair specified the need to "connect" with all of life in useful ways, as explained below.  Much later, as they were forced west, the salvation offered by the original Gamwing turned to redemption paid for by their suffering.

Elkhair said the rite began in the spring when crops were planted.  Yet the actual 12-day ritual was not held until the fall after "the crops are good" to "give thanks to God ... For what good they have seen, they attend the meeting house to extend it for another year."  Each of the 12 days represented one of the "tiers" or levels between the earth and the Creator, who sat in the 12th one.  At each level was and is a being whose face, vertically half red and half black with white eyebrows, was carved and painted on one of the ten support posts along the inside walls.  The last two faces were on the east and west sides of the center "main guide post" (p 10).  At each level, one of these sky keepers received "the service" and passed it above to the next one until it finally reached the Creator.  These carved faces, which had not been a feature of the ancient Gamwing, were the result of a visit in a time of stress.

During a long war, the big house was destroyed and the Delawares could not hold a Gamwing.  A warning earthquake began that lasted a year until, with growing alarm, the chief decided to combine 2 bark houses and hold a service.  These two separate structures justified the dualities which pervaded the entire rite.  "All day long, they shook hands with each other," but the earth still shook, trees sunk into the earth, and deep pools filled the holes.  After 6 months, the tremors lessened and Delawares began to build a big house across the river, presumably because it was pure [untainted by human refuse] land.

The new hall was ready in the spring and the Gamwing moved there.  Every night, Delawares heard the sounds of sky keepers coming closer.  Two elders arose and asked, "Can anyone here who is gifted by those people find out what they want?"  A man got up and volunteered.  Two old men accompanied him into the forest, where they met the false faces (sky keepers), who said, "God sent us down this spring to tell you Delawares to halt the meeting and to plant corn and crops.  From now on, hold the Gamwing in the fall and we will drive deer to hunters as food for those carrying on the meeting.  Carve the look of our faces upon the posts inside the big house.  When you get the faces down representing our looks, we will put the power in them that is the same as the power in ourselves."  As proof of this message, the earthquake stopped.

The Gamwing was ever after celebrated in the fall.  During days 4-7, special hunters went out to receive the deer driven to them by the sky keepers, especially Məsing who lived in the first level above the earth in a floating mountain range.  Before the hunters departed from inside the big house, each put his right toe upon the left foot of his neighbor and the chief reminded them of the message from the sky keepers.[47]  Then, to remind the sky keepers themselves, the chief put finely shredded tobacco into the fires to indicate the Delawares were "for sure and in earnest."  As the hunters left, two singers repeated the agreement in song, the strongest means of expression between beings.

After the hunters returned with venison for subsequent meals, the ritual intensified and included events like the measuring of turtle shell rattles with strings of wampum beads.  Visionaries always used the left hand when making gestures because it was holy.  Between recitations, six

---

[47]  This vivid linking of feet, since the hands held weapons and food, was a connection to indicate these hunters were of one mind and intent.

ushers moved along the sides to make sweeping gestures with turkey wings held in the left hand. Every man with a proven vision, received as a child, sang and recited about his "animal who turned into the appearance of a person." Two singers, called Geese, echoed his song as relatives and friends walked behind him in a show of support. When finished, the man stood beside the center post, extended his "kind thoughts to the people," and personally thanked everyone and "God he is able to perform his duty in the meeting house."

The last or 12th night, women gifted with visions recited and sang. Everyone wore their best clothes because they were then with the Creator. Similarly, grease and red paint were applied with a finger by men ushers to the carved faces and ritual objects, while women ushers did the same to the attending Delawares. The women visionaries went outside, lined up, and came inside with a man on either side of their leader. As they entered, these men cried out "Kwiya," the women answered "Huuuu," and the men inside responded with "Hoooo," holding up their right hands. Unlike the men who each sang one song per vision, the lead woman sang 6 songs (received as a set from her spirit), the second sang 4, the third sang 2, and others sang one each. The ushers, first the women then the men, sang along with the women. If an usher did not know the song or could not sing, he or she hired a substitute for a yard of wampum beads. The women's recitations ended when the man who accompanied the head woman sang 12 songs, with delayed backup from the Geese, pausing 12 times along the oval route until he was at the east door and led the women out with everyone inside crying "Hiiii" and raising their right hands. These men and women were then given venison to eat.

Inside, the ushers swept the route using turkey wings in the left hand. The chief announced that the rite would end at noon the next day. Then the host took the turtle shell rattle, sang, and passed the rattle on. Any male visionary sang when it got to him, seconded by the Geese ("deerskin drummers"), until the rattle reached their spot. Then that night ended and the rattle rested in front of the drum until the next day, when the rattle resumed its course and men sang until it got to the host on the opposite side.

There, a chosen man sang the last 12 songs. He sat for the first 10, then stood up along with everyone else, moving forward to "crowd" around the center post. At end of the twelfth song, everyone held up the left hand and cried out "Hiiii" and "Hoooo."

They went back to their seats while a woman usher passed out a few wampum beads to everyone to use for "extending thanks to God." The hides of the deer killed by the hunters were brought in and given away. A doeskin went to the oldest woman of the hunter's clan and a buckskin to the oldest man. Any remaining food was distributed among as many people as possible, kin, elders, and anyone else attending. All of the prayersticks, rattles, and other sacra were collected in the middle of the house. The ushers were each given a yard of strung wampum.

At the very end, "the chief tells them (the people) what good they have done since they were there, + during the time they were in earnest about their work, + their good will will be a benefit to them from heaven. So those attendants [ushers] hold those beads instead of cutting them up." The leader or host held one end. Everyone then filed outside, stood in a line facing east, and recited prayer words, alternating from one end of the line to the other until they met in the middle and the rite concluded for another year.

Elkhair took great pains to emphasize that the Gamwing was concerned with "good" and "God" and, moreover, he illustrated what this meant throughout his account. To paraphrase

Elkhair's intention, good followed from the mandate to "only connect" by forging links throughout the cosmos in the most personal way possible, literally by touching to extend and manage the flow of power. These links could be either direct by body contact or indirect through the various means of transfer via word, gift, offering, proxy, token, and, most of all, song – the most emotional and satisfying transference.

The many dynamic contacts and connections specified by Elkhair included passing the service upward between levels, shaking hands, meeting with the sky keepers, receiving gifts of power from them, driving deer to the hunters, touching feet by departing hunters, burning tobacco, painting with a finger, touching shoulders around the center post, giving hides from young to old clan members, and, especially, handing out strings or beads of wampum.

Wampum was intended to be strung together and so it was an apt metaphor for connectedness. Moreover, the shape of each bead of wampum as a hollow tube represented the kind of link that was being made: a conduit piping to channel the flow of power among particular beings and their fixed abodes, to persons and places. In this regard, therefore, it is all the more telling that the Delaware word for wampum is grammatically animate. It both circulated and connected, since, strung together, it measured the length of turtle shells during the Gamwing. Altogether, the rite connected Delawares with Our Creator, providing the means of and for tribal continuity and salvation among all of creation.

## Comparisons

Comparison of the Unami and Munsee rites confirms their common origin and subsequent divergence. Both "tribes" used a rectangular building with a central post, double fires, and a leader who sat in the middle of the north side. Among the Munsee, the drum and singers were located between the post and the west fire, but the Unami placed them in the middle of the south side, across from the leader. The spot between the east fire and center post was considered especially sacred. In general, Munsees historically have shifted from a Unami-style Big House toward that of an Iroquois longhouse with stoves, benches, and windows, yet many of the colonial descriptions suggest that Munsee rather than Unami practices were the older forms.

Munsee assigned most active roles to men, such as the sweepers, although there was a clear balancing of men and of women throughout their ritual series, both in details and through all-pervasive moieties. Unami more thoroughly balanced men and women in all positions, as with their sweepers, who were also distributed by matriclans, and by more diffuse symbolic equations. For both Munsee and Unami, men were the majority of visionaries, but the Munsee fixed their number. Unami women, accompanied by men, and young men recited at the end of the rite, but Munsee women, if they recited at all, seem to have been adjuncts to men, as described by Torry. The association of Munsee women with wampum is especially intriguing since Beata preached against such use of wampum during the Delaware religious fervor in Indiana.

While faces and hides were attached directly onto the Munsee center post and faces were carved into the Unami post, the masked performers were regarded as later additions to both ceremonies, under the inspiration of the Creator or of Məsing himself – during a time of distress. The faces on Unami side posts were also considered to have been later additions.

Within the walls of each Big House, the bare floor and center post represented the turtle and tree which (who) generated life while surrounded by sea and sky. As nodes within this relational network, visionaries reaffirmed their links with the Creator and other sources of power, embodying the vitality of the cosmos and assuring continued Delaware wellbeing despite ever-stressful interference from overbearing outside forces.

# NATIVE ACCOUNTS ~ Ontario ~ 14

## Munsee

When Munsee fled to Canada, they settled two communities, apart from Christian Moraviantown, where the Big House was celebrated. These were Munseytown and the neighborhood called Smoothtown among the Iroquois of the Six Nations Reserve along the Grand River. Even at Moraviantown, old beliefs continued, according to Mrs. Jamesson, who visited Moravian Delaware at Thames in 1835 and reported of the minister "only a small portion of the tribe under his care and tuition could be called Christians" (Witthoft 1949: 14).

While the comparative studies by Harrington and the exemplary monograph by Speck are well known, there is also an eye-witness account of a Munseytown ceremony.[48] We therefore begin with it.

## Munseytown – Torry

In 1825, Reverend Alvin Torry (1871: 109-113), along with Peter Jones, famous Ojibwe convert and Methodist minister, and "five of our most zealous and reliable Missionaries" went to Munceytown, Ontario with hopes for a mission.[49]

... we found the Indians preparing for their annual religious feast. They brought to the council-house, a little of all they had raised during the summer, as an offering to the Great Spirit ... Their council-house was from thirty to forty feet long, and eighteen wide, with no windows, chimney or hole, for the smoke to escape, that I could perceive. It had a door at each end, with a broad alley running through the center, from one door to the other. A pole, about six inches in diameter extended on either side [of] the alley, the length of the house. They had collected large quantities of wild grass, dried it, and placed it inside the poles, for the Indians to sit or lie upon. A large post was placed midway from the doors, and running to the roof. As soon as it became dark, one of the leading chiefs called for all men and women to hasten in to the house. This they immediately did, the men taking one side of the house, and the women the other. Fires had been kindled within four feet of each door, which gave light enough to see the way through the house. I, with my company, was invited in, and we accepted the invitation. We took sides with the men, who by this time were all seated. At the center post was seated one of their most intelligent looking Indians, with his head ornamented with beautiful feathers, and with other marks of distinction upon him. He was called their Commissary, and he had, properly speaking, a secretary by his side. Back of these, were seated a number of Indians,

---

[48] This citation was called to my attention by George Hamell, with thanks.
[49] Cf. Donald Smith (1987: 84-90), although there is no mention of the rite or the building by Peter Jones.

who had before them a pile of deer skins. Each one held in his hand a stick similar to a drum stick.

After all were in their places, the doors were ordered to be shut, and the fires smothered with hemlock in such a manner as to stop their blazing. This was done by two smart looking young Indians, and now, nothing was to be seen or felt, but smoke, and it seemed for a time, as though I should suffocate. I put my face into my hands, laid them upon my knees, as I was sitting on the ground, and tried to keep my eyes shut as closely as possible. In every part of the house was heard coughing and sighing. In about six minutes the doors were opened, and gradually the smoke disappeared. One of the chiefs now stepped out into the alley. He had a turtle shell in his hand; this shell contained wampum, and shining beads. He began shaking it slowly at first, and dancing moderately.

Opposite him, sprang up a fine looking woman with wampum in her hands. She kept step with the chief, who increased his speed, and his efforts to shake the shell, until he was dancing with all his might, the woman meanwhile keeping up with him. This they continued for some time. Finally, the chief took his seat, the woman, walking up to the center-post, laid down the wampum which she held in her hand, and then took her seat.

During the whole of these exercises, the men with their drumsticks kept beating upon the deer-skins, which made considerable noise. Directly, another chief made his appearance, with the shell of wampum, and commenced shaking and dancing, as the other had done. He also was accompanied by a woman as before; and thus these exercises lasted all night. A little while before daylight appeared, several men and women were requested to leave the house, and set the kettles, which contained their meat, &c, over the fires.

The young Indians, for the occasion, had brought in twelve yearling bucks. These were dressed, and cut in small pieces. But the heads of the twelve bucks were neither skinned nor dressed in any shape, but were thrown in with the rest of the meat, as they were first taken from the animals. With their meat they had boiled corn, potatoes, squashes, and beans; and when it was all cooked, they brought it into the council-house, where one of the chiefs distributed it to those who were present. To each person he gave <u>one</u> piece of meat, but to me he gave <u>two</u>. Their succotash, which they seemed to enjoy so much, was more than I could eat. None of it was salted, for they were entirely "out of" the article.[50] As near as I could determine, the twelve deer heads were given to those who used the drumsticks. After devouring the twelve deers, and eating up all their succotash, the leading chiefs marched out of, and around the house, with their eyes upraised, and in a loud tone of voice, crying hoo! hoo! hoo! and thus ended this night's feast.

I now supposed they were through with their pagan worship for the present; but I was soon informed that they were preparing for another night's worship, in which the devil, or "bad spirit" was to be invoked. In this, they put on false faces, which they called their "grandfather's faces." These made them look very frightful. I said to some nearest me, "that no good to worship the devil." This spread like wild-fire among the warriors, and in a few moments they put on cloudy faces, and showed by their actions and looks, that they

---

[50] The same word meant 'salt' and 'penis' so a ritual taboo was probably involved in this lack of the condiment.

were much displeased with me, for condemning their proceedings. However, the Con[o]y chief, Turkey, informed them they must prepare to meet me in council in about two hours.

## Munceytown – Harrington

Also at Munceytown, from John Wolf and his nephew Nellis Timothy, Harrington (1921: 127-8) heard about the origin of the Munsee Big House. They told him that God came down to earth and instructed the Delaware how to worship, setting procedures for the Big House Rite. Afterward, He rose into the air, carrying twelve shining sumac sticks, dropping them, one at a time, as he went higher through twelve levels. As He let go of the twelfth one, He disappeared accompanied by a thunder-like boom caused by the heavens closing behind Him.

To celebrate this rite, a Big House, with doors on the east and west ends, was built around a center post decorated with carved human faces. Nearby, another short post held a fresh deerskin with head and antlers placed there after the return of the hunters. Twice a year, this Big House was used for tribal ceremonies. During June, one night was devoted to thanksgiving for new vegetation, and the consumption of a fresh strawberry drink, like Iroquois do at their Strawberry Dance. During winter, a twelve day renewal rite was held in the Big House, during one night of which the strawberry drink was also served, made from dried berries put aside in the Spring.

Inside the Big House, long poles were laid along the sides, as Torry described, between seating and dancing areas. According to Harrington, the sitting area was covered with special leaves, not hay as other sources report. Twelve peeled and painted sumac sticks, representing the prayersticks dropped by God, were set along the poles, where they could be picked up and used to beat time against the dividers by self-selected volunteers. A turtle shell was placed at the base of the center post. Previously, new bark bowls and spoons were made to use whenever food was served.

During the twelve day rite, people went in through the east door and out of the west one. When the two fireplaces were cleaned, the ashes were taken out through the west door. Four singers sat near the center post, each holding a carved beater in one hand and the corner of a square, folded, deerskin drum in the other. Harrington reported that the beaters had carved faces, like those of the Oklahoma Delaware, but Speck reported another style of drumsticks. No masks were used.

Once the date was set, every Munsee visionary was sent a stick to invite him to participate. Hunters went to get 12 deer, which were butchered and stewed by four young men in a separate cookhouse.

Events began when old men used a fire-drill to start the twin fires in the Big House. When all were seated, the interior was purified by dense smoke, which Torry found so uncomfortable, from hemlock boughs thrown on the fires. Helpers swept the floor with turkey wings.

Then, the speaker rose and gave a sermon full of moral injunctions for humans, thanking God (called *Patumawas*) and everything else in creation. During the June rite, special attention was paid to the newly-planted crops. Bear fat was thrown into both fires as an offering before the fresh strawberry drink was passed around.

Next, visionaries took the floor in turn. The first reciter picked up the turtle shell and began his account and song. Supporters, anyone intending to join in behind him to dance in place, had to give a gift of wampum, ranging from a bead to a string depending on the quantity they had at their disposal. A recitation ended with the word "kwi!." Then the visionary went around the Big House to shake hands with everyone. After he sat down, the shell was passed to the next man willing to recite. During the course of each night, the prayer cry "Ho-o-o" was repeated twelve times.

Having only had a light supper before going in, everyone was hungry by midnight, when the four cooks carried around baskets of boiled meat and corn bread. Recitations resumed until dawn when breakfast, served in new bowls, was eaten using new spoons.

On the last night, a final speech encouraged everyone to do right, and prayers asked that all might live through another year. Filing out of the west door and marching around the building toward the front, everyone lined up facing east. Each person raised his or her hands and called "Ho-o-o" twelve times. This ended the ceremony. Most families went home, but hunters left immediately for the winter hunt, blessed for success.

## Smoothtown – Wampum

For the Smoothtown community of mixed Munsee and Mahikan, we begin with the description by John Wampum (Chief Waubuno 1845),[51] who collaborated with George "Smoke" Johnson, a Mohawk Anglican leader, in the brutal attack on that building (below). As a member of the community, Waubuno abetted its conversion from the traditional religion after the baptism of "fifteen Indians and two chiefs" meeting "in a long pagan temple, in the centre of which was a large post, and at the eastern and western sides of this post was a large idol" (1845: 38, 40). Significantly, even this break with ancient traditions took place within a big house, like other major historical events as perceived and reported by the Delaware themselves.

According to Wampum, in a section called "Parallel Between the Ten Lost Tribes and the American Indians" (1845: 26-28), tribes held annual first food feasts like "those of Mosaic ritual." In particular, every six months, Munsee ancestors prepared twelve deer and consumed them during a ceremony lasting a day and night to cleanse themselves from sin.

The major Munsee rite was a great Fall feast of first fruits, like that seen by Torry, when people brought some of all the crops they harvested to the "temple" to be cooked by women. This building was rectangular, with east and west doors and two fires. Inside, people sat on the ground during ceremonies. The center post was hung with deerskins, and, at its base, the wampum used for rites was kept buried. During services, two singers sat near the post, drumming on a bundle of undressed deerhides. Two young men, serving as doorkeepers, began each night by adding hemlock boughs to the fires and waving blankets to purify the interior with billowing smoke.

When the smudge subsided, an old chief rose and shook a turtle shell rattle. He returned thanks to the Great Spirit for the growth and ripening of corn. Next, he began to dance, sing, and shake the rattle, accompanied by the two drummers, until he finished his recitation. Then he sat and passed the rattle to the next reciter. Each in turn recounted the mercies of the Great Spirit, with the entire night spent in the recitation of dreams. During intervals, some people went out of the west door, "making a wailing noise to the moon," and returned through the east door, like a Summoning. In the morning, meat and soup was served to all. Wampum concluded, "These feasts often lasted 12

---

[51] This account also appears in Harrington (1921: 143-4, 202), with note 7 discussing Wampum's plagiarism from Peter Jones.

days and 12 nights, and Indians call it nee-shaw-neechk-togho-quanoo-maun, or ween-da-much-teen. No drinking or improper conduct is allowed. The utmost solemnity prevails" (1845: 28).

## Smoothtown - Anthony to Harrington

From Michael Anthony, Harrington (1921: 140-1) heard that in a later period, after the destruction and abandonment of their Big House, the Smoothtown faithful borrowed the Cayuga longhouse in the Spring and Fall to recite their dreams and to celebrate a general thanksgiving. These rites used a rectangular drum of folded deerskins, four beaters carved with human faces, and six painted sticks.

> The carved heads on the drumsticks meant that human beings were giving thanks; the lengthwise painting of the sticks, half black and half red, implied that men and women were together in thanksgiving, the black representing the warriors, the red the women. ... The dyes for producing the colors were made by boiling bark, the black being soft maple (sexi'kiminsi), and the red, red alder bark (wito'pi).

Poles rested along the edge between the dancing and seating areas. Three prayersticks were placed along the pole on each side, six in all. Anyone who felt particularly happy could come up and use a stick to beat time.

When the leader gave thanks to God and all creation, he used wampum strings and bunches, laid out on a bench, to prompt him, beginning with the Creator and, taking up each of the other twelve in turn, addressed the others. After each had received thanks and a prayer, the leader handed the wampum strand to a helper to lay it aside. These mnemonics, each with a different combination of white and purple beads, represented (1) Earth, (2) Plants, (3) Streams and Waters, (4) Corn, Beans, and Vegetables, (5) Wild Birds and Beasts, (6) Winds, (7) Sun, (8) Moon, (9) Sky, (10) Stars, (11) Thunder and Rain, (12) Spirits, and (13) Great Spirit.

When he finished, the speaker urged all present to enjoy themselves. A man was selected to distributed little wampum bunches (about 3 beads) "as invitations to join in the dancing that followed." If not specifically invited, someone could ask for a bunch to be able to dance in place along the side.

Anthony was vague about the details of recitations, although he had heard that a turtle shell rattle was used and that one old man told about a duck that was half black and half white. The reciter swayed his body to and fro, while dancers behind him shuffled sideways. Between verses, the four drummers kneeling at a drum sang a plaintive song.

## Smoothtown - Moses and Peters to Speck

The major study of Canadian Delaware ceremonialism and symbolism remains Speck (1945), written near the end of his career when he could apply the full sweep of his remarkable lifetime of comparative research. Helped by the insights of Jesse Moses and Nekatcit (Nicodemus Peters), the monograph is especially rich on the internal organization of the rite.[5]

Munsee came into Canada from the Cattaraugus Seneca, by way of Buffalo Creek, after a charge of witchcraft was raised against the Munsee by Handsome Lake (Tanner 1988: 103). They crossed at Niagara Falls to the north shore of Lake Ontario. According to the famous Montour family, the first Delaware settlement in Canada was at Dunnville, near the mouth of the Grand River, where their Big House had a dirt floor, no benches, and two open fires. While there, cholera spared only 90 Delaware out of about 300. For their own health, these survivors moved upriver to their present home.

At Smoothtown, the Big House was fifty feet long and thirty feet wide, with a shingled roof and walls formed of squared logs chinked with white clay (formerly moss) to prevent witches from entering between the cracks or peeking inside. This was an entirely magical preventative since the Big House had windows set in the center of both the north and the south sides. The floor was once bare earth, but more recently was made of hewn logs, set lengthwise, with every fourth board pinioned to the floor beams. When the floor was earthen, two fires were located under roof vents east or west of the center post, but, after 1835, iron stoves occupied these locations. The east and west doorways had plank doors. In ancient times, attenders sat on hay, skins, and blankets placed on the dirt floor. More recently, like the Cayuga Iroquois, benches were built and installed for the men on the west and for the women on the east, nearest the door used by each gender.

The crux of the Smoothtown Big House was the center post, an entire tree trunk complete with bark, hung with a red mask on the east side and a white mask on the west one (1945: 39). This post was believed to extend to the hand of the Creator, whose face was represented by the masks. The Munsee started using such masks after they felt dejected and wandered near a rocky crag that looked like a face. The leaders took this as a sign from the Creator to mend their ways and everafter have made wooden images of this face to hang on the center post as a reminder (1945: 42). Though unstated by Speck or his sources, the presence of two faces, white and red, was probably explained as aspects of the same image seen at dawn or sunset. Such celestial factors were important for Delaware.

Overall, "The Munsee-Mahikan Big House is a sky projection upon earth, specifically the constellation Ursa Major projected upon the floor of the Big House sanctuary" (1945: 32). As the Great Bear (Ursa Major) seasonally rotated around the north star, so the Delaware moved around the center post. In the Canadian Maritimes, Wabanaki attributed the "autumnal reddening of the forest foliage to the tinting of the leaves by the blood of the celestial bear slain at this turn of the seasons by the star-hunters, and the white mantle of early winter snow upon the earth to a coating of white bear's grease falling down when the sky-hunters first use the fat of the slain bear" (1945: 57).

The Smoothtown Big House and ceremonies were arranged by moiety, respectively called Wapanachki or Unami halves.

The Wapanachki lived in the east, the Unami in the west. In an early era of their relations the two tribes fought. Finally they reached a mutual agreement to cease conflict and to stay together (1945: 21, cf 24).

Their separate longhouses were merged to create the alignments of the Smoothtown hall near Boston Creek. Accordingly, the Wapanachki were symbolized by single west-facing white masks on the west side of the center post and over the east door, and the Unami by an east-facing red mask on east side of the center post and another over the west door. Interestingly, Delaware at Oshweken, a modern town on the Iroquois reserve, used the term Unami to refer both to their kinspeople in the West (Oklahoma) and those at Moraviantown, who were also sometimes called Unalachtigo speakers, presumably with reference to their past as converted refugees.

These moieties also had attributes of gender, with men on the west and women on the east, and of totem, as Wolves or Turtles. Those to the east, variously Mahikan, Munsee, and later those at Oshweken, were associated as Wolves, while the Unami Delaware were considered Turtles. Among the members of the Lower Cayuga longhouse, the same moieties prevailed. These associations were also consistent with a general equation of red with warriors and violence, or of white with women and peace, reinforced by a reversal of these among the Cayuga at the Sour Springs longhouse.

> The men occupy the western half of the building, that is the Munsee (and Unami) side with the red mask as its patron, the women the east half or Wapanachki side under the white mask.... Comparing the sex-color symbolism of these Delawares with that of the Lower Cayuga, their century and a half associates, we find that the latter seat their males on the west side and females on the east side, while the Sour Springs Cayuga reverse the directions again (1945: 23).

At Smoothtown, the major annual festivals were the Bear Sacrifice, celebrating the New Year for twelve days during late January or early February, and the Green Corn, held for seven days in September to give thanks for the coming harvest and to mark the beginning of the hunting season. Writing about 1624, Nicholaes Van Wassenaer noted that tribes along the Hudson River, ancestors to those at Smoothtown, also celebrated a midwinter and a preharvest maize rite as major events (Witthoft 1949: 11).

Other seasonal rites, held in this Canadian Big House after the Bear Sacrifice, included a March gathering to pray for a bountiful flow of maple sap, when, during the day, the Hoop and Pole game was played between men representing the opposite moieties. After a day and night of prayers, the Men's Dance was held. One of the men recited his vision, then a chief gave a final sermon. In May, there was a planting ceremony.

June was marked by the Strawberry Dance during one long day. At some point, the chief threw wampum beads on the floor of the Big House and children scrambled for them, imitating a wild turkey picking berries so as to make them "expert and swift in picking berries in the season being ushered in" (1945: 28), much like the Gathering of the Unami rite. During that evening, a Men's Dance was held, a visionary recited, and the chief gave a sermon.

Some Munsee matrilines owned dolls, apparently hosting dances for them in the Fall, but little is known about these ceremonial feedings (Harrington 1921: 166-171).

September included the Green Corn Ceremony for seven days and nights. Three men, each wearing a huskface mask, led by a fourth maskless man with staff, came into the Big House through both doors, crawled toward the center post, making sweeping gestures, and purged the Big House. Every night there was a sermon by the chief and a series of social dances. At the end of the last night, just before sunrise, the women walked around the center-post, left by the west door, and moved along the south side of the building toward the east door, where the men were waiting. In raised hands, women carried cornbread cakes, which men grabbed until all were taken. Finally, men and women went into the Big House through the east door and heard a sermon by the chief, which ended the Green Corn for that year.

At midwinter, the Bear Sacrifice was held. Throughout North America, by virtue of being ritually thanked and welcomed after being killed, bear souls would be reborn in cubs the next year. The mid-winter Bear Sacrifice Rite was such a celebration on a tribal scale.

These events were set in motion when an old woman dreamed about the location of a bear den, whose occupant was predestined for the rite. After she described the place, twelve hunters went to the den, roused the bear, and drove it toward the Big House, where it ran inside, through the east door, to the center post, and was killed by the chief, who immediately began a long prayer of thanks. The body was carried around the inside, followed by men who came in through the west door and women who came through the east one. If the bear was uncooperative, it was killed and carried into the Big House, through the east door, with all following behind. Then, the twelve hunters, called captains, helped to skin and butcher the bear. The hide was fastened to the east side of the post because bears were believed to hibernate in dens on the east sides of trees. The bear's nose was positioned at the base of the red mask, and the whole pelt was wrapped around the post.

The chief appointed helpers to butcher the bear, along with two women to wash and boil the meat in the cookhouse. Two sweepers and two singers also served as male officials during the ceremony. Each sat on a bench made from a split log with two legs at each end of its rounded bottom. Two parallel benches, painted red and used by the singers, were set east-west just west of the center post, while the sweeper's benches were painted white and set north-south near each door. Each sweeper tended the fire near his seat, adding wood as needed. For sweeping, eagle or turkey wings were used formerly, splint brooms more recently. Because he was custodian of the turtle shell rattle, the east sweeper outranked the west one, who had charge of the drum and beaters.

The chief sat on a white bench in front of the north window, across from the center post, with the turtle shell rattle placed before him, where "it somehow represented the tiny star Alcor close to Mizar in the analogue between the floor plan of the Big House and the Great Bear constellation" (1945: 71).

The turtle shell was always positioned as though headed west, whether resting on the north side at the feet of the chief or stationed just south of center post. The east sweeper had the task of putting the turtle shell before the chief, while the west sweeper moved it back to the south side after recitations.

The formal Bear Sacrifice consisted of two parts, each lasting five days. For the first five evenings, everyone went into the Big House to hear a sermon by the chief, who successively began about an hour later and ended an hour earlier. The chief spoke until the moon rose above the tree tops, when the gathering was dismissed.

The first night, before the sermon, a Pulling (Tug-of-War) Contest was held, with six men on each end of a long pole and the chief standing at its middle. The sides and betting was intended to be men against women, with the team of men on the east end representing females. The wagers consisted of food and trinkets, as was done in the Cayuga longhouses.

On the first or fifth night, after the sermon, the sweepers served bear meat, which was passed as a sacrament along each side, beginning with the women in the northeast half, then women of the southeast half, men in the northwest quarter, and men on the southwest half. The bear stew lacked both salt and maize, in keeping with the hunting associations of the rite. At Munseytown, Rev. Torry was told that the community was "out of" salt when he was served, but this was a polite subterfuge.

On the fifth night, the bear bones were burned in the east fire, and vision recitations began, their potency believed to increase as the moon waxed. The sweeper at the east door placed the drum and 4 beaters between the center post and the west fire, where the drummers sat. He carried the turtle shell to the bench on the southwest side where the reciters were sitting. Each, in turn, took up the rattle, holding it with the carapace against the palm of the right hand, and advanced toward the center post, going counter-clockwise around it once while expressing his vision and song. The drummers repeated each of his verses, holding the drum at the corners with their free hands. Remembered visionaries included Bullhorn, Kaya'ckwec, Julian Montour, Moses Cornelius, and Popotakan (Peter Klingerschmidt, the captive ancestor of Nicodemus Peters). When each finished and returned to his seat, he pushed the rattle to the man on his left, moving it westward. When all who desired to do so had recited, the sweeper at the west door took the shell to the chief.

After the recitations, three distinctive dances were held. First was the Men's Dance with men in single file behind a leader, moving counterclockwise along an oval path starting from the men's seats and going around the center post between the fires. The accompanying song made reference to boys who rose into the sky and became stars [the Pleiades]. Next was the Mixed Dance of men and women going around the outside of the center post and the fires. Then came the Women's Dance led by a male singer with the women dancing around the center post as the men had. These three dances were accompanied by the same folded deerskin drum used for the recitations and were held in "fulfillment of the wishes of the Creator ... in a time of religious revival following a crisis long ago" (1945: 72).

If time remained each night, social dances were held until the moon faded away with the dawn. After the fifth night, the early evening was devoted to recitations, and the late night was spent in dances named for animals, masked performances, ceremonial games, and social dances. The Robin, Raccoon, and Nighthawk Dances were accompanied by a water drum and cowhorn rattle.

The water drum was also used for the succeeding Məsing Dance by members of the Mazink guild on each of the last five nights. Twelve men, six wearing white masks of the Wapanachki moiety coming through the west door and six in red masks of the Unami moiety coming through east door, moved in groups of three along the north and south sides of the Big House to converge on the center post and to begin their dance. Each shook a snapping turtle rattle and moved in a crouch, motioning along the floor, to exorcise the Big House. Three times during this cleansing, the Mazinks shifted into the War Dance, ending with a whoop. After the third War Dance, they all ran out of the Big House, through the respective door of their moiety.

After an ensuing silence, social dances began, such as the Round Dance. At the end of each night, as dawn approached, the sweepers swept with their brooms from the center post to the doors, following everyone else outside.

The tenth night ended with the Nighthawk Dance, performed by two to four men wearing only loincloths. In the past, each carried a turtle shell rattle in the right hand, but, more recently, they used a horn rattle. In the left hand were formerly nighthawk wings, since replaced by feather wands. Like the Eagle Dance, Nighthawk was danced with squatting hops. Gifts, especially corn cakes, were given to the dancers as a way to ask blessings from the Creator. When given, each donor pounded on the floor with a staff that told the dancers to freeze in place while he or she gave a prayer. The gift was then put with the others, while the dancing and singing resumed. At the very end, brooms were used for a last sweep and any remaining bear meat was given away, concluding the Bear ceremony for that year.

Several events and portents marked the demise of most Munsee traditional ceremonies, along with their special building. About 1832, the masks affixed to the post in the Big House were attacked with axes by George H. M. Johnson, assisted by John Wampum, who was quoted above. Johnson was a Mohawk convert and father of the famous Canadian author, Pauline Johnson, whose sister kept one of the Delaware masks in her possession for some years.

Among the portents was the refusal of the last predestined bear to enter the Big House, which was taken as a sign that the sacrifice was meant to come to an end. Accordingly, a holy man named Red (MaXkok) "terminated the ceremonial life of the band about 1850, at which time he crushed the sacred turtle-shell rattle and declared an end to the annual sacrifice rite of the Six Nations Delawares" (1945: 52, cf 62).

Even so, a token rite continued in ever-more attenuated form. After the Big House on Boston Creek was abandoned, a simple purification observance was held every Fall, when the first bear was killed, by some Smoothtown Delaware gathered in a home, often that of William Montour. As bears became scarce, the rite was held using a pig as a substitute, just as the Oklahoma Delaware also replaced bear meat with pork. Eventually all Munsee rites ceased. After a lapse of some years, in 1905, Anglican Delaware, recalling their New Year Bear ceremony, began an Annual Tea Meeting during the winter season. These Anglicans were well aware of the earlier rite because their chapel, founded in 1839, preserved relics from the Big House, such as one of the half log benches.

---

# Endnote

[5] By the time of this study, Speck (1937: 26; 1945: 20) appreciated that gender symbolism was the most pervasive feature in Delaware culture, although he confused some relationships, such as the equation of men, black, and left, or of women, red, and right, etc. My own work builds systematically on this insight, provided to Speck by George Anderson, although I studied his charts only late in my own research.

An arrangement of symbols and functions associated with sex in Delaware thought could be shown as follows (Speck 1937: 26).

| MALE | Abstract Associations | FEMALE |
|---|---|---|
| The color red | | The color black |
| life | | death (the beyond) |
| east | | west |
| day | | night |
| right-hand side | | left-hand side |

Big House Associations

| East half | West half |
|---|---|
| east door | west door |
| east fire | west fire |
| image of Great Spirit on | image of Great Spirit |
| on east side of center post | west side of center post |

Functions and Privileges

Balanced participation in all rites and dances

Balanced ritual and dance leadership (approximate)

Balanced sponsorship of ceremonies

Balanced performance of offices as "attendants" (a'shkas)

Balanced dance-path sweeping

Balanced reception of "payment" (sacrifice) of wampum for
ceremonial services

Balanced control of ceremonial equipment in east and west sides of Big House

| | |
|---|---|
| Conducting ceremonial hunt | Preparing ceremonial foods |
| (symbol of animal economy | (symbol of plant economy |
| as male sphere) | as female sphere) |
| Singing and praying aloud | Silent supplication |
| Giving ceremonial prayer-call | Occasionally giving prayer-call |
| Controlling harvest rite | Corn Harvest Ceremony |
| Dancing on outside of dance | Dancing on inside column |
| column in Big House | in Big House |
| (inside in Doll Dance and | (outside in Doll and Buffalo ) |
| and Buffalo Dance) | |
| Nightly recitation of visions | Recitation allowed only on last |
| | day of Big House Ceremony |
| Use of musical instruments | |
| (hide-drum and rattle) | |
| Moral "purity" during ceremonial | Moral and catamenial "purity" |

*Dichotomy of sex in the seating arrangements during ceremonies in the Big House is subordinated to the classified grouping of the ceremonial divisions, Turkey, Wolf, Tortoise, and secondarily to which of the three groups is sponsoring the celebration. [original note by Speck]

# OKLAHOMA SETTING ~ 15

While the Christian Delaware willingly moved from Kansas to Oklahoma, the Big House people did not. A delegation, led by Captain Falleaf, stayed in Kansas until US commissioners, early in June of 1868, convinced them to join the Christian Delaware already in the Cherokee Nation. Described as destitute, this fifth of the tribe was provided with money, to pay their moving expenses, from the sale of their Kansas lands and its improvements.

Captain Anderson Sarcoxie, signer of a 13 June 1867 petition to protest joining with the Cherokee, settled with another group on the Caney River, west of the 96th meridian defining the eastern edge of Cherokee land. "The principal cause of his dissatisfaction was his objection to have his tribe merged into and become part of the Cherokee nation (as all Indians have to do who locate east of 96) and thereby lose his national organization, name, and power" (Manypenny 1865).[52]

Settled on the Caney, these Delaware were again in conflict with Osages. Further, made unwelcome by Cherokee homesteaders, in 1869, about 300 Big House Delaware (a third of the tribe) moved east to the Neosho River, outside the specified boundary, among the Peoria (Brown 1973), Miami, and Quapaw. While the Osage had been enemies since the time Delawares stayed in Missouri, the Miami had been willing, at least for a time, to share their land in Indiana with the Delaware. Thus, these conservatives moved from hostile to friendly territory at opposite sides of the Delaware reserved lands. These Neosho Delaware built log cabin homesteads and a school between 1871-73, although they were supposed to "care but little about civilization and progress."

Coaxed back to the Caney region, they built the old Big House associated with Colonel Jackson. On the Neosho petitions, Jackson signed after James Simons (Adams ms.). His military title was acquired, informally, while commanding Indian scouts during the Civil War. Jackson died on 24 May 1904 according to his tombstone.

The Old Big House was built along the Caney River near modern Copan, previously called Larston and Weldon. This building (site 34 Wn 46, used 1867-1902(?), Rohn and Smith ms: 97) was decorated on the inside support posts with faces carved in bas relief like the mask used by Məsing.

About the time that Jackson died (contrary to the dates given by Adams and Harrington),[53] a New Big House (34 Wn 19, used 1902(?)-24) was built nearby, decorated with intaglio faces, and associated with Charlie Elkhair (1848-1935), the last leader of the fluent traditionalists. In 1913, it was remodeled and roofed with handsplit shingles.

Other traditional leaders from this period named by Charlie Webber (IPH 49: 105), who became better informed after working with Frank Speck, were Bill Swannock, Boston Bullette, Widow Lee, Isaac Wilson, Captain Curlyhead, Delaware Charlie, Jim Gibson, William Wilson, William Longbone, Julius Fouts, George Wilson, Charlie Machine (Mawatise), Edgar Halfmoon, and Willie Brown.

---

[52] Thomas Moneypenny to Charles Mix, 6 June 1865, BIA, Letters Received.

[53] This 1904 date is taken from Jackson's tombstone and is more reliable than later dates cited in the literature.

## The Building

The Oklahoma building known as the Big House, sometimes called the Delaware church, was rectangular in form, with a door on each end and a peaked roof. According to measurements taken in 1913 by M. R. Harrington, the last building, associated with Elkhair, was 40 feet along the east to west length, 26 1/2 feet from north to south, over 6 feet tall at the eaves, and 14 feet high at the ridge line. It was built of logs, each 10 feet long, held in place by upright posts 9 inches in diameter set on either side of the sequence of three joints between each of the four log rows. Each of these three paired posts was locked together by a notched wooden brace set near the top, and each inside post bore an incised or intaglio human face. The most reliable sources insist that these faces, both the older carved bas relief and newer incised, were only on the posts inside of the building, never on the outside posts as a few recent elders have claimed.

While exterior faces were totally inappropriate to the intention of the rite of concentrating the universe inside the building, there is some contrary evidence. The University Museum in Philadelphia preserves in its collections a model of the Big House made by Harrington and William Orchard after the former returned from Oklahoma. It has etched masks on the outer side of the posts and carved ones on the inside. Since it was intended for display, the outside ones may have been added for dramatic effect. Alternatively, the two Big House styles may have been fused for purposes of illustration. Accession records were mute on the maker's reasoning.[54]

Published dates for the use of the two Oklahoma churches indicate some overlap, but this probably reflected delays in construction rather than concurrent usage (Rohn and Smith ms.). The earlier Big House (site 34 Wn 46) dated from 1867-1902 and the later one (site 34 Wn 19) from 1902-1924, with some refurbishing and a new roof of handsplit shingles added in 1913. Prewitt (1981: 48) suggested and Elkhair, in his 1912 account to Truman Michelson, implied that there was a period when the ritual lapsed between Big Houses. It seems likely that the second Big House was built in anticipation of the transfer of authority from the aged Jackson to Elkhair, the last such transfer since the ceremony lapsed a decade before Elkhair himself died in 1935.

The walls were stacked logs with interlocking corners and mud plugging the gaps and cracks. During the ceremony, a four foot square of white cloth was tacked onto the center of the north wall, providing a backdrop for the display of strings of wampum beads used toward the end of the rite. A wooden bucket, hung on the center of the opposite or south wall, contained water infused with red oak bark used by the singers, called Geese, to soothe their parched throats. The chinking and other details of building upkeep were the responsibility of the _ashkas-uk_ [aškas∧k] or "ushers," who began camping a week before everyone else to put everything in good repair by the time the campers arrived.

The ends of the building held the doorways, each gap bordered by a pair of interlocking posts that also had mask-like faces on the inner surfaces. In all, there were twelve of these faces inside the building, ten on the uprights and one each on the east and west sides of the center post,

---

[54] Another Big House Model, made by traditionalist Rueben Wilson decades later, also has outside faces (Weslager 1972: 419), but the living elders all insisted this was not the case with the Big House they knew as children.

not on all four sides as Adams claimed, at least in Oklahoma. Each was painted so that a viewer saw a mask's right half as red and left half as black.

In color and form these faces were identical with the wooden mask worn as part of the Məsing outfit. According to early sources, these faces represented the deities called skykeepers, in charge of each of the twelve tiers that intervened between earth and the Creator. These beings were vital to the rite since each conveyed the prayers of the Delaware from a lower to a higher level to reach the Creator. At an earlier time, a different face might have been addressed each night, but no direct evidence of this has survived. Still, the repetition of twelve faces, keepers, and tiers over a 12-day rite is more than suggestive.

Lucy Blalock and Nora Dean specified that the masks varied in size according to the diameter of the support post. Those at the doors were the smallest, those on the sides were medium, and the two on the center post were the largest. In order to match the masks with the twelve layers, however, the count would have to begin with Məsing and move counterclockwise from east to north to west to south before reaching the center post, where the double masks represented different aspects of the Creator. In the Canadian Munsee Big Houses, there were only four masks, two of red and two of white, representing the Creator at sunset and dawn. The split masks of the Unami seem to represent noon or midnight since black stood for night and red for day.

Each of the two doorways had very different functions during the rite since everyone entered and left by the east door, covered only with a skin or canvas curtain, while the west door was kept securely fastened or blocked, except on the ninth day when it was opened to allow ushers to carry out the old fireplace ashes and to deposit them on the ash pile just outside this door. Since the Munsee entered their Big House by the east door and left by the west one, and the Delaware believed that all life, exemplified by turtles, constantly traveled to the west, the abode of the dead, this sealing of the west door represented a denial of death for at least the duration of the rite. Also, a recurrent prayer during the ceremonies was a sincere wish that all those attending a Gamwing be blessed to live healthy lives for the coming year. In more ancient times, the host and other officials of the rite were probably positioned on this west end, physically situated between their people and outer forces.

The building's ridge line consisted of two 20 foot posts, about the same diameter as the side uprights, abutting in the middle above the center post. Spaced stringers ran from the ridge, slightly overhanging the side walls. Shingles, handsplit by a work team of men, were overlapped to cover the roof. In the ancient days when the Big House served as the town hall for a community, this covering would have been bark slabs along a peaked roof. Since a curved, quonset, barrel-style roof was an Iroquois characteristic, the Delaware use of a peaked roof set them apart, architecturally expressing ancient antagonisms.

While the peaked roof of the big house has been traced to the introduction of the log cabin, a more likely source can be seen in the long A-frame multi-family home used by Manitoba Ojibwa and most often mentioned in their mythology. It even had doors at each end and fireplaces along the center line of the floor. Two families living across from each other shared the same fire, with the boys sleeping near the father and girls near the mother so that females clustered near the doors (Hallowell 1992: 105).

The last center post was a large, squared timber of burr oak specially selected and hauled from Coon Creek (east of Dewey) to the site of the newer building near Copan. It was probably the single most important part of the construction, along with the prepared earthen floor, since it represented the world tree binding heavens and earth, the vertical axis of the cosmos. In recent memory there were only two carved faces, located on east and west sides, to anthropomorphize this axis, aligning it with the Delaware, the skykeepers, and the Creator. Its Lenape name recognized an identification with spirits and the world tree: _Məsingak^w_ = "_Məsing +-ak^w_", the ending signifying "upright tree." Throughout recorded history, posts with carved faces were particularly venerated by the Delaware (Speck 1950, Krusche 1986, Miller 1991). Today, Delaware elders show equal reverence when they visit the Big House center post preserved in the Philbrook Museum in Tulsa, and the one recently put on display at the new Noble Museum at Norman.

Image #8 ~ Center post in last Oklahoma Big House (by Vincenzo Petrullo)

The earthen floor was divided into a smooth, oval, central area and a covering of hay scattered around the edges as padding to make sitting more comfortable. The oval area included the center post and two fires located to the east and the west. Firewood was stacked just outside the east door, handy for the ushers who kept the fires burning all night.[55] The most sacred spot in the house was located between the center post and the east fire, which probably represented the place where the world tree bent over and touched the earth to create the First Woman, according to the Origin

---

[55] Much has been made of the accuracy of the Big House paintings done for Harrington in December 1918 by Ernest Spybuck (1928-1949), a Shawnee artist married to a Delaware. Native and professional colleagues called them a faithful visual record so, at first, I accepted them uncritically, ignoring the report by Speck (1937: 22) from George Anderson, who noticed that the audience should have been standing. Indeed, closer inspection shows that the paintings are not entirely accurate. For example, the view of the inside of the Big House has the woman usher with a broom not a turkey wing, the audience sitting not standing during the recitation, and the visionary with right not left hand raised. The outside view may have been printed in reverse since it has the mortar on the north not the south, and the pile of firewood is backward, also the cupboard is empty. Still, the paintings have great nostalgic value for many elders, who accept them uncritically as the valued work of a native artist (Callander and Slivka 1984).

Saga. Ritual events, such as the Gathering, held at that spot during the twelve day rite also confirm this.

The central oval was clearly intended to represent the earth resting on the back of the world turtle, suggesting continuity for the belief outlined to Jasper Danckers by Hans, three hundred years before, in the general area of New York City. The turtle itself was also evoked by the box turtle shell rattle used in turn by each visionary and passed by hand through the audience.

The ceremony was conducted by a man located on the north side of the building near the center post. He was called *Tamiket* in Lenape, meaning "the one who brings in, enters, or introduces." Since this phrase is awkward in English, I have substituted, as a near equivalent, the term "host," which is appropriate because his clan sponsored the rite and he took charge on its behalf of the welfare of the congregation. Until his death in 1935, Charlie Elkhair acted as host because he was the traditionalist chief. He was a leader of the Wolf clan, numerically the largest among the Oklahoma Delaware. As Elkhair grew more feeble, however, the routine of the rite was handled by other well-respected visionaries. Eventually, the roles of chief and of host became distinct, with the aged chief giving formal prayers at the start and end of the entire rite and on every night in between, at the request of the host. In the past, chiefs functioned as priests during communal rituals, because, as senior members of clan and village, they possessed sanction, knowledge, and authority in all areas.

In Kansas and Oklahoma until 1904, the Big House host was Colonel Jackson. At a much earlier period, of course, the council hall would have also been the official residence of the town chief, consciously equating the chiefship with the building. The last vestiges of this were the two successive Big Houses in Oklahoma, each during the tenure of Jackson or Elkhair.

In Oklahoma, after an informal caucus of chief, host, and respected elders, a date was set for the day that people were to set up camps around the Big House. Two messengers were sent to each homestead where traditionalists lived, announcing this date, inviting visionaries to attend, and selecting respected but "empty" people – those without a vision – to serve as usher~aides. Often the same ones worked year after year because anyone who served for 12 years guaranteed themselves a quick journey to heaven at death. Since there were twelve levels in the sky between earth and the Creator, helpers who swept the floor between recitations literally could say they had "swept their way to heaven" during their twelve years in office.

When the messengers visited Delaware farms and homesteads, they were accompanied by a man dressed in pants and shirt of bearskin and wearing a wooden mask. He represented Məsing, patron of nature and an intermediary between earth and sky. As the messengers traveled, the Məsing went with them either on horseback or in a buggy. While some men were better than others at embodying Məsing, any man could wear the mask and clothing when they were available. There did not seem to have been any particularly well-known impersonator. The outfit was inherited through a matriline, but this family apparently had no more claim on wearing it than any other Delaware. During the rite, the full costume hung from a secluded tree west of camp, where any man could put it on to startle and amuse the campers or to toughen up the children by scaring them. When the hunters (appointed for three days during the rite to supply the camp with meat) were away, Məsing visited inside the Big House while special hunting songs were sung there daily. He played no role in the evening recitations, and so was not fully incorporated into the rite, probably because there was a separate dance to honor Məsing. Speck was told that Məsing's addition to the

Oklahoma rite was a "mistake." Certainly, in Canada, Mazink (as the Munsee name this being) did not figure in the Munseytown rite, although twelve masked dancers did appear at Smoothtown.

The most strenuous work during the Oklahoma ceremonial was performed by six assistants, known as *ashkasuk* (singular, *aškas*). Most recently, they were six men and women who lacked a vision, but, anciently, they were probably selected on the basis of status, gender, and matriclan. With the lapse of clan-based versions, clanship became less important in the selection of the aides. Now, in English, these aides are often called ushers because this English word is close in sound, meaning, and religious connotations to their Lenape name.

Therefore, it will be used here, despite its Christian overtones, even more pronounced when they were called "deacons," which was upsetting to some of the older traditionalists, who well remember the intolerance of Delaware preachers toward their aboriginal traditions. In general, however, responding to pressure and criticism from their converted kin, traditionalists have long tried to emphasize the equal or greater worth of their rite by using English religious terminology.

Similarly, I have the sense that behavior during the rite became more staid, influenced by Protestant practices, further deflecting attacks of "paganism." In its earlier form, as described in Indiana, recitations were much more athletic, with the visionary using his or her body to mime the characteristics of a spirit power. Such behavior can still be seen during the visionary recitations of other tribes, such as the winter dances of the Salish in Washington State and British Columbia (Miller 1988, 1999).

As the helpers were called ushers, the building itself was designated the Delaware church. In an ecumenical sense, of course, it was a church, although used less frequently than many Christian ones, but it was also much more. As the focus of national religion, instead of being a neighborhood church, it was a tribal one, not unlike Catholic regard for Saint Peter's Basilica in Rome, albeit further heightened by an increasing absence of any equivalent Delaware parish churches during recent centuries.

While the rite has been somewhat modified to appease Christian critics, its origins were not post-contact. The rite well reflected crucial features of Delaware culture, and became the epitome of those beliefs. The ushers were selected from the ranks of those Delaware who were "empty" (without a vision), in recognition of the personal value accorded everyone. Traditionally, they were a male and female pair from each of the Canine, Fowl, and Turtle clans. More than other participants, these ushers represented the genders at the crux of Delaware culture and the Gamwing itself.

Other ritual officials included two men well versed in the vision songs of all the men and women reciters. This pair sat nightly on the south side, across from the host and behind a folded deerskin drum, repeating, after a slight delay, the phrasings of each visionary. Their repetitious echoing gained these singer-drummers the name of *taleka*, "Canadian geese," because of the way these birds call back and forth, passing on the sound of the flight leader with a pause between each repeat.

In addition to the host, ushers, and Geese (singers), the actual performers were the mature visionaries with acknowledged claims to a vision and song, as confirmed by community consensus and their own proper conduct and proven success. Women visionaries, while historically fewer in number, could prove themselves at an earlier age than men by being capable wives and mothers. Thus, while some women could be accepted as approved visionaries before thirty, men only began to sing and recite when approaching fifty, by which time they were grandfathers training younger generations.

During the rite, the clans had fixed seating places on the floor. In the past, the seating of a matriclan, further segregated by gender, depended on the membership of the chief or host in charge. His clan sat behind him along the north wall, while the other clans sat on either side of the drummers. In modern memory, however, Oklahoma clan and gender seating was invariable, year after year, based on hosting by the Wolf clan. Adams implied this by placing the Wolf clanspeople along the north side, but the Turtles and Turkeys occupied other positions than the south and west, where he located them.

Clanship distinguished traditional from Christian Delaware. As a matrilineal system, membership passed from mother to children within three groups whose Lenape names and associations identify them as Turtle, Fowl, or Canine. Their emblems were usually an outlined turtle seen from above, a turkey foot, or a wolf paw. The Lenape names of these clans, moreover, indicate that they were generic categories linking Turtle with water, Wolf with other canines roaming the land, and Turkey with fowl roosting in trees or flying through the air (Chapter 6).

In the last Oklahoma Big House, entering by the east door, the Canine women sat at that end, north of the door, Canine men along the north side, the host in the middle, Turtle women along the west end, Turtle men in the southwest, singers in the middle, Fowl men in the southeast, and Fowl women along the east end, south of the door. It is especially noteworthy that the women sat along the ends with the men toward the inside, females forming a bracket around the males. This arrangement reversed ordinary gender symbolism – women inside and men outside – but was consistent with other reversals setting the Big House apart from Delaware mundane affairs.[56]

For example, outside, the ushers set up their tents east of the building, with the three men on the north and the trio of women on the south, the direction called Grandmother. These tent positions were rank-ordered so that the senior ushers were nearest the Big House and the most junior ones furthest away. These reversed inside the Big House, the male aides were responsible for the south side and the females for the north half.

Such reversals were not unique to the Delaware. They occur in all human societies, as well as tribes ranging from Southwestern Pueblos (Miller 1972b) to other Algonkians. For instance, Adrian Tanner (1979: 218, # 8) noted that in the Shaking Tent seances so important among tribes of northern America and Siberia (Miller 1990: 130-135), polarities were reversed so that the spiritual was inside and the physical-mundane was outside, setting these uniquely apart from usual spatial organizations. Similarly, the Naskapi built a long tent with double doors reminiscent of the Big House for their hunt rituals, insisting on covering or plugging all holes in its walls to keep honored spirits in and dangerous ones out (Speck 1935: 220, # 20).

More examples could be cited, but these are sufficient to indicate the special status of the Big House as a model of the universe turned inside-out. The potency of the ritual was such that the cosmos was realigned and power so concentrated inside that participants could easily direct their thoughts to the Creator, the ultimate source of everything.

---

[56] In all cases, however, the line of men moved ahead of the line of women, expressing their priority.

This inversion also occurred in miniature in terms of the drum used by the singers during the nightly recitations. The drum was a folded deerskin, fur inside, forming a rectangle about a yard long with two slats tied lengthwise along the top and two along the bottom to add resonance. The inside was also stuffed with hair, sometimes hay, adding further to the reversal.

For the first eight nights, each singer used a slat drumstick incised with an X at the top. On the ninth night, they switched to slat beaters embossed with a mask face, one of the two also having carved breasts. In other words, depictions of human faces extended from the center post (representing the world tree) to these latter drumsticks, evoking Man and Woman, while the posts and sticks represented branches of the world tree stretching between sky and earth. Both inverted rectangles, the Big House and the drum emphasized an inside-out universe.

## Outside Environs

The area outside the Big House was arranged according to the usual pattern, men associated with the outside and the women with the inside, as aspects of a universe organized into concentric rings of womanly features, limited to domestic space, or manly associates, extending outward and upward to the Creator.

Camps were arranged along the sides of the building, with most public activities localized east of the Big House, where the usher camps bordered the work area.[57] Outside, along the east to west axis, was a central cooking fire, with a frame, three feet high, set over it to hold cooking pots. The women ushers prepared meals and served them to the host's own clanspeople three times a day and to the congregation at the end of each night. Farther east was a tree trimmed to stubby branches and set up to hold the deer and other meat killed by the official hunters. On the north side was a scaffold, called the cupboard, with several, usually three, shelves to hold dry goods in bulk, such as flour, coffee, sugar, salt, beans, and some canned goods. On the south side were a kitchen table used to prepare food before cooking, and a mortar, hollowed from a tree stump, used with five foot wooden pestles to pound cornmeal.

Accordingly, the meat pole, associated with men and hunting, was on the outermost edge while the mortar, associated with women, maize, and domesticity, was innermost. Much of the food supply was on the north with the men aides, while the work table for processing food and the cooking area was on the south near the female ushers.

The fire was in the center, serving as a mediator. As described by Abraham Luckenbach, a Moravian missionary among the Delaware on the White River, the best-known Indiana Big House had three fires inside the building. Since the building had only two in recent memory, as Kinietz (1940: 119) noted, this outside cooking fire was the third along the east-west axis. This shift did not change the internal symbolism, since the two inside ones represented men or women, while this third one was their mediation.

In sum, the officials, building, and environs of the Big House set the stage for the ritual drama, filling twelve nights, of recitations by acknowledged male visionaries until women gifted

---

[57] Lucy Blalock recalled that children were encouraged to play in the dirt around the camps because they would find lost wampum beads that could be strung for reuse in the Gamwing.

with power songs recited on the last day.  The rite ended with a dance in concentric circles inside the church and a north-south lineup for final prayers outside in the field.

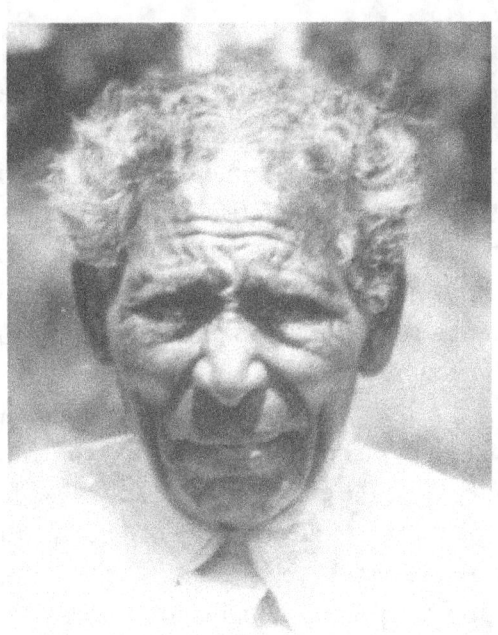

Image #9 ~  Chief Charlie Elkhair

# OKLAHOMA RITE ~ 16

The Big House Rite was once known by the distinctive term of *ngamuin*, *gamwing* = "feasting," but now both the building and the rite share the same designation of *xingwikawn*, literally *xing-* "big," *wi-* a connective, *-kawn* "house."[58]

Actually, the Big House was the most integrative of a series of family and tribal rites celebrated by ancient Delaware. Family Rites (Bear, Otter, and Doll Dances) were presumably held in the spring, much as rituals to open the medicine bundles were and are held by other tribes to mark the reawakening of the earth and to pray for the advance of growth and summer warmth. The Tribal Rites, which became progressively incorporated into the historic Big House Rite, included the Spring ballgames, the Fall preharvest Green Corn (Maize), and the Fall Məsing rite.

The modern version of the Big House, envisioned in Indiana, initially was a spring ritual, but soon it was shifted to the fall, a more appropriate time to express thanksgiving to the Creator for his continuing bounty. As such, it was the culmination of a ritual series begun by the native football games (played men against women with a deerskin oval) to hasten the growth and maturation of plants, and ended with the Maize preharvest celebration. The Big House was held after the harvest, about mid-October, marking an overlap in economic contributions by women and by men. It came both at the end of the agricultural year and at the start of the hunting season, signaled by changing deciduous leaf colors and the appearance of certain constellations. Schlesier (1987: 179) suggested that holding the rite at night allowed Ursa Major (and the Pleiades) to be in sight. Also, Adams, in the account above, specified that the rite was held during the full moon. Therefore, the rite was both an ending and a beginning much as the harvest rite once signaled the transfer of crops into storage, a sacrifice of summer growth for human nourishment during the winter.

Like others in the ritual series, the Big House emphasized the complementarity of life and death, of plant and animal, and of woman and man. Moreover, it represented a particular ordering of the universe into nested sets of matrices with members characterized as exclusively specific, inclusively generic, and inclosively categoric – all epitomized by the triad of Woman, Man, and Mind. In ordinary contexts, Man was inclusive, representing both genders; Woman was exclusive, set apart; and Mind was inclosive, binding the genders together within a unified cosmos.

Traditional families expected the two official messengers (inviters) to visit in early October to announce the date to set up camps. Within a week of this date, the ushers, who agreed to serve after being asked by the messengers, gathered at the site to make repairs, scatter a layer of fresh hay along the inside walls, and generally clean and tidy up the surroundings in time for the encampment. Each family arrived sometime during the day specified, camping at their usual place. Sleeping

---

[58] Another folk etymology, intriguing for its symbolism, is xing- "big," -wik- "house," -aon "fog." Big Fog House would be akin to terms like Rainbow and Shimmering House, used in the Southeast for sacred precincts and rotunda to invoke their hazy, primordial associations. The Yuchi call their square ground, supposedly the site of the first Busk, the Rainbow House (Speck 1909, cf Jackson 2003).

arrangements kept couples apart because, as Adams indicated, sexual continence was required as an act of devotion.

During the ritual, days were counted from high noon (noonrise), but recitations did not start until dusky dark each evening. Throughout Native America, the power of spirits was believed to wax and wane during each day, being weakest from dawn to noon, increasing until sometime around midnight, and then weakening again. The Delaware, therefore, scheduled their recitations for the time when spirits were requickening, and especially likely to be strong and helpful. Those spirits who were malevolent were excluded (exorcised) by ritual precautions from the sacred space.

The full rite lasted for twelve days because 12 expressed completeness, also the resolution of the pattern numbers 3 and 4 favored by the Delaware. The rite was divided into four periods, each of three days duration, with each day itself also marking one level in the passage through the sky until heaven was reached on the last day, when everyone dressed in finery for the only time during the rite. On the last day both men and women recited, fusing the genders in the abode of *Kishaylamukɔng*, "The One Who Thought Our Creation" – the Mind deified.

Similarly, the full ceremony started with the kindling of sacred fires by a chaste man using a pump fire drill, an act rich in symbolism. Many tribes (among them the Hopi (Fewkes 1920), Pawnee (Murie 1981), Yahi, and Skagit) equated the kindling of fire with coitus, the drill shaft = male and the indented base = female. Presumably, the Delaware also attributed the same symbolism to fire making, beginning the ceremony with the an equal fusion of genders as occurred during the concentric dancing at the end.

Each of the four periods in the rite had a particular function: the first an introduction, the second a hunt for nourishment, the third a renewal, and the fourth an intensification while approaching the deity.[59]

## Days 1-3    Period One:  Introduction (Layers 1-3, Turtle)

At twilight, an usher walked through the camps calling for everyone to come into the Big House, where two fires had just been lit by an honored man, often Julius Fouts (Fox), using a large pump-drill fire starter. The loud humming noise (for which it was named in Lenape) served to warn away women and children, who could not be present when the new fires ignited. Thus, while women were excluded, men performed a ritualized union of the genders, symbolizing manly inclusiveness. On the east and west sides of the central pillar and upon the ten side posts were carved faces, twelve in all, each painted red on their left side and black on their right side, representing the skykeepers.

---

[59] My account emphasizes a narrative flow of events, based on a decade and a half of studying various, sometimes conflicting, accounts by Harrington (1921), Speck (1931, 1937), Elkhair (circa 1912), Dean (1974), Adams (1890, 1906), McCracken (1956), Gilliland (1947), Goddard (1978), and Jones (1973). Gilliland is the source for my statement that days were counted from noonrise and the singers were wary of female recitations because their songs were not as well known. Careful documentation of data, sources, and conflicts occurs in Miller (1980a), which compares the different descriptions to arrive at the structure of the rite explored in greater detail in this book. Grumet (2001) assembles these, with some current native commentary.

The fires were located to the east and west sides of the central timber supporting the peaked roof.  While the fires were fed, people came inside with padding, such as blankets and shawls, to spread over a wide strip of hay piled along the walls, leaving a central oval of bare earth.  Children attending the service stayed only on the hay; they were kept away from the bare floor because it was sacred and thereby dangerous to those without power of their own to protect them.

People sat by gender within sections reserved for clans (Canine, Fowl, and Turtle) inherited through the mother.  When everyone was seated, an usher closed the flap over the eastern doorway. The six ushers, a man and woman from each clan, took their positions near the east door, three men on the north side and three women on the south.

The host, representing the sponsoring clan, usually Wolf, began the ceremony by praying or asking Chief Elkhair to pray, expressing thanks to the Creator and many specific features of the universe.  The overall prayer asked for the continued wellbeing of Delaware and everything else. After the prayer, the host began the procedure, repeated that night and every night thereafter, of reciting a figurative account of his meeting with an immortal (his *mǝnitu* - spirit, guardian, ally), interspersing his narrative with verses of the song he was given at the time of his vision (Voegelin 1941a).

An usher placed a single rattle – made from a box turtle shell with kernels sealed inside and a leather strap stretched along the length of its curved back – on the ground beside the sitting host, who picked it up, stood, and moved into the bare oval.  Placing his right hand between the strap and carapace, he shook it firmly and heard two answering beats from the two drummers to indicate that they were ready.  Called Geese, these musicians led the men in echoing, after a slight delay, the words and song of the visionary.  Everyone stood while he spoke and sang of his experiences.

Delivery was typically on a high tone from which the voice fell at the end of each segment.  In this pause, the phrase was echoed by every male present, led by the drummers ... In certain cases the drummers might highlight a passage by playing a loud tremolo, as in Elkhair's narrative, when they used this device to underscore his reference to Thunder-beings (Robert Adams 1977: 25).

The host walked in a counterclockwise spiral, shaking the rattle from side to side during his chant.  At intervals, he shouted "kwi" and switched to a verse of his song, moving the rattle up and down.  Overall, these motions formed an axis in three directions.

In rows behind him, a separate line for men and another for women, adults followed to offer encouragement.  Males echoed each phrase of the visionary, but women remained silent.  At the last word, the visionary stopped wherever he was, those following him raised their left hands in thanksgiving, and all returned to their seats.  When Chief Elkhair finished his narrative, however, he stood with his back to the center post, extending his left palm to shake hands with everyone who had followed him.

After this first recitation, two women ushers went to the outside cooking fire to prepare a venison stew, simmering it all night to be served in the morning.

Between recitations, the rattle was passed through the audience, while a man and a woman usher swept the length of the building with fans made of entire turkey wings.  Because of the symbolic associations, the woman probably used a right wing, and the male usher a left one.

Starting from alternating sides, they bent at the waist and made brushing motions. Nora Dean remembered the man sweeping from west to east and the woman from east to west.

At an earlier time, they may have alternated sides because there were shorter intervals between recitations and this was more efficient. Sweeping for 12 years meant that, at death, an usher would quickly pass through the 12 sky levels to be with the Creator. In this way, someone who was "empty" could receive some of the post-mortem advantages of a visionary.

Moreover, the posture of the aide bending over with feathers in hand resembled the dancers in the Calumet ritual, diffused from Caddoan tribes and important for peacekeeping and intertribal relations among Woodland and Plains tribes. Among the Iroquois, who adopted the ritual, it was known as the Eagle Dance (Fenton 1953), while the Munsee adopted it as the Nighthawk Dance.

After the length of the floor had been swept, people could leave or enter the building before the next recitation began and the east door was again covered. During these intermissions, old men might call out "let's all smoke," and share tobacco.

The rattle was carried back to the seating place and passed along. "Always handled by the thong and never pushed along the ground, the sacred rattle passed from one worshiper to the next – sometimes handed beneath the knees..." (Adams 1977: 26). If the shell made any noise, while hovering just off the ground, the Geese would strike the drum in response, embarrassing anyone who was not going to recite. Nora said that mild chuckles from the audience also added to the discomfort of a clumsy handler. The rattle moved to the left, counterclockwise from the east. Recitations formerly continued all night because of the large number of visionaries, each performance lasting about half an hour, but during the early 1900s, there were so few visionaries that men had to recite twice each night to fill the time until midnight. Aboriginally, as described in the chapter on the Homeland, each town had its own Big House or hall to accommodate its own visionaries so the night was filled with many recitations. The Munsee limited visionaries to a fixed number of men, often twelve, and so determined the length of the services.[60]

When the rattle reached a visionary, he shook it, stood, and received two beats in reply from the drummers. Walking onto the earthen oval, his recitation was similar to others, with each one making vague reference to his own experience with an immortal.

As morning approached, the service drew to a close. The host asked everyone to stand, hold up their left hands, and call out the prayer word "Hoooo" twelve times. Then ushers brought in the venison stew and served it before everyone left for a morning rest or nap. Extended periods of sleep were not allowed during the entire rite because everyone was supposed to be constantly alert, praying and giving thanks.

During the day, the Big House served as a retreat for men and boys, who relaxed, tended the fires, and practiced special "Long Winged Being Songs" addressed to the Thunderers, powerful birdlike immortals living in the sky. During the day, boys learned details of the rite and practiced for future roles. Women and girls stayed in their camps, preparing meals, caring for families, and visiting.

---

[60] Munsee could limit the number of visionaries reciting at these public ceremonies because, like the present Coast Salish, visionaries sponsored recitations in their own homes, giving them private outlets for religious expression among a small group of supporters.

## Days 4-6     Period Two:  The Hunt (Levels 4-6, Wolf)

At noon on the fourth day, hunters assembled in the Big House, where they were served lunch by the women ushers.  This special hunt was requested by the host and organized by the senior male usher, who assembled willing hunters and often was elected to be their leader.

After eating, the hunters formed an east-west line facing north, with the right foot of each lightly resting on the left foot of his neighbor.  For balance, each leaned on a gun (formerly a bow?) held upright between his feet.  In this way, the hunters formed a linked set ready to leave through the east door on their right.  In this pose, the host instructed them about the importance of supplying meat for the camp, while the Geese sang about the promise made by Məsing and the skykeepers to drive deer toward the hunters at such times.

These skykeepers, each occupying one of the twelve levels between earth and heaven, were represented by the twelve faces carved on the interior posts and by a wooden mask of the same design worn by a man dressed as Məsing, the lowest sky keeper.  While the host instructed the hunters, Məsing stood near the center, silently blessing the hunters.  The host placed 12 pinches of tobacco into the fires, six in the west one and then six in the east flames, as offerings for each of the 12 skykeepers.

Women ushers gave each hunter a food packet of meat and cornbread for the trip.  The leader could not return to camp until noon of the seventh day.  When deer were killed the first day out, they were returned to the camp, announced by a rifle shot for each one slain to indicate prompt blessings; otherwise, the venison and hides were brought back on the seventh day.  All deer were given to the cooks, who gutted and skinned each one before hanging it on the meat pole, a tree with trimmed branches east of the Big House.  The men ushers did the cleaning, hanging, and butchering; while women ushers did the cooking.  The hunter who made each kill promised that hide to an elder, buckskins to old men and doeskins to old women.

Because of the close ties between Məsing and deer, venison was a sacramental food.  At the last few services, however, farming and homesteading had so damaged the local ecology that venison was replaced with beef purchased from a local butcher.  For a time before all Delaware rituals lapsed, beef was reluctantly substituted for venison as pork was for bear meat.  Eventually, however, it became prohibitively expensive to feed the entire camp for two weeks.[61]

On the fourth night, additional events took place during the early evening.  Held respectively outside and inside the building, these were the Summoning (wiltin, also called "name-calling") and the Gathering (mawãsi, mawansi, "berry picking").

For the Summoning, the host and elders selected six worthy men and asked an usher to go through the camp calling out the Lenape name of each.  Ordinarily, these names were carefully guarded and never said aloud to prevent their use in sorcery because every name was intimately associated with its owner.  In lieu of names, Delaware used kin terms, nicknames, and affectionate

---

[61]  The Shawnee, while extremely conservative in their traditions, have allowed small animals like squirrels, always more abundant, to be used as ceremonial food, helping to perpetuate the sacred aspects of food sharing at their rituals.  While the large mammals have been all but exterminated, smaller ones continue to thrive in Oklahoma, and are still served during Shawnee rituals.

slang to refer to each other. Nevertheless, the sanctity of the Big House provided sufficient protection that names could be safely if selectively used there in public. As a man heard his name, he responded, "I am here," and went into the Big House. The usher reported back, "Now he has heard you." A yard of strung wampum was presented to the six men to divide among themselves, at the very sacred spot between the center post and east fire, before they went out and prayed "Hoooo" 12 times beside the meat pole. Since the event was held while the hunters were away, the intent of the Summoning was probably to remind the skykeepers of their promise to provide meat to the Delaware attending the Big House. That it was originally a Wolf clan rite is indicated by early reports of men squatting on their haunches and howling near the meat pole in exchange for wampum.

The Gathering was held just after everyone was seated inside, prior to the recitations. Ushers were called to the sacred spot, where wampum beads were scattered on the ground. The aides knelt down and rapidly began to toss beads, using the left hand, into their own mouths while humming. This awkward and comical feat produced mild laughter among the audience whenever beads fell out. Among the Munsee, a similar rite in June had youngsters act like turkeys picking berries to assure that they would have necessary skills for gathering wild foods. Among the Powhatan of Virginia, scattering beads was symbolic of plenty.[62]

Recitations continued nightly. By noon on the sixth day, the returned hunters assembled in the Big House and were thanked by the host before disbanding to their family camps. The Geese and Məsing also gave them welcome and thanks. No tobacco offerings were made in the fires.

## Days 7-9   Period Three: Renewal (Layers 7-9, Turkey)

On the seventh night, everyone who had a turtle shell rattle brought it to the Big House for the Measuring. These shells were placed in a row before the host, who then cut strings of wampum equal to the length of each one. Every owner then came forward, in turn, to take both the string and rattle, shaking it so everyone could hear how it sounded. If it was "off," sounding dull or indistinct, listeners could laugh quietly. Since not all visionaries recited in the Big House – as was the case of Willy Longbone, who sang as one of the Geese, and others – the Measuring provided a public forum for acknowledging all turtle shell owners, who by virtue of such possession had to be visionaries. While only one rattle was used during the Oklahoma rite, in the past, a series of rattles may have been used and the Measuring may have consecrated each one for ritual use. Also, the event provided a means for honoring the turtle by its namesake clan. Later evenings might also include a Summoning and a Gathering.

---

[62] Powhatan practices suggest the use of beads in the Gamwing also evoked plenty. At a wedding, a string of beads was broken over the heads of the couple (Roundtree 1989: 90). After the leader called Powhatan had his fields planted for him, he walked backwards and flung beads to his people, who scrambled for them (Roundtree 1989: 110). At the funeral of a weroance or leader, his family threw beads to the poor, who lunged to get them (Roundtree 1989: 111). These usages suggest an equation of beads with bounty, plenty, and abundance. The Gathering in the Gamwing could have had similar meaning.

On the ninth night, during a Summoning, the ushers introduced special paraphernalia: two forked drumsticks with carved faces, 12 prayersticks, and two folded bark dishes holding red paint or deer grease. The drummers each switched to one of these anthropomorphic beaters for the remaining nights.

Each of the final nights began with the prayersticks being distributed to a rapid drum beat. Six of the sticks were plain and six had a continuous spiral burned along their length. The ushers passing out the prayersticks had to be careful in their haste to distribute them evenly. Half of the plain sticks had to be on the north side and the other three on the south, with the holders forming pairs across from each other. If this did not happen, then the ushers had to gather up the sticks and pass them out again. Each person, old or young, holding a prayerstick used it to beat time, waving it in rhythm with the drum, during the nightly recitations until the ushers collected them in the morning.

Presumably these sticks represented branches of the world tree, since the participants were now symbolically quite high in this Cedar. The decorated sticks were said to represent the beginning prayer word "Hoooo," and the plain ones were the ending prayer "Haaay," both believed to have originated from the cries of innocent children traumatized by a continuous earthquake that frightened the ancient Delaware into reviving the Big House after it had lapsed.

During an intermission, the ushers brought out folded bark dishes holding red paint or grease. The women aides marked the faces of everyone on the north side, while the three men did the same for those on the south. Everyone received an undercoating of grease and a diagonal red line along the left cheek. The undercoat helped to make the paint less irritating than a direct application would have been. Women also had paint applied to the part down the middle of their hair. The paint was a mild irritant helping everyone to stay awake and alert. A male usher painted a red diagonal on the left or black cheek of each of the 12 carved faces. The two faces on the center post were so high that he had to jump up several times to reach them.

## Days 10-12 Period Four: Intensification (Levels 10-12, Tree)

The tenth evening began with greater intensity as the inside was cleaned and renewed. During the afternoon, the west door was opened (for the only time) to carry out ashes from the fires, and to add them to the ashheap of past embers. New fires were kindled with the pump drill, while women and children again were excluded. Red cedar boughs were placed in the fires to fill the inside with purifying smoke. Reverend Torry described a similar smudging among the Munsee. During interludes, old men continued to call for tobacco and smoke.

In contrast to tobacco smoke, which included and welcomed spirits, cedar smoke excluded or exorcised them. In short, burning tobacco attracted them, while cedar repelled them, so smoking tobacco was limited to the old, who were close to the spirits anyway, and forbidden to the young as dangerous or unwise. After funerals and periods of unhappiness, it is still Delaware practice to burn cedar needles and brush the body, especially the eyes, with the smoke to banish unpleasant thoughts and associations with the dead. Nora Dean also did this after visiting a museum and handling artifacts. Since these had belonged to the dead, their ghosts might still be lingering around them, so the cedar smoke provided protection.

The tenth night continued as before. An usher called everyone inside before men visionaries recounted their narratives and lyrics. The eleventh night was the same, but began with a stronger purification, dense cedar smoke filling the house.

The last night, a shallow wooden bowl was placed just inside the east door and everyone dropped a few wampum beads into it when entering. After all were seated, the bowl was taken to the host, who scattered the beads for a Gathering. Ushers painted everyone's left cheek, along with the 12 carved faces, drumsticks, turtle shells, and deerskins taken by the hunters.

During that night, women visionaries prepared to recite, dressed in their best finery. After the inside had been purified with cedar smoke, female visionaries lined up outside the door behind a senior woman flanked between two gifted men. When all were ready, these men called out "*kwiya*" and the women responded "*Haaay*" 12 times, indicating that they were prayerful. The east door flap was raised, the Geese beat the drum, and the women marched in as everyone held up their right hands and the men cried "*Hoooo.*" Each woman then recited in turn, alternating chanted lines with sung verses, accompanied by a male visionary dancing beside her on the inside near the center post. The drummers echoed their remarks, rather wary because they were less familiar with the women's songs. Adults followed them on their circuit, with the line of women near the post and that of men near the walls. In other words, except for the paired reciters (woman outside and man inside), men resumed their inclusive position on the outside, and women their exclusive one on the inside.

Since the sky was a manly realm, the arrival of the women from the outside took the assembly back to earth. According to the legend of the Pleiades boys, their frantic parents and other villagers threw soiled female undergarments (or menstrual pads) at the rising youths. When one was hit, he fell back to earth. Eventually, only seven remained in the sky, rising ever higher until they became the stars known as the "bunched together ones" (Pleiades). Accordingly, women and objects associated with them did not belong in the sky. Menstruation could be particularly damaging to men and the cosmic order, not because it was polluting but rather because it had a contrary power of its own.

By entering the Big House and reciting, these women both served to give thanks to the Creator and to restore the normal order of women inside and men out. Female visionaries represented a transition in terms of the spatial arrangement of the genders lined up behind them. After the women recited, the host reasserted male priority by leading the final songs and prayers.

In the morning, while the host sang 12 songs while shaking the rattle, the ushers cleaned out the fireplaces and swept the floor. As the tenth song began, everyone stood in concentric rings facing inward, men outside and women inside, slowly moving toward the center post. For the twelfth song, all raised their left hands and shouted "Haaay," then "Hoooo."

Then everyone sat down while the ushers collected the prayersticks, passed out wampum beads, gave the deerskins to those elders previously designated, and distributed any remaining deer meat to relatives of the host and then to others while it lasted. When these activities were completed, the host called the ushers into the center and gave them a yard of wampum, which they took outside near the cooking fire and cut up into equal sections. Meanwhile, the host gave a long prayer to the Creator, especially lengthy because it thanked all aspects of the universe, ending with a fervent plea that everyone stay well through the coming year, when the next rite would repeat the prayer again. During the Munsee ceremony, twelve strands of wampum were used to pray for specific aspects of the universe, with a final one directed to the Creator.

At the end, filing out of the Big House, with all holding a few wampum beads in their mouths, everyone went beyond the meat pole to form a north to south line facing east, the agile kneeling and the elders standing up. All raised the right hand, and repeated the prayer word *"Hoooo"* ten times. For the last two prayers, the prayer words were passed from one end to the other, men at the south end shouting *"Haaay,"* someone in the middle calling *natanuk*[w] ("watch out"), and men on the north end responding with *"Hoooo."* For the twelfth prayer, the man at the north shouted *"Hooo"* and each neighbor in turn repeated it along the line until it reached the south end. The man in the middle called "watch out," and the last man responded by beginning the shout of *"Haaay,"* which passed along the line. After the word has been conveyed with pauses from person to person, north to south and back again, it reached the middle and the rite concluded for another year.

According to Speck (1931) these two sounds were the essence of prayer, so the use of *"Hoooo"* and *"Haaay"* was never random or arbitrary. The *"Hoooo"* was used more frequently, associated with the spiraled prayersticks, left hand, north, and sky. Presumably these striped sticks represent the sky layers, especially the upper branches of the world tree. The word *"Haaay"* was associated with women, plain prayersticks, right hand, south, and earth, particularly since the plain ones were subjected to greater restrictions when passed out.

The final concentric dance (called *lantkan*) toward the center post stood in marked contrast to the linear arrangements otherwise typical of the rite. Its name derived from the terms for "standard" (*lan-*), the root of Lenape, and "dance" (*-kan*). Modern Delaware describe it as the core of the rite, presumably ancient since it concentrated on the center post and restored the ordinary expectations of women inside and men out, moving toward a center, fusing men and women with the post that bridged earth and sky.

The singers themselves represented one of the most potent images of all, sitting behind the drum, exactly as the Creator was believed to sit eternally in heaven, directing the universe by his thoughts. Thus, the beat of the drum also evoked life and thought, whose pulse or rhythm was well represented in song. Throughout Native America, song was believed to be the purest expression of the supernatural since it was rhythmic, sensate, and intuitively understandable across species and locations.

In addition to symbolism within the rite, for the larger Delaware ritual context, the Gamwing itself was the culmination of a series of annual rituals, the responsibility of particular families and positions, gifted by appropriate *manituwak*. Now that such personal revelations have lapsed in Oklahoma, so has the transmission of rituals conducted by families.[63]

---

[63] Other tribes have solved this problem of acquiring guardian spirits in the modern world by making them inheritable in family lines. Many of the Salish communities in the Northwest do this today.

Image #10 ~ Nora and Lucy charting color terms
at Quapaw camps (by Jim Rementer)

# REFLECTIONS ~ 17

Increasingly over recent centuries, the Gamwing of the Delaware has been redeeming themselves and their culture as it increasingly assumed the primary role of giving thanks to their universe and all of its components. By fulfilling this national duty, Delawares were exemplifying the "good life" of connectedness and assuring their own salvation. As such, the rite provided the means for humans and other "persons" to interconnect so as to work together to renew the world by returning to primordial conditions when it was "thin" and interactions that much easier. These persons included a variety of beings, each with distinctive characteristics.

Visionaries reciting in the Gamwing, who lead in a variety of contexts, were known as the "gifted" because one or more of the beings called *mənituwak* decided to share a modicum of power (*mənituwakan*) with that human, either man or woman. In origin and outcome, this power is most identified with the pulsing thought of the Creator, spreading and returning in ripples and beams, which are further equated with light.

Moreover, this analysis of the history and religion of the Gamwing also emphasized the role of culture, which provided the logical circuitry, the boundaries and passages of taboos and tokens, that aligned the flowing of power among these interlinked persons (See Appendices). While power flows along the rings and rays of a web-like system, it is further constrained by the matrix of threeway contrasts. In other words, the rays are exclusive, the rings inclusive, and the nexus (tysic) at the center is inclosive, the source and summary of the power binding together this universe.[64]

For Delawares, this webbing is cone-shaped with the tysic at the peak, where the creator sits eternally in the twelfth and highest heaven. Skykeepers occupy each of the lower rings, maintaining communication with each other and the Creator, whose central link throughout this cosmos is the cedar tree growing on the back of the turtle floating in the sea, an image attested for four hundred years.

Today, as in the past, Delaware elders insist on the continuity of their culture, while recognizing that, as traditions passed out of everyday usage, they became ritualized within the Gamwing. Hence, the continuity of their past and of this ritual became mutually interdependent.

Because so much of Delaware culture, and its traditions, have been previously treated in piecemeal fashion (cut up and divided by topics and interests), a holistic approach, emphasizing a concern with religion, history, and culture, is necessary to understand the process whereby Delaware have survived against impossible odds.

Modern Delaware elders, like those of other tribes, often criticize young, inexperienced, or oblivious tribal members because they have selected names from past tribal rolls, used several colors of paint on their faces if women, put salt in food they brought to funeral feasts, or traced

---

[64] This model of power as like a spider web emerging and returning to the mind (heart) of a Creator is nearly universal in the Americas, though rarely reported (Miller 1980b: 1980c). Not surprisingly, among cooperative societies, the web was mostly flat, while among hierarchical societies, it was peaked into a cone. In all instances, the nexus was a tysic occupied by a Creator, whether man, woman, neither, or both.

descent and clanship through both parents. As should be clear, all these actions violated matrix relationships within the categoric inclosive, especially specific exclusive restrictions applying to Woman.

While such reinterpretations will long continue, especially as the obvious cultural inventory becomes depleted and its tangible emanations are further modified, it is important that these mistakes were compromises between those that are distinctively Delaware and those that are acceptable to white America. After all, living in a winter wikwam, taking scalps, or remaining monolingual in Lenape would be too extreme, disruptive, or uncomfortable for a Delaware to function in the modern world, despite strong romantic desires to return to traditions.

While ethnic Delaware viewed their acts as isolated ones, serving to validate their ancestry and personal worth, traditionalist elders saw them as parts of an intermeshing, consistent whole, whose totality was mocked by attention to details removed from proper context. As systems, they teach us about the human condition; while as diluted or dismantled remnants, they encouraged confusion. Yet, these attempts, however attenuated, express hope. Any effort can forge a new context and meaning, one more coherent than those provided by moribund or borrowed perspectives. Significantly, these efforts provide meaning for new continuities, and, thereby, reinvigorate Delaware culture. With only a center post and an oval dirt floor, the Delaware rebuilt a universe, not once but many times.

This contrast between cultural and ethnic Delawares, like that between the gifted and "empty," should not be overdrawn to indicate a perceived fragmentation of our common tradition. Rather, I would argue, it is not so much a shattering as a weakening of consistency. Certainly, the echo still informs the Delaware community, except that most Delawares, lacking fluency in Lenape or a traditional ritual life, remain unaware of its all-embracing reverberations. Overall, throughout Delaware history, the culture has been collapsing to generics with the loss of its specifics. The end result, therefore, is not "shreds and patches," but foundations.

In the final summing up, after half a millennium, therefore, Delaware culture has been stripped to its essentials, leaving at its heart the personal core of Turtle and Tree, Man and Woman, and, most of all, Our Creator.

Appendix **A**

# DELAWARE ALTERNATIVE CLASSIFICATIONS ~ 18

This article is intended to augment the extensive literature on Delaware (Lenape), and more generally Algonkian, species designations and taxonomies which has been developing over the past two centuries. After a review of the earlier sources and my own fieldwork, I will present eight classifications of taxonomies by form, habitat, color, movement, sound, use, relationship, and appearance. Finally, the regularities found in these classifications and taxa will be discussed. Throughout the paper 'classification' will refer to a collection of taxa sharing at least one attribute in common and 'taxon' will refer to a class or group of individuals and species presumed by Delaware speakers to be related.

Concern with Delaware ethnoscience can be said to have begun with Peter Kalm, a student of Carl von Linne, sent to America by the Swedish Academy of Sciences in 1747 to record Delaware plant usage (Herman 1950: 46). A long list of Delaware biological terms was recorded by David Zeisberger in his diary of 1781 (1910) and appeared in his dictionary (1887). However, by this time the Delaware had left their East Coast homeland and the new Ohio ecology may have altered some of the species terminology but probably not the taxa. In a letter, John Heckewelder (1876: 399-400) included four words that continue to serve as form taxa: gook from /xkuk/ <u>snake</u>, names from /nʌamɛs/ <u>fish</u>, chum from / -xʌm/ <u>animal</u>, and wehellen from / -ehəle / <u>bird</u>. Modern field workers can appreciate the frustrations that Heckewelder (1876: 319) experienced in collecting such terms:

> Whenever I found the Indians disposed to attend to my enquiries, I would point to particular objects and repeat my formulary, and the answers that they. gave I immediately wrote down in a book which I kept for the purpose; at last, when I had written about half a dozen sheets, I found that I had more than a dozen names for "tree," as many for "fish, " and so on with other things, and yet I had not a single generic name. What was still worse, when I pointed to something, repeating the name or one of the names by which I had been taught to call it, I was sure to excite a laugh; and when, in order to be set right, I put the question....I would receive for answer a new word or name which I had never heard before.

Unlike Heckewelder however, most observers concentrated on species names. Many of these species names are included in a Delaware dictionary assembled from various sources by Brinton and Anthony (1888). Chamberlain [p435] (1901) included some Delaware species in his discussion of Algonkian animal names. Most recently, Mahr (1949, 1954, 1959, 1960, 1961, 1962) has subjected all of the biological terms recorded by Zeisberger to analysis by historical and comparative linguistic methods in order to produce a semantic analysis which showed that each name reflected the particular use of the species. In other words, he gives utilitarian reasons for many of the species names. Speck (1931, 1937) included species and taxa names in some of the texts he recorded from Charles Webber. However, some of these terms are unknown to my sources and others they translate differently. Tantaquidgeon (1972) and Hill (1971) discuss Delaware plant usage. Weslager (1973) summarized information on Delaware herbal use for a popular audience. But all of these sources group the species by English and not Delaware classifications.

The details of the eight classifications about to be presented have been worked out with Mrs. Nora Thompson Dean, a most meticulous, knowledgeable, and concerned speaker of the Unami dialect of Delaware. Many of the terms she gave me have been checked with Mrs. Lucy Parks Blalock, a fluent and careful speaker of the same dialect.

I began the research in 1972 by asking Mrs. Dean every term that seemed biological in the Zeisberger and Brinton-Anthony dictionaries. Although a start, the procedure was largely unrewarding. Beginning with the few words she substantiated, I expanded the list by asking for analogies and contrasts for each term through correspondence and fieldtrips to northeastern Oklahoma. While in the field I could also listen to Mrs. Dean use the terms, ask her for the taxon and name of an animal we had just seen, and occasionally try to use an appropriate term myself.

In addition to Mrs. Dean and Mrs. Blalock, who both supplied terms and served to cross-check each other, some taxa were also checked with Edward Leonard Thompson, Tom Wilson, and Mrs. Anna Brown Parks. All of these Unami speakers are also fluent in English so that it was always possible to supply intuitively satisfying English equivalents for the Unami terms. While English and Unami speakers can recognize the same taxonomic distinctions, there seem to be important semantic differences behind the two systems. I will discuss the semantics of the Unami system in the conclusion.

While there is a phonemic system for Delaware (Voegelin 1946:130), 1 have chosen to present the forms phonetically using a transcription checked .by James Rementer to conform to one he has been using informally for the past ten years (Hill 1972: 17). His system is already familiar to several Unami speakers. Although length is phonemic in Delaware, I have tended to ignore it in the surface phonetics. The 1anguage also has an important inanimate/animate grammatical distinction, which can be clearly seen in plurals. The inanimate plural ends in a vowel, while the animate ends in a vowel and final /-k/. All taxa but <u>plants</u> /skiko/ are animate. Mrs. Dean has translated the single third person animate form as <u>one(s)</u> or <u>one(s)</u> who. Plurals are given in parentheses.

While I am unable to show the five or six taxonomic levels suggested [p436] by Berlin, Breedlove, and Raven (1973) for folk classifications generally, there are two terms, which serve as what they call a unique beginner, which subsume the eight classifications and their taxa. Mrs. Dean and Mrs. Blalock regard the two words as synonyms, however, persistent questioning revealed a fine distinction:

lehəlexɛt(čik) <u>alive one(s)</u> derived from the word for breath or breathing
pəmawsit(čik) <u>living one(s)</u>

The species and taxa under these unique beginners can have any of four attributes:

pənayltndamʌweit(čik)  <u>one(s) with the ability to think</u>

lixsuwakʌnit (čik)  <u>one(s) with language</u>

nthənitcanit(čik)  <u>one(s) who can reproduce themselves</u> which includes all form taxa but deities.

kãsɪləsit(čik)  <u>one(s) with spiritual power to do great things on earth</u>  These are mostly deities although some of this power can also be conferred on humans by specific deities.

Species and taxa might also possess both, one, or none of two spirits.  The first is a soul which resembles a spark and the second is a ghost which resembles a transparent skeleton.  The former journeys to the Creator after death and the latter remains on earth.  I refrain from giving the terms for these because they are sensitive to Delaware traditionalists.

The Delaware seem to recognize at least eight alternative classifications based on form, habitat, color, movement, sound, use, relationship, and appearance.  These will now be described.

Form:  ɛlhʌkat(čik) or ɛlčɛsit(čik)  <u>their shape(s)</u>, is the primary classification of living things among the Delaware, as it is in all folk taxonomies.  It is divided into seven major taxa.

A.  manitu(ʌk)  <u>deities</u>  As a group they are immortal, have the ability to alter things and events by their thoughts, can confer powers on humans, and possess both a body soul and language.

kišelamukɔŋ  <u>the one who created us by his thoughts</u>, the Creator who alone can create things and events by his very thoughts.  He is described as eternally sitting in the twelfth or highest heaven.

mahtantu  <u>bad spirit</u>, the Evil One or Devil.

pɛthakhuwe(yok)  the <u>thunderer(s)</u>  Large birds with the heads of old or young men who live in the sky and control thunder and lightning.

məxaxkuk  <u>red snake</u>  An enormous, horned red snake who lived in the ocean until he was killed and pieces of him divided among various tribes as tribal palladia.

wewtunəwɛs(ʌk)  <u>drawer(s) under</u>.  Serpentine male spirits who live in all bodies of water.  They were born of a girl who neglected to cover her genitals when she bathed.

wemahtekənis  <u>all over the woods one</u>  A leather-clad man about three feet high who is very agile and lives wherever he can find a wooded area.  He confers powers of strength and stamina.

tehtɔŋələmhaləwes  <u>the one who leads people astray</u>, the will-o-the wisp. [p437]

mʌsingʷ  A bear-like being who is guardian of game animals and vegetation.

ɔhtas(ʌk)  <u>dolls</u>  These are represented by carved wooden dolls formerly inherited in certain families and believed to be alive.

ɔwiyalahsu  <u>a whirlwind</u>

kaoxən  <u>a cyclone</u> or <u>tornado</u>

manitutət(ʌk)  <u>little people</u>.  They are about a foot high and can either cause painful injuries or grant the power of great stamina or the ability to cure without the aid of medicines.

ilawənιtu <u>war spirit</u>, any comet.

<u>Jupiter</u>  (kečipənɛs) and <u>Mars</u>  (mʌxalʌŋw) might be considered deities but Mrs. Dean was not positive that they were.

ãsisktayɛsʌk  <u>bunched together ones</u>.  The Pleiades, who were originally seven Delaware boys lifted into the sky by their purity or innocence.

ɛlantuwiɛk<sup>w</sup> Vocative name for the four directional spirits.

    luwanʌntu  <u>Grandfather North</u>, who is closely associated with snow and icicles. When these are bothered, he sends more snow and cold weather.

    šawnaxawəš  <u>Grandmother South</u>.  Alternating warm and cold blasts of wind mean that South and North are trying out their powers.

    wɛhɛnjiopvŋ  <u>Grandfather East</u>.

    ehəliwsikakw  <u>Grandfather West</u>.


B.  awɛn(čik)  <u>person(s)</u>, having the attributes of thought, language, reproduction, soul, ghost, and bipedalism.


    Neutral Terms:

mɛxkeɔkəsit(čik)  <u>Red(s)</u>, subdivided by tribes

weɔpsit(čik)  <u>White(s)</u>, subdivided by European countries

nɛskəsit(čék)  <u>Black(s)</u>, not subdivided

wisawsit(čik)  <u>Yellow(s)</u>, not subdivided,


    Deprecating Terms:

awɛnhakɛ(ɔk)  <u>wild tribes</u> for Indians

šəwʌnʌkw(ɔk)  <u>salt person(s)</u> for Whites

səkahkolɛs(ak)  <u>black person(s)</u> for Blacks.


    Derogatory Terms:

ɔping<sup>w</sup> <u>opossum</u>,  literally <u>white face</u>, for Whites

kvmhɔkw(ɔk)  <u>cloud(s)</u> for Blacks.


Mrs. Dean also includes three characters from Delaware mythology within this taxon:


    hmuwe  A <u>giant</u> cannibal.

    məkihape  <u>pimply face</u>.  An orphan finally taken in by an old couple who watched him grow into a wise hunter and scout.

    wɛhixamukɛs  A humorous but wise man who is noted for the fact that he always took metaphors literally.

C. xʌskwim <u>corn</u>. Usually called Mother Corn, it possesses thoughts, a language, and a soul. Five species are named:

puhwɛm <u>white flour corn</u>

sɛhsapsiŋ <u>blue corn</u> [p438]

pisim <u>sweet corn</u>

pɛphɔksiŋ <u>popcorn</u>

šəwanʌhkwim <u>White Man corn</u>, <u>field corn</u>.

D. -xʌm <u>animal</u>, with the attributes of thought, reproduction, four legs and fur. Animals can take pity on people and ask deities to give these people powers. Some species (such as dogs, eagles, crows, otters) were singled out by Mrs. Dean as having languages, powers, and souls of their own.

awsit (čik) <u>wild one(s)</u>
    lənwexʌm(uk) <u>male animal(s)</u>
    xkwexʌm(uk) female <u>animal(s)</u>
        nusexʌm (uk) <u>nursing female(s)</u>
    wəskxʌm(uk) <u>young animal(s)</u>
    kikexʌm (uk) <u>old animal(s).</u>
tkawsit(čik) <u>tame one(s)</u>
    lənuwexʌm(uk) <u>castrated male animal (s)</u>
    wɛlxus(ʌk) <u>intact male animal (s)</u>
      The rest of the terms duplicate those listed above under the awsitčik.

The list of the subtaxa of animals is as follows:

ayɛsəs(ʌk) <u>land mammal(s)</u> specifically, although the term can be stretched to
    include animals generally.
tahkox(ʌk) <u>turtle(s)</u>
xkuk(ʌk) <u>snake(s)</u>
kəkahtaliakwe(yok) <u>lizard (s)</u>
čahkol(ʌk) <u>frog(s)</u>
kaxkxʌkəs(ʌk) <u>toad(s)</u> literally <u>dry waist.</u>
nʌmɛ̌s(ʌk) <u>fish(es), sea mammal(s), shellfish(es)</u>
muxwɛs(ʌk) <u>bug(s)</u>
    piskewəni muxwɛsʌk <u>night bugs.</u>

E. -ehɩle <u>bird</u> is characterized by thought, reproduction, wings, feathers, and a language of their own. As noted above, some bird species can take pity on humans and ask deities to transfer powers to these people.

lənuwehɪle  <u>male bird (s)</u>
xkwehəle(yok)  <u>female bird (s)</u>
wəskihɪle(yok)  <u>young bird(s)</u>
kikehəle(yok)  <u>old bird(s)</u>.

Two bird subtaxa have been identified:

pale•(ok)  <u>fowl</u>, gallinaceous birds
čulɛ̃ns(ʌk)  <u>migratory</u> and <u>predatory birds</u>

piskewəni čulɛ̃ns(ʌk)  <u>night birds</u>, especially

kukhus(ʌk)  <u>owl(s)</u>
pipisilvŋɔn (ʌk)  <u>bat(s)</u>, literally <u>wrinkle wing.</u>

F.  hɪtukw (hɪtkuk)  <u>tree(s)</u> which have the attributes of thought, reproduction, kinship with the Delaware, leaves, and a language and powers of their own.  As the example of rosinweed indicates, Mrs. Dean seems to regard any plant over human height as a tree.  This taxon can be sub-divided on the basis of two suffixes:  [p439]

-akw  is used for trees with straight trunks that do not bear fruit, with the exception of peach trees.
kələkənikʌnakw  <u>common sumac</u>
puhwɛsənakw  <u>elderberry</u>
pkuwakw  <u>rosinweed</u>
xaxakw  <u>sycamore</u>
pilkəšakw  <u>peach tree</u>
-mɛ̃ši  is used for branching trees which bear fruit:
mwɪmɔ̃ši  <u>excrement tree</u>, wild black cherry

tɪtpanɪmɔ̃ši  <u>bitter nut tree</u>, hickory

ɔkhatimuši  <u>mulberry</u>

tʌkwimɔ̃ši i <u>round fruit tree</u>, black walnut.

G.  skikw (skiko)  <u>plant (s)</u>, <u>grasses</u>, <u>weeds</u>.  Except for <u>medicine plants</u>, this taxon lacks thought, language, and powers. Its attributes are ubiquity and being shorter than a human adult.  Mrs. Dean translates this label as <u>plants</u>, but acculturated speakers preferred the term <u>weeds</u>.  This label does in fact serve as the basis for the translation borrowing /skikwimiŋ/ <u>hayseed,</u> which is a term Delaware speakers apply to many rural Whites.  There are two subtaxa:

čəphɪk (a) <u>root(s)</u>
bisuni skiko  <u>medicine plants</u>, which have the ability to think, speak their own language, cure the sick, and alter events for good or evil.

The separation of corn, trees, and plants was consistently made by three Delaware speakers in each of two card sortings. I placed the species names given in the Hill (1971) ethnobotany on index cards. The Delaware word was written in black and the English translation in red; because of the eight colors named by the Delaware, these two are aesthetically and ritually preferred. Each speaker sorted the cards, first to divide them into whatever groupings they wished and, second, to place them in groups that had Delaware names. In both cases, each speaker distinguished corn and trees. Plants were also regarded as distinct but were always further sub-divided into root and medicine subtaxa. The category of 'food' also emerged in these sortings and eventually led to the use classification.

Species are placed in one of the following taxa on the basis of preferred or usual habitat, εndalawsitčik where they live, although an individual could be placed in another taxon during its appearance in a different ecological context from that it normally inhabited.

> hukweyuŋ εndalawsit(čik) one(s) who live above
>
> xkwithakamika εndalawsit(čik)  one(s) who live on the earth.  This form
> > alternates with the more literal form:  pəmhakamit(čik)  earth liver(s).
> > Both of these forms include the following:
>
> bi εndalawsit(čik) ones who live in the water
> > > bixʌm water animal, specifically whales.
> > > biyaehitle water bird
>
> tekəntŋ εndalawsitčik ones who live in the woods
>
> ε•kwi hakiŋ εndalawsitčik ones who live underground [p440]

Species are placed in the color taxa (εliksitčik  their colors) by their predominant color /likte/. Delaware colors are classified much like those j English, with these exceptions. Black tends to include the spectrum from dark purple to dark red. This means that Delaware colors tend to be slightly lighter than the English values. Yellow includes most of the orange shades. For example, /wisaɔpaltıs/ yellow apple means a Golden Delicious to Mrs. Dean but an orange to Mrs. Blalock. There are eight color taxa:

> mʌxksit(čik)  red one(s)
>
> səksit(čik)  black one(s)
>
> askaskwsit(čik)  green one(s)
>
> wisawsit(čik)  yellow one(s)
>
> aonsit(čik)  blue one(s)
>
> weɔpsit(čik)  white one(s)
>
> wipuŋwsit(čik)  grey one(s)
>
> čʌkingwεmiktεit(čik)  the color of pokeberry one(s), purple.

The movement classification, εlayhɔsitčik  their actions or movements, is limited to beings capable of movement, especially animals. Inclusion is based on the characteristic movements of the species. However, it is the particular movement that is important and as such an individual can be temporarily placed in an untypical taxon during its distinctive behavior.

pəmuxsit(čik)  crawler(s)

ɛlakihəlat(čik)  hopper(s) or jumper(s)

kənthwit(čik)  flier(s)

pəməsksɛt(čik)  walker(s)

ahkusit(čik)  climber(s)

lɛmbamehəlat(čik)  trotter(s)

kɛšamehəlat(čik)  runner (s)

ašuwihəlat(čik)  swimmer(s)

činktɛhwɛt(čik)  sunner(s), one sunning itself.

On several occasions while eliciting for the form classification, Mrs. Dean gave me the crawlers term as meaning reptiles (turtles, snakes, lizards, and toads). I think this is an instance of English affecting Delaware usage. However, by asking for analogies and contrasts for the crawlers this movement classification filled out, This may mean that Delaware terms with closer English equivalents have remained in use while those uniquely Delaware have faded from use but are not unrecoverable.

The placement of animals in the sound classification, ɛlixsitčik  their sounds depends first on their distinctive cries or sounds, although if a particular animal happens to be physically present it will be temporarily classed on the basis of its current utterances. A species might also overlap several taxa if it can make a range of sounds,

kənjimwit(čik)  crower(s)

məkikɛt(čik)  bark(ers)

məlimwit(čit)  crier(s), sobber(s), lower(s)

whulit(čik)  howler(s)

asuwit(čik)  singer(s)

The use classification, ɛli hnʌkalwəsitčik  the way they are used, [p441] emphasizes the possible usefulness of all or part of various species, especially of plants:

bison  medicine

mehʌmičiŋ  food

məneokʌn (a)  potables

wehupɔŋ  smokeables especially tobacco (kwsatay)

mɛhəmanitasik  that from which something is made, raw materials kwvlakʌn(a) forbidden or taboo one(s)

nučkwe  useless one(s).

In the relationship classification, ɛlʌəŋumʌtčik  our relatives, the Delaware have extended most of their lineal kinship terms with associations of authority to the natural and supernatural world:

muxomsənanʌk <u>our grandfathers:</u> tobacco, the Thunderers, fire, mʌsingw, male turtles, the male wooden dolls, whirlwind, and the directions north, east, and west. Also included are male bears together with water in large bodies or running free.

nuhʌmənanʌk <u>our grandmothers:</u> female turtles and bears, female wooden dolls kept formerly in certain families.

kahɛsɪnanʌk <u>our mothers:</u> corn, the earth, and water in wells, springs, or containers.

kuxəna <u>our father:</u> used only for the Creator

xãsəna <u>our elder brother:</u> the sun

nitis <u>male friend</u> with a male speaking: trees and medicines

ničus <u>my female friend</u> with a woman speaking: trees and medicines.

Mrs. Dean explained these terms for friend in the classification by saying that over time a friend comes to be considered a relative. Formerly friends of different sexes used sibling terms.

In the appearance classification, ɛl•inakwsitčik <u>the way they look</u>, we find taxa derived from surface coverings and physical features of the species. Because each taxon concentrates on a visual detail, species generally overlap several of them. The list of taxa remains incomplete because Mrs. Dean could not recall the term for <u>scaled ones:</u>

mikwənit(čik) <u>feathered one(s)</u>

wixʌwɛsit(čik) <u>furred one(s)</u>

olʌxʌkayit(čik) <u>skin shedder(s)</u>

xɛsit(čik) <u>hide skinned one(s)</u>

supsit(čik) <u>naked ones</u>: humans and worms

wipit•it(čik) <u>one(s) with teeth</u>

hwɪkʌšsit(čik) <u>one(s) with nails, claws, hooves</u>

wɛšəməwit(čik) <u>one(s) with tails</u>

kəmbʌhkwit(čik) <u>one(s) with leaves</u>

This then completes the description of the eight classifications and their representative taxa.

It now remains to find the regularities which characterize the Delaware taxonomic system. These are the recurrence of three contrasts, which are increasingly more general: <u>wildness</u> / <u>tameness</u> (awsuwakʌn / tkawsuwakʌn), <u>land</u> / <u>water</u> (Ø / bi), and <u>man</u> / <u>woman</u> (lenu / xkwe). [p442]

The wild/ tame contrast applies more to individuals and species than to taxa. The contrast is most obvious in the animal form taxa, but it can be extended to others. Tameness has more to do with frequent proximity to humans than with domestication. Wildness has to do with remoteness

174

or unfamiliarity to humans. For example, any animal kept as a pet or which is remarkably docile around humans is considered to be tame: bears are wild but a pet cub is tame, dogs are tame but a dog which shuns humans is wild, and while fish are wild, a goldfish is tame. Indian tribes distant from the Delaware are also considered wild. The Delaware concept of wildness is close to the English one, but that of tameness is broader than that of English speakers.

The land/water contrast applies to taxa and subtaxa. The land taxa are linguistically unmarked, while the water taxa are marked by the initial /bi/. While there are distinct terms for water animals and water birds, the word /bi/ can also be added to the names of other taxa, species and individuals providing that a preference or familiarity with water justifies the addition.

The most general contrast in Delaware taxonomy is that of man/ woman Every taxon of the Delaware either includes both male and female members or is recognized as consisting of only one sex; for example, Mother Corn. In fact, the man/ woman contrast can be considered the semantic core of the entire taxonomy. This is shown by an analysis of the words and concepts used by the Delaware. It is the terms that specifically mean man and woman which are used to express sex differences: /lənuwexʌm/ actually means man animal as /xkwehɪle/ literally means woman bird. In other words, the Delaware recognize 'living ones' by analogy to humans, specifically adult Delaware. After I had reached this conclusion, I found a similar observation made by Heckewelder (1876: 254):

> All beings endowed by the Creator with the power of volition and self-motion, they [the Delaware] view in a manner as a great society of which they are the head, whom they are appointed, indeed, to govern, but between whom and themselves intimate ties of connection and relationship may exist, or at least did exist at the beginning of time. They are, in fact, according to their opinions, only the first among equals, the legitimate hereditary sovereigns of the whole animated race, of which they are themselves a constituent part. Hence, in their languages, these inflections of their nouns which we call genders, are not, as with us, descriptive of the masculine and feminine species, but of the animate and inanimate kinds. Indeed they go so far as to include trees and plants within the first of these descriptions. All animated nature, in whatever degree, is in their eyes a great whole, from which they have not yet ventured to separate themselves. They do not exclude other animals from their world of spirits, the place to which they expect to go after death. (*emphasis original*)

The recognition that the animate refers to 'the powers of volition and self- motion' has recently also been made by Black (1969: 18) for the animate in Ojibwa, a related Algonkian language: "Movement, especially self-propelled, is the most heavily stressed feature in these [Ojibwa] reactions to gender choices in novel situations." The reference to the Creator is instructive since he is ultimately the source of all life and thought. The thoughts of the Creator are his most powerful attribute, possessed in lesser ability by deities, people, [p443] corn, animals, trees, and medicine plants. With thought seems to go the possession of spiritual powers. A proper regard for these powers requires the selective avoidance of reproduction, which is considered to be contaminating. This injunction specifically applies to humans since the rest of nature seems better able to control powers. Languages are also recognized for most taxa. While some use the Delaware language, others have their very own. However, I have the impression that with proper ritual preparation and intent, a human could be taught any and all of these languages by a sympathetic natural speaker. Many taxa also have a soul. While I have not given the actual Delaware word, it is important to note that it is derived from the Delaware name for themselves (lenape). Thus we can see a metaphorical human existing within these beings. As these data indicate Delaware adults did serve as the nexus or mediation of the animate world.

In addition to the classifications and taxa, Delaware speakers also recognize a few songs or sayings as characteristic of particular species. The sound of a cat purring is described in Delaware as təl, təl, etc., but the purring itself represents a sentence: "I killed a mouse this long (sɔkɛn pukwɛs nthəla)." The robin says "I have repeatedly sewn my former husband a breech cloth." The sound of the cry of horned owls is described as hu, hu, hu' but they are saying "Kweshkweletis will eat all of you (kwəškwəltis muhukuwa)" in order to frighten children. Blackbirds have a complete song, appropriate only for winter telling, that says they like to steal from fields and they feel strong all winter long. Weslager (1973: 75) reports a song from Mrs. Dean used to call rattlesnakes to do harm. Delaware traditionalists also have several sayings about the eating or behavior of chickens. For example, gizzards and eggs should not be eaten by the young, and if a hen crows it must be killed immediately. People are also told not to mock a crow or their quilts and blankets will burn up.

These are most of the examples told to me by Mrs. Dean, Mrs. Blalock, and Thompson. I conclude with them in order to show the richness of the folk biology still used by the Delaware.

## WORKS CITED #A

Berlin, Brent; Dennis Breedlove and Peter Raven  1973  General Principles of Classification and Nomenclature in Folk Biology.  AA 75: 214-42.

Black, M  1969 A Note on Gender in Eliciting Ojibwa Semantic Structures.  AL 11: 177-86.

Brinton, DG and A. S. Anthony  1888  A Lenape-English Dictionary.  Philadelphia.

Chamberlain, A  1901  Significations of Certain Algonquian Animal-Names.  AA 3: 669-83.

Harrington, MR  1921  Religion and Ceremonies of the Lenape.  Museum of the American Indian, Indian Notes and Monographs 19.

Heckewelder, J  1876  History, Manners, and Customs of the Indian Nations Who Once Inhabited Pennsylvania and Neighboring States.  Philadelphia.

Herman, M  1950  A Reconstruction of Aboriginal Delaware Culture from Contemporary Sources.  Kroeber Anthropological Society Papers 1: 45-77.

Hill, GA  1971  Delaware Ethnobotany.  Oklahoma Anthropological Society Newsletter 19 (3): 3-18.

Mahr, A

  1949  A Chapter of Early Ohio Natural History.  Ohio Journal of Science 49 (2): 45-69.

  1954  Aboriginal Culture Traits As Reflected in 18th-Century Delaware Indian Tree Names. Ohio Journal of Science 54: 6, 380-7.

1955  Eighteenth-Century Terminology of Delaware Indian Cultivation and Use of Maize:  A Semantic Analysis.  Ethnohistory 2: 3, 209-40.

1959  Practical Reasons for Algonkian Indian Stream and Place Names.  Ohio Journal of Science 59: 6, 365-74.

1960  Anatomical Terminology of the Eighteenth- Century Delaware Indians:  A Study in Semantics.  AL 2: 5, 1-65.

1961  Semantic Evaluation.  AL 3: 5, 1-46.

1962  Delaware Terms for Plants and Animals in the Eastern Ohio Country:  A Study in Semantics.  AL 4: 5, 1-48.

Speck, F

1931  A Study of the Delaware Big House Ceremony.  Publications of the Pennsylvania Historical Commission 2.  Harrisburg.

1937  Oklahoma Delaware Ceremonies, Feasts and Dances.  Memoirs of the American Philosophical Society 7.  Philadelphia.

Tantaquidgeon, G  1972  Folk Medicine of the Delaware and Related Algonkian Indians.  The Pennsylvania Historical and Museum Commission Anthropological Series 3.  Harrisburg.  (original 1942)

Voegelin, CF  1946  Delaware, An Eastern Algonquian Language in Linguistic Structures of Native America, edited by Harry Hoijer.  VFPA 6.

Weslager, CA  1973  Magic Medicines of the Indians.  Signet Books.  New York.

Zeisberger, D  1887  Zeisberger's Indian Dictionary, edited by E. N. Horsford.  Cambridge, Massachusetts.

1910  History of the North American Indian.  Ohio Archaeological and Historical Quarterly XIX: 1-2, 1-189, edited by A. B. Hulbert and W. N. Schwarze.  Columbus.

Originally published:

Anthropological Linguistics 17 (9): 534-544   1975

Appendix **B**

# DELAWARE ANATOMY ~ 19
## Linguistic, Social, and Medical Aspects

The members of any human society will vary with regard to their control and understanding of different areas of knowledge because of factors such as intelligence, interest, curiosity, and profession. Specialized careers in hunting, fishing, trapping, foraging, and farming will require detailed knowledge of relevant aspects of the natural world. However, it has been my experience both in fieldwork and in reading, that medical personnel generally possess a fuller understanding and comprehension of the system of folk science than most other members of their society. A career in a native medical system seems to require a more expansive view of the world than other, more economically oriented, careers.

But it is also the case that no feature of nature, biology, or general knowledge is ever accepted in its own right. Initially it must be something culturally recognized and thus incorporated into a logical system. One of the vital tasks of human culture and of the human mind is to filter human experience and to code empirical knowledge. Both the empirical knowledge and the logical system, as reflected in the psychological consequences of the training, self-assurance, and routine behaviors of specialists, contribute significantly to the confidence that others have in their effectiveness. Medical specialists in the native and the industrial worlds are particularly good examples of this.

While an important function of such specialists is to provide a systematic portrait of the order in the world, this order is already suggested by vocabulary items and sociolinguistic usages. As discussed by Brown and others (1976), this understanding takes the forms of taxonomies and partonomies. A taxonomy is a system based on the hierarchic inclusion of conventally named segregates (taxa), while a partonomy is a system based on a hierarchical relationship among inclusions (parta). McClure (1975), among others, distinguishes [p145] a taxonomy as typically characterized by 'kind of' relationships and partonomies as typically characterized by 'part of' relationships.

Miller (1975) has presented the complex taxonomy of all 'living or alive ones' preserved by the few remaining speakers of Unami Lenape or Delaware living in northeastern Oklahoma.[65] The taxonomy consists of eight overlapping classifications based on form, habitat, color,

---

[65] The Delaware or Lenape Nation originally occupied the valley of the Delaware River on the mid-Atlantic slope. They were divided into at least two political divisions: the Munsi in the north and the Unami in the south. A third group, sometimes called the Unalachtigo in the historical records, may have been further south than the Unami. Most Lenape had left the East Coast by 1700. Alter passing through Pennsylvania, Ohio, Indiana, and Kansas, the Unami settled north of Tulsa, Oklahoma. A splinter Unami group had joined the Caddo and adopted a Plains lifestyle in Texas before they settled near Anadarko, Oklahoma. Most Munsi fled to Canada and are presently located in several Ontario communities.

movement, sound or cry, use, kinship, and appearance; each of which are cross-cut by the contrasts of men / women, wild / tame, and land / water.

The present paper will present the comprehensive partonomy of anatomy as provided by a modern Unami specialist, Mrs. Nora Thompson Dean, and checked with another fluent speaker, Mrs. Lucy Parks Blalock. The primary referent is the human body, but some comparative terms referring to animals and plants will also be provided. My Lenape sources were also conscientious enough to discuss with me other linguistic, social, and medical applications which will be provided in separate sections.

Other anthropologists have remarked that modesty usually prohibits anatomical knowledge from crossing sex lines. Therefore, some discussion of my fieldwork and these Delaware data seems to be necessary.

Over the past five years, I have been increasingly more convinced that Mrs. Dean is the most articulate and knowledgeable source for things Delaware, at least in northeastern Oklahoma, if not also elsewhere. She is one of the last practicing herbalists. Earlier in her life, she worked as a health professional in a small Kansas clinic and then later in an Oklahoma old age home. Her even earlier interest in anatomy was the result of growing up on a farm, where she participated in the butchering of livestock. Her data were later checked with Mrs. Blalock, who is a fluent and careful Unami speaker, although not a native specialist.

The data were actually collected several times with different methods. The terms were first elicited in Lenape without careful attention to details. Later I collected as full a list of parta as possible, read them back to Mrs. Dean, and asked her to mark the location and limits of each term on diagrams of male and female bodies from a general health text xeroxed through the generosity of the Bartlesville Public Library and Mr. Gene Winn. Over the intervening winter, I improved my own knowledge of human anatomy and pathology before I analyzed the partonomy and returned to the field with an earlier version of this paper.

At that time, Mrs. Dean was ill and seeking several medical opinions. I had also recently been exposed to the dehumanizing and singularly uninformative role that Western medicine reserves for its patients. With these common experiences, our conversations would sometimes turn to medical topics. The slang and obscene uses of anatomical terms were known to me, but it was not until I found a list of them in the field notes of Frank Speck that I could comfortably raise the topic. Mrs. Dean had mentioned various of the social aspects several years previously. I reviewed them with her when we went over the final version of this paper. I was also able to ask specific question based on my knowledge of autopsies, only to learn that Mrs. Dean was unaware of some features of human anatomy: for example, the size [p146] difference of the lungs.

Several factors account for Mrs. Dean's willingness to ignore our sex differences and to provide me with Delaware anatomical knowledge. Among them are her general concern that the record on the Delaware be as accurate as possible, her clinical training in Western medicine, the age difference between us, and our own personal relationship of trust and kinship. As my clan mother, I sometimes address her by the Lenape term which literally means little mother but which is usually translated into English as aunt.

Mrs. Dean and I were initially concerned that someone might misconstrue the references to 'ringworm' and other diseases associated with uncleanliness or to obscenities, but we have decided that an accurate record, no matter how human, is preferable to an edited or a biased one.

As taxonomies are divided into taxon (taxa), so, following Brown and others (1976), the partonomy will be divided into parton (parta). Brown and others have argued that the general principles of biological folk classification presented by Berlin and others (1973) actually have the status of universal principles of classification. These can be used for such non-biological taxonomies as those for American 'automobile' and 'tool', for Finnish 'winter vehicle', for Thai 'spirit-ghost', for Huasteca 'male body', for the diagnosis of ' skin disease' among the Subanun of Mindanao, for 'beer' in Munich, and for the 'Bucket' or city jail of Seattle tramps.

These taxonomies and partonomies rarely exceed five hierarchical levels in depth. Berlin and others (1973) call these levels, in decreasing inclusiveness: unique beginner, life form, generic, specific, and varietal. Corollary with these levels are principles of nomenclature. The higher levels have 'primary lexemes' or unitary labels, which can be productive or unproductive. A productive primary lexeme can usually be linguistically analyzed or literally translated to show a category subordination. Unproductive primary lexemes can not be analyzed unambiguously. Lower levels have 'secondary lexemes', which can be analyzed as derivative of primary lexemes. Brown and others (1976: 75) provide this chart:

| HIERARCHIC LEVEL | TAXONOMIC CATEGORY | NOMENCLATURE STATUS |
| --- | --- | --- |
| Level 0 – L0 | Unique Beginner – UB | unanalyzable primary lexeme |
| Level 1 – L1 | life form – lf | productive primary lexeme |
| Level 2 – L2 | Generic – gn | unproductive primary lexeme |
| Level 3 – L3 | Specific – sp | secondary lexeme |
| Level 4 – L4 | Varietal – vr | |

While we must be extremely cautious in using these categories for fear of skewing or biasing or forcing the data, I will accept them as heuristic devices to be accepted or rejected on the basis of available data.

For example, my finished partonomy was compared to the paper on Delaware anatomical terms by Mahr (1960), who painstakingly used the dictionary composed by the Reverend David Zeisberger in about 1782 as the source for his etymologies of anatomical parta in conjunction with his general interest in semantic analysis. While many of my parta also occur in Mahr, indicating a long time depth for the Unami terms, the entire body of Zeisberger terms appears to me to be a hopeless jumble of several Delaware [p147] dialects and inept transcriptions. Mahr also errors in imposing English (and German) categories on the Delaware system. For example, Mahr (1960: 5, 6) assumed the Lenape recognized only five senses and divided the body parta into head and neck, trunk and extremities, and internal organs. I also find unlikely (1960: 26) his conclusion that several etymologies indicate that the Delaware had an ideal model of the human body as squatting and bent forward. Mrs. Dean told me she visualizes the human body as standing with arms at the sides. On the other hand, Mahr is correct with both his observations that the heart is the seat both of human emotion and of human reasoning (1960: 6) and that "Hunters as they we re, the Delaware frequently cut open an animal, thus becoming acquainted with the various tissues and substances of the mammalian body; and also with the fact that these were essentially the same in the body of man (sic)" (1960: 2). Both of these observations accord with my field data.

For reasons discussed below, each Lenape parton is given in the singular with the plural in parenthesis). English translations will usually be given in the singular. Delaware has a very important animate / inanimate grammatical distinction best seen in plurals. Inanimate forms are linguistically unmarked, ending with a vowel in the plural; while animate forms are marked by a final -k in addition to the plural vowel ending. Delaware also has only one third person form, which I will translate as <u>someone</u> or <u>someone who</u> for the animate and as <u>something</u> or <u>it</u> for the inanimate.

1.  L0  hɔkay(a) <u>body</u>
    LI  wil  head
        L2  təm(bʌ)  <u>brain</u>
           xayʌndep(a)  <u>scalp</u>, not to be confused with manukɔla  <u>someone was</u>
      <u>scalped</u>
           L3  milʌxk (mixɛkɛna)  <u>hair</u>
               ɔlɛkʷ  <u>dandruff</u>
           lawxkalay  <u>forehead</u>
           hwɪtawk(a)  <u>ear</u>
           wəškiŋʷ(ɔ)  <u>face</u>
               mamawn(a)  <u>eyebrow</u>
               weškiŋʷ (ɔ)  <u>eyes</u>, the <u>face</u> term seems to have
                  replaced an archaic form nataɛpi(a)  literally,
                  <u>something for looking,</u>

           L4  rnilxiŋɔn(a)  <u>eyelash</u>
             biŋ čan(a)  <u>eyeball</u>
               L5  məlišeŋɔkʌn  matter in the eye
                  səpiŋ (o)  <u>tear</u>, literally, <u>sap from the eyes</u>
              wanʌnuw(a)  <u>cheek</u>
              hwikiyɔn(a)  <u>nose</u>
                 sʌnikʷ  <u>snot</u>, <u>nasal mucus</u>
                 kwəskwɪnɛ  <u>to sneeze</u>
      3L  tun(a)  <u>mouth</u>
        4L  šetun(a)  <u>lips</u>
          wilanu(wa)  <u>tongue</u> [p148]
             kɛhkəndakhwikʌn  <u>uvula</u>, literally,

something that pushes
5L sukwinakʌn(a) <u>spit</u>, <u>sputum</u>
kɔxsəma to <u>snore</u>
kšapaɛ to <u>yawn</u>
pɔikham to <u>hiccup</u>
muxkčila to <u>belch</u>
dušəwilɛxɛ <u>I gasp</u>, <u>irregular respiration</u>

wipit(a) <u>tooth</u>
ɛnda tuŋanikea• <u>incisors</u>, literally, <u>where my teeth are</u>
<u>small</u>
ɛnda•hkin•anikea• <u>canines</u>, literally, <u>where my teeth are</u>
<u>sharp</u>
ɛnda pahk•anikea• <u>molars</u>, literally, <u>where my teeth are</u>
<u>flat</u>
6L ɔlanike <u>cavities</u>, literally, <u>someone has holes in</u>
<u>the teeth</u>
tawmbikʌn(a) jaw
witunay(a) <u>whiskers</u>, <u>insect antennae</u>
hwɪkwi(a) <u>chin</u>
xkwɛk•ʌŋʌn(ʌk) <u>neck</u>
k̊ʷəndakʌn(a) <u>throat</u>
1L tuhwɛpi (a) <u>trunk</u>
2L nikani tuhwɛpiŋ <u>front of the trunk</u> (grammatical form not in common
use)
3L tulhay <u>chest</u>, a triangular area with its base at the neck
and apex in the upper belly region
4L tulhaixhʌn(a) <u>sternum</u>, literally, <u>chest bone</u>
3L nunakʌn(a) <u>breasts</u>, literally, <u>milk bone</u>, also occurs as
a bound form -nɛ
xkelixʌn(a) <u>rib</u>, <u>side</u>
ahsiluŋɔn(a) <u>armpit</u>
təlamʌŋʌn(a) <u>shoulder and upper arm</u>
naxk(a) <u>forearm and hand</u>, from elbow to finger tips
4L wiskɔn(a) <u>elbow</u>, an exclusively human parton
mayayələnj(a) <u>right hand</u>, literally, <u>true, exact</u>
<u>hand</u> [66]

---

[66] When I began fieldwork in Oklahoma, none of the six fluent Unami speakers could remember
the term for the right hand. The term I was given translated as "not left." Then, in a series
of visits between Anadarko Delaware and the Unami, during which words and cultural data
were exchanged and shared, this word for the right hand was reintroduced from Anadarko.

amɛmʌndələnj(a) <u>left hand</u>
5L ɛnda siak̊ʷələnj(a) <u>finger</u>, literally, <u>where my
hand splits</u>
6L kitələnj(a) <u>thumb</u>, literally, <u>big finger</u>
7L kithuk̊ʷələnj(a) <u>palmar aspect of
thumb</u>
lɛlawələnj(a) <u>middle finger</u>
mɛkələnj(a) <u>pinky</u>, literally, <u>last
finger</u>
hwikʌš(a) <u>nails, hooves, claws</u>
8L lənapeokʌni sʌhkihələnj(a) <u>lunula</u>, literally, <u>soul
finger</u>. These are the lighter semicircles at the base of the
nails, which are closely watched as [p149] the more faded
they are, the sicker someone is until they disappear at death.
mutay(a) <u>belly, stomach</u>
4L wilhwi <u>navel</u>, an area with a two inch diameter
pɛhpamapisia my <u>waist</u>, also the bound form -hakɛ
as in xiŋhɔkɛ <u>pregnancy</u>, literally, <u>big waist</u>
2L ʷtɛŋ tuhwɛpiŋ <u>back of the trunk</u> (grammatical form not in common
use)
3L upxkɔn(a) <u>back</u>, also occurs as the bound form -ipxkone, includes
from the back of the neck to the base of the spine.
4L dəki <u>shoulder blade area</u>
ɔwikan(a) <u>spine</u>, <u>backbone</u>
5L pəpek̊ʷsu(ʌk) <u>kidney</u>, because it is attached to the
spine.
sukʌn(a) <u>lower back</u>, <u>small of the back</u>
2L lamuŋwi tuhwɛpiŋ <u>inside of the trunk</u> (grammatical form not
in common use)
3L tɛh(ak) <u>heart</u>
hopʌn(a) <u>lung</u>
mutay(a) <u>stomach</u>, <u>bowels generally</u>, for humans and most
animals. The <u>stomach of a pig</u> is hɔkahtɛs and <u>cow tripe</u> is
winaxaxkay.
4L wɛlʌkši (a) <u>intestines</u>
xɔy (a) <u>spleen</u>
xkwən (a) liver
wishwitakʌn (a) <u>gall bladder</u>, literally, <u>bile container</u>
5L wishwi <u>bile</u>. A Delaware wrote to the anthropologist Frank
Speck (APS: 932) to say that deer do not have a gall bladder and as
a result sleep only once a year. Actually, however, while deer do
lack a gall bladder, they sleep quite regularly.

1L ɛnda tahčǝsia <u>crotch</u>, literally, <u>where I am divided</u> (ɛkɔktiɛ under the
buttocks is a slightly vulgar form, not used in mixed company)

2L wixa (wixʌk) <u>pubic hair</u>

škitakʌn (a) <u>bladder</u>, literally, <u>urine container</u>

3L škɪh <u>urine</u>

lǝxutakʌn(a) <u>scrotum</u>, literally, <u>testicle container</u>

lǝxu(ak) <u>testicles</u>, in Unami slang: hopǝnis(ak) <u>potato.</u>

škiyɔn(ak) <u>penis</u>, in Unami slang: sikhay <u>salt</u> and kɛkunǝm(a)
<u>someone's thing</u>. Related terms are nipʌhtasu it has been made to
stand erect and nipʌhta someone has an <u>erection</u>. Goddard (1974:
175 #35) lists <u>Jew's harp</u> as Munsi Delaware slang for penis.
Brinton-Anthony (1888: 81) list mengwe <u>foreskin</u> but this term
has lapsed except as a designation for the enemy Iroquois people.

spǝlaš semen [p150]

ma•x(ak) <u>female genitalia</u>, including the vulva, vagina,
womb.

kɛkunǝm(a) literally <u>someone's thing</u> used in slang.

min(a) <u>clitoris</u>, literally, <u>berry</u>

alawixǝnǝwakʌn <u>menstruation</u>, literally, <u>can not</u>
<u>cook</u> (an abstract state)

1L hwikat (a) <u>leg</u>, from hip to ankle

2L pom(a) thigh, ham

3L wasiti(a) buttock

4L sputi anus, with the bound form -šɛti

5L mwičti <u>feces</u>, with the shortened to form mwih
and the bound form –či(a).

5L pukti <u>fart</u>, <u>flatus</u>

6L piskḱᵂti <u>silent fart</u>, literally, <u>like a</u>
<u>night hawk</u>

2L gǝtuǩᵂ (ǩᵂǝntkuʌk) <u>my knee</u>, exclusively human parton

wiču(ʌk) <u>calf</u>

hnikxkɔn(a) <u>shin</u>

ɛnda tʌŋk•ata• <u>ankle</u>, literally, <u>where my leg is small</u>

1L sit (a) foot

2L ʌŋɔn (a) heel

ɛnda kɛntsita• <u>where the ball of my foot is</u>

ɛnda pʌksita• <u>where my sole is</u>

ɛnda puksita• <u>where my foot bends or breaks</u>, <u>instep</u>

ɛnda siaǩᵂsita• <u>where my foot splits</u>, <u>toes</u>

3L kithukwɛsit(a) <u>big toe</u>

4L hwikʌš(a) <u>nails</u>, <u>hooves</u>, <u>claws</u>

1L lamuŋwi hɔkay(a) <u>inside of the body</u> (grammatical form not in common use)

2L ʷčɛt(a) <u>muscle</u>

hatəs(a) <u>ligaments</u>, <u>tendons</u>

wilsu <u>fat</u>

mukəm(ʌk) <u>blood vessels</u>

    3L mɛxkilək mukəm(ʌk) <u>aorta</u>, literally, <u>biggest vessel</u>

    xkʌn(a) <u>bone</u>, with the bound form: -ikʌne. The word for skeleton will not be given for religious reasons. The word also refers to ghost and to mention it is to 'make the spirits cry' and may even draw someone from the afterworld to cause the death of a loved one.

        pahkʌsun <u>marrow</u> (no plural)

2L tšpʌtke•ɛk <u>joint</u>, literally, <u>place of separation</u>

hmuk̃ʷ <u>blood</u>, itself a spirit which leaves the body at death to form a spheroid which wanders the earth forever.

lənapeokʌn <u>soul</u> or <u>body spirit</u>. The most powerful medical specialists have seen it as a spark or a miniature person. Death is caused when this soul leaves the body.

čičʌŋʷ(a) <u>image</u>, a word used by Christian missionaries to refer to souls of converted Delaware. Mrs. Dean and Mrs. Blalock know this as the word for <u>mirror</u>. [p151]

1L kɔtčʌmiŋ hɔkay(a) <u>outside of the body</u> (grammatical form, uncommon use)

    2L xɛs(a) <u>skin</u>

        3L milʌxk (mixɛkɛna) <u>hair</u>

        taptiksəwakʌn <u>sweat</u>

These Delaware parta conform to the principles of nomenclature outlined above, even with the occasional six or seven levels of depth. More generally, these terms bear upon two linguistic considerations: our understanding of the animate / inanimate distinction and the sociolinguistic use of insults.

In one sense, the animate / inanimate distinction is suggestive of the taxonomy / partonomy contrast. As a general rule, animate forms refer to wholes and inanimate ones to parts or to pieces. Yet a closer look at the anatomical parta show that some of these have animate plurals: <u>body</u>, <u>neck</u>, <u>knee</u>, <u>calf</u>, <u>pubic hair</u>, <u>penis</u>, <u>testicles</u>, <u>female genitalia, heart</u>, <u>kidney</u>, and <u>blood vessel</u>. Miller (1975: 442), following Heckewelder and Black, has argued that the animate specifically refers to the ability of self-motion or self-propulsion. These parta further strengthen this contention. While the entire body is self-propelled, the means of propulsion seems to be localized in the lower leg. As Mrs. Dean told me, the Delaware words for <u>leg</u> and <u>foot</u> apply to both people and animals, while those for <u>elbow</u>, <u>knee</u> and <u>ankle</u> apply only to humans. Of these, the animateness of the <u>knees</u> seems to be particularly related to their ability to mobilize the entire body. Similarly the <u>neck</u> has the ability to move the <u>head</u>. The animateness of the <u>genitals</u> seems also to be related to movement and the creation of life. Mahr (1960: 46,45) saw the Delaware for testicles as "primarily meaning moving inside the body, by means of breath, [which] quite naturally presented itself as the perpetual slow- rhythm up-and-down movement of the testicles in the scrotum." His etymology for <u>female genitalia</u> is "copulating (movement) device." The muscular action of the penis seems related to its animateness. Pubic hair is probably animate because of its proximity to the genitals. The animateness of <u>kidneys</u> and of <u>blood vessels</u> seems to be related to their contiguity with the blood spirit and the beat of the pulse. The <u>heart</u> is animate because of the heart beat, especially obvious during the butchering of freshly killed animals.

In short, the animateness of these parta seems to be related to the rhythmic actions of breath, blood, and muscle in the body. White medicine attributes much of this rhythmic mobility to muscular action, even of the testicles; while the Delaware seem to regard this and all mobility as the ultimate result of willful action on the part of spiritual entities, such as the mind and the soul.

There is an unconfirmed but general impression that Native American languages lack either proverbs or profanity. While I can say nothing about proverbs, the Delaware version of profanity is related to the domain of anatomy.

A Delaware named Charlie Webber wrote to Frank Speck (APS: 1178) that profanity was an ancient practice for the Delaware among people who had not [p152] been properly raised. Mrs. Dean also said that a woman should not use profanity while her father was alive out of respect for him. This helps to explain why the old women were especially noted for their frequent use of profanity or obscenities. Nevertheless, the constant use of profanity was said to cause a disease called məli• hukwɛni (a ring of pus around the neck). Unlike other American Indian languages, such as Nootkan and Kwakiutl of the Wakashan stock, which derive their terms of insult and profanity from besmirching someone's pedigree or from wishing them dead in creative ways, Delaware insult by using anatomical terms. As with English, Delaware pejoratives are explicitly genital and, thus, are better described as obscenities rather than profanities. Many are sex specific:

čitkɔle  <u>shut up testicles</u> said by one male to another male
čitkoxa  <u>shut up vulva</u> by female to female
čitkwəšɛtia  <u>shut your anus</u> by either sex to either sex.

Other obscenities were supplied to Speck (APS: 1178) by Webber. These were reviewed and transcribed with the help of Mrs. Dean. She felt that some of them may have been Munsi and not Unami forms.

mwialahkay  <u>excrement penis</u>, said by male to male
sputalʌkai  <u>anus be damned</u>, said by female to female
sput•ax  <u>anus vulva</u>, usually female to female, but sometimes by either sex to
   either sex
malʌštiye  <u>sticky anus</u>, <u>syrupy buttocks</u>, a general purpose exclamation.

Mrs. Dean also supplied other exclamations:

Wah  expresses surprise
kɛsa  exclaimed at hearing or seeing something nasty
puxɔ•  for an obnoxious smell
pʰwit  conveys a strong sense of disbelief, a stronger form of 'hogwash'
awɛ•  expresses pain or being tired

Positive expressions include

pιsi  yes, certainly
ɛ̃ɛ̃•  yes
xιta  it must be

Negative expressions include

ku  no
mata  no, not
ku tha  no
ku nəlɛ•  not true
mata nəlɛ•  not so

In all then, while Lenape have many exclamations which convey a range of meanings, the most concrete and specific choices available are those which are anatomical and specifically genital.

While Lenape speakers of the present generation lack an integrated system of folk physiognomy, certain features of anatomy are singled out for personality and character assessment. These are most important in the selection of marriage partners. [p153] A Delaware intent on marrying a full blood Indian woman was cautioned to inspect her as circumspectly as possible for the following features:

eyelids — the more epicanthic fold, the more Indian.
ear size — if she has small ears, she is stingy.
wrist — examining the wrist will show whether she is a virgin.
neck length — the more Indian, the shorter the neck.
underarms — a full blood will have no underarm hair.
waist — a full blood will have no distinct waist.
rump size — the more Indian, the straighter the line of the back.
second toe — if this is the longest toe (a Morton' s toe), she can't be dominated.
body hair — the less, the more Indian.
general appearance — she should be seen before she has had time to fix herself
         up, 'before breakfast'.

A Delaware intent on a full blood husband should check

> eyelids — for epicanthic fold
> ear size — for stinginess
> musculature — the more smooth and slight, the more Indian
> body hair — the less, the more full blood
> ability — especially hunting ability depending on keen sight, hearing, and stealth

In addition, older Delaware remember expressions which equate characteristics of a person's mouth and voice with his or her genitals. For example, a woman with a high, squeaky voice is said to have a mattery genitalia.

Further, there is a general belief that a high forehead betokens considerable intelligence. This belief was taken seriously enough that formerly when tribal chiefs and elders met in council, each would shave his hairline back a few inches.

In the realm of traditional Delaware medicine, we can see the applied as well as the classificatory functions of Delaware folk science, especially as it relates to anatomy. Health and disease are relative concepts, very much depending on cultural considerations. Anthropologists and Delaware are well aware of this fact and so divide traditional Delaware medical practice and hygiene beliefs from those of Whites. White or Western medicine is only now beginning to generally realize this relativity.

An English physician has written "We utilize the concept of disease as if this notion has substance. However, in the final analysis disease has no existence outside the bodies of those that suffer from it, and the primary obligation of medical practitioners is to ameliorate the patients' illness, combating the disease being only a second-order function" (Wood 1970: 23). More philosophically, Kleinman (1974: 212) has said "Since Plato, there has been a persistent and more or less unspecified ideal in the West of an anthropological medicine, a kind of medical science and practice that would be concerned unashamedly with such problems as human nature and other Critical aspects of philosophical anthropology, a medical science conceived [p154] in radically human terms, just as medical systems have traditionally been structured, and taking its place as an essential part of the human sciences."

Delaware perceptions of Western medicine have changed over time. Most Delaware I talked with said that White doctors were initially called kɛhkitənikɛs someone who hurts you (in diagnosis). Later they were called wɛlamʌlsuhalwɛs someone who makes people feel well, although this term was not limited to White practitioners. When most Delaware had learned to speak English, the term daktəl was substituted. Since the Lenape language has no /r/ sound, daktəl is an approximation of the English word 'doctor'. Even now, traditional Delaware will still use the term daktəl with a blend of nostalgia and jest. Those who still remember the old Oklahoma daktəls have remarked to me that while White medicine has increasingly refined its chemical and cosmetic techniques, it has also decreased its psychologically comforting abilities. Older Delaware particularly object to the vagueness and seeming indecision with which modern daktəls deliver their diagnosis; a vagueness which seems to be necessitated by the increase in malpractice suits. Even so, Delaware have told me that adequate White medical care requires that the daktəl be a personal friend or be personally interested in the case. (I originally assumed that this opinion was linked to indigent considerations and the ministrations of the Indian Health Service. However, it seems to be a more generally American phenomenon in that most of my younger, and some of my older university colleagues hold the same opinion.)[67]

The Delaware recognize a category of diseases (šəwanʌkwi lʌŋələwakʌn) introduced by Whites and as such best treated by a daktəl. These include contagious or epidemic diseases:

šəwanʌhkwi lʌŋələwakʌn  White person disease

      təspehɪleɔkʌn  small pox

      maxkpehlɪleɔkʌn measles

      apčihɪleokʌn  whooping cough

      ɔxukɔŋələnwakʌn  tuberculosis

      mahčʌŋələwakʌn  venereal disease

In addition, the Delaware recognize other diseases, such as poison ivy, which occur among Whites hut not among Indians.

Except for herbal lore, the traditional Delaware medical system has almost fully lapsed at present. Hence, Delaware suffering from the more severe traditional diseases, such as witchcraft, must seek cures from specialists in other tribes. Creek and Cherokee doctors are said to be especially effective. Creek patients, however, seem to prefer Shawnee doctors. The surviving Delaware herbal lore has been discussed by Tantaquidgeon (1972), Hill (1971), and Weslager (1973). Most of the older Delaware still remember parts of the traditional medical system. Mrs. Dean has the most complete memory of the system I have found.

Delaware traditional medicine had a religious justification, expressed as the power of animals and plants to cure or to harm people. The powers of these creatures derive directly from the various deities (manituʌk) and ultimately all power derives from the Creator, 'The One Who Created Us By His Thoughts'. Various substances, especially menstrual blood and human [p155] hair, can also be put to evil purposes.

Paralleling this hierarchy of access to supernatural power are levels of medical specialization. Every Delaware had some hereditary herbal or curative knowledge of the sort that Americans call 'home remedies'. These are usually some sort of laxative (ɛhɛšikakwən).

---

[67] From one perspective, this statement hints that physicians can cure anyone if they really want to; but from another, it assumes that patients need the help of a concerned healer before they can begin their own recovery. It has been said that "any medical practice that is not actually harmful will relieve symptoms a good deal of the time, [making] it possible to avoid a fruitless discussion of whether singing and hallucinating are a more or less effective curing method than a belief in the Virgin of Lourdes or in little white pills" (Siskind 1973: 209, note 5). According to Weil (1972) the real culprit is not White medicine per se, but rather allopathic medicine because it is specifically concerned with the treatment of disease symptoms and not of individuals, with externals and not essences. Weil's cogent plea for a nonallopathic medicine seeking the etiology of disease and illness in mental states seems very compatible with the concerns of traditional Delaware medicine.

Higher levels of specialization require 'being gifted' by a guardian spirit or partner. There were three grades of specialization. The first was the herbalist: wathakɛs(ʌk) <u>someone who understands plants</u> (and their uses). The second was the <u>sweat doctor</u> nɛntpikɛs(ʌk), who cured a patient by using a sweat lodge (piməwakʌn) and various liquids, especially məlʌnčpe, a mixture of herbs that induces vomiting. At the highest level is the <u>Indian doctor</u> məteınu(wak) or mətexkwe(yok), from mətakʌn <u>hex, spell, curse</u> plus lınu <u>man</u> or xkwe <u>woman</u>. This was the real specialist, deriving his or her power and cures only from guardian spirits. Formerly, some training by a skillful and experienced predecessor may have been involved.

While the <u>power</u> (lantuwakʌn) itself is neutral, the Indian doctor could use it for both good or evil purposes. In addition to these specialists, and in contrast to those people who were <u>empty</u> (alʌxsu), there were Delaware who were gifted by a <u>guardian spirit vision</u> (lingwehəleɔkʌn) at puberty and who then concentrated this acquired power into a <u>medicine bundle</u> (bisuni wiɔhšun), consisting of metonymic items representative of the partner and its power, such as hides, pelts, claws, paws, beads, and plants. Some people also made <u>love bundles</u> (ehɔltuwi wiɔhšun) to influence the affections of others. Still others sought to benefit themselves with <u>witch bundles</u> (nučihwei wiɔhšun). There was also a very special class of visionaries who were gifted with the ability to cure without any aids at all (ahasuma). Sarah (Sally) Wilson Thompson, Mrs. Dean's mother, had this ability. What distinguishes most of these specialists, as a group, is their ability to <u>cause a cure</u> (gikɛyʌwakʌn(a), kikeha <u>you cure him</u>).

Delaware recognize several types of illnesses:

1ʌŋgələwakʌn(a) <u>disease of any severity</u>
    palsuwakʌn(a) <u>physical illness</u> or <u>sickness</u>
        palsuhalkʷən(a) <u>debilitating illness</u>, 'it makes one real sick'
        məšihəweɔkʌn(a) <u>contagious disease</u>
    sakomalsəwakʌn(a) <u>being in discomfort</u>
        pasahtayɛ• <u>someone with gas</u>
    mahtapasikʌn(a) <u>bad medicine</u>
    alawatəmweɔkʌn(a) <u>mental illness, loss of mental faculties</u>
    nučihəweokʌn(a) <u>witchcraft</u>
    mətakʌn(a) a <u>hex</u>

Witchcraft is held responsible for any unusual or chronic disease. Witches are called either nutčihweyok <u>pesterers</u> or nɛthənipapwisʌk <u>night travelers</u>. They were the owners of the witch bundles, among whose ingredients was a <u>bad thing</u> (mahči kɛko) which caused harm to people. The witch was motivated to cause this harm out of anger, jealousy, envy, hatred, or general nastiness. Witch bundles were passed down after the original Visionary composed them according to the instructions of a guardian spirit. [p156] Vital ingredients always include wampum, human hair, and the bones of a fresh victim. The tuition for learning witchcraft was always the death of a loved one. Instruction ran in family lines, but anyone could request to receive instruction provided they were willing to pay the fee of a human life. Sometimes, a witch would ask someone if they would like to learn witchcraft in order to get wealthy and provide another's life in payment.

Each of the vital ingredients has a justification. The wampum beads and strings convey a sense of the wealth and ill-gotten gains attributed to witches. The human bones, fresh and otherwise, convey a sense of the powers and successes of the witch. The human hair is related to the universal symbolism of body dirt outlined by Edmund Leach (1967: 1, 7, 103) in his seminal essay Magical Hair: Everyone takes it for granted that verbal expletives in almost any language derive their magical potency from association either with sexual or excretory function or with God. The theory propounded in this essay is that the magical power of 'body dirt' (including head hair) is of precisely the same kind…. Finally I have made the point that hair, as a separable part of the body, is not only a symbol of aggression but a 'thing in itself', a material piece of aggression." The hair in a Delaware witch bundle is of the same piece. It is a representation of the aggressive hostility of witches, complete with sexual overtones. Similar sexual overtones lie behind the reasoning that witchcraft was ineffective on Whites because they ate too much salt, which is also a slang term for penis.

Less chronic, but nevertheless fatal, diseases are caused by improper conduct. Proper conduct exemplifies the ideal Delaware life (pilawsəwakʌn) a clean, holy, chaste life; in contrast to niskawsəwakʌn: a bad, evil, promiscuous life. Dangers to the clean life include becoming physically or spiritually dirty through sexual relations and contact with menstrual blood (niskənəman), mistreating animals, and eating food which has been eaten or touched by animals. Cats are especially dangerous because they are said to have bad mouths (mahčətuna). Mistreated cats and other animals will sometimes cause boils filled with hair. Improper conduct at rituals or failure to perform them causes insanity and congenital malformations. "The cause of insanity is attributed to the failure of a family to perform certain inherited ceremonials" (Tantaquidgeon 1972: 7). Paralysis can result from encountering a ghost. A permanently twisted mouth (pimtun) results from tampering with a grave (təmaksuwakʌnike the place of the pitiful people) or eating in the dark.

Delaware recognize several diseases related to spiritual and moral pollution:

> mutələwakʌn defilement
> niskiha• to spiritually dirty someone
> matapaməweokʌn causing a relapse or worsening by looking at
>   someone after having sex or seeing a corpse
> šikɔndamən someone tasted or wanted the food so much that the
>   nourishment was taken out of it
> mikolahɛ a mother who makes a baby sick by not following the
>   post-partem correction or restrictions [p157]

Before discussing specific diseases of the body, it is important to note that a healthy Delaware individual has six senses localized in six organs:

pənaylɪndaməweokʌn <u>thinking</u>, in the heart
pəndaməweokʌn <u>hearing</u>, in the ears
nɛməweɔkʌn <u>seeing</u>, in the eyes
məlaməweokʌn <u>smelling</u>, in the nose
wtəndamaweɔkʌn <u>tasting</u>, in the mouth
aməndaməweɔkʌn <u>touching</u>, on the skin

Specific diseases or illnesses of the body include the following:

<u>body</u> hɔkay(a)

    šiomʌndəməweokʌn <u>general numbness</u>, <u>paralysis</u>
    šipənəsəwakʌn <u>numbness</u>
    mačihəleokʌn <u>relapse</u>
    mahk̑ʷisəweokʌn <u>swelling</u>
    maingaluk̑ʷ <u>gravitation</u>, <u>referred pain</u>
    kšɛlɛxeokʌn <u>fever</u>, <u>hot all over</u> (kšəlɛxin <u>someone has a fever</u>)
    nɛhənupəneɔkʌn <u>chills</u>
    winamʌndəmweokʌn <u>soreness</u>, <u>aching</u>
    kikitsuwakʌn <u>soreness</u>
    ahɛlindəmawakʌn <u>intense pain</u>
    wisʌhkamalsəwakʌn <u>extreme stinging pain</u>
    ɔhčipisuweokʌn <u>convulsions</u>, <u>epilepsy</u>
    nʌŋihaleokʌn <u>palsy</u>, <u>trembling disease</u>
    kiwsuwakʌn <u>drunkenness</u>
    šiomalsəwakʌn <u>weakness</u>
    hilusəwʌŋɛl <u>rheumatism</u>, literally, <u>old man' s disease</u>
    mɛtatʌməweɔkʌn dying of old age
    ʌŋəlawakʌn <u>death</u>

<u>head</u> wil

    wilinɛɔkʌn <u>head ache</u>
    sapʌleʌntpeokʌn <u>baldness</u>
    kionʌskweokʌn <u>dizziness</u>

<u>face</u>, <u>eye</u> wəškiŋʷ

    mʌmkihtəliŋweɔkʌn <u>acne</u>, literally, <u>sore face</u>
    kəkhakihəleokʌn <u>chappedness</u>, literally, <u>cracked face</u>
    sukšeŋwɛ <u>someone has a blackened eye</u>
    ahpimškiŋweɔkʌn <u>cross-eyedness</u>
    pimɛliŋwe <u>someone has an eye that looks to one side</u>

ahkɛpiŋweɔkʌn  blindness

tuhənəšɛŋ<sup>w</sup>  a sty

hmuǩ<sup>w</sup>šeŋ<sup>w</sup>e  someone has bloodshot eyes


nose  hwikiyɔn

 hmukwitʌm  nosebleed

 saniǩ<sup>w</sup>ineɔkʌn  head cold, literally, snot aching

 g<sup>w</sup>əsǩ<sup>w</sup>ine  I sneeze


ear  hwɪtawk

 ahkɛxeɔkʌn  deafness


mouth  tun [p158]

 pisəlixsuwakʌn  hoarseness, literally, wrinkled voice

 nɛnahka1it  someone who stutters

 aluhu  someone who is choked

 lɛxɛwsu  someone who pants

 alətən  halitosis, literally, rotten mouth

 xuǩ<sup>w</sup>inakʌn  spit heavy with mucus, mucoid sputum

 məlʌndʌmweɔkʌn  vomit

 daluhwi  I choke

 dɛčkakoli  I have something caught between my teeth

 wipitinɛɔkʌn  toothache

 ǩ<sup>w</sup>əndakʌninɛɔkʌn  throat ache

 dukpɛkilahtʌ  I swallowed something liquid and it went down too slowly and
  painfully

 bičilahta  I swallowed something and it went down the wrong throat,
  aspiration of food or liquid

 xukwinɛɔkʌn  cold, literally, coughing disease

trunk  tuhwɛpi

 tulhayinɛɔkʌn  chest aching

 kolalhwɛ•  gurgling in the chest

 ɔwikʌninɛokʌn  shoulder aching

 upxkɔninɛɔkʌn  back aching

 sukʌninɛokʌn  an ache in the small of the back

 puhɔkɛ•  someone is humpbacked

 ɔhtnɛɔkʌn  stomach ache, with diarrhea

 mutɛnɛɔkʌn  stomach ache

 xkukčaktʌn(a)  stomach worms, literally, stomach snakes

 nalʌihəle mutay  settle the stomach

 pk<sup>w</sup>utčɛ  someone who is ruptured, hernia

ahoxahkəsʌwakʌn  over-sexiness

pasahtayɛ•  someone with gas

pasu  someone is bloated

šapwihəleɔkʌn  diarrhea, dysentery

> piməwalehəle  diarrhea from eating green or unripe fruit or a particular
> food, literally, someone who is tilted

pɔsktəweokʌn  constipation, literally, stopped up

bənčtiɛpala  I gave someone an enema

ktanehəmalke  something (a food or medicine) caused intermenstrual bleeding, a
> resumption of menstruation between periods, literally, it threw you out

kukhusəwakʌn  onset of menstruation, derived from the word for owl (*kukhus*)

leg  hwikat

> hwɪkatineɔkʌn  leg ache, caused by 'growing pains' and cured by putting an old
> woman's garter on the youth s leg, also any general leg ache

> puk•atexin  someone broke their own leg

> kek̆ʷəluk•wihəleɔkʌn  lameness  [p159]

> ɔk̆ʷčəsitat  club foot, someone with a crooked foot

> čilihəlɛ•  someone has a sprain

> aləsiteokʌn  athlete's feet, literally, rotten feet

> mahk̆ʷisu  someone is swollen, as in the leg, or area of injury, edema

heart  tɛh

> wəlamʌlsəwakʌn  feeling well

> wəteləndʌmawakʌn  happiness, satisfaction

> aholtəwakʌn  love, strong affection

> čipɛləndəmawakʌn  feeling strange or astonishment

> aləwatəmweɔkʌn  loss of mental faculties

> nəwiʌkskamʌlsi  I have mixed feelings

> nəwiʌkskeləndʌm  I have mixed emotions

> sʌkweltndʌməwakʌn  worrying

> šiɛləndʌmʌweokʌn  depression, sadness

> k̆ʷilaleləndʌməwakʌn  being in a deep quandry

> pahseɔtəmawakʌn  half-wittedness

> mim̃sʌweɔtʌmawakʌn  child-mindedness

> kpʌteɔŋələwakʌn  insanity

> ɔxpahəlɛ  someone regains consciousness or returns to a normal mental state after
> a bout with alcoholism or insanity

> manuŋsəwakʌn  anger

> šiŋgaltawakʌn  hatred

> kʌŋwiltəwakʌn  jealousy

> k̆ʷitəmawakʌn  fear, awe

skin xɛs

>  maxkaləl <u>chafed</u> or <u>galled</u>, literally, <u>someone who turns red</u>
>  zəkhɪksi <u>sunburn</u>, literally, <u>I am blackened by solar heat</u>
>  sʌnʌk̇ʷtis <u>wart</u>, <u>mole</u>
>  lusəwakʌn(a) burn
>  wise <u>sore</u>, <u>scrape</u>
>  məki <u>scab</u>
>  ɛhɛndawisɛk <u>scar</u>

When the Delaware body system (partonomy) and its applications are compared to other anatomical systems, some interesting differences and underlying similarities emerge. Among those which I will consider are the cultural emphasis given to anatomical knowledge, different sequences of topographical ordering of items (parta), and the role of the specialist as sage and curer.

According to the paleo-pathologist E.H. Ackerknecht (1943), much of what we now call 'folk science' is extremely scanty on physiological function. As examples, he cited cultural beliefs that deny any link between sexual intercourse and pregnancy or that place the vital principal in the stomach, kidney fat, larynx, pelvis, or big toe. He argued that the butchering of game or the practice of cannibalism did not contribute to the store of anatomical information because people were intent on things other than gaining knowledge. He strengthened his position with reference to the autopsies typically [p160] performed in Samoa and in parts of Siberia and Africa to determine the cause of death, especially from sorcery, where specific organs are unknown and anatomical details invented. I would prefer to modify this position, however, as we have seen, the Delaware did correctly observe that the deer has no gall bladder and attribute behavioral consequence to this, albeit the wrong one. Further, I was told that 'old time' Delaware were able to check a person's body temperature by taking their pulse. Nevertheless, Ackerkneckt (1943: 338) rightly concludes that 'only in the context of a culture pattern oriented towards a kind of 'science', do dissections furnish anatomical knowledge'. A superb example of this is provided by the Aleutian Islanders.

Anatomical knowledge is a strong cultural focus for the Aleuts. Marsh and Laughlin (1956) were able to list 19 pages of anatomical terminology, which they say was derived from five sources: (1) their extreme pragmatic orientation to the environment and skill at concentrated observation brought to bear on the butchering of fowl, fish, and mammal carcasses; (2) a well developed belief in the value of empiricism and experimentation; (3) the practice of human autopsies by native medical specialists and the observations of native midwives; (4) an interest in comparative anatomy per se, using sea otter and seal carcasses because of their clear morphological resemblance to humans; and (5) the practice of dry mummification of the dead. Laughlin (1972: 141) provides examples of Aleut pragmatic experimentation: two villages agreed to raise the boating team of each on either steamed or boiled food, later the teams raced to see which food gave better wind and endurance; also, two children were raised by different methods to see which gave the better resulting child.

The key to the Aleut cultural emphasis on anatomy seems to be the class of medical specialists, who doctored with a form of acupuncture, which unlike the Chinese system of 365 vital points, required a special prognosis for each patient. The anthropologists found the native doctors and midwives most adept at anatomical knowledge, with hunters less so. Limited surgery was done, sutured with sinew. There were important sex differences in treatment. Massage was mostly used by women as part of the treatment for pregnancy and childbirth. Native physicians would let blood only from men, because the blood of a woman was unclean to a man. Aleuts know enough human physiology to understand morphological development and use pressure points. Many Aleut men had some knowledge of human anatomy because Aleut warriors would dismember enemies, owls, and hawks to prevent their souls from avenging their deaths. In contrast, Aleut mummified their own dead in order that the soul or spirit remain with the body to help the descendants.

Aleut also metaphorically name islands, throwing boards, kayaks, and fish weirs in whole or in part with anatomical terms. As the Aleut language has singular, dual, and plural number, they quite explicitly designate the jaw as dual, both for animal jaws which separate at the symphysis and for the fused human mandible. Marsh and Laughlin (1956: 67, note 35) decided not to include Aleut slang and obscene usages, although they report that these exist. Laughlin (1968) reports that Aleut use their anatomical knowledge in [p161] training exercises for children, especially for hunting from a kayak, and in the observation of pet wild animal young. Such observation and learning was vital: "An Eskimo may wound a bear and then drive him down to a stream where he can be killed and boated home, thus eliminating backpacking some 1, 200 pounds through difficult country" (1968: 309).

While the Delaware clearly place less cultural emphasis on anatomy than the Aleut, when there was a more viable Delaware society in the past, physicians and hunters could have provided a fuller account than I was able to record.[68] Some variability in the exact peripheries of these *parta* would have also been present, although the reoccurrence of the same *parton* or *taxon* at different levels (such as Delaware face) is a regular feature of folk classification (Brown and others 1976: 83) and thus does not represent a break-down of an earlier Delaware system. Landar and Gasagrande (1962) have noted the sort of periphery variability I have suggested for Delaware of past generations among present day Navaho. The Delaware may have also practiced some comparative anatomy since early sources indicate that they were well aware of the morphological and behavioral closeness between humans and bears (Miller 1982).

Actually, it is not that Delaware anatomical knowledge has been preserved into the present, but rather that one of its lower level specialists is alive and using the system. Other native speakers of Delaware exist, but their anatomical knowledge is far less systematic and useful. Another significant aspect of this system is that its presentation represents one of the few times in the literature when a full set of anatomical terms was transmitted across the sexes. Landar and Casagrande (1962: 371) and Marsh and Laughlin (1956: 42) remark that modesty

---

68 Further comparison indicates that two terminological styles are not represented in the Delaware partonomy: (1) the application of lexical suffixes in Halkomelem in order to create neat etymological systems such as that described for the Bella Coola (Saunders and Davis 1974) and (2) the reoccurrence of parallel formations such as that of the Upper Stalo where palms and soles are respectively the face of the hand and the face of the foot (Galloway 1976: 45). Both of these are Salishan languages.

often maintains anatomical knowledge within the same sex, much as Delaware obscenities are used.

Because the Delaware topographic sequence duplicates that of the White folk system, the possibility of other sequences might go unrecognized. Delaware and White American topography runs from top to bottom. Other logical systems are possible: bottom to top, and circular. These are reported in the literature. Among the Navaho of Arizona (Werner and Begishe 1966: 247, note 2), whose Genesis has humans emerging from the ground like plants, "the proper order of the creation of the human body by the Holy People is: Foot, Leg, Hip, Trunk, Shoulder, Arm, Hand, Neck, and Head. " A Tlingit of Yakutat, Alaska named the 'eight bones or joints' of the body as: left elbow, left shoulder, right shoulder, right elbow, right hip, right knee, left knee, and left hip (de Laguna 1972: 761). Some indeterminacy in the Tlingit terms can be expected as in this language nouns have no plurals.

In addition to such linear and circular sequences, auxiliary sequences are also possible, especially those involving distinctions between right/left and center/periphery. The almost universal priority of right to left suggests that most sequences will emphasize the right side. The Tlingit sequence noted above is distinctive because other evidence indicates that the Tlingit otherwise give priority to the right. Rare priority of the left has been reported for the Keres Pueblos and the Delaware (Miller 1972). The priority of the center to the periphery also seems to be pan-human. This may also [p162] explain the physiological and the intellectual importance that the Delaware attribute to the heart. But this is not unique, given the importance of the heart in early India, Greece, China, Egypt, and Mexico (Danek 1975: 68). The hearts of Renaissance French and English kings were even buried separately from the body and received special veneration (Giesey 1960: 20). In Western medicine, autopsies proceed from center to periphery (from proximal to distal in the argot) and top to bottom. 'Some etymologists assume that words denoting 'centrality', 'belief', and even 'firmness' might be derived, in some Indo-European languages at least, from the same root as 'heart' (1975: 68).

Lastly, we come to a consideration of the specialist in anatomical knowledge as a sage and curer. The Delaware system has, of course, atrophied. Nevertheless, the fullest partonomy was provided by a practicing herbalist. In a functioning traditional system, the importance of the specialist is even clearer. Among the Desana of Colombia (Reichel-Dolmatoff 1971: 175ff), the highest ranking members of each village are the priest and the shaman. These men are almost alone in having a complete cultural knowledge of the Desana world such that they believe the world to be based on male/female biocosmic energy flow. They also are able to act on this belief. For the Desana, diseases are caused by natural sources, by contact with agents such as pubic hair, and by 'wrappings'. In the latter case, the patient is enveloped in mystical bindings or wrappings caused by mythic creatures or enemy intent. These diseases are psychosomatic with hysterical overtones which are clearly related to the various strong cultural mechanisms repressing human sexuality, with the intention of promoting animal sexuality and multiplication so vital to these hunting people. After the disease has been diagnosed by a specialist, the cure is performed as a complex but explicit evocation of coitus and rebirth, executed through phallic personifications and gesturings from the center to the extremities of the patient (Reichel-Dolmatoff 1971: 185, 181). The effectiveness of the cure depends on the shared beliefs of patient and curer, and the confidence of the former in the special mystical, cognitive, and systematic abilities of the latter.

The crux of each domain of knowledge seems to be its specialists, who regularize and routinize the system for themselves and, by extension, for the other members of their community. In fact, native conferences on nomenclature are not unknown (Miller 1975a). These specialists give order and meaning to their domain — if not to the whole world – and confidence to others. This psychological effect is a consequence of their intellectual and behavioral functions. Any skepticism, especially from White specialists, is unwarranted. It is not that an old woman' s garter cures <u>leg ache</u> for the Delaware, but rather that it renders concrete and objective the mystical and practical powers of the specialist curer, the concern of the larger social network, and the resolve of the patient. As Kleinman (1974: 208) has said "the acts of ordering, naming, interpreting, and offering therapy for illness are aspects of symbolic reality common to both the sick individual, the healer, and their society. Anthropological studies have continuously [p163] reiterated the ability of native specialists working in social and cultural contexts to treat, to kill, and to cure their patients." In his now classic study, Cannon (1942) showed that social pressure can be finely applied to over-stress an individual into a 'voodoo death'. Jelik (1974: 28) has also stressed the 'lethal outcome of severe anxiety states'. Conversely, Levi- Strauss (1967) has suggested that skillful psychology and social structure can permit a Panaman Cuna shaman to produce a successful childbirth by a chanted poem, or a priesthood in the Pueblo of Zuni, New Mexico to produce a recognized witch from a rejected suitor.

In all then, an important feature of human knowledge, whether technical or folk, and its cultural emphasis and utility, is that each domain has its specialists recruited on the basis of natural propensities and trained through a process of rigorous apprenticeship and self-motivated curiosity to become a focus of public service and manipulation, a nexus of social supports and pressures, and a source for individual catharsis.

# WORKS CITED #B

Ackerknecht, EH 1943 Primitive Autopsies and the History of Anatomy, <u>Bulletin of the History of Medicine</u> 13 (3): 334-9.

Berlin, Brent, Dennis Breedlove, and Peter Raven 1973 General Principles of Classification and Nomenclature in Folk Biology. <u>AA</u> 75: 214-42.

Brown, Cecil, John Kolar, Barbara Torrey, Tipawan Truong-Quang, and Philip Volkman 1976 Some General Principles of Biological and Non-Biological Folk Classification. <u>American Ethnologist</u> 3: 73-85.

Cannon, Walter 1942 'Voodoo' Death. <u>AA</u> 44: 169-81.

Danek, Karel 1975 Some Remarks Illustrating the Dawn of Cardiology. <u>Nordisk Medicinhistorisk Aarsbok</u>: 61-70.

de Laguna, Frederica 1972 <u>Under Mount Saint Elias</u>: The History and Culture of the Yakutat Tlingit. Washington: Smithsonian Contributions to Anthropology, Volume 7, in three parts.

Galloway, Brent 1976 Anatomy in Upper Stab Halkomelem, A Morphosememic Study. Paper presented at the 11th International Conference on Salishan Languages. Seattle, Washington.

Giesey, Ralph 1960 The Royal Funeral Ceremony in Renaissance France. Geneve: Librairie E Droz, Travaux D' Humanisme Et Rennaissance.

Goddard, Ives 1974 Dutch Loanwords in Delaware. A Delaware Indian Symposium. Herbert Kraft, ed. Harrisburg: The Pennsylvania Historical and Museum Commission, Anthropological Series #4.

Hill, George 1971 Delaware Ethnobotany. Oklahoma Anthropological [p164] Society Newsletter 19 (3): 3-18.

Jelik, Wolfgang 1974 Salish Indian Mental Health and Culture Change: Psychohygienic and Therapeutic Aspects of the Guardian Spirit Ceremonial. Toronto: Holt, Rinehart, and Winston of Canada, Ltd.

Kleinman, Arthur 1974 Medicine's Symbolic Reality: On a Central Problem In The Philosophy of Medicine. Inquiry 16: 206-313.

Landar, Herbert and Joseph Casagrande 1962 Navaho Anatomical Reference. Ethnology 1 (3): 70-3.

Laughlin, William
    1968 Hunting: An Integrating Biobehavior System And Its Evolutionary Importance: 304-320. Man the Hunter. Richard Lee and Irven Devore, eds. Chicago: Aldine Publishing Co.
    1972 The Aleut-Eskimo Community: 125-143. The North American Indians: A Source-Book. Roger Owen, James Deetz, and Anthony Fisher, eds. Toronto: Collier-MacMillian Canada, Ltd.

Leach, Edmund 1967 Magical Hair: 77-108. Myth and Cosmos. John Middleton, ed. Garden City: The Natural History Press. American Museum Source-books in Anthropology.

Levi-Strauss, Claude 1967 Structural Anthropology: 161-201. Translated by Claire Jacobson and Brooke Grundfest Schoef. Garden City: Anchor Books.

Mahr, August 1960 Anatomical Terminology of the Eighteenth-Century Delaware Indians: A Study in Semantics. AL 2 (5): 1-65.

Marsh, Gordon and William Laughlin 1956 Human Anatomical Knowledge Among the Aleutian Islanders. SJA 12: 38-78.

McClure, Erica 1975 Ethno-Anatomy: The Structure of the Domain. AL 17: 78-88.

Miller, Jay
    1972 The Priority of the Left. Man 7: 646-7.
    1975 Delaware Alternative Classifications. AL 17: 434-44.
    1975a Addendum On Ethno-Taxonomic Congresses. AA 77 (4): 887.
    1982 People, Berdaches, And Left-Handed Bears: Human Variation In Native North America. Journal of Anthropological Research 38 (3), 274-287.

Reichel-Dolmatoff, Gerardo 1971 Amazonian Cosmos: The Sexual and Religious Symbolism of the Tukano Indians. Chicago: University of Chicago Press.

Saunders, Ross and Philip Davis 1974 Bella Coola Head Bone Nomenclature. Journal of Anthropological Research 30: 174-190. [p165]

Siskind, Janet 1973 To Hunt in the Morning. Oxford University Press.

Speck, Frank  APS  Collected materials stored in the Library of the American Philosophical Society, Philadelphia.  Delaware material in boxes 8 and 9.  Manuscript numbers given in the text.

Tantaquidgeon, Gladys  1972  <u>Folk Medicine of the Delaware and Related Algonkian Indians</u>. Harrisburg: The Pennsylvania Historical and Museum Commission, Anthropological Series #3. (original: 1942).

Weil, Andrew  1972  <u>The Natural Mind</u>.  Boston: Houghton Mifflin Co.

Werner, Oswald and Kenneth Begishe  1966  A Lexical Typology of Navajo Anatomical Terms I; The Foot.  <u>IJAL</u> 34: 247-65.

Weslager, Clinton  1973  <u>Magic Medicines of the Indians</u>.  New York: New American Library.

Wood, Philip  1970  Peculiarities of Medical Characteristics for Taxonomic Purposes.  <u>The Classification Society Bulletin</u> 2: 23-8.

## Endnotes

*For a paper devoted to categorization, it seems only appropriate for me to differentiate my debts of gratitude to Delaware, physicians, and others.

Delawares:  special appreciation must go to my Lenape friends and relatives, but most especially to Nora Thompson Dean, Lucy Parks Blalock, Leonard Thompson, and Jim Rememter.

Physicians:  my interest and understanding of the medical aspects of the partonomy has been fostered by references from the late Robert G. Bull, by the assistance of the University of Washington Pathology Department chaired by Earl Benditt and especially the help of Tom Norris and his young, able staff, by the careful reading of Thaworn Hangledarom, and by the karma of Doug Allderdice.  Some assistance and terminology was provided by George R. Kennedy and William J. Russum of Bartlesville, Oklahoma.

Others:  as always, my severest critics and loyalest supporters have been selected colleagues in Anthropology, at Monday Nite, and under sail or paddle.  Particular thanks must go to the intellectual elite of Saratoga, Wyoming.

Originally published in >>

Anthropological Linguistics, Vol. 19 (4): 144-166

## Summary

| Orafices | | Products | |
|---|---|---|---|
| skin | xɛs | | |
| ears | hwɪtawk(a) | | |
| eyes | wəškiŋ$^w$ | səpiŋ$^w$(o) | tear(s) |
| nose | hwikiyɔn(a) | hmukwitʌm | nosebleed; |
| nostrils | | sʌnik$^w$ | snot, nasal mucus |
| mouth | tun(a) | sukwinakʌn(a) | spit, mehʌmičŋi  food |
| breasts | nunakʌn(a) | nunakʌn | milk, nipples |
| navel | wilhwi | | |
| penis | škiyɔn(ak) | ških, spəlaš | urine, semen |
| vulva | maax(ak) | hmuk | blood |
| anus | sputi | mwičti | feces |

201

Appendix **C**

# Women's Dance: Origins and Expressions ~ 20

## Abstract

The Women's Dance stands out among the other Woodlands "social dances" because only women crowd before the singers and occupy the line moving around the central fire in the hallowed square ground. For the other dances, the names and actions appropriate to each of these festive night events clearly indicate that each is dedicated to another fellow being (by species or tribe) in their cultural universe. The origin saga for the Women's Dance, reported here for the first time on the basis of two versions provided by a Caddo-Delaware elder, shows a link to the Orpheus motif as a failed plea to return a mother from the dead. Richly meaningful to the communities that maintain the dance, these women's dance traditions also say much about the solidarity of women throughout Native North America.

Today, about 4000 Caddo have their tribal headquarters near Binger, north of Anadarko, Oklahoma, where they have lived since fleeing Texas in 1859. Among the few elders still speaking Caddo (as well as Delaware and other native languages) in the 1980s, the daughters of the late Chief Enoch Hoag, Lillie Hoag Whitehorn and Esther Hoag Homovich, were particularly helpful in providing continuity with the Caddo (and Delaware) past (Miller 1996). That one family, albeit a chiefly one, could represent so well two such diverse traditions bespeaks the catastrophes of European land hunger and violence.

The Delaware (Lenape) homeland was the namesake river of the Northeast. They were divided, at least, into the Monsey to the north and the Unami to the south. A distinct coastal division quickly succumbed to diseases. Three matriclans were and are known as Wolf, Turkey, and Turtle, but these are likely the surviving triple phratries of many named clans. Driven successively westward from New Jersey to Ohio, Indiana, Ontario, Missouri, Kansas, Texas, and Oklahoma, Delaware communities still live in Wisconsin, Ontario, and Oklahoma. In Oklahoma live both the main body of Unami (Eastern Delawares) and a second group of Unami (Western Delawares) who had allied in Texas with the Caddos.

The prehistoric Caddos were the westernmost of the Mississippian mound builders, with an array of priests, mounds, and ranked towns. Once the aboriginal occupants of major tributaries, Caddos suffered greatly from European-derived epidemics, which took a heavy toll. Survivors relocated to form confederacies such as the Cadohadacho at the great bend of the Red River in the southwestern corner of Arkansas, the Natchitoches of Louisiana near Shreveport, and the Hasinai along the Neches drainages of East Texas. Neighbors included the Natchez and Tunica, other important mound temple using nations. Nearest Osage enemies, the Cahinnio Caddo along the upper Ouachita River concentrated into a single town of 100 cabins (near Camden, Arkansas) by 1687, but eventually joined the other confederacies.

Caddoans did not have clans, though their priests and doctors were organized into specialist guilds named for animals. Very numerous, communities included graded economic, social, and religious ranks. Kinship was bilateral, and residence matrilocal, with village endogamy. In keeping with this complexity, the Caddo language uses polite forms indicating rank and status that include the title of <u>sah</u>, translated as Ms. or Mrs. to indicate a woman, and <u>tsah</u> as Mr.

The importance of women is well illustrated by the epic about the creation of Moon (Neesh), the Caddo culture hero. A mother and her two daughters were living together when the pregnant one was killed by a monster and a drop of her blood was nourished into the miraculous birth of Moon. In time this family went to live in the sky. As distinct from the usual practice, Caddos address Thunder as "grandmother" (below). They call the Earth "mother," but do so using a kin term borrowed from the Osage to mean "my own mother."

Grandmother Thunder was not alone. Both Thunder and Lightning were once linked with twin boys, the sons of the Creator, called the <u>kokonikis</u> or <u>koninisi</u> ("little ones"). They were believed to occupy a single or double building containing a central fire and two small storage trunks. The Spanish called the priestly leaders of the Hasinai Caddos the shinesi, probably derived from the title Tsah Neesh ("Mr Moon"). While other town priests had temple mounds, only the grand shinesi had this twin's shrine near his main temple. It was burned down among the Hasinai during an attack by Yowani Choctaw in 1714.

While Caddos today perform the Women Dance, its origins are set among the Delawares, for whom the Thunders are a group of young and old males.

## Choreography

Woman's Dance is one of the named social dances, each with special song texts and movements. In the past, these were distinctive of community and tribe, but they are now being lost in favor of more generic Stomp Dances. As the name implies, they include all the community – women, men, and children. By general understanding, each of these dances honors and propitiates the named species or entity (e.g. Jackson and Levine 2002 for Garfish). Among the most specialized, only females participate in the Women's Dance. It occurs among Woodland tribes (Delaware, Shawnee, Kickapoo, Sauk, Seneca-Cayuga (Mingo)), as well as those like the Caddo who are influenced by participation in this network.

In their remarkable history of the Hasinai Caddoan Confederacy, Newkumet and Meredith (1988: 46-50) divide the topics among chapters that are named for illustrative social dances. Chapter VI is Women's Dance: Family Relationships. Two dozen songs occupy phases either of standing or shuffling near a drum or of double-stepping counterclockwise around a central fire. Women sing with a drummer as well as alone. At the very end, men join in, each facing a woman partner and dancing backwards until their positions reverse.

Donald Ahdunko (1926- ), a Delaware-Caddo, has had 400 songs in his repertoire recorded for posterity by Tom Blanchard (http://members.tripod.com/~BlanchardT/, accessed by Dr Jason Jackson on 11/3/2003). His Woman Dance, done exclusively by women moving counterclockwise, has three distinct parts – "swing and sway," "back and forth" and "dancing."

The women actively participate in the singing during the fires. Ahdunko vaguely recalled a fourth part that once allowed men to join in (above).

Shawnee call all of these "Nighttime dances" (Howard 1981: 309-312, photos Plates 39, 41, 44, 45). At the White Oak ground in 1970, Women's Dance began the all night festivities, lasting from 9pm to 8am. The Women's had three variants – straight, cluster, side. For straight, women are in single file, circling the fire counterclockwise, stepping toe-heel left, toe-heel right. For cluster, the women form rows facing a drummer seated in the middle of one side, singing along with him. For side, also called "dove" or shuffle, women in a ring face toward the central fire, balancing back on the heels and swinging the toes out at 45 degrees to the right, balancing again, swinging the heels out at 45 degrees to the right, and so on. Iroquois women are famous for their skill at this feat, known as Enskanye.

The Delaware versions have been called row, shuffle, and file dances (double tapping twice left then twice right (LLRR)), where "The head dancer may clowningly bob and pirouette" (Roark-Calnek 1977: 247). Texts "may combine vocables and words which often have the sense of courtship or sexual joking. Two old Absentee Shawnee songs went: "You fight with your woman, I wish it was me," and "I'm going with you wherever you go, even if it's looking for horses" (Roark-Calnek 1977: 247).

Literally called "the answer for the woman," this dance was described by Nora Dean, the consummate Unami Delaware elder, as having five phases accompanied by drum and rattle (Adams 1977: 111). These are straight ahead, twisting the torso from side to side; sideways shuffle; short steps in file; sideways steps; and cluster moving back and forth, singing "alewi kiluna" (We're the greatest). The actual sequencing may vary depending on the drummer and head dancer. Adams (1977: 131, 142-155) provides a summary analysis of Woman Dance Songs, as well as a transcriptions that include four by Lillie Whitehorn (Adams 1977: 143, 150, 154, 155).

In general, therefore, Women's Dance has three phases. The first has the women clustering around a water drum struck by a male singer. The second has the women shuffling back and forth. The third has the women dancing in file, led by elders that moved by double taps of each foot around the inner edge of the square lit by a central fire. Animated by a sense of fun and good cheer, these women lure the soul back among them. In an occasional fourth part, men and women face off and pivot in each other's directions, confirming the role of couples in the continuity of the group.

In all, the drum presumably evokes the sound of Thunder (below). The cluster summons the deceased mother, the shuffle anxiously awaits her arrival, and the line in file provides an opportunity to entice her to materialize among them and rejoin her family and abandoned baby. This was never to occur physically but instead only in spiritual terms.

## Origin Of The Women Dance:
### Three Versions by Lillie Hoag Whitehorn

On two separate occasions, drawing on different sources, Lilly was taped by Jay Miller telling this epic in English. In 1979, she told it in Lenape, and a translation by Bruce Pearson and Jim Rementer was kindly provided by them. The first English version, attributed to Lillie's older sister, Josephine, identifies the killing force as Thunder and sets the pattern number at 3. The call of a turkey sets the action in motion. The later one by her mother, told properly in the Spring context of these events, identifies the force as Lightning and the pattern number as 4. This latter has more to recommend it as accounting for more of the features of this dance. The translation adds considerable detail about the type of hoe, the mother's constant supervision of her boy, the blackening effects of the blast on the woman's body, the use of a gourd rattle to hold her soul, and the formations of the dance by women in double line and in a circle to bring her back.

12 Dec 1986, Attributed to Josephine Hoag

One time, there was a couple. There was a couple. There was a young man and a young lady. They lived by themselves, kind of away from the folks. Just a little ways.

It was getting along about toward Spring. Maybe it was early Spring, when the corn was growing, just getting good. It rains all the time.

They had a little baby boy learning how to crawl. It was a boy. He could crawl and sit, but he could not walk yet.

Then, one time, this man, he heard a turkey. He heard a turkey, distant, you know.

He went and got his bow and arrow. He was going to get that turkey. He went out. At the same time, I guess, it was going to rain. He went out, anyway.

They were still in there. These two were still asleep. Finally, that lady, she got up. She thought to herself, she would go out to that patch while the baby was asleep. She could go out there and finish that hoeing. She had hoeing to do. That was early, early in the morning, before breakfast, while that man is gone out, but she would be back in time. She left the baby there and she went out. Her garden patch was just a little ways from there. She had squaw [field] corn there. They call it lə̀nxaskʷim[69]. She went out there and got her hoe. (Well, them days, they didn't have no [iron] hoe. They used to use deer joint, jawbone of a deer. They used that for to scratch the ground with. They hoe with it.) She went over there.

Meanwhile, she seen there was a cloud coming, coming up. She thought she could beat it back before it got there. But that was too quick for her. But, anyways, she worked a little ways. When she worked a little ways, that cloud was over her already. (I've seen this done. Well, sometimes rain will, it'll come up so fast that you don't know [until it hits you].)

It stormed and it thundered. It thundered. Maybe so many times. One time there, that thunder hit her, killed her. She was hit back here on her neck, burned all over, on clear [down] to her back. She was laying there.

In the meantime, this man, he come back to their place. He seen that baby. He was crawling outside. He was crying. He was all wet. He [Father] picked it up, and he thought there was something wrong. He picked it up and he looked in there [inside the wikwam]. Nobody. Gone. He was wondering where she went to. She never did do anything like that. So, he gets the baby.

---

[69] The prefix len- is the same as that of the tribal name and means "standard, usual, common, real" while the rest of the word is the name for corn (maize) itself.

In the meantime, it was kind of sliding down, this rain [falling on a slant]. He went over there. He tracked it, and he couldn't see nothing. He went a little ways. Some places it showed where she went. Then he come up to her. She was lying there. She was dead. She was burnt. Lightning had struck her. He just cried.

He come back. He left from there and took the baby to the village, to his folks, and he told 'em what happened. And so they come. (Now, this is just a story.)

So, he come back. He got that baby over there, and he come back. And the others, they told 'em about it and they told those putchel [pučəl = attendants, ushers]. They got them to notify the people and notify the chief. They come and they got her and they took her to where they live. They brought her in. Then they all got together. They got all together with the chief and everybody in the village there. They were discussing about what happened.

This one man, he tells the chief, "I could, I could bring her back. (This was way back in ancient times.) I could bring her back. Only one thing. You all got to do like I tell you. If you do wrong, you'll be missing somewhere, and I can not do it no more. That's going to end it all. Just that one time." They talked about it. He said, "I have a gourd, a little bitty gourd. I keep that." (I don't know, maybe that's what Delawares call it. Maybe so. It means a certain thing. But always, maybe, for instance, you could say mikušiken. It's something that old people keep. A [sacred] bundle.) He said, "I got that."

They told him all right. Try it. He's going to try it. He said, "I'm going to be gone 4 days. I'm going to the East. Nobody follow me. I'm going East. I'm going to be gone 4 days. Then I'll come back and I'll have her with me, stored in there, in that gourd. Her soul in that little gourd."

Anyway, he come back. He come back and then the chief called up a council. Everybody got together. They set a certain date. When he brought her back, they talk it over. Everybody was waiting.

He said, "We going to have a dance. Dance 4 nights. 4 nights. The third one [in line], it'll be her. These 2 leaders, they go [ahead], one by one, and she'll be the third one, then another one." Then he told that man [husband], "You stand on the side with that baby. You going to be standing there and holding that baby. She's going to come and when she sees you (She won't see you the first time, but the second round), then she'll come up to you. She's going to try to get that baby from you. Don't you give it to her." He said, "If you give it to her, you'll never get it back. She's going to take it with her. You'll never get it back. Don't you turn it loose. No matter how much she beg."

So (I guess), he told 'em to line up. They all dance the Women Dance. Them women, they all dress up. They had certain women to be leaders. They start off them songs. They didn't see her till third time. Afterwards (you know). When they sang that song, sure enough, it was her. She was there. He said, when he was talking that time, "When you all see her, meet up with her, don't any of you go up to her and cry to her. Don't cry to her. You just hold yourself back. Don't do that. If you do that, you'll spoil the whole thing." So they didn't. Nobody.

Anyway, this man [husband], he goes and she comes out, and tries to take that baby from him. But he won't turn it loose. She told him, "Let it go. I want to hold it. Hold it a little." He said, "No." He just held on to it. Then, while she was doing that, while they were at it like that, there was another old man that lived way out to himself. He was never among that clan, always way out to himself. And he come up. He cry. He goes right up to her and he cries to her. He told her, "My little granddaughter, I'm so happy to see that you come back."

He started crying and telling her he's glad to see her. And that minute, she was gone. That killed the whole thing. That's what he [the shaman] meant.

Five months later, in the midst of Spring itself, Lily returned to the epic again, but this time used the version told by her mother. It is important to know that it was triggered by a discussion of the clans. Specifically, she recalled what her mother had said about boys having their matriclan emblem tattooed on their chest so they could be readily identified among the huge population. Daughters, of course, carried their clan inherently. The prelude to Nellie's version was the following.

## Tattoos

They say. It could be Delawares, cause there's a Delaware story to that. It is not at all Kickapoo. My mother said there used to be three clans of Delawares. They were in the villages. There was tukʷsit, pukuongu, and pəlay. [Wolf, Turtle, and Turkey by emblem.] There was. And she told me. Pukuongu, them boys, they were all tattooed, right here on the chest. So I guess there used to be a lot of Delawares. So if a Delaware child got lost, they can't find his folks, they take him to the village were the Pukuongu live. They turn him loose there and he find his folks. They find out that way where he belongs. That's what my mother used to say. She tell me most about. Then them pəlay, she didn't much say much about pəley, and them tukʷsit. She said, tukʷsit is like dog-foot clan or coyot. Pəlay is Fowl clan that flies up in the air. My grandmother belonged to that. She belonged to the Fowl. But our grandpa, Kasiya, he belonged to the tukʷsit – so that's what we are. She didn't tell me that, whether this woman was tukʷsit or what. But anyway, she said that, Years ago …

27 April 1987  Attributed to Nellie Thomas Hoag

Long years ago, they were all in villages, each one of a certain group. But this here couple, they kind of live away from these people.

One time now, they say, this young man, he heard a turkey [gobble]. He heard a turkey out there. He went after it. He made up his mind, he'd go to get it. So he gets to go after it while she was still [asleep]. I guess, she knew that he got up and went after it.

And they had a little baby boy that could kind of crawl, and, you know, sit up.

But she went. When this man went, she gets up too. That baby was still asleep, and she left there. She thought she had so much to hoe yet. She could hoe that out right quick before he gets back. And so, she goes out there. (They say, they used to have a hoe made out of the jawbone of a deer. They used that for hoe.) She went to her corn patch and she had a little more [to do]. When she look back that way, here, that rain was coming. It didn't look bad. It was coming, so she got over there. She started hoeing. All at once, it come so quick, so fast. (I guess this lightning didn't give her no chance.) When it lightninged, it hit her. It killed her right out there, and it start sprinkling. Started sprinkling. She was already dead. She was hit from the back. She was dead.

Finally, that man, he come home. (They didn't say whether he had turkey or not.) Anyway, he come home. He come home. He seen that baby. He seen that baby. It was crawling out, crawling outdoors from that wikwam, or whatever it was. Looking for his mother. He was crying. He was all wet. He was crying. This man, he goes over there and picks it up. He wondered. There's something wrong here. So, he (meantime, this rain it kind of stopped. It was going that way. It stopped) he took the baby, and he looked around, and he didn't see nobody. He had that baby.

He was thinking, "I wonder what could [have] happen to her." So he went around there, and then he thought, then he got to thinking, and he kept tracking. It showed one place there where she stepped. Her track. He went on a little while and he seen another track. Then he knew something was wrong, but he didn't see nothing yet. Then he went on. When he got there, there she was. She was lying there. She was dead. That lightning killed her.

Oh, he felt bad. He come back. He went to his folks, her people. Told 'em about it. They all come in and they brought her home to where they live. They don't know what they're going to do. Talking about it. They said, Well, the best thing would be to notify the head chiefs, to let them know, to tell them what happened. Course, they never did have that to happen like that.

So, anyway, he told 'em about it. Then they sent a word to one man. He was kind of a prophet like (you could say). He come. They hold councils and they talk about it. He said, he said, "I could try. I could try it. I could give it a try." And then he start telling what they must do. He said, "Let there be a dance. Women Dance. There must be, he named a certain woman that's going to be the leader, that's got to take lead in that dance." So, so, they said, all right. There was 2, 4 of these women, and this woman was the leader, and then the next ones. He said, "When I get her," he said, "she'll be the fourth one." When he bring her back. Course, they talked it over and this man, that was going to try it, why, he said, "If everything goes well, it'll be all right. If something goes wrong, then I can not do that no more. I lost that way." And he said, "Let there be 4 nights dance, and you all get singers to sing that song. They told him, "All right."

Then he told this man [the husband], "You be there with the baby. She's going to come to you while you're standing there. When she sees you, don't you give her that child. If you give it to her, she's going to take it with her. You can't get it back. (That means it's going to die.) You keep it. You hold it tight, don't you turn it loose."

So they got ready. They said, "All right." This man, he went. He took his gourd and he went East. He was gone for so many days, and when he came back, they were ready to have that dance.

The first two nights, nothing happened. Then the third night. Then the fourth night. Here she was, she was dancing with them women. She was the fourth lady from that first. That man, he was standing there looking on with that child. They danced several times.

Here that old man that lived way out to himself, he come and he seen her. He grab her while she was talking to that man (you know), her husband, trying to get that baby from him. He grab her and he told her, "Oh, little grand daughter, I'm glad to see you. You come back." That minute, she was gone. That ended the whole thing. But she didn't get the baby. They said that's the way that dance was. That's why some of those dance songs, they kind of sound sad. Some of them. That's the way that went.

Translated from Lenape, 1979, attributed to Nellie Thomas Hoag

This is a story that was told to me about when they sing exclusively for the women when they dance. My late mother told us this a great while ago about the origin of the singing for the women when they dance.

Long ago, the Delawares lived in three parts, the Turkey clan, the Wolf clan, and then the Turtle clan. The Turtle clanspeople are my clan. Then, it was said, they lived together, but by themselves. There was a man and a woman who lived by themselves a short distance away, and they had a little son who was just then beginning to crawl. Then one day the man told his wife, "I want to go hunting, I want to go hunting, I am going to look for a turkey." The woman said, "That's good."

The man left, and the woman stayed home with her little son. The boy was just now beginning to crawl, and he could stand occasionally, but he couldn't walk yet. Then it began to look like rain, and was getting cloudy. Then the woman went outdoors, or rather, she went out. Then she got her hoe and went to the garden. It was the old type of hoe like the Delawares used before they had iron as it was made out of a deer's jaw. That was what they used to use when they made a garden. She went to the garden to hoe her corn which hadn't yet started to tassel. Then the woman thought, "I could cut down or pull up some of the grass [weeds] in the garden." Then the woman went there. It was just a short distance to where their garden was, and she began to work.

Then it was just about to rain, and all at once it thundered. Then that woman was struck by the thunders. It then began slowly to rain. Before long, it rained hard, and it thundered repeatedly.

That child must have been asleep over there in the house. Then he awoke and began to look for his mother. When he couldn't find her, he crawled outside. Then he began to cry. About that time, the man returned home. Suddenly he saw his little son crawling toward him, so he picked him up. He thought, "Whatever is wrong with him?" Something was wrong because the woman never left her son.

So he picked him up and carried him inside, he was really wet. Then it slowly began to stop raining. He went outside, carrying his son, and he began to hunt for his wife. Then he remembered that she liked to go to the garden. Then they went there, and then they got there they found the woman. She was lying there dead, as it was there that the thunders struck her. She was really burned and she looked very black. Then the man went and got his little son and carried him. They left to go to where his relatives lived, and he went to tell them. They then all notified each other at that place. The chief was notified and all the people. Then they held a council. They went after the deceased woman and brought her. The deceased one was really burned when she was struck by the thunders. Then they had a council.

They were surprised because she was struck by those thunders. One man said, "I could bring her back." The man said, "I know what I could do to bring her back." Then he said, "That's it!" Then he said, "But for four days I will be gone," he said, "I will be gone for four days. I will go to the east. I will hold this little gourd rattle. This is what I will hold," he said. "Then if that woman is to be brought back you will hold a dance, you will have a dance," he said. He said, "All the women will be two at a time behind each other. The old women will lead," he said. "Then it will seem like when the women are in fours we will see that woman on the fourth [day?]," he said, when he brings her back. "Then they will have a dance," he said, "the men will sing, and the women will dance in a circle," he said. Then when they have this dance for four times at night," he said, "she will be there, she will be there, that will be her. The man will carry his little son," he said. "Then when the woman steps aside she will tell her husband, 'Give me our little son.' Don't give him to her," he said, "because if he hands him to her she will never again return, and she will take him to where a person goes forever," he said. "Don't anyone cry," he said. "If anyone cries he will ruin it and I can never bring her back. He will ruin it for me, and in the future I cannot bring anyone back." Then he said, "You all have a dance!"

It really happened [the dance]. Then they had held a dance for four days. On the fourth day when it was night the woman returned and there with the people she danced, she danced with those women. Then she saw her husband, and she stepped to one side. She told him, "Give me our little son. I love him, my little son, I want to see him." The man tightly held onto his son. While they were doing that [dancing] an old man who lived separately came toward them. He was not often there among the people, he was always separate. He came there and he said, "Grandchild," he began to cry. He said, "Grandchild, you have truly come back. I am glad to see you." When he did that, when he told his granddaughter that then that deceased woman disappeared. She was not seen again, never was there again.

Now this is where it comes from when they have the Delaware Woman Dance. This then is the length of the story. This is what I heard from my late mother and grandmother when they told stories. My Delaware name is Wèndataèxkwe [Where the Flowers Come From Woman]. My grandmother named me that. I am half Caddo. My late father a chief was named was named Enoch Hoag, and he was the last chief of the Caddo. That is my tribe of the Caddo. I am half Caddo and half Delaware woman. My mother was a Delaware woman and her name was Kweihtiti in Delaware. In English her name was Nellie Thomas Hoag.

## Motivations

By combining these three versions, a clearer context for the dance emerges. Her sister Josephine identified Thunder, the intensely burned body, and 3 as the pattern number. Her mother Nellie provided more plausible details, specifying Lightning as blackening the body and numberings by 4 behind paired women leaders.

## Turkey

The turkey that lured the father away has military aspects since its waddle is said to be a scalp(s) lock taken in war (Hall 1997: 171). Among the Caddo, the Turkey Dance is the primary vehicle for expressing their history (Newkumet and Meredith 1988: 102-6; Sabo 2003). Though turkeys can not fly high into the sky (and contra the anglo-American image), their wisdom, valor, and gobble do link them with the Thunders in the sky for much of Native America.

## Thunder

The source for a vindictive Thunder was the Southeast not the Woodlands, by comparison among Delawares, Caddos, and Natchez.  In Delaware tradition, Thunders were seven beings with birdlike bodies and human heads.  The deep, rumbling booms were made by the elderly and the quick, flashing cracks by youngsters.  Boys and men have visited them, usually by riding up on a huge cloud of steam (Newcomb 1956: 73, Miller 1975).  But women are never mentioned in connection with these very male beings.

In diametric contrast, the Caddo recognized Grandmother Thunder, as well as the *kokonikis* ("little ones") of Thunder and Lightning, who parallel the Pueblo war god twins of the Southwest.  Their sky associations linked them with birds, and Lighting is said to have a long sharp nose.  Such a nose-as-beak linkage recalls the "long nose face" that appears on paired shell ear pendants (Williams and Goggin 1956), and on the masks with two-foot noses reported hanging in a Calusa temple near the tip of Florida (Hann 1991: 195).

Of particular note, in a Natchez tale, after Thunder, who seems to be solitary, blasted a person with lightning, he hung body parts in his house.  He was away so much that a big Frog kept his fire, which also smoked this drying meat.  While waiting between tasks, Frog burrowed into the floor.  Sometimes, however, this meat got angry and shouted back.  Then Thunder had Frog bury it so "In that way he had made mounds of earth" containing human remains (Swanton 1929: 239-240).

## Water

Returning to a consideration of the Women's Dance epic, we have to ask, Why would Thunder kill this woman?  Among Delaware, it may have been enough that she was female and a mother to draw the ire of celibate Thunder.  Moreover, despite constant attention, she neglected her son just this once to work in the field.  Throughout the Americas, great antipathy existed between the Thunder of the sky and the Snakes of the water.  Often these are cast as Thunderbirds and Underwater Panthers, who combine attributes of many species but were generally serpentine.  If the woman was Turtle Clan, she might have been a hapless victim of this water association.

Moreover, in the most famous example of spiritual retribution, the origin epic of the Midewiwin, Wolf is killed by the Underwater Beings for hunting overzealously and killing more game than he or Hare (Nanabush) actually needed.  Thus, it may be that the woman was keeping too big a garden, but this seems unlikely.  Instead, she may have failed to watch the weather, a foremost consideration among all farmers, and thus suffered for her inattention by getting caught out in a thunderstorm.  Therefore, the woman was partially to blame for her own death.  That this is the most likely scenario is indicated by her second chance to come back.

It is expressly a time of Spring rains.  Struck in the neck, her entire body is burned, much like the smoked meat hung in the house of the Natchez Thunder.  After the shaman returns with her soul inside his special gourd rattle, she took the last (or fourth) place in the dance line, behind the senior women. Only women dance. She only became manifest at the ending rounds of the dance, with only a last (or fourth) one to go. Her husband holds their baby boy as a lure. He is not included in the dance. Everything is spoiled, however, when the old hermit enters the town. Either he weeps for the woman, and she vanishes; or he reminds her of her own death. In the sister's version, first, she is taken in the rain, and, second, in a flood of tears, both watery conditions hostile to Thunder. Both parents are punished, the wife by death and the husband by grief, though, in hope of the future, the baby lives.

## Alabama Mama

It is suggestive to look at another story famous in the Southeast concerning an absent mother, that of the Alabama Sky Skiff (Swanton 1929: 138-139). Its outcome is more successful for on-going maternal relations.

In short form, sky people repeatedly come down to earth, singing and laughing in a canoe. They play stickball for hours. Then they went back up. A man watched their visits. He captured one of the woman when she chased an out-of-bounds ball. They married and had children. When they got older, their mother kept having them ask their father to hunt away from home. Meanwhile, the woman made a canoe and tried to take her family heavenward. The husband prevented her just in time. Next the woman made two canoes, put herself in the big one and her children in the little one. The husband rescued his children, but the wife escaped.

The children pleaded to visit their mother so the father took them aloft. An old woman told them that this woman was dancing. The family was fed from a dish of never-ending squash. An old corncob was broken up and the pieces were given to the children. When they saw their mother dance by, they threw these at her. The first few times they missed, but then they hit her. She recognized her own children and returned to earth with them. They lived together for a time, but then the mother and children returned to the sky. After an interval, the father followed but on his way up, he looked down and immediately fell to his death.

In northern latitudes, only the three circumpolar constellations appear to swing down to earth and rise into the sky (Williamson 1992). These are the Big Dipper (Ursa Major), Little Dipper (Ursa Minor), and Cassiopeia. Since the length of time on the ground was enough for a ballgame, which could last hours, only Ursa Major for Summer and Cassiopeia for early and late Spring would fit. The annual harvest Green Corn (Busk) and the ballgames, however, are Summer events so it has to be the Big Dipper. As confirmation, the Alabama native name for the bowl of this constellation is indeed "canoe, watercraft" or Boat Stars.

In late July, the Big Dipper in the Alabama homeland appears to set at 1am and rises just after dawn. On the autumnal equinox, the sun rises at 6am and sets at 6pm, with an hour and twenty minutes of twilight, when the Big Dipper begins to set. The small canoe holding the children is probably one of the three stars in the handle, all of them bright. And they do indeed follow along with the body of the dipper's bowl.

During the Busk, Alabamas (Swanton 1928b: 602) placed a taboo on the touching, eating, and using of corn. By fasting, praying, and purifying, people prepare to eat the new corn. Old pottery, clothes, and presumably stored food was discarded.

The Alabama Busk was held in June and until then "it was wrong to touch" the corn. Each family brought roasted ears to the square, where they were placed on a cane-covered scaffold four feet high.[70] Everyone danced until midnight, the women forming an inner ring near the fire and the men in an outer ring. Anyone who did not participate was ostracized. Some of the roasted ears were shelled, "and a few men took a handful [of kernels] apiece and threw it over the house. This was done four times." They ate what was left. A pot of medicine was brewed and heated. Then a man blew into it through a cane tube to make it bubble and receive special prayers. Men drank this medicine and then retired to purge.

The next dawn, a new fire was kindled in the woods and brought into the square. Women took embers from it to restart their kitchen fires. Each of the four nights of the Busk, roasted ears were brought to the scaffold, everyone danced until midnight when handfuls of kernels were thrown over the house.

## Conclusions

Women Dance concerns the solidarity of women throughout Native North America. As only women give birth, so here only women dance. Throughout there is a strong sense of planning for the inevitable. In her own lead-in to her mother's versions, Lilly talked about matri-clans and their emblems tattooed onto boy members, marking there membership in dye as that of women is traced in blood. In the cited Alabama story, mother and children stay together in the sky, but this is not the case for this Delaware epic.

Similarly the social dances (named Garfish, Turkey, Tick, Bean, Bell, Duck, Alligator, Quail, Quapaw, Turtle, Morning, Snake, etc) are (or were) held to convey regard for the named species or quality. Their inherent qualities and differences are celebrated by humans enjoying themselves.

What is inevitable and distinct is honored. It is taken for granted by any audience of the Orpheus saga, with its ultimately failed plea for the return of a wife or mother from the dead. Since these souls nevertheless become ancestors, though maybe not direct ones, death itself becomes accepted as part of the fabric of the universe.

In all, these dances are distillations of tribal regard for otherness. Much as clans are pseudo-species, so too are differences among species themselves as well as beings of many forms and qualities. Women Dance is about womanhood. The best of mothers, nevertheless leaves her crawling child to hoe up her field before a rain. Food came before family.

Her fate rested on a conflict in alignments. Her husband, who was probably Turkey clan, was drawn off by his desires as a hunter, lured, falsely or not, by the call of a turkey. Such a gobble was also a war cry of humans and of Thunders on attack. The wife, probably of the Turtle clan, trusted in the Spring rains to nourish her crop. So, leaving her baby boy, she took up her jawbone hoe and stood in the open field to be charred by the fatal bolt.

---

[70] This placement of the corn atop a scaffold recalls the first stages in some Southeast burial ritual, where the body is left on a platform to decompose before the bones are prepared for the temple.

Men play pivotal (if tragic) roles in the epic, but they orbit around the core of women. It is only the women who dance, the more surely to attract back the ghost mother. Men are away or apart. Before her own death, the husband had departed their home and she had left the boy behind. After her burial, the medicine man showed the ghost the way back, held within a gourd rattle. Ultimately, despite dire warnings, the old man frustrated all attempts to bring her back, except as an ancestor.

Yet even so, women stay together, helping each other and celebrating the Women Dance, in a world where males are both dangerous and fickle despite the best of intentions all around.

## WORKS CITED #C

Adams, Robert   1977   Songs of Our Grandfathers:  Music of the Unami Delaware Indians. Seatttle:  University of Washington, Ethnomusicology MA.

Hall, Robert   1997   An Archaeology of the Soul.  North American Indian Belief and Ritual. Urbana:  University of Illinois Press.

Hann, John
   1988   Apalachee:  The Land Between the Rivers.  Gainesville:  University of Florida Press.
   1991   Missions to the Calusa.  Gainesville:  University of Florida Press.

Howard, James   1981   Shawnee!  The Ceremonialism of a Native Indian Tribe and Its Cultural Background.  Athens:  Ohio University Press.

Jackson, Jason, and Victoria Lindsay Levine   2002   Singing for Garfish:  Music and Woodland Communities in Eastern Oklahoma.  Ethnomusicology 46 (2): 284-305.

Miller, Jay
   1975   Delaware Alternative Classifications.  Anthropological Linguistics 17 (9): 434-444.  [Appendix A]
   1996   Changing Moons:  A History of Caddo Religion.  Plains Anthropologist 41 (157): 243-259.

Newcomb, William   1956   The Culture and Acculturation of the Delaware Indians.  Ann Arbor: Museum of Anthropology, Anthropological Papers 10.

Newkumet, Vynola Beaver, and Howard Meredith   1988   Hasinai ~ A Traditional History of the Caddo Confederacy.  College Station:  Texas A&M University Press.

Roark-Calnek, Sue   1977   Indian Way in Oklahoma:  Transactions in Honor and Legitimacy. Bryn Mawr College:  Anthropology PhD.

Sabo III, George   2003   Dancing into the Past:  Colonial Legacies in Modern Caddo Indian Ceremony.  The Arkansas Historical Quarterly LXII (4 Winter): 423-445.

Swanton, John
   1928   Religious Beliefs and Medical Practices of the Creek Indians.  Bureau of American Ethnology, Annual Report 42 for 1924-25.
   1929   Myths and Tales of the Southeastern Indians.  Bureau of American Ethnology, Bulletin 88.

Weltfish, Gene 1977 <u>Lost Universe</u>. <u>Pawnee Life and Culture</u>. Lincoln: University of Nebraska Press.

Williams, Stephen, and John Goggin 1956 "The Long-Nosed God Mask." <u>Missouri Archaeologist</u> 18 (3).

Williamson, Ray 1992 The Celestial Skiff: An Alabama Myth of the Stars: 52-66. <u>Earth & Sky</u>. <u>Vision of the Cosmos in Native American Folkore</u>. Ray Williamson and Claire Farrer, eds. Albuquerque: University of New Mexico Press.

On the Web >>

<u>Origin of the Delaware Woman Dance - Parts One & Two</u> [Xkweyok Enta Naxkuhëmënt Enta Këntkahtit] Told by Lillie Hoag Whitehorn (1902 - 1994) to Bruce Pearson and Jim Rementer in 1977. Lillie was a member of the Delaware Tribe of Western Oklahoma (now The Delaware Nation), and half Caddo through her father, Enoch Hoag, Caddo Chief. http://talk-lenape.org/story.php?story=44

## ABBREVIATIONS USED

AA = American Anthropologist
AL = Anthropological Linguistics
DIOH = The Doris Duke Indian Oral History Collection, Western History Collections, University of Oklahoma Library
BAE-AR = Bureau of American Ethnology, Annual Report
BAE-B = Bureau of American Ethnology, Bulletin
IJAL = International Journal of American Linguistics
IPH = Indian - Pioneer History Foreman Collection Oklahoma Historical Society 113 volumes (no #45)
JAF = Journal of American Folklore
MNE = Man In The Northeast.

# Bibliography ~ 21

Abel, Anna 1904 Indian Reservations in Kansas and the Extinguishment of Their Title. Transactions of the Kansas State Historical Society 8: 72-109.

Aberle, David 1974 Historical Reconstruction and its Explanatory Role in Comparative Ethnology, a Study in Method. Comparative Studies in Honor of Harold E Driver and Essays in His Honor: 63-79. Joseph G Jorgensen, ed New Haven: HRAF Press..

Acrelius, Isreal 1874 A History of New Sweden; or, The Settlements on The River Delaware. Translated by William Reynolds. Philadelphia: The Historical Society of Pennsylvania .

Adair, James 1930 History of the American Indian. Samuel Cole Williams, ed. New York: Promontory Press.

Adams, Richard C 1890 Notes on Delaware Indians in Report Of Indians Taxed And Not Taxed United States Census for 1890, Volume 10.

   1904 Ancient Religion of the Delaware Indians, Observations and Reflections. Washington: The Law Reporter Publishing Co.

   1905 A Brief History of the Delaware Indians. Washington: 59th Congress, 1st Session, Document 501 June 22.

   1906 Legends of the Delaware Indians and Picture Writing . Washington, D C.

   ms Legal Notes on Delaware History, Humanities Research Center, University of Texas at Austin (Microfilm on file with the Delaware Tribe of Western Oklahoma, Anadarko).

Adams, Robert 1977 Songs of Our Grandfathers: Music of the Unami Delaware Indians. MA Thesis. University of Washington.

Adams, William 1963 Shonto: A Study of the Role of the Trader in a Modern Navaho Community. BAE-B 188.

Alford, Thomas Wildcat 1979 Civilization, and The Story of the Absentee Shawnees. Norman: University of Oklahoma Press. [1936]

Allen, Rosemary 1953 Changing Social Organization and Kinship Among the Alaskan Haida. Anthropological Papers of the University of Alaska 1: 5-11.

Allen, Walser 1981 Who Are The Moravians? The Story of the Moravian Church, A World-Wide Fellowship. Bethlehem, Pa: Moravian Church, Dept of Publications.

American Museum of Natural History Erustus T Tefft Collection Inventory (1904-41, Muncey Delaware and other tribes).

Andrews, KR, NP Canny, and PEH Hair 1978 The Westward Enterprise, English Activities in Ireland, the Atlantic, and America 1480-1650. Liverpool University Press.

Aubin, George 1975 A Proto-Algonquian Dictionary. Ottawa: Mercury Series, Canadian Ethnology Service, Paper 29.

Axtell, James, ed 1981 The Indian Peoples of Eastern America, A Documentary History of the Sexes. Oxford University Press.

Barker, George Interview by J W Tyner DIOH, Volume 30 T-371-1.

Barker, Martin, and Roger Sabin 1995 The Lasting of the Mohicans ~ History of an American Myth. Jackson: University Press of Mississippi.

Barlow, William and David Powell  1986  'The Late Dr Ward of Indiana':  Rafinesque's Source of the Walam Olum.  Indiana Magazine of History 82 (2): 185-193.

Barnes, Carol  1968  Subsistence and Social Organization of the Delaware Indians:  1600 A D. Bulletin of the Philadelphia Anthropological Society 20 (1): 15-29.

Barnett, Homer  1953  Innovation:  The Basis of Cultural Change.  New York:  McGraw-Hill Book Company.

Barry, Louise  1972  The Beginnings of the West ~ Annals of the Kansas Gateway to the American West, 1540-1854.  Topeka:  Kansas State Historical Society .

Barton, Benjamin Smith  1798  New Views of the Origin of the Tribes and Nations of America. Philadelphia:  John Bioren for the author.
    1805  Vary Curious Tradition of Some of Our Indians, Relative to Serpents.  The Philadelphia Medical and Physical Journal II, Part 1: 166-171.

Bateson, Gregory  1958  Naven.  Stanford University Press.  [1936]

Bayard, Rev Ralph  1957  The South Missouri Diocese In Embryo, 1824.  Bulletin of the Missouri Historical Society XIV (1): 7-32.

Bean, Lowell  1974  Mukat's People:  The Cahuilla Indians of Southern California.  Berkeley: University of California Press.

Beatty, Charles  1962  Journals of Charles Beatty, 1762-69.  Guy Soulliard Klett, ed.  University Park:  Pennsylvania State University Press.

Becker, Marshall  1980  Lenape Archaeology:  Archaeological and Ethnohistoric Considerations in Light of Recent Excavations.  Pennsylvania Archaeologist 50 (4): 19-30.
    1983  The Boundary Between the Lenape and the Munsee:  The Forks of the Delaware as Buffer Zone.  Man In The Northeast 26: 1-20.
    ms  The Lenape Southern Boundary:  Cultural Interaction and Change in the Early Contact Period, 1550-1610.

Benedict, Ruth  1923  The Guardian Spirit Complex  AA Memoir 29.
    1932  Configurations of Culture in North America  AA 34: 1-27.

Berlin, Isiah  1953  The Hedgehog and the Fox:  An Essay on Tolstoy's View of History. London:  Weidenfeld and Nicolson.

Beverley, Robert  1947  The History and Present State of Virginia.  Louis B Wright, ed.  Chapel Hill:  The University  of North Carolina Press for The Institute of Early American History and Culture.

Bierhorst, John  1995  Mythology of the Lenape ~ Guide and Texts.  Tucson:  University of Arizona Press.

Black, Mary  1969  A Note on Gender in Eliciting Ojibwa Semantic Structures  AL 11 (6): 177-186.

Bleeker, Sonia  1953  The Delaware Indians:  Eastern Fishermen and Farmers.  New York: William Morrow and Co.

Blodgett, Harold  1935  Samson Occum.  Dartmouth College:  Manuscript Series 3.

Bloomfield, Leonard  1946  Algonquian: 85-129.  in Hoijer, ed.

Boon, James  1972  From Symbolism to Structuralism.  New York:  Harper Torchbooks .

Boyd, Garland  Interview by J W Tyner, DIOH, Volume 30 T-555.

Brasser, Ted 1974 <u>Riding on the Frontier's Crest</u>: <u>Mahican Culture and Culture Change</u>. Ottawa: National Musuem of Man, Mercury Series, Ethnology Division Paper 13.

Brawer, Catherine Coleman, General Ed 1983 <u>Many Trails</u>: <u>Indians of the Lower Hudson Valley</u>. Katonah, New York: The Katonah Gallery Catalog for Exhibition of March 13-May 22.

Brickell, John 1842 Narrative <u>American Pioneer</u> 1: 43-56. Cincinnati: J S Williams.

Briggs, Argye 1954 <u>Both Banks of the River</u>. Grand Rapids: William Eerdmans Publishing Co.

Brinton, Daniel 1985 <u>The Lenape and Their Legends; with the Complete Texts and Symbols of the Walam Olum</u>. Philadelphia: Library of Aboriginal American Literature V.
    1888 Lenape Conversations. JAF 1: 37-43.
    1969 <u>The Lenape and Their Legends</u>. New York: AMS Press. [1884]

Brinton, Daniel and Reverend Albert Seqaqkind Anthony 1888 <u>A Lenape-English Dictionary</u>. Philadelphia: The Historical Society of Pennsylvania.

Brock, Elsie Interview IPH 16.

Brown, Margaret Kimball 1973 Cultural Transformation among the Illinois: The Application of a Systems Model to Archaeological and Ethnohistorical Data. Michigan State University: Ph D Dissertation.

Callander, Lee A and Ruth Slivka 1984 <u>Shawnee Home Life</u>: <u>The Paintings of Ernest Spybuck</u>. New York: Museum of the American Indian.

Callender, Charles 1962 <u>Social Organization of the Central Algonkian Indians</u> Milwaukee Public Museum Publications in Anthropology 7.

Calloway, Colin 1987 <u>Crown and Calumet ~ British Indian Relations, 1783-1815</u>. Norman: University of Oklahoma Press.
    1989 Simon Girty: Interpreter and Intermediary. <u>Being and Becoming Indian</u>: <u>Biographical Studies of North American Frontiers</u>: 38-58. James Clifton, ed. Chicago: Dorsey Press.

Campesi, Jack 1974 Ethnic Identity and Boundary Maintenance in Three Oneida Communities. PhD Dissertation, State University of New York at Albany.

Cartwright, Willena 1952 American Indian Beadwork Designs. Cambridge: 13th International Congress of Americanists 21: 127-135.

Ceci, Lynn 1978 Watchers of the Pleiades: Ethnoastronomy among Native Cultivators in Northeastern North America. <u>Ethnohistory</u> 25 (4): 301-317.
    1982 The Value of Wampum among the New York Iroquois: A Case Study in Artifact Analysis. <u>Journal of Anthropological Research</u> 38 (1): 97-107.

Cecil, Samuel, Isaac Cartwright, and George Eddy 1905 Indian Torture Post In Delaware County. <u>The Indiana Magazine of History</u> 1 (1): 176-9; 3 (2), 96-7 (1907).

Chafe, Wallace 1961 <u>Seneca Thanksgiving Rituals</u>. BAE-B 183.

Chamberlain, Alexander 1890 The Thunderbird Amongst The Algonkins. AA 03: 51-54.
    1901 Significations of Certain Algonquian Animal-Names AA 3: 669-683.

Chase, Thomas Christopher 1982 Christian Frederick Post, 1715-1785: Missionary and Diplomat to the Indians of America. Pennsylvania State University: D Ed.

Cole, Fannie 1912 Pioneer Life in Kansas. Kansas State Historical Society Collections 12: 353-58.

Cranor, Ruby 1974 <u>Talking Tombstones</u>, Pioneers of Washington County. Bartlesville Print Shop.

Custer, Jay 1984 <u>Delaware Prehistoric Archaeology</u>, An Ecological Approach. Newark: University of Delaware Press.

Cross, Dorothy 1941 <u>The Archaeology of New Jersey, Volume One</u>. Trenton: The State Museum.

   1956 <u>The Archaeology of New Jersey, Volume Two: The Abbott Farm</u>. Trenton: The State Musuem.

Dankers, Jasper 1966 <u>Journal of a Voyage to New York (New Netherland) and a Tour in Several American Colonies in 1679-80</u>. Ann Arbor: University Microfilms.

Daly, Richard Heywood 1985 Housing Metaphors – A Study of the Role of the Longhouse in the Persistence of Iroquois Culture. University of Toronto: Ph D.

Danckaerts, Jasper 1969 <u>Diary of Our Second Trip from Holland to New Netherland, 1683</u>. Upper Saddle River, New Jersey: The Cregg Press.

Darnell, Regna 1990 <u>Edward Sapir: Linguist, Anthropologist, Humanist</u>. Berkeley: University of California Press.

Dauenhauer, Nora and Richard 1987 <u>Haa Shuka</u> ~ <u>Our Ancestors</u> ~ <u>Tlingit Oral Narratives</u>. Seattle: University of Washington Press.

Davidson, John Nelson 1893 <u>MUH-HE-KA-NE-OK, A History of the Stockbridge Nation</u>. Milwaukee: Silas Chapman.

   1900 The Coming of the New York Indians to Wisconsin. The State Historical Society of Wisconsin: 153-185.

Davis, Anna Anderson Interview by Katherine Red Corn, DIOH, Volume 31 T-298.

Davis, William Floyd Interview, IPH 105.

Day, Katie Interview, IPH 2.

De Laet, Johannes 1967 New World (excerpts): 29-60. in Jameson, ed .

De Schweinitz, Edmund 1871 <u>The Life and Times of David Zeisberger, the Western Pioneer and Apostle to the Indians</u>. Philadelphia: J B Lippincott and Co.

De Valinger, Leon 1938 <u>Colonial Military Organization in Delaware 1638-1776</u>. Wilmington: Delaware Trecentenary Commission.

Dean, Nora Thompson 1975 A Reply to 'A Further Note on Delaware Clan Names' MNE 9: 63-65.

   ms Interview by Katherine Red Corn, DIOH, Volume 31 T-296.

Dean, Thomas 1918 Journal of Thomas Dean, A Voyage to Indiana in 1817. John Candee Dean and Randle C Dean, eds. Indiana Historical Society Publications 6 (2): 271-345.

Deardorff, Merle 1946 Zeisberger's Allegheny River Indian Towns. <u>Pennsylvania Archaeologist</u> 16 (1): 2-19.

Denny, Major E 1860 A Military Journal, 1781-95, Appendix II: Delaware Vocabulary, Fort M'Intosh, January 1785. Memoirs of the Historical Society of Pennsylvania 7: 478-81.

Denton, Daniel 1937 <u>A Brief Description of New York: Formerly Called New Netherlands</u>. Columbia University Press for the Facsimile Press Society [1670].

Dodge, Colonel Richard Irving 1882 Our Wild Indians: Thirty-Three Years' Personal Experience Among the Red Men of the Great West. Hartford, Conn: A D Worthington and Co.

Donck, Adriaen Van Der 1968 A Description of the New Netherlands. Thomas O'Donnell, ed. Syracuse University Press.

Donehoo, George 1928 A History of the Indian Villages and Place Names in Pennsylvania, with numerous Historical notes and References. Harrisburg: Pennsylvania Historical and Museum Commission.

Douglas, Mary 1970 Purity and Danger: An Analysis of Concepts of Pollution and Taboo. London: Pelican Books.

Douglass, Robert S 1912 History of Southeast Missouri ~ A Narrative Account of Its Historical Progress, Its People, and Its Principal Interests. Chicago: The Lewis Publishing Co, 2 Volumes.

Dowd, Gregory 1992 A Spirited Resistance: The North American Indian Struggle for Unity, 1745-1815. Baltimore: Johns Hopkins University Press.

Drake, Benjamin 1852 Life of Tecumseh and His Brother The Prophet, With a Historical Sketch. Cincinnati: HS & J.

Draper, Lyman Microfilm of Manuscript Collection. Wisconsin Historical Society.

Drechsel, Emanuel 1981 A Preliminary Sociolinguistic Comparison of Four Indigenous Pidgin Languages of North America (With Notes Towards a Sociolinguistic Typology in American Indian Linguistics. AL 23 (3): 93-112.

Driver, Harold 1961 Indians of North America. University of Chicago Press.

Dunlap, A R and C A Weslager 1958 Typonymy of the Delaware Valley as Revealed by an early Seventeenth Century Dutch Map. Bulletin of The Archaeological Society of New Jersey 15-16: 1-13.

Dunn, Jacob Pratt 1909 True Indian Stories, With Glossary of Indiana Indian Names. Indianapolis: Sentinel Publishing Co.

Ehrmann, Jacques, ed 1970 Structuralism. New York: Anchor Books.

El Guindi, Fadwa 1973 The Internal Structure of the Zapotec Conceptual System. Journal of Symbolic Anthropology 1: 15-34.

El Reno News 1899 Osage-Delaware Smoke. July 7: Column 6.

Elkhair, Charles 1912 Delaware Meeting House: 1-18. in Michelson ms-a.

Elmendorf, William 1960 The Structure of Twana Culture, with Comparative Notes of the Structure of Yurok Culture by A L Kroeber. Pullman, Washington: Research Studies 27 (3), Monographic Suppliment 2.

Esarey, Logan 1922 Governor's Messages and Letters. Messages and Letters of William Henry Harrison. Volume 1, 1800-1811. Indiana Historical Collections 7.

Evans-Pritchard, EE 1974 Nuer Religion. Oxford: University Press.

Ewing, Douglas 1982 Pleasing The Spirits ~ A Catalogue of a Collection of American Indian Art. New York: Ghylen Press.

Falleaf, Fred Interview by Katherine Red Corn and J W Tyner, DIOH, Volume 31 T-299 (7pp), T-377 (5pp), T-377-2 (30pp), T-512 (2pp), Y-512-1 (22pp).

Farley, Alan 1955 The Delaware Indians in Kansas, 1829-1867. Kansas City: Kansas City Posse of the Westerners. 16pp.

Fenton, William 1940 Problems Arising from the Historic Northeastern Position of the Iroquois in Essays in Historical Anthropology in Honor of John Swanton. Smithsonian Miscellaneous Collections 100: 159-251.

1941a Iroquois Suicide: A Study in the Stability of a Cultural Pattern BAE-B 128: 79-137.

1941b Tonawanda Longhouse Ceremonies: Ninety Years After Lewis Henry Morgan. BAE-B 128: 139-166.

1950 The Roll Call of Iroquois Chiefs: A Study of a Mneumonic Cane from the Six Nations Reserve. Smithsonian Miscellaneous Collections 3 (15), Publication 3995.

1953 The Iroquois Eagle Dance, An Offshoot of the Calumet Dance. BAE-B 156.

1957 American Indian and White Relations To 1830 ~ Needs And Opportunities for Study. Chapel Hill: University of North Carolina Press.

2000 The Great Law and the Longhouse: a political history of the Iroquois Confederacy. Norman: University of Oklahoma Press.

Fenton, William, ed 1951 Symposium on Local Diversity in Iroquois Culture. BAE-B 149.

Fenton, William and John Gulick 1961 Symposium on Cherokee and Iroquois Culture. BAE-B 180.

Ferguson, Roger 1972 The White River Indiana Delawares: An Ethnohistorical Synthesis, 1795-1867. Ball State University: D Ed.

Fernandez, James 1974 The Mission of Metaphor in Expressive Culture. Current Anthropology 15 (2), 119-145.

Fewkes, Jesse Walter 1920 Fire Worship of the Hopi Indians. Annual Report of the Smithsonian Institution: 58-610.

1928 Report of the Fieldwork of J N B Hewett. BAE-AR 42.

Fienup-Riordan, Ann 1988 The Yup'ik Eskimos as Described in the Travel Journals and Ethnographic Accounts of John and Edith Kilbuck, 1885-1900. Kingston, Ontario: The Limestone Press.

1990 Eskimo Essays ~ Yup'ik Lives and How We See Them. New Brunswick NJ: Rutgers University Press.

1991 The Real People and the Children of Thunder. The Yup'ik Encounter with Moravian Missionaries John and Edith Killbuck. Norman: University of Oklahoma Press.

1994 Boundaries and Passages Rule and Ritual in Yup'ik Eskimo Oral Tradition. Norman: University of Oklahoma Press.

Firth, Raymond 1965 A Note on Mediators. Ethnology 4 (3): 386-388.

Fischler, Benjamin, and Jean French 1991 The Middle Woodland To Late Woodland Transition in the Upper Delaware Valley: New Information from the Smithfield Beach Site (36Mr5): 145-163 in David Orr and Douglas Campana, eds.

Fitting, James, ed 1973 The Development of North American Archaeology. Garden City: Anchor Books .

Flannery, Regina 1939 An Analysis of Coastal Algonquian Culture. The Catholic University of America, Anthropological Series 7.

Fliegel, Carl John  1970  Index to the Records of the Moravian Missions Among the Indians of North America.  New Haven:  Research Publications.

Fogelson, Raymond, ed  1976  Contributions to Anthropology ~ Selected Papers of A Irving Hallowell.  University of Chicago Press.

Foreman, Carolyn Thomas  1946  Black Beaver.  The Chronicles of Oklahoma 24 (3): 269-92.

Foreman, Grant  1930  Indians and Pioneers, The Story of the American Southwest Before 1830.  New Haven:  Yale University Press.

    1946  The Last Trek Of The Indians.  Chicago:  University Press.

Foster, Lawrence  1935  Negro-Indian Relationships in the Southeast.  University of Pennsylvania Thesis in Anthropology.

Fowler, Don  1975  Notes on Inquiries in Anthropology:  A Bibliographic Essay:15-32.  Toward A Science Of Man:  Essays in the History of Anthropology.  Timothy Thoreson, ed.  The Hague:  Mouton.

Freeman, John and Murphy Smith  1966  Guide to Manuscripts in the American Philosophical Society.  Memoir of the American Philosophical Society 65.

Frisch, Jack  1977  Cognatic Kinship Organization Among the Northeastern Algonkians.  Halifax:  Saint Mary's University, Department of Anthropology, Occasional Papers in Anthropology 2.

Gardiner, Howard  1974  The Quest For Mind.  New York:  Vintage Books.

Gibson, Hugh  1837  An Account of the Captivity of Hugh Gibson Among the Delaware Indians of the Big Beaver and Muskingum, From the Latter Part of July 1756, To the Beginning of April, 1759  Collections of the Massachusetts Historical Society VI: 141-153.

Gill, Harold, and George Curtis III, eds.  A Man Apart ~ The Journal of Nicholas Cresswell, 1774-1781.  Latham:  Lexington Books.

Gill, Sam  1982  Beyond the Primitive:  The Religions of Nonliterate Peoples.  Englewood Cliffs:  Prentice-Hall.

    1982a  Native American Religions:  An Introduction.  Belmont, CA:  Wadsworth Publishing Co.

    1987  Native American Religious Action:  A Performance Approach to Religion.  Columbia:  University of South Carolina Press.

    1987a  Mother Earth:  An American Story.  University of Chicago Press.

Gilliland, Lula Mae Gibson  1947  Big House Notes.  National Anthropological Archives # 3873.

Gipson, Lawrence Henry  1938  The Moravian Indian Mission on White River ~ Diaries and Letters  May 5, 1799 to November 2, 1806.  Translated from the German of the Original Manuscript by Harry E Stocker, Herman T Frueauff, and Samuel C Zeller.  Indianapolis:  Indian Historical Bureau.

Gehring, Charles and Robert Grumet  1987  Observations of the Indians from Jasper Danckaert's Journal, 1679-1680  William and Mary Quarterly 44: 104-120.

Goddard, Ives  1971 The Ethnohistorical Implications of Early Delaware Linguistic Materials  MNE 1: 14-26.

    1973 Delaware Kinship Terminology (With Comparative Notes)  Studies in Linguistics 23: 39-56.

    1974a Dutch Loan Words in Delaware: 153-160.  in Kraft 1974.

1974b  A Further Note on Delaware Clan Names  MNE 7: 106-109.

1975a  A Brief Comment on Mrs Dean's 'Reply'  MNE 9: 65-67.

1975b  Algonquian, Wiyot, and Yurok:  Proving a Distant Genetic Relationship: 249-262. in M Dale Kinkade, Kenneth L Hale, and Oswald Werner, eds.

1978  Delaware.  Handbook of North American Indians, Northeast.  Bruce Trigger, ed. DC:  Volume 15: 213-239.

1979  Delaware Big House Ceremonial.  Native North American Spirituality of the Eastern Woodlands ~ Sacred Myths, Dreams, Visions, Speeches, Healing Formulas, Rituals and Ceremonials, Chapter III: 104-124.  Elisabeth Tooker, ed.  New York: Paulist Press.

Goldman, Irving  1963  The Cubeo, Indians of the Northwest Amazon.  Urbana:  Illinois Studies in Anthropology 2.

1975  The Mouth Of Heaven:  An Introduction to Kwakiutl Religious Thought.  New York:  John Wiley and Sons.

Gowing, Clara  1912  Life Among the Delaware Indians, 1859- 1864.  Collections of the Kansas State Historical Society 12: 183-193.

Gray, Elma  1956  Wilderness Christians, The Moravian Mission to the Delaware Indians. Ithaca:  Cornell University Press.

Gregg, Josiah  1974  Commerce On The Prairies.  Max Morehead, ed.  Norman:  University of Oklahoma Press  [1844].

Greenberg, Joseph  1975  Language Universals.  The Hague:  Mouton.

Griaule, Marcel  1975  Conversations With Ogotemmeli:  An Introduction to Dogon Religious Ideas.  Oxford:  University Press.

Grinde, Donald  1977  The Iroquois and the Founding of the American Revolution.  San Francisco:  The Indian Historian Press.

Grinter, Moses  ms  Records of the Moses Grinter Logbook (Daily sales records to the Delaware Indians at Grinter House at Kaw River, Kansas from April 1855 to October 1860).

Grumet, Robert  1979  We Are Not So Great Fools: Changes in Upper Delawarean Socio-Political Life, 1630-1758.  Rutgers University:  PhD Dissertation.

1980 Sunksquaws, Shamans, and Tradeswomen:  Middle Atlantic Coastal Algonkian Women During the 17th and 18th Centuries.  Women and Colonization ~ Anthropological Perspectives: 43-62.  Mona Etienne and Eleanor Leacock, eds.  New York:  Praeger.

1989 The Lenapes.  New York:  Chelsea House Publishers.

1991 The People of Minisink ~ Papers from the 1989 Delaware Water Gap Symposium: 175-250.  David Orr and Douglas Campana, eds.  Philadelphia:  National Park Service.

Grumet, Robert, ed.  2001  Voices from the Delaware Big House Ceremony.  Norman: University of Oklahoma Press.

Guilday, John  1973  Vertebrate Remains from the Westheimer Site, Schoharie County, New York.  Aboriginal Settlement Patterns in the Northeast.  William Ritchie and Robert Funk. New York State Museum and Science Service, Memoir 20: 149.

Haas, Mary  1944  Men's and Women's Speech in Koasati.  Language 20: 142-149.

1965  'Other-Culture' vs 'Own-Culture':  Some Thoughts on L White's Query.  AA 67 (6): 1556-1559.

1969  'Exclusive' and Inclusive':  A Look at Early Usage.  IJAL 35 (1): 1-6.

Haines, Francis 1946 Tom Hill – Delaware Scout. California Historical Society Quarterly, 25 (2): 139-148.

Hale, Duane K 1984a Turtle Tales: Oral Traditions of the Delaware Tribe of Western Oklahoma. Anadarko: Delaware Tribe of Western Oklahoma Press.

　　1984b Cooley's Traditional Stories of the Delaware. Anadarko: Delaware Tribe of Western Oklahoma Press.

　　1987 Peacemakers on the Frontier: A History of the Delaware Tribe of Western Oklahoma. Anadarko: Delaware Tribe of Western Oklahoma Press.

Hall, Julia Interview, IPH 63.

Hall, Robert 1977 An Anthropocentric Perspective for Eastern United States Prehistory. American Antiquity 42 (4): 499-518.

Hallowell, A Irving 1926 Bear Ceremonialism in the Northern Hemisphere. AA 28 (1): 1-175.

　　1942 The Role of Conjuring in Saulteaux Society. Philadelphia Anthropological Society Publications 2.

　　1951 Frank Gouldsmith Speck, 1881-1950. AA 53 (1): 67-87.

　　1967 Culture and Experience. New York: Schocken Books.

　　1992 The Ojibwa of Berens River, Manitoba. Edited with a Preface and Afterword by Jennifer SH Brown. Case Studies in Cultural Anthropology Harcourt Brace Jovanovich College Publishers.

Hanna, Charles A 1911 The Wilderness Trail. New York: G P Putnam and Sons, 2 Volumes.

Harrington, Mark Raymond 1908 Vestiges of Material Culture among the Canadian Delawares. AA 10 (3): 408-418.

　　1910 Some Customs of the Delaware Indians. The Museum Journal 1 (3): 52-60 December.

　　1913 A Preliminary Sketch of Lenape Culture. AA 15: 208- 235.

　　1921 Religion and Ceremonies of the Lenape. Museum of the American Indian, Heye Foundation, Indian Notes and Monographs 19.

　　1963 The Indians of New Jersey: Dickon among the Lenapes. New Brunswick: Rutgers University Press. [1938]

　　ms Draft on Delaware social organization and ethnography. Museum of the American Indian, Heye Foundation.

Harris, Zellig 1947 Structural Restatements: II (Delaware). IJAL 13 (3): 175-186.

Hauptman, Laurence and Jack Campisi, eds 1978 Neighbors and Intruders: An Ethnohistorical Exploration of the Indians of Hudson's River. National Museum of Man, Mercury Series, Canadian Ethnology Service Paper 39.

Heckewelder, John 1820 A Narrative of the Mission of the United Brethren Among the Delaware and Mohegan Indians, From Its Commencement, In the year 1740, to The Close of the Year 1808. Philadelphia: McCarthy and Davis.

　　1833 Names Which the Lenni Lenape or Delaware Indians Had Given to Rivers, Streams, Places, etc, etc within the now states of Pennsylvania, New Jersey, Maryland, and Virginia; (with a list of Distinguished Names). American Philosophical Society, Article XI: 351-396.

　　1884 Map and Description of Northeastern Ohio, 1796. Western Reserve and Northern Ohio Historical Society. Tract 64: 333-340.

1876 <u>History, Manners, and Customs of the Indian Nations Who Once Inhabited Pennsylvania, and Neighboring States</u>. Philadelphia: Publication Fund of the Historical Society of Pennsylvania. [1817]

ms A Short Account of the Emigration of the Nation of Indians, Calling Themselves Lenni Lenape. American Philosophical Society # 890 (74-13-1).

Herman, Mary 1950 A Reconstruction of Aboriginal Delaware Culture from Contemporary Sources <u>Kroeber Anthropological Society Papers</u> 1: 45-77 .

1956 Wampum as a Money in Northeastern North America. <u>Ethnohistory</u> 3 (1): 21-33.

Hewett, J N B 1928 <u>Iroquoian Cosmology</u>, Second Part, BAE-AR 43: 449-819.

Heye, George and George Pepper 1915 <u>Explorations of a Munsee Cemetery near Montague, New Jersey</u>. Museum of the American Indian, Heye Foundation, Contributions 2.

Hickerson, Harold 1970 <u>The Chippewa and Their Neighbors: A Study in Ethnohistory</u>. Holt, Rinehart, and Winston; Studies in Anthropological Method.

1988 <u>The Chippewa and Their Neighbors: A Study in Ethnohistory Revised and Expanded</u>. Review Essay and Bibliographic Supplement by Jennifer S H Brown and Laura L Peers. Prospect Heights, Illinois: Waveland Press.

Hicks, Lawrence Interview, IPH 5 ??.

Hill, George 1971 Delaware Ethnobotany. Oklahoma Anthropological Society Newsletter 19 (3): 3-18.

Hill, Leonard 1957 <u>John Johnston and The Indians in the Land of the Three Miamis</u>. Columbus, Ohio: Stoneman Press .

Hinsley, Curtis M 1981 <u>Savages and Scientists ~ The Smithsonian Institution and the Development of American Anthropology 1846-1910</u>. DC: Smithsonian Institution Press .

Hockett, Charles 1966 What Algonquian Is Really Like. IJAL 32 (1): 59-73.

Hoffman, Bernard 1967 Ancient Tribes Revisited: A Summary of Indian Distribution and Movement in the Northeastern United States from 1534 to 1779, Parts I-III. <u>Ethnohistory</u> 14 (1-2): 1-46.

Hoijer, Harry, ed 1946 <u>Linguistic Structures of Native America</u>. Viking Fund Publications in Anthropology 6.

Holmer, Niles G 1946 John Campanius' Lutheran Catechism in the Delaware Language. Upsala: Essays and Studies on American Language and Literature.

Honigmann, John 1976 <u>The Development of Anthropological Ideas</u>. Homewood, Illinois: The Dorsey Press.

Howard, James 1975 The Nanticoke-Delaware Skeleton Dance. <u>American Indian Quarterly</u> 2 (1): 1-13.

1976 Ceremonial Dress of the Delaware Man. Bulletin of the Archaeological Society of New Jersey 33: 1-45.

1981 <u>Shawnee! The Ceremonialism of a Native Indian Tribe and Its Cultural Background</u>. Athens: Ohio University Press.

Huebner, Francis 1902 <u>Charles Killbuck, An Indian's Story of the Border Wars of the American Revolution</u>. Washington: The Herbert Publishing Co.

Hugh-Jones, Stephen 1979 <u>The Palm and the Pleiades: Initiation and Cosmology in Northwestern Amazonia</u>. Cambridge Studies in Social Anthropology.

Hultkrantz, Ake  1981  Belief and Worship in Native North America.  Christopher Vecsey, ed. Syracuse University Press.

    1987  Native Religions Of North America ~ The Power of Visions and Fertility.  New York:  Harper and Row.

Hunter, Charles  1971  The Delaware Nativist Revival of the Mid-Eighteenth Century. Ethnohistory 18 (1): 39-49.

Hunter, William  1954  John Hays Diary and Journal of 1760.  PA 24 (2): 63-83.

    1974  A Note on the Unalachtigo: 147-152.  in Kraft 1974.

    p.c.  Letters to Nora Dean 14 Sept 1971; 6 May, 29 May, 12 Nov of 1974.

Hrdlicka, Ales  1916  Physical Anthropology of the Lenape or Delawares, and of the Eastern Indians in General.  Museum of the American Indian, Heye Foundation, Contribution 3.

Inglis, Richard and George MacDonald  1979  Skeena River Prehistory.  National Museum of Canada, Mercury Series, Archaeological Survey of Canada Paper 87.

Jackson, Jason  2003  Yuchi Ceremonial Life ~ Performance, Meaning, and Tradition in a Contemporry American Indian Community.  Lincoln:  University Of Nebraska Press.

Jameson, J Franklin, ed  1967  Narratives of New Netherland, 1609-64.  New York:  Barnes and Noble, Inc. [1909]

Jemison, Mary  1961  A Narrative of the Life of Mrs Mary Jemison.  James Seaver, ed.  New York:  Corinth Books. [1824]

Jennings, Francis  1965  The Delaware Interregnum.  Pennsylvania Magazine of History and Biography 89 (2): 174-198.

    1968  Glory, Death, and Transfiguration:  The Susquehannock Indians in the Seventeenth Century.  Proceedings of the American Philosophical Society 112 (1): 15-53.

    1975  The Invasion of America:  Indians, Colonialism, and the Cant of Conquest.  New York:  WW Norton and Co.

    1984  The Ambiguous Iroquois Empire:  The Covenant Chain Confederation of Indian Tribes With English Colonies From Its Beginnings to the Lancaster Treaty of 1744  New York:  W W Norton and Co.

    1988  Empire of Fortune:  Crowns, Colonies, and Tribes in the Seven Years War in America.  New York:  WW Norton and Co.

Johnson, Amandus  1911  The Swedish Settlements on the Delaware, Their History and Relation to the Indians, Dutch, and English.  2 Volumes.

    1914  The Swedes in America, 1638-1900, Volumes I-IV.  Volume I:  The Swedes on the Delaware, 1638-1664.  Philadelphia:  The Lenape Press.

    1915  The Indians and Their Culture as Described in Swedish and Dutch Records from 1614-1664.  International Congress of Americanists 19: 277-282.

Johnson, Mike  1973  Floral Beadwork in North America.  American Indian Crafts and Culture 7 (8): 2-9, 7 (9): 2-7, 7 (10): 2-9.

Jorgensen, Joseph  Salish Language and Culture ~ A Statistical Analysis of Internal Relationships, History, and Evolution.  Indiana University Language Science Monographs 3.

Jones, David  1865  A Journal of Two Visits Made to Some Nations Of Indians on the West Side of the River Ohio, in the Years 1772 and 1773.  New York:  Joseph Sabin.

Jones, Electa  1854  Stockbridge, Past and Present, Or, Records of an Old Mission Station. Springfield: Samuel Bowles and Co.

Jones, Rev Peter  1970  History of the Ojebway Indians; with special reference to their conversion to Christianity. Freeport, NY: Books for Libraries Press. [1861]

Jones, Ruthe Blalock 1973 Hi'ngwikan: Delaware Big House Ceremony.

Kalm, Peter 1972 Travels Into North America. Barre, Massachusetts: The Imprint Society.

Kappler, Charles J 1903 Indian Treaties, 1778-1883. DC: Government Printing Office.

Keesing, Roger 1974 Theories of Culture. Annual Review of Anthropology # 9536: 73-97.

Kenny, James 1913 Journal of 1761-1763. John W Jordan, ed. Pennsylvania Magazine of History and Biography 37: 1-47, 152-201.

Kent, Barry, Ira Smith, and Catherine McCann, eds.  1971  Foundations of Pennsylvanian Prehistory. Anthropological Series of the Pennsylvania Historical and Museum Commission 1.

Kinietz, Vernon  1940  European Civilization as a Determinant of Native Indian Customs.  AA 42: 116-121.

1946 Delaware Culture Chronology Indianapolis: Indiana Historical Society, Prehistory Research Series 3 (1): 1-143.

1947  Chippewa Village, The Story of Katikitegon.  Cranbrook Institute of Science, Bulletin 25.

Klein, Laura and Lillian Ackerman  1995  Women and Power in Native North America. Norman: University of Oklahoma Press.

Kohn, Rita, and W Lynwood Montell  1997  Always A People ~ Oral Histories of Contemporary Woodland Indians. Bloomington: Indiana University Press.

Kraft, Herbert, ed 1974 A Delaware Indian Symposium. Harrisburg: Pennsylvania History and Museum Commission, Anthropological Series 4.

1986 The Lenape ~ Archaeology, History, and Ethnography. Newark: Collections of the New Jersey Historical Society, Vol 21.

2001  The Lenape-Delaware Indian Heritage ~ 10,000 BC to AD 2000.  Self-Published, Lenape Books .

Krusche, Rolf  1986  The Origin of the Mask Concept in the Eastern Woodlands of North America. MNE 31: 1-47.

Kuper, Adam  1973  Anthropologists and Anthropology, the British School 1922-1972.  New York: Pica Press.

Kurath, Gertrude 1964 Iroquois Music and Dance. BAE-B 187.

1970 Music and Dance of the Tewa Pueblos. Santa Fe: Museum of New Mexico Press.

La Barre, Weston 1969 The Peyote Cult. New York: Schocken Books.

Landes, Ruth 1968a Ojibwa Religion and the Midewiwin. Madison: University of Wisconsin Press.

1968b  The Mystic Lake Sioux:  Sociology of the Mdewakantonwan Santee.  Madison: University of Wisconsin Press.

1970 The Prairie Potawatomi: Tradition and Ritual in the Twentieth Century. Madison: University of Wisconsin Press.

Lane, Michael, ed 1970 Introduction to Structuralism. New York: Basic Books.

Larrabee, Edward 1976 Recurrent Themes and Sequences in North American Indian-European Culture Contact. Transactions of the American Philosophical Society, Volume 66, Part 7.

Latorre, Felipe and Dolores Latorre 1976 The Mexican Kickapoo Indians. Austin: University of Texas Press.

Leach, Edmund 1965 Political Systems of Highland Burma. Boston: Beacon Press.
     1970 Claude Levi-Strauss. New York: Viking Press .

Leach, Edmund, ed 1968 The Structural Study of Myth and Totemism. London: Tavistock Publications.

Leeth, John 1904 A Short Biography of John Leeth, With an Account of His Life among the Indians. Reuben Gold Thwaites, ed. Cleveland: The Burrows Brothers Co.

Levi-Strauss, Claude 1944 Reciprocity and Hierarchy. AA 46: 266-268.
     1967 Structural Anthropology. Claire Jacobson and Brooke Grundfest Schoepf, trans. Garden City: Anchor Books.
     1976 Structural Anthropology, Volume Two. Translated by Monique Layton. New York: Basic Books.
     1979 The Origin of Table Manners ~ Introduction to the Science of Mythology 3. Translated by John and Doreen Weightman. New York: Harper Colophon Books.
     1981 The Naked Man ~ Introduction to the Science of Mythology 4. Translated by John and Doreen Weightman. New York: Harper Colophon Books.

Liljeblad, Sven 1969 The Religious Attitude of the Shoshonean Indians. Rendezvous: Idaho State University Journal of Arts and Letters IV (1): 47-58.

Lilly, Eli, ed 1954 Walam Olum or Red Score, The Migration Legend of the Lenni Lenape or Delaware Indians. Indianapolis: Indiana Historical Society.

Lindestrom, Peter 1925 Geographica Americae, with an Account of the Delaware Indians Based on Surveys and Notes Made in 1654-1656. Amandus Johnson, ed. Philadelphia: The Swedish Colonial Society. [1691]

Long, Major Stephen 1923 An Account of an Expedition from Pittsburgh to the Rocky Mountains, Performed in the Years 1819 and '20, By Order of the Hon JC Calhoun, Sec'y of War. Compiled by Edwin James, Botanist and Geologist for the Expedition. Philadelphia: H C Carey and I Lea.

Lord, Mary 19xx Interview by J W Tyner, DIOH, Volume 31, T-335 (3pp), T-335-1 (17pp).

Loskiel, George Henry 1794 History of the Mission of the United Brethren among the Indians of North America. London: Brethren's Society for the Furtherance of the Gospel.

Lutz, Rev JJ 1906 The Delaware Mission. The Methodist Missions among the Indian Tribes in Kansas. Transactions of the Kansas State Historical Society 9: 160-230.

McCartlin, Glenn and James Rementer 1986 Some Additional Lenape Indian Medicines. Bulletin of the Archaeological Society of New Jersey 40: 15-20.

McCoy, Isaac 1840 History of the Baptist Indian Missions: Embracing Remarks on the Former and Present Conditions of the Aboriginal Tribes, Their Settlement within the Indian Territory and Their Future Prospects. Washington: William M Morrison.

McCullough, John 1888 A Narrative of Captivity. Indian Narratives I, A Selection of Narratives of Outrages: 252-301. Archibald Loudon, ed. Carlisle, Pa. [1808]

McCutchen, David  1993  The Red Record ~ The Wallam Olum.  Garden City Park:  Avery Publishing Co.

McCracken, Horace  1956  The Delaware Big House.  The Chronicles of Oklahoma 34: 183-192.

McLaughlin, Andrew  1891  Lewis Cass.  Cambridge, Mass:  The Riverside Press, American Statesmen Series.

Macksey, Richard and Eugenio Donato, eds.  1975  The Structuralist Controversy:  The Languages of Criticism and the Sciences of Man.  Baltimore:  The Johns Hopkins University Press.

MacLeod, William Christie  1922  The Family Hunting Territory and Lenape Political Organization.  AA 24 (4): 448-463.

Mahr, August  1949  A Chapter of Early Ohio Natural History.  Ohio Journal of Science 49 (2): 45-69.

   1951  Materica Medica.  Ohio State Archaeology and Historical Quarterly 60 (4): 331-354.

   1953  John Heckewaelder's 'Toads' (April 25th, 1773).  The Ohio Journal of Science 53 (4): 217-219.

   1954  Aboriginal Culture Traits as Reflected in 18th Century Delaware Indian Tree Names.  Ohio Journal of Science 54 (6): 380-387.

   1955  Eighteenth Century Terminology of Delaware Indian Cultivation and Use of Maize/ A Semantic Analysis.  Ethnohistory 2 (3): 209-240.

   1959  Practical Reasons for Algonkian Indian Stream and Place Names.  Ohio Journal of Science 59 (6): 365-374.

   1960  Anatomical Terminology of the Eighteenth Century Delaware Indians ~ A Study in Semantics.  AL 2 (5): 1-65.

   1961  Semantic Evolution.  AL 3 (5): 1-46.

   1962  Delaware Terms for Plants and Animals in the Eastern Ohio Country:  A Study in Semantics.  AL 4 (5): 1-48.

Maier, Pauline  1971  Review of The Mathers:  Three Generations of Puritan Intellectuals (1596-1728) by Robert Mindlekauff.  New York Times Book Review Section, June 20, 1971.

Malinowski, Bronislaw  1954  Magic, Science, and Religion.  Garden City:  Anchor Books. [1948]

Masthay, Carl, ed  1991  Schmick's Mahican Dictionary.  American Philosophical Society, Memoir 197.

Michelson, Truman  ms-a  Ethnological and Linguistic Field Notes from the Munsee in Kansas and the Delaware in Oklahoma, 1912  National Anthropological Archives #2776 .

   ms-b  Canadian Munsee Linguistic and Ethnological Notes, 1922  National Anthropological Archives #1635: 33-54.

Miller, David R  1979  A Guide To The Ohio Valley - Great Lakes Ethnohistory Archives Indiana University:  Glenn A Black Laboratory of Archaeology.  Research Reports 4.

Miller, Jay  1972a  The Anthropology of Keres Identity.  PhD Dissertation: Rutgers University.

   1972b  Priority of the Left.  Man 7 (4): 646-647.

   1973a  Triads in Delaware Culture.  Eastern States Archaeological Federation Bulletin 32: 18.

1973b  Delaware Clan Names.  MNE 6: 57-60.

1974a  Why the World Is on the Back of a Turtle.  Man 9 (2): 306-308.

1974b  The Delaware as Women:  A Symbolic Solution.  American Ethnologist  1 (3): 507-514.

1974c The Unalachtigo?  Pennsylvania Archaeologist 44 (4): 7-8.

1975a  The Cultural View of Delaware Clan Names as Contrasted with a Linguistic View. MNE 6: 60-63.

1975b  Delaware Alternative Classifications.  AL 17 (9): 434-444.

1975c  $K^w ulakan$:  The Delaware Side of Their Movement West.  Pennsylvania Archaeologist 45 (4): 45-46.

1975d  Addendum on Ethno-Taxonomic Congresses.  AA 77 (4): 887.

1976a  Review of A Delaware Indian Symposium.  edited by Herbert Kraft.  American Antiquity 41 (2): 245-248.

1976b  The Delaware Doll Dance.  MNE 12: 80-84.

1977  Delaware Anatomy.  AL 19 (4): 144-166.

1978  Delaware Language and Culture.  Papers of the 1978 Mid-America Linguistics Conference: 23-31.  Ralph Cooley, John Dunn, and Melvin Barnes, eds.  Norman: University of Oklahoma Press.

1979  A 'Strucon' Model of Delaware Culture and the Positioning of Mediators.  American Ethnologist 6 (4): 791-802.

1980a  A Structural Analysis of the Delaware Big House Rite.  University of Oklahoma, Publication in Anthropology 21 (2): 107-133.

1980b  High Minded High Gods in North America.  Anthropos 75: 916-919.

1980c  The Matter of the (Thoughtful) Heart:  Centrality, Focality, or Overlap.  Journal of Anthropological Research 36 (3): 338-342.

1982  People, Berdaches, and Left-Handed Bears:  Human Variation in Native America. Journal of Anthropological Research  38: 274-287.

1988  Shamanic Odyssey:  The Lushootseed Journey to the Land of the Dead.  Ballena Press Anthropology Papers 32.

1989a  The Early Years of Watomika (James Bouchard), Delaware and Jesuit.  American Indian Quarterly 13 (2): 165-188.

1989b  Delaware Traditions from Kansas, Nahkoman to Isaac McCoy.  Plains Anthropologist 34 (123): 1-6.

1991a  Delaware Personhood.  MNE 42: 17-27.

1991b  Delaware Masking.  MNE 41: 105-110.

1992  Earthmaker ~ Tribal Stories from Native North America.  New York:  Perigree Books.

1994a  The Delaware.  Chicago:  Childrens Press.

1994b The 1806 Purge Among the Indiana Delaware:  Sorcery, Gender, Boundaries, and Legitimacy.  Ethnohistory 41 (4): 245-266.

1994  Delaware: 169-70, Native America in the Twentieth Century:  An Encyclopedia. NY:  Garland Publishing.

1997a <u>Tsimshian Culture: A Light Through The Ages</u>. Lincoln: University Of Nebraska Press. Paperback 2001.

1997b Old Religion Among the Delawares. <u>Ethnohistory</u> 44(1), 113-134.

1999a <u>Lushootseed Culture And The Shamanic Odyssey: An Anchored Radiance</u>. Lincoln: University of Nebraska Press.

1999b Teedyuskung, <u>American National Biography</u>, 21: 425-426. John A Garraty and Mark C Carnes, eds. Oxford University Press.

Miller, Jay, ed 1990 <u>Mourning Dove: A Salishan Autobiography</u>. Lincoln: University of Nebraska Press.

Miller, Jay and Nora Thompson Dean 1978 A Personal Account of the Delaware Big House Rite. <u>Pennsylvania Archaeologist</u> 48 (1-2): 39-43.

Mills, Antonia, and Richard Slobodin 1994 <u>Amerindian Rebirth: Reincarnation Belief among North American Indians and Inuit</u>. University of Toronto Press.

Mitchell, S H 1895 <u>The Indian Chief, Journeycake</u>. Philadelphia: American Baptist Publication Society.

Mochon, Marion Johnson 1968 <u>Stockbridge-Munsee Cultural Adapations</u>: Assimilated Indians. Proceedings of the American Philosophical Society 112 (3): 182-219.

Mooney, James 1900 <u>Myths of the Cherokee</u>. Bureau of American Ethnology, Annual Report 19.

Moore, John 1974 Cheyenne Political History, 1820-1894. <u>Ethnohistory</u> 21 (4): 329-359.

Moravian Historical Society 1860 <u>A Memorial of the Dedication of Monuments Erected by the Moravian Historical Society to Mark the Sites of Ancient Missionary Stations in New York and Connecticut</u>. Philadephia: J B Lippincott and Co .

Morgan, Lewis Henry 1959 <u>Indian Journals</u>. Leslie White, ed. Ann Arbor: University of Michigan Press. [1859]

1963 <u>Ancient Society</u>. Eleanor Leacock, ed. New York: The World Publishing Co. [1877]

1972 <u>The League of the Iroquois</u>. Secaucus: the Citadel Press. [1851]

Morison, Samuel Eliot 1972 <u>The Oxford History of the American People</u>. New York: Mentor Books, 3 Volumes.

Morrison, Kenneth.

1985 Discourse and the Accommodation of Values: Toward a Revision of Mission History. <u>Journal of the American Academy of Religion</u> 53 (3): 365-382.

1986 Montagnais Missionization in Early New France: The Syncretic Imperative. <u>American Indian Culture and Research Journal</u> 10 (3): 1-23.

1979 Towards A History of Intimate Encounters: Algonkian Folklore, Jesuit Missionaries, and Kiwakwe, the Cannibal Giant. <u>American Indian Culture and Research Journal</u> 3 (4): 51-80.

1981 The Mythological Sources of Abenaki Catholicism: A Case Study of the Social History of Power. <u>Religion</u> 11: 235-263.

1990 Baptism and Alliance: The Symbolic Mediations of Religious Syncretism. <u>Ethnohistory</u> 37 (4): 416-37.

1992 Beyond the Supernatural: Language and Religious Action. <u>Religion</u> 22: 201-205.

1992a Sharing the Flower: A Non-Supernaturalistic Theory of Grace. Religion 22: 207-219.

Mulkearn, Lois 1949 The Biography of a Forgotten Book - Pownall's Topographical Description of North America. The Papers of the Bibliographical Society of America 43: 63-74.

Muller, Herbert F 1952 The Uses of the Past ~ Profiles of Former Societies. Oxford University Press.

1958 The Loom of History. New York: Harper and Brothers.

Murdock, George Peter 1965 Algonkian Social Organization. Context and Meaning in Cultural Anthropology: 24-35. Melford Spiro, ed. New York: Free Press.

Murie, James 1981 Ceremonies of the Pawnee Part I: The Skiri; Part II: The South Bands. Douglas Parks, ed. Smithsonian Contributions To Anthropology 27.

Murphy, Robert 1971 The Dialectics of Social Life: Alarms and Excursions in Anthropological Theory. New York: Basic Books .

Myers, Albert, ed 1912 Narratives of Early Pennsylvania, West New Jersey and Delaware, 1630-1707. New York: Charles Scribner's Sons. [1967 Reprint, Barnes and Noble]

Needham, Rodney 1973 Right and Left: Essays in Dual Symbolic Classification. Chicago: University Press.

1980 Reconnaissances. Toronto: University Press.

Nelson, James David 1963 Herrnhut: Friedrich Schleiermacher's Spiritual Homeland. University of Chicago, School of Divinity: PhD 2 Volumes.

Nelson, William, ed 1902 The New Jersey Coast In Three Centuries. Volume 1: History of the New Jersey Coast with Genealogical and Historical-Biographical Appendix. Chicago: The Lewis Publishing Co.

1904 Personal Names of Indians of New Jersey; Being a list of 650 such names, gleaned mostly from Indian deeds of the Seventeenth century. The Paterson History Club.

Newcomb, William 1955 A Note on Cherokee-Delaware Pan-Indianism. AA 57 (3): 1042-45.

1956 The Culture and Acculturation of the Delaware Indians. University of Michigan, Museum of Anthropology, Anthropological Papers 10.

1956a The Peyote Cult of the Delaware Indians. The Texas Journal of Science 8 (2): 202-11.

1978 The Indians of Texas, From Prehistoric to Modern Times. Austin: University of Texas Press. [1961]

New Jersey 1972 Drainage Basin Map of New Jersey. Department of Environmental Protection, Bureau of Geology and Topography, Division of Water Resources.

Obermeyer, Brice 2009 Delaware Tribe in a Cherokee Nation. Lincoln: University of Nebraska Press.

Oestreicher, David 1988 Surviving Historic Traditions Of The Unami Delaware. Paper Delivered at the Delaware Cultural Exchange, New Philadelphia, Ohio 1-5 June.

1994 Unmasking the Walam Olum: A 19th Century Hoax. Bulletin of the Archaeological Society of New Jersey 49: 1-44.

Olmstead, Earl P 1991 Blackcoats Among The Delaware ~ David Zeisberger on the Ohio Frontier. Kent State University Press.

Ortiz, Alfonso 1969 <u>The Tewa World</u>. Chicago: University Press.

Ortner, Sherry 1973 On Key Symbols. AA 75 (5): 1338-1346.

    1974 Is Female to Male as Nature is to Culture. <u>Woman, Culture, and Society</u>: 67-87. Michelle Rosaldo and Louise Lamphere, eds. Stanford: University Press.

Parker, Arthur 1922 <u>The Archeological History of New York</u>. New York State Museum Bulletins 235-236, 237-238.

Parkman, Francis 1964 <u>The Oregon Trail</u>. New York: Airmont Publishing Co. [1847]

Parks, Ruth Interview, IPH 8.

Parsons, Elsie Clews 1941 Notes On the Caddo. AA 42 (3), Part 2, AA Memoir 57.

Patton, Rev William 1954 Journal of a Visit to the Indian Missions, Missouri Conference. Missouri Historical Society Bulletin X (2): 166-180.

Peale, Arthur 1931 <u>Uncas and the Mohegan-Pequot</u>. Boston: Meador Publishing Co.

Pearson, Bruce 1973 A Grammar of Delaware: Semantics, Morpho-Syntax, Lexicon, and Phonology. University of California at Berkeley: Ph D Dissertation.

Perry, ET 1846 <u>Selected Hymns</u> with Their Translations in the Delaware Language on the Opposite Page. Indian Manual Labor School.

Perry, Lynette, and Manny Skolnick 1999 <u>Keeper of the Delaware Dolls</u>. Norman: University of Oklahoma Press.

Penn, William 1970 <u>William Penn's Own Account of the Lenni Lenape or Delaware Indians</u>. Albert Cook Myers, ed. Revised. Wallingford, Pa: The Middle Atlantic Press.

Petrullo, Vincenzo 1934 <u>The Diabolic Root, A Study of Peyotism, The New Indian Religion, Among the Delawares</u>. Philadelphia: University of Pennsylvania Press.

    ms-a Doll Dance.

    ms-b Peyote Teaches.

    ms-c A Birthday Peyote Meeting .

Philbrook Art Museum 1980 Native American Art At Philbrook. August 17 - September 21. Tulsa, Oklahoma.

Philhower, Charles nd <u>Indian Lore of New Jersey</u>. Trenton Sunday News.

Phillips, P Lee 1911 The Rare Map of Virginia and Maryland By Augustine Herrman, the First Lord of Bohemia Manor, Maryland: A Bibliographical Account. Washington: WH Lowdermilk and Co.

Piaget, Jean 1970 <u>Structuralism</u>. New York: Basic Books .

Penick, James Lal 1981 <u>The New Madrid Earthquakes</u>. Columbia: University of Missouri Press.

Pollak, Janet 1971 The Abbott Phase: A Hopewellian Manifestation in the Delaware Valley Temple University: MA Thesis.

    1976 Middle Woodland Settlement Patterns in the Central Delaware Valley: The Abbott Phase Components in the Abbott Farm Historic District and Vicinity. New Jersey Academy of Science Meetings, Rutgers University, April 3.

Post, Christian Frederick 1759 The Journal of Christian Frederick Post, in his Journey from Philadelphia to the Ohio, on a Message from the Government of Pennsylvania to the Delaware, Shawanese and Mingo Indians settled there, and formerly in Alliance with the English [July 15 - September 20, 1758]: 130-171. in Thomson 1759.

Pownall, Thomas 1949 A Typological Description of the Dominions of the United States of America. Lois Mulkearn, ed. Pittsburgh: University of Pittsburgh Press. [1776, Revised 1784]

Prewitt, Terry 1981 Tradition and Culture Change in the Oklahoma Delaware Big House Community: 1867-1924. University of Tulsa: Laboratory of Archaeology, Contributions in Archaeology 9.

Prince, Dyneley 1912 An Ancient New Jersey Indian Jargon. AA 14: 508-524.

Purchas, Samuel 1617 Purchas His Pilgrimage. London.

Rafinesque, C S 1828 Letter of 5 April 1828. Cherokee Phoenix 1 (2) (30 July 1828).

    1832 93 The Last Indians of New Jersey. Atlantic Journal and Friend of Knowledge, Winter 1 (4): 128-29. Philadelphia.

Raufer, Sister Maria Ilma 1966 Black Robes and Indians on the Last Frontier: A Story of Heroism. Milwaukee: The Bruce Publishing Co.

Redman, Martha Interview by JW Tyner, DIOH, Volume 31, T-572 (2pp), T-572-4 (11pp).

Reichel-Dolmatoff, Gerardo 1971 Amazonian Cosmos: The Sexual and Religious Symbolism of the Tukano Indians. Chicago: University Press.

Reichel, William 1872 Names which the Leni Lenape of Delaware Indians gave to Rivers, Streams and Locations within the states of Pennsylvania, New Jersey, Maryland, and Virginia with their Significations. Nazareth: Transactions of the Moravian Historical Society: 227-282 .

Ritchie, William 1949 The Bell-Philhower Site. Indianapolis: Indiana Historical Society, Prehistory Research Series 3 (2): 1-244.

    1969 The Archaeology of New York State. Garden City, New York: The Natural History Press.

Ristow, Walter 1972 Augustine Hermann's Map of Virginia and Maryland. A La Carte, Selected Papers on Maps and Atlases: 96-101. Washington: Library of Congress.

Roarch, Harry 1970 Charles Journeycake: Indian Statesman and Christian Leader. A Dissertation of the Central Baptist Theological Seminary. Dalles: Taylor Publishing Co. [1948]

Roark-Calnek, Sue 1977 Indian Way In Oklahoma: Transactions In Honor and Legitimacy. Bryn Mawr: PhD Dissertation.

    1978 The Delaware Moral Economy: Transactions and Transformations in Ritual Exchange. Acts of the XLI International Congress of Americanists 5: 327-33 Paris.

    1980 Delaware Religion and Ethnic Identity: The Last Fifty Years. University of Oklahoma, Papers in Anthropology 21 (2): 135-152.

Rogers, Joseph Interview by J W Tyner, DIOH, Volume 31 T-572 (3pp), T-572-1 (16pp).

Rohn, Arthur 1975 A Stockaded Basketmaker III Village at Yellow Jacket, Colorado. The Kiva 40 (3): 113-119 .

Rohn, Arthur and Marian Smith ms An Assessment of the Archaeological Resources and an Evaluation of the Impact of Construction of the Copan Dam and Lake. Army Corps of Engineers: Tulsa District Contract DACW 56-72-C-0064.

Rondthaler, Rev Edward 1847 Life of John Heckewelder. Philadelphia: Townsend Ward.

Romig, Rev Jerome 1910 The Chippewa and Munsee (or Christian) Indians of Franklin County, Kansas. Kansas State Historical Society Collections 11: 314-323.

Rossi, Ino, ed 1974 The Unconscious In Culture. New York: EP Dutton and Co.

Rostlund, Erhard 1952 Freshwater Fish and Fishing in Native North America. Berkeley: University of California Publications in Geography 9.

Roundtree, Helen 1989 The Powhatan Indians of Virginia. Norman: University of Oklahoma Press.

    1990 Pocahontas's People. Norman: University of Oklahoma Press.

Royce, Charles 1899 Indian Land Cessions in the United States. BAE-AR 18 for 1896-7, Part 2: 523-997, 174 Plates.

Ruttenber, E M 1872 History of the Indian Tribes of Hudson's River. Albany: J Munsell.

Ryden, Stig 1963 Discovery in the Skokloster Collection of a Seventeenth Century Indian Head Dress From Delaware. Ethnos 2-4: 107-121.

Sachs, Karen 1976 State Bias and Women's Status. AA 78 (3): 565-569.

Saladin D'Anglure, Bernard 1994 From Foetus to Shaman: The Construction of an Inuit Third Sex. chapter 6: 82-106. in Mills and Slobodin, eds.

Saler, Benson 1977 Supernatural as a Western Category ~ An Appreciation of A Irving Hallowell. Dennison Nash, ed. Ethnos 5 (1): 31-53.

Sanderson, Eric 2009 Mannahatta ~ A Natural History of New York City. NY: Abrams.

Sapir, Edward 1915 Abnormal Types of Speech in Nootka. Ottawa: Canadian Department of Mines, Geological Survey Memoir, Anthropology Series 62 (5): 1-21.

Schattschneider, Allen 1982 Through Five Hundred Years: A Popular History of the Moravian Church. Bethlehem, Pa: Comenius Press of the Moravian Church of America.

Schlesier, Karl 1987 The Wolves of Heaven ~ Cheyenne Shamanism, Ceremonies, and Prehistoric Origins. Norman: University of Oklahoma Press.

    1990 Rethinking the Midewiwin and The Plains Ceremonial Called the Sun Dance. Plains Anthropologist 35 (127): 1-27.

Schoolcraft, Henry 1854 Passages of a Tour in the Semi-Alpine Region Transversed by De Soto, West of the Mississippi river, in 1542: From the Original Journal, Nov 1818 - Feb 1819. Information Respecting the History, Manners, and Prospects of the Indian Tribes of the United States IV: 278-200.

Schultz, George 1972 An Indian Canaan, Isaac McCoy and the Vision of an Indian State. Norman: University of Oklahoma Press.

Schutt, Amy 2007 Peoples of the River Valleys ~ The Odyssey of the Delaware Indians. Philadelphia: University of Pennsylvania Press.

Schrabisch, Max 1930 Archaeology of Delaware River Valley: Between Hancock and Dingman's Ferry in Wayne and Pike Counties. Harrisburg: Publications of the Pennsylvania Historical Commission 1.

Secondine, Isaac Interview IPH 9.

Siebert, Frank T 1967 The Original Home of the Proto-Algonquian Languages. Contributions to Anthropology: Linguistics I (Algonquian). National Museum of Canada, Bulletin 214, Anthropological Series 78: 13-47.

Simmons, William S  Cautantowwit's House, An Indian Burial Ground On The Island Of Conanicut In Narrigansett Bay. Providence:  Brown University Press.

Sinclair, AT  1909  Tatooing of the North American Indians.  AA 11: 362-400.

Skinner, Alanson  1925  Tree-Dweller Bundle Of The Wahpeton Dakota.  Indian Notes 2 (1): 66-73.

Skolnick, Sharon (Okee-Chee) and Manny  1997  Where Courage Is Like a Wild Horse:  The World of an Indian Orphanage.  Lincoln:  University of Nebraska Press.

Smith, DeCost  1948  Martyrs of the Oblong and Little Nine.  Caldwell, Idaho:  Caxton Printers.

Smith, Donald B  1987  Sacred Feathers ~ The Reverend Peter Jones (Kahkewaquonaby) and the Mississauga Indians.  Lincoln:  University of Nebraska Press.

Smith, Marian  1940  The Puyallup-Nisqually.  New York:  Columbia University Contributions to Anthropology 32.

1941  The Coast Salish of Puget Sound.  AA 43: 197-211.

Snake, Bessie Hunter  Interview by Letha Barksdale, DIOH, Volume 31 T-88 (26pp).

Speck, Frank  1915  The Nanticoke Community of Delaware.  Museum of the American Indian, Heye Foundation, Contribution 2: 1-43.

1919  The Functions of Wampum among the Eastern Algonkians.  AA Memoirs 6: 3-71.

1924  The Ethnic Position of the Southeastern Algonkian.  AA 26 (2): 184-200.

1925  The Penn Wampum Belts.  Leaflets of the Museum of the American Indian, Heye Foundation, # 4.

1927  The Nanticoke and Conoy Indians.  The Historical Society of Delaware, New Series 1.

1928  Native Tribes and Dialects of Connecticut:  A Mohegan - Pequot Diary by Fidelia Fielding.  BAE-AR 43: 199-287.

1931  A Study of the Delaware Big House Ceremony.  Harrisburg:  Publications of the Pennsylvania Historical Commission 2.

1933  Notes on the Life of John Wilson, the Revealer of Peyote, as Recalled by His Nephew, George Anderson.  The General Magazine and Historical Chronicle 35: 539-556.

1935  Naskapi, The Savage Hunters of the Labrador Peninsula.  Norman:  University of Oklahoma Press.

1937  Oklahoma Delaware Ceremonies, Feasts and Dances.  Memoirs of the American Philosophical Society 7.

1943  The Wapanachki Delaware and the English:  Their Past as Viewed by an Ethnologist.  The Pennsylvania Magazine of History and Biography 67 (4): 319-344 October.

1945  The Iroquois:  A Study in Cultural Evolution.  Cranbrook Institute of Science Bulletin 23.

1946a  The Delaware Indians as Women:  Were the Original Pennsylvanians Politically Emasculated?  Pennsylvania Magazine of History and Biography 70: 377-389.

1946b  Bird Nomenclature and Song Interpretation of the Canadian Delaware:  An essay in ethno-ornithology.  Journal of the Washington Academy of Sciences 36 (8): 249-258.

1948  Critical Comments on 'Delaware Culture Chronology'.  AA 50: 723-724.

1949    Midwinter Rites of the Cayuga Longhouse.    Philadelphia:    University of Pennsylvania Press .

1950   Concerning Iconology and the Masking Complex in Eastern North America. University Museum Bulletin 15 (1): 1-57.

APS   Collected Papers, Stored in the Library of the American Philosophical Society, Philadelphia. Delaware Material in Boxes 8 and 9 (Manuscript numbers given in the text, # 912, # 921, #932).

Speck, Frank and Jesse Moses  1945  The Celestial Bear Comes Down To Earth. Reading Public Museum and Art Gallery, Scientific Publication 7 .

Spencer, Oliver M  1968  The Indian Captivity of OM Spencer. Milo Milton Quaife, ed.  New York:  The Citadel Press  [1834].

Spicer, Edward  1969  A Short History of the Indians of the United States.  New York:  D Van Nostrand and Co.

Earnest Sprybuck (1828-1949), Shawnee  1960  The Chronicles of Oklahoma 38 (1): 29-30.

Stein, Rolf  1972  Tibetan Civilization. Translated by J E S Driver.  Stanford:  University Press.

Stewart, Ty  1973  Oklahoma Delaware Women's Dance Clothes.  American Indian Crafts and Culture 7 (6): 4-22.

Stone, Irving  1956  Men To Match My Mountains, The Opening of the Far West, 1840-1900. Garden City:  Doubleday and Co.

Straus, Anne  1975  Northern Cheyenne Ethnopsychology.  Ethnos 5 (3): 326-357.

1976  Being Human In the Cheyenne Way.  PhD Dissertation, University of Chicago.

Tanner, Adrian  1979  Bringing Home Animals, Religious Ideology and Mode of Production of the Mistassini Cree Hunters.  London:  C Hurst and Co.

Tanner, Helen Hornbeck  1974  Caddoan Indians, IV.  American Indian Ethnohistory.  New York:  Garland Publishing, Inc.

1978a  The Glaize in 1792:  A Composite Indian Community.  Ethnohistory 25 (1): 15-39.

1978b  Cherokees in the Ohio Country.  Journal of Cherokee Studies 3 (2): 94-102.

1979  Coocoochee:  Mohawk Medicine Woman.  American Indian Culture and Research Journal 3 (3): 23-41.

Tanner, Helen Hornbeck, ed  1987  Atlas of Great Lakes Indian History. Norman:  University of Oklahoma Press.

Tantaquidgeon, Gladys  1972  Folk Medicines of the Delaware and Related Algonkian Indians. Harrisburg:  Pennsylvania Historical and Museum Commission, Anthropological Series 3. [1942]

Temple, Wayne  1958  Indian Villages of the Illinois Country.  Springfield:  Illinois State Museum, Scientific Papers, Volume 2, Part 2.

Thomason, Sarah Grey  1980  On Interpreting 'The Indian Interpreter'.  Language in Society 9 (2): 167-193.

Thompson, Charles  1937  Sons of the Wilderness, John and William Conner.  Indianapolis: Indiana Historical Society Publication 12.

Thomson, Charles  1759  An Inquiry into the Causes of the Alienation of the Delaware and Shawanese Indians from the British Interest, and into the Measures Taken for Recovering Their Friendship. London:  J Wilkie.

Thurman, Melburn 1973a Supplementary Material on the Life of John Wilson, The Revealer of Peyote. Ethnohistory 20 (3): 279-287.

1973b The Delaware Indians: A Study in Ethnohistory. PhD Dissertation. University of California, Santa Barbara.

Thwaites, Rueben Gold 1904 Original Journals of the Lewis and Clark Expedition, 1804-1806. New York: Dodd, Mead and Co 7 Volumes, Atlas.

Tomlinson, William 1859 Kansas In 1858, Being Chiefly A History of the Recent Troubles in the Territory. A Night With The Delawares, Chapter II: 28-38. New York: H Dayton.

Tong, Marvin 1959 The Indian Heritage of Christian County. Christian County, Its First Hundred Years: 199-211. Jefferson County, Missouri: Von Hoffman Press.

Tooker, Elizabeth 1970a The Iroquois Ceremonial of Midwinter. Syracuse University Press.

1970b Northern Iroquoian Sociopolitical Organization. AA 72 (1): 90-97.

1979 Native North American Spirituality of the Eastern Woodlands: Sacred Myths, Dreams, Visions, Speeches, Healing Formulas, Rituals, and Ceremonies. New York: Paulist Press.

Torry, Rev Alvin 1871 Autobiography of Rev Alvin Torry, First Missionary to the Six Nations and the Northwestern Tribes of British North America. Fourth Edition. Rev William Hosmer, ed. Auburn: William J Moses.

Tricentenary Commission of the State of Connecticut 1933 The Indians of Conncticut. Yale University Press.

Trigger, Bruce 1976 Children of Aataentsic: A History of the Huron People to 1660. Montreal: McGill-Queens Press, 2 Volumes.

1978 Iroquoian Matriliny Pennsylvania Archaeologist 48 (1-2): 55-56.

Trowbridge, Charles Christopher [1824] Traditions of the Lenee Lenaupee or Delawares. Transcript in the possession of James Rementer.

TP C C Trowbridge Papers Delaware Traditions. Rackham Building, Michigan Historical Collections, University of Michigan.

TC C C Trowbridge Collection, Detroit Public Library.

1939 Shawnese Traditions. Vernon Kinietz and Erminie W Voegelin, ed. University of Michigan, Museum of Anthropology, Occasional Contributions 9.

Turner, Edith 1994 Behind Inupiaq Reincarnation: Cosmological Cycling. Chapter 5: 67-81. Mills and Slobodin.

United States Government 1903 Memorial of the Delaware Indians Residing in the Cherokee Nation Praying Relief Relative to Their Rights in and Ownership of Certain Lands within the Boundaries of Said Nation. 58th Congress, First Session, Senate Document 16, November 23.

1904a Memorial of the Delaware Indians Residing in the Cherokee Nation Praying Relief Relative to Their Rights in and Ownership of Certain Lands within the Boundaries of Said Nation. 58th Congress, First Session, Senate Document 58, January 4.

1904b Memorial from Richard C Adams, Representing the Delaware Indians, Concerning the Dawes Commission and Its Action in Connection with the Making of the Delaware Segregation, etc. 58th Congress, Second Session, Senate Document 58, part two January 4: 1-8.

1904c  Letter from the Secretary of the Interior in Response to the Senate Resolution of January 11, 1904, Transmitting Papers and Copies of Reports of the Commission to the Five Civilized Tribes Relative to the Allotment of Lands in the Cherokee Nation to the Delaware Indians. 58th Congress, Second Session ,Senate Document 104.

1904d  A Memorial of Members of the Dawes Commission to the Senate of the United States of America. 58th Congress, Second Session, Senate Document 106, January 20: 1-5.

1904e  Memorial of the Delaware Indians Residing in the Cherokee Nation in Support of Their Claims for Payment of the Difference between Gold and Silver Coin and the Currency in which Payments Were Made to Them during the Years 1862-1878. 58th Congress, Second Session, Senate Document 211, March 17.

1904f  Letter from the Secretary of the Treasury, Submitting, in Response to Senate Resolution of March 23, 1904, a Statement Showing the Difference in Value between Coin and Currency on Payments Made by the US to Delaware Indians from and including the Year 1862 to and including the Year 1876. 58th Congress, Second Session, March 24.

Unrau, William  1978  The Kansa Indians: A History of the Wind People, 1673-1873. Norman: University of Oklahoma Press.

1979  The Emigrant Indians of Kansas: A Critical Bibliography. Bloomington: Indiana University Press for the Newberry Library.

Van Der Donck, Adriaen  1968  A Description of the New Netherlands. Thomas O'Donnell, ed. Syracuse University Press. [1655]

Voegelin, Carl  1939  The Lenape and Munsee Dialects of Delaware, An Algonquian Language. Proceedings of the Indiana Academy of Science 49: 34-37.

1941a  Word Distortions in Delaware Big House and Walam Olum Songs. Proceedings of the Indiana Academy of Sciences 51: 48-54.

1941b  Proto-Algonquian Consonant Clusters in Delaware. Language 17: 143-147.

1945  Delaware Texts. IJAL 11 (2): 105-119.

1946  Delaware, An Eastern Algonquian Language: 130-157. in Hoijer, ed.

Voegelin, Carl, John Yegerlehner, and Florence Robinett  1954  Shawnee Laws: Perceptual Statements for the Language and for the Content. Language and Culture Harry Hoijer, ed. AA Memoir 79: 32-46.

Voight, Virginia Frances  1965  Mohegan Chief ~ The Story of Harold Tantaquidgeon. New York: Funk and Wagnalls Co.

Volk, Ernest  1911  Archaeology of the Delaware Valley. Harvard: Papers of the Peabody Museum of American Archaeology and Ethnology 5.

Wacker, Peter  1968  The Musconetcong Valley of New Jersey, A Historical Geography. New Brunswick: Rutgers University Press.

Walker, Willard  1975  The Proto-Algonquians: 633-647. in M Dale Kinkade, Kenneth Hale, and Oswald Werner, eds.

Wallace, Anthony F C  1947  Women, Land, and Society: Three Aspects of Aboriginal Delaware Life. Pennsylvania Archaeologist 17 (1-2): 1-35.

1949  King of the Delaware: Teedyuscung, 1700-1763. Philadelphia: University of Pennsylvania Press.

1952   The Modal Personality Structure of the Tuscarora Indians as Revealed by the Rorschach Test.  BAE-B 150.

1956  New Religions among the Delaware Indians, 1600-1900.  Southwestern Journal of Anthropology 12 (1): 1-21.

1957   Political Organization and Land Tenure Among the Northeastern Indians, 1600-1830.  Southwestern Journal of Anthropology 13: 301-321.

2012  Tuscarora ~ A History.  Albany:  SUNY Press.

Wallace, Paul AW   1952   John Heckewelder's Indians and the Fenimore Cooper Tradition.  Proceedings of the American Philosophical Society 92 (4): 46-504.

1958  Thirty Thousand Miles with John Heckewlder.  University of Pittsburgh Press.

1975   Indians in Pennsylvania.  Harrisburg:  The Pennsyvania Historical and Museum Commission.

Washburn, Wilcomb  1976  Introduction, VI Cultural Change: 477-479.  in Fogelson, ed.

Washington, Cyrus  Interview, IPH 11.

Watanabe, Hitoshi   1973   The Ainu Ecosystem, Environment and Group Structure.  Seattle:  University of Washington Press, Memoirs of th American Ethnological Society 54.

Watson, James and Harold Nelson  1967  Body-Environment Transactions:  A Standard Model for Cross-Cultural Analyses.  Southwestern Journal of Anthropology 23 (3): 292-309.

Chief Waubuno [John Wampum]  1845  The Traditions of the Delawares  London:  Bowers Brothers Printers .

Webber, Charlie  Interview, IPH 49.

Weinman, Paul  1969  A Bibliography of the Iroquian Literature.  New York State Museum and Science Service, Bulletin 411.

Weslager, Clinton  1943  Delaware's Forgotten Folk:  The Story of the Moors and Nanticoke.  Philadelphia:  University of Pennsylvania Press.

1950  Indians of the Eastern Shore of Maryland and Virginia.  The Eastern Shore of Maryland and Virginia, Volume I, Chapter 3: 39-69.  Charles Clark, ed.  Lewis Historical Publishing Co.

1961   Dutch Explorers, Traders and Settlers in the Delaware Valley, 1609-1664.  Philadelphia:  University of Pennsylvania Press.

1971  Name-Giving among the Delaware Indians.  Names 19 (4): 268-283.

1972  The Delaware Indians:  A History.  New Brunswick:  Rutgers University Press .

1973  Magic Medicines of the Indians.  New York:  New American Library.

1974   Enrollment of the Chippewa and Delaware-Munsies Living in Franklin County, Kansas, May 31, 1900.  The Kansas Historical Quarterly 40 (2): 234-241.

1975  More About The Unalachtigo.  Pennsylvania Archaeologist 45 (3): 40-44 .

1978a   The Delaware Indian Westward Migration, with Trowbridge-Cass Texts.  Wallingford, Pa:  The Middle Atlantic Press.

1978b   The Delawares, A Critical Bibliography.   Indiana University Press for the Newberry Library, Chicago.

1985   Lenape Ethnology From William Penn's Relation of 1683.   Bulletin of the Archaeological Society of Delaware 18: 1-28.

Wheeler-Voegelin, Erminie 1941 The Place of Agriculture in the Subsistence Economy of the Shawnee. Papers of the Michigan Academy of Science, Arts and Letters 24: 513-520.

1944 Mortuary Customs of the Shawnee and Other Eastern Tribes. Indianapolis: Indiana Historical Society, Prehistory Research Series 11 (4): 225-444.

1959 Documents on the Delawares, from John Ettwein to George Washington and John Heckewelder to Peter Du Ponceau. Ethnohistory 6 (1): 42-81, 186.

Wherry, James 1979 Eastern Algonquian Relationships to Proto-Algonquian Social Organization. Halifax: Saint Mary's University, Department of Anthropology, Occasional Papers in Anthropology 5.

Whiting, Beatrice 1950 Paiute Sorcery. Viking Fund Publications in Anthropology 15.

Wilson, Terry P 1988 The Osage. New York: Chelsea House .

White, Richard 1991 The Middle Ground ~ Indians, Empires, and Republics in the Great Lakes Region, 1650-1815. Cambridge University Press.

Wilkes, Charles 1845 Narrative of the US Exploring Expedition. Philadelphia: Lea and Blanchard, Volume IV.

Williams, Lorraine 1980 The Delaware Indians, A Study Combining Archaeology, Ethnohistory and Ethnography. Trenton: New Jersey State Museum.

Wissler, Clark, ed 1909 Indians of Greater New York and the Lower Hudson Anthropological Papers of the American Museum of Natural History 3 .

Witthoft, John 1949 Green Corn Ceremonialism in the Eastern Woodlands. University of Michigan, Museum of Anthropology, Occasional Contributions 13.

1965 Indian Prehistory of Pennsylvania, Harrisburg: Pennsylvania Historical and Museum Commission.

1967 The American Indian As Hunter, Harrisburg: Pennsylvania Historical and Museum Commission, Reprints in Anthropology 6.

Zeisberger, David 1885 Diary Among the Indians of Ohio 1781-98. Translated from German and Edited by Eugene Bliss. Cincinnati: Robert Clarke and Co for the Historical and Philosophical Society of Ohio, 2 Volumes.

1887 Zeisberger's Indian Dictionary Eben Norton Horsford, ed Cambridge, Massachusetts.

1910 History of the Northern American Indian Archer Butler Hulbert and Reverend William Nathaniel Schwarze, eds Columbus: Ohio Archaeological and Historical Quarterly 19 (1-2): 1-189.

Oklahoma Big House

Rev Zeisberger introduces Delaware Spelling Book first school text, By Hal Sherman

Last Night of Gamwing in Ohio, by Hal Sherman

Index

# Images

By page and image #

Typo-gnomes are constant, Corrections Welcome

Wanishi

Sold @ amazon.com

ACCULTURATING AMELIA ~ Round Valley 1937 California
ALASKA EDGE ISLAND ~ Siberian Yupiks of St Lawrence Island
ALLIED MOUNDS ~ Touching the Earth, Modeling the World, Reaching the Sky
ANIMAL PEOPLE ADVENTURES ~ Native North American Tribal Stories
AT BAY ~ Cultures Converging through Southwest Washington                         > 5
BALLARD BULWARK ~
CHACO ECHOES ~ Pervasive Keresan Priesthoods
CHACOKIA ~ Chaco, Cahokia, Cities & Ceremonies ~ Bundles & Blood Lines Centuries Ago
CHINOOK CONCERNS ~ Emma Millett Luscier, Isabella Bertrand, Verne Ray
CIRCLING FOUR CORNERS ~ Re-Viewing Native American Indiens                        > 10
CROSSING ~ LINES: An Educational Memoir of Native North America
DEL-AWARE ~ Lenape Legacies
DELAWARE INTEGRITY ~ Rituals, Removals, Reforms by Lenape Indiens
DISCLAIMING TREATIES I ~ Puget Tribes 1927 Testimonies
DISCLAIMING TREATIES II ~ Puget Tribes 1927 Testimonies                          > 15
ELDERS' DIALOG ~ Ed Davis & Vi Hilbert Discuss Native Puget Sound Language, Culture, & Heritage
EVERGREEN ETHNOGRAPHIES ~ Hoh, Chehalis, Suquamish, and Snoqualmi of Western Washington
FEDERAL FISH FILES ~ Swindell 1942 Treaty Rights Report
GEORGE GIBBS NORTHWEST ARRAY ~ Full Reports, Place Names, Word List, Artifact Names, and Guide
GRASSROOTS JANET ~ Advancing Salish and Traditional Cultures                     > 20
HERMAN HAEBERLIN REGAINED ~ Anthropology and Artifacts of Puget Sound 1916-17
HERSTORY NW ~ Women Upholding Native Traditions
INDIEN ~ ETHNOGRAPHY: Cultural Traditions of Native North America
INDIEN ~ ETHNOLOGY: Grounded, Gendered, Meaningful Cultural Traditions
LESCHI IN LOVE ~ A Novel of Native Puget Sound  > x2                             > 25
MARCO MUCK MASKS ~ Frank Cushing on Marshes and Mounds
MINTER BAY ~ Land, Lore, Loss, and Lucre in the South Salish Sea
NATIVE MET HOW ~ Improving Posterity
OLD LUKH ~ A Novel of Native Puget Sound Daily Life, Places, and Stories
OVER THE FALLS ~ Sdoqwalbixw Survivance Surrounding Seattle                      > 30
PACIFIC PLATEAU PORTRAYALS ~ People Places Ponderings
RAY'S ARRAY ~ Raymond D Fogelson's Works
RIGHTING NATIVE PLACES ~ Adventures in Northwest Geography
SAHAPTINS STUDIES ~ Columbia River Plateau, Cora Du Bois, Homer Garner Barnett, Gerald Raymond Desmond
SDOQWALBIXW                                                                      > 35
SOUND SALISH STRAITS ~ Central Salish Sea Cultures
UNSETTLING SEATTLE ~ Arresting Local Talent and Academic Illiteracy
WRITING WORDS IN WARY WORLDS ~ World Wide Improved Spellings of Native America Languages > 38

## JONA Memoirs

RESCUES, RANTS, & RESEARCHES ~ A Re-View of Jay Miller's Writings on Northwest Indien Cultures ~ #9
TRIBAL TRIO of the Northwest Coast by Kenneth D Tollefson ~ #10
INTERWEAVING COAST SALISH CULTURAL SYSTEMS ~ Collected Works of Pamela Thorsen Amoss ~ #14

## University of Nebraska Press

ANCESTRAL MOUNDS ~ Vitality and Volatility Crossing Native North America 2015
HONNE ~ The Spirit of the Chehalis 2015